NAKBA

CULTURES OF HISTORY

NICHOLAS DIRKS, *Series Editor*

The death of history, reported at the end of the twentieth century, was clearly premature. It has become a hotly contested battleground in struggles over identity, citizenship, and claims of recognition and rights. Each new national history proclaims itself as ancient and universal, while the contingent character of its focus raises questions about the universality and objectivity of any historical tradition. Globalization and the American hegemony have created cultural, social, local, and national backlashes. Cultures of History is a new series of books that investigates the forms, understandings, genres, and histories of history, taking history as the primary text of modern life and the foundational basis for state, society, and nation.

Shail Mayaram, *Against History, Against State: Counterperspectives from the Margins*

Tapati Guha-Thakurta, *Monuments, Objects, Histories: Institutions of Art in Colonial and Postcolonial India*

Charles Hirschkind, *The Ethical Soundscape: Cassette Sermons and Islamic Counterpublics*

Prachi Deshpande, *Creative Pasts: Historical Memory and Identity in Western India, 1700–1960*

Bear, Laura, *Lines of the Nation: Indian Railway Workers, Bureaucracy, and the Intimate Historical Self*

NAKBA

PALESTINE, 1948, AND
THE CLAIMS OF MEMORY

Edited by

AHMAD H. SA'DI & LILA ABU-LUGHOD

COLUMBIA UNIVERSITY PRESS

NEW YORK

COLUMBIA UNIVERSITY PRESS
Publishers Since 1893

New York   Chichester, West Sussex
Copyright © 2007 Columbia University Press
All rights reserved

Library of Congress Cataloging-in-Publication Data

Nakba : Palestine, 1948, and the claims of memory /
Ahmad H. Sa'di, Lila Abu-Lughod editors.
p. cm.
Includes bibliographical references and index.
ISBN 978-0-231-13578-8 (cloth : alk. paper)—ISBN 978-0-231-13579-5 (pbk. : alk. paper)—
ISBN 978-0-231-50970-1 (electronic)
1. Israel-Arab War, 1948–1949—Personal narratives, Palestinian Arab. 2. Israel-
Arab War, 1948–1949—Historiography. 3. Israel-Arab War, 1948–1949—Influence.
4. Refugees, Palestinian Arab—Biography. 5. Israel-Arab War, 1948–1949—Atrocities.
6. Disasters—Psychological aspects. 7. Collective memory—Palestine. I. Sa'di, Ahmad H.,
1958– II. Abu-Lughod, Lila. III. Title

DS126.9.N35 2007
956.04'2—dc22

2006029175

∞ Columbia University Press books are printed on permanent and durable acid-free paper.

Printed in the United States of America.

References to Internet Web Sites (URLs) were accurate at the time of writing. Neither the
author nor Columbia University Press is responsible for Web sites that may have expired or
changed since the book was prepared.

BOOK DESIGNED BY VIN DANG

CONTENTS

LIST OF ILLUSTRATIONS

ACKNOWLEDGMENTS

This book has been a truly collective endeavor. We thank all the contributors for their thoughtful and well-researched chapters and for their patience with us, both when we asked for revisions in the hopes of making this a truly significant book, and when we took longer than expected to bring the whole volume together. We also want to thank those who had hoped to contribute chapters but could not in the end.

In the process of pulling together such a complex work, we benefited from the advice and the generous and careful assistance of many. We had good advice from several anonymous reviewers for the presses to whom we submitted the proposal and the book, as well as from Kate Wahl. We are also grateful to Joey Beinin, Marianne Hirsch, Zachary Lockman, and Ted Swedenburg for insightful and detailed comments that improved the manuscript in key ways. Our editor, Peter Dimock, who believes that history can be popular and that knowledge of the past can make a difference, gave us consistent encouragement. Anne Routon and Kabir Dandona were efficient in processing the manuscript, and we are very grateful for the careful and sympathetic copyediting of Leslie Bialler. We are also grateful to Lori Allen, Karen Austrian, Amahl Bishara, Nadia Guessous, Andrew Hao, Munir Fakher Eldin, Naomi Schiller, and especially Mona Soleiman and Vina Tran for help with research, ideas, references, illustrations, and the myriad details of preparing the manuscript.

Finally, thanks to Professor Barbara Mann for helping standardize the trans-literations from Hebrew.

We thank Imco Brouwer, scientific organizer of the Sixth Mediterranean Social and Political Research Meeting of the Mediterranean Program of the Robert Schuman Centre for Advanced Studies at the European University Institute, held in Montecatini Terme, March 2005. He was supportive when we mounted a workshop on "Al-Nakba in Palestinian Collective Memory" at which versions of six of the chapters were presented. Although we had begun the book before the workshop, the discussions there and the contributions of the other participants clarified our thinking about and enriched our knowledge of the significance of the Nakba.

Ahmad and Lila met at her father's funeral in Jaffa and it is his spirit of investigation and struggle that has animated us as we worked. Lila is also grateful to her mother, Janet Abu-Lughod, who herself dedicated some of her formidable energy and keen intellect to understanding what happened in 1948. Although her life, through her husband, was irrevocably marked by the Nakba, she has always been unsparing in her judgment of history and driven by a deep sense of justice that is all her own. Lila thanks her for insisting that one should not dwell only on the past when a new Nakba is taking place before our eyes. Tim Mitchell has been encouraging throughout, reading and commenting on chapters and sharing his knowledge while Adie and JJ must be thanked for putting up with a mother who spent a lot of time at the computer, sometimes crying while she worked.

Ahmad is particularly grateful to the late Edward Said for his encouragement in beginning the project; he thanks Paul Kelemen for reading earlier drafts, which encompassed his thoughts on Palestinian memory of the Nakba, and Sylvia Saba-Sa'di for reading and commenting on various drafts of the articles as well as accompanying the project from its beginning to conclusion, bearing with him the ups and downs that are part of academic work. Sylvia, along with his children, Yara and Sari, provided him with a congenial environment for thinking and writing about this disturbing topic.

Edward Said inscribed a copy of his book *Reflections on Exile and Other Essays* to Ibrahim Abu-Lughod in February 2001 with the words: "To my dear old friend and comrade Ibrahim, who shares the fate(s) of illness and terminal Palestinianism." We dedicate this book to their memory, in hopes of carrying on their efforts to forge a better future for others.

NOTE ON TRANSLITERATIONS

It is difficult to decide how specific to be in transliterating from other languages in a book that is intended for a general audience and whose main import is theoretical. For the Arabic, we decided to use a simplified version of the transliteration system recommended by the *International Journal of Middle East Studies*. We use no diacritics, including indications of long vowels, except to mark the ayn by a single open quotation mark and the hamza by a single close quotation mark. The assumption is that readers who know Arabic will recognize the words and others will not be interested in the details. We use the standard form for the most common place names, such as Deir Yassin, Jaffa, and Saida, since many have written in English about them. For authors' names, we also often follow their preference for publication in English, even if this does not conform to standard transliteration systems. For the destroyed Palestinian villages, we have followed the spellings used by Walid Khalidi and his team of researchers, as presented in *All that Remains* (1992). The Hebrew transliterations follow the standard form, except that we do not use diacritics.

The main challenge has been how to treat the Palestinian dialect, especially for those who rely on oral sources. In almost all cases, we have used the more standard Arabic form, thus writing Umm (mother) rather than Imm, as it would be pronounced. Very occasionally we have expressed a name with an "eh" at the end, rather than the classical "a," to better capture how a name would be pronounced.

Fifty years on
I am trying to tell the story
of what was lost
before my birth

the story of what was there
before the stone house fell
        mortar blasted loose
        rocks carted away for new purposes, or smashed
        the land declared clean, empty

before the oranges bowed in grief
blossoms sifting to the ground like snow
quickly melting

before my father clamped his teeth
        hard
            on the pit of exile
slammed shut the door to his eyes. . . .

LISA SUHAIR MAJAJ
from "Fifty Years On/Stones in an Unfinished Wall"
Ripe Guava: Voices of Women of Color (Fall 1999–Spring 2000)

Exile, in the words of Wallace Stevens, is "a mind of winter" in which
the pathos of summer and autumn as much as the potential of spring
are nearby but unobtainable. Perhaps this is another way of saying that
a life of exile moves according to a different calendar.

EDWARD W. SAID,
Reflections on Exile and Other Essays
(Cambridge: Harvard University Press, 2000), p. 186.

NAKBA

Figure 1 Palestinian refugee, "'Baqa'a Camp, Jordan, 1967.

Introduction

THE CLAIMS OF MEMORY

Lila Abu-Lughod & *Ahmad H. Sa'di*

In the kind of story that repeats itself among Palestinians, Rema Hammami, an anthropologist and second-generation Palestinian refugee, describes how she felt when she found herself for the first time standing before what she was certain was her grandfather's former house in Jaffa:

> When I saw the arches, I had a sudden shock of recognition based on an old family photograph taken in front of this veranda, which back then had a huge asparagus fern growing up one side. . . . It showed a large family, with young girls in white frocks and bows in their hair lined up in the front row. I always noticed how innocent they looked. . . .
>
> The gate was open so I walked in. . . . It was full of people who somehow didn't enter my field of vision: I was remapping the *liwan's* (sitting room) former reality, a process that excluded objects and people not part of that earlier moment. Then someone spoke to me in Hebrew, and I was brought out of my dream. A woman in a white medical coat was asking me things I didn't understand. I looked around and realized that the *liwan* was full of retarded children. When I answered in English, the woman walked off and returned with a large blond Germanic looking matron, also in a white coat. . . . She asked me what I wanted, and I replied that this was my grandfather's house and I just wanted to look at it. For some reason I was surprised at her reaction, which was nervousness and agitation.
>
> (TAMARI AND HAMMAMI 1998: 68–9)

After suspiciously testing the truthfulness of her story, (to which Rema gave living evidence—her aunt who had grown up in the house sitting in the car outside, too disturbed to come in), the woman ushered her into the manager's office. He told Rema:

> "Here, I want to show you something." I followed him to the landing where he indicated an odd colored frieze on the wall. He asked me to look closely and then proceeded to explain with what seemed to be glee that the frieze depicted the return of the Jewish people to the Land of Israel and the creation of the Jewish state. He ended with a kind of hymn to the success of the Zionist dream. I was speechless at what I could only take as a form of sadism, and mumbled something like: "Look, I just want to look around the house."
>
> (IBID: 69)

This unsettling encounter is pregnant with meaning for a book on Palestinian memory. We have in the grandfather's house an instance of a site to which memory attaches, one of the kinds of objects that Pierre Nora (1989) famously refers to as *"les lieux de mémoire."* We have in the second-generation "return" to the site of the parents' and grandparents' former life, the imaginative workings of "postmemory" provoked by a historical family photograph (Hirsch 1997). We have in Rema's initial wanderings and searching for traces the juxtaposition of a dreamy past made of stories and innocent photographs with a harsh present. We have, sitting in the car outside, the traumatized survivor who cannot bear to face the violators of her presence in what they have now made theirs. The events of the Palestinian expulsion in 1948 have rendered the old family home a place of painful memory and a symbol of what has been taken. Finally, we have in Rema's submission to the suspicions of the woman in the white coat and the manager's didactic lecture on Jewish redemption in Israel the humbling confrontation with the dominant narrative of the victor, in which an alternative truth cannot even be mumbled.

This book is about what the events and aftermath of 1948 have meant for Palestinians, as refracted through their memories, individual and collective, rendered public through being elicited by researchers, volunteered creatively, or presented in conventionalized memorial practices. We are not as concerned about what these memories tell us about the past (although we think they contribute rich material to the ongoing historical reconstruction of the events of 1947 and 1948) as we are with the work they do, and can do, in the present. Although we are aware that such memory work can burden present generations whose own traumas might be made to seem like mere echoes, or who want to forget—as Augé (2004) notes, wishing for oblivion—we also see strong evidence that making memories public affirms identity, tames trauma, and asserts Palestinian political and moral claims to justice, redress, and the right to return. We look especially hard at how memories are produced, when people are silent and when collective memory proliferates, and what forms Palestinian memories of the cataclysmic events of 1948 that are known simply as "the catastrophe" (al-nakba) take. We share with the many scholars who have now reflected deeply on the question of memory the conviction that no memory is pure, unmediated, or spontaneous. Yet we believe that Palestinian memory is particularly poignant because it struggles with and against a still much-contested present.

The Nakba

The 1948 War that led to the creation of the State of Israel also resulted in the devastation of Palestinian society. At least 80 percent of the Palestinians who lived in the major part of Palestine upon which Israel was established— more than 77 percent of Palestine's territory—became refugees.[1] Their fate hung on the decisions of politicians in the countries to which they fled or bureaucrats in international agencies. The minority of Palestinians—anywhere from 60,000 to 156,000, depending on the sources—who remained behind became nominal citizens of the newly established Jewish state, subject to a separate system of military administration by a government that also confiscated the bulk of their lands. The Palestinians in the West Bank, whether refugees from other parts of Palestine or native to the area, came under the repressive regime of the Hashemites, the rulers of Jordan, while those residing in the Gaza Strip, bordering Egypt, came under an uncaring Egyptian administration. Then, in 1967, Israel brought both of these regions under military occupation (see Hadawi, 1967, 1988; I. Abu-Lughod, 1971; W. Khalidi, 1971; Said, 1979; Pappé, 2004).

For Palestinians, the 1948 War led indeed to a "catastrophe." A society disintegrated, a people dispersed, and a complex and historically changing but taken for granted communal life was ended violently. The Nakba has thus become, both in Palestinian memory and history, the demarcation line between two qualitatively opposing periods. After 1948, the lives of the Palestinians at the individual, community, and national level were dramatically and irreversibly changed.

Yet this destruction of Palestinian society was overshadowed by the heavy presence of what was represented and understood internationally as a birth or rebirth. The death-rebirth dialectic, a philosophical conception with enormous purchase in both religious and secular Western thought, was applied to the Jewish people. The 1948 War that led to the creation of the State of Israel was made to symbolize their rebirth within a decade after their persecution in Europe and subjection to the Nazi genocide. Israel's creation was represented, and sometimes conceived, as an act of restitution that resolved this dialectic, bringing good out of evil. The Palestinians were excluded from the unfolding of this history. Their catastrophe was either disregarded or reduced to a question of ill-fated refugees, similar to the many millions around the world—those who wandered in Europe following the end of World War II or those forced to flee the violence that accompanied the partition of India. Excluded from history as the remnant of a nation whose right to independence, statehood, and even existence was denied, Palestinian refugees were seen, at best, as a humanitarian case, deserving what they often experienced as the demeaning support of UN agencies (see Peteet 2005).

Elias Sanbar, a Palestinian historian and writer, articulates this strange exclusion in the shadow of a powerful counternarrative in his essay "Out of Place, Out of Time":

> The contemporary history of the Palestinians turns on a key date: 1948. That year, a country and its people disappeared from maps and dictionaries. . . . "The Palestinian people does not exist," said the new masters, and henceforth the Palestinians would be referred to by general, conveniently vague terms, as either "refugees," or in the case of a small minority that had managed to escape the generalized expulsion, "Israeli Arabs." A long absence was beginning
>
> (SANBAR 2001: 87).

Although Palestinians had various forms of identity before 1948, including a sense of themselves as Palestinians, there is little doubt that the catastrophe, in all its dimensions, has not just determined their lives but has since then become the key site of Palestinian collective memory and national identity (Doumani 1992; R. Khalidi 1997; Sa'di 2002). Our purpose in this book is to critically examine this potent and painful site of memory in light of the larger comparative literature on memory, history, and trauma. We are concerned with what Palestinian memory has in common with other community memory and what may be distinctive. As we explore below, the special character of Palestinian memory lies in the key experiences of their radical and abrupt displacement from life *in situ*, the continuing violence and lack of resolution they must endure, and the political nature of the deliberate erasure of their story, which gives birth to the stubborn dissidence of their memory-work.

Memory and History

The Nakba is often reckoned as the beginning of contemporary Palestinian history, a history of catastrophic changes, violent suppression, and refusal to disappear. It is the focal point for what might be called Palestinian time. The Nakba is the point of reference for other events, past and future. The Balfour Declaration of 1917 gains its significance from being followed by the Nakba. Landmark events in Palestinian history such as Black September (Jordan, 1970), the massacre at Sabra and Shatila (Lebanon, 1982), Land Day (Israel, 1976), and the first and second intifadas (1987–1993; 2000–present) would not have occurred if they had not been preceded by the Nakba, to which they refer back. The Nakba has become a key event in the Palestinian calendar—the baseline for personal histories and the sorting of generations.[2] Moreover, it is the creator of an unsettled inner time. It deflects Palestinians from the flow of social time[3] into their own specific history and often into a melancholic existence, as Bresheeth explores in his chapter on recent Palestinian cinema, or a ghostly nostalgia, as Al-Qattan in his chapter suggests. For writer Fawaz Turki, this internalization of the Nakba leads him to say that he could not escape it, "For it always comes back, that past, as if it were an ache, an ache from a sickness a man didn't know he had. Like the smell of ripened figs at a Perth supermarket that would place me, for one blissful moment, under that big fig tree in the backyard of our house in Haifa. Like the taste of sea salt in my mouth as I swam in the Indian Ocean that would take me back to the Mediterranean, our own ancient sea" (Turki 1998: 10). The Nakba is the point to which Palestinians return when they reach the age at which they want to sum up their lives. The structure of the following appraisal by a Palestinian refugee from Mar Ilyas Camp in Lebanon, of the refugees' condition in 1994, is typical:

> How did we get to this point? Our reality today is the worst it has ever been, from all standpoints. It was understandable that we would be in a bad situation in 1948 and during the years following. But that we should go back to zero forty-five years after the Catastrophe raises a number of questions. How is it possible

that our people, who never stinted in sacrificing themselves, are confronted today
with such a future?

(AQL 1995: 55)

The essays in this book rely on oral testimony and personal memory
made public. The authors, not tied to state archives or official bodies or institutions, and not professional historians, attempt something other than producing an authoritative Palestinian history of 1948, or even a counter-history
of the events of 1948. Those unfamiliar with the history of 1948 should read
the Afterword of this book first. Benjamin and Kracauer, among other theorists of history and memory, have suggested that history is partial and always
written by the victors (Gilloch, 2002; Kracauer, 1995). The narratives, documents, and archives of the victors, as well as the realities they have imposed
on the ground, are what, in the final analysis, count as historical truth. The
frieze that Rema Hammami was shown casts a shadow over the story of the
victims of Zionism (Said 1979).

Yet Kracauer (1995) gives us an opening for memory. He argues that the
powerful cannot fully impose their will in constituting the hegemonic discourse about certain historical events or in determining the reading of reality.
He reminds us that "There are always holes in the wall for us to evade and
the improbable to slip in" (p. 8). Memory is one of the few weapons available
to those against whom the tide of history has turned. It can slip in to rattle
the wall. Palestinian memory is, by dint of its preservation and social production under the conditions of its silencing by the thundering story of Zionism,
dissident memory, counter-memory. It contributes to a counter-history.

Paolo Jedlowski's general understanding of the relationship between
power and memory can illuminate for us the potential of Palestinian counter-
memory. He argues that "memory is not only what serves the identity of a
group and its present interests, but also the depository of traces that may be
valid both in defetishizing the existing and in understanding the processes that
have led to the present as it is now, and to the criticism of this very present
in the name of forgotten desires, aspirations or traumas" (Jedlowski 2001: 36).
If memory is often mobilized to buttress and bind states and nations, as so
much of the literature on the deliberate deployments of memory for positive
projects of power and history-making suggests, memories can also call into
question the status quo. Palestinians' memories of the Nakba, which provide
a nagging counter-story of the myth of the birth of Israel, can indeed be said
to criticize the present in the name of a trauma that has hardly begun to be

recognized by those outside the Arab world and that awaits some form of redress. For many Palestinians, the Nakba is the touchstone of a hope for a reconstituted or refigured Palestine and a claim to rights.

If for so many reasons this is not a book of history proper, neither is it merely a collection of individual testimonials or personal reflections. Instead, it is a sustained examination of the nature, shapes, and determinants of Palestinian collective, social, or cultural memory. We are not particularly concerned with the term used, even though each of these terms has a different genealogy and theoretical range, as Olick and Robbins (1998) so masterfully outline in their review of memory studies. What we do want to stress is that we are dealing with memories made public, in recognizable cultural forms, and from within particular social milieus. Unlike many who study memory, especially the brilliant analysts of Holocaust memory, we are not much concerned with the psychodynamics of memory and certainly not with projecting such dynamics onto a collective, a people.[4] Rather we focus on the forms—or what Olick and Robbins (1998: 112) call the "mnemonic practices"—and the politics of Palestinian discourses of the Nakba. With Halbwachs, we believe we are in the realm of collective memory in that for Palestinians, like others, "it is in society that people normally acquire their memories . . . [and] recall, recognize, and localize their memories" (Halbwachs 1992: 38) but also insofar as the painful memories recounted are part of an active past that helps form Palestinian identity (Olick and Robbins 1998: 111; Sa'di 2002). Also with Halbwachs, we see a dialectical relationship between individual and social group. The Durkheimian thinker asserts that individual memories are social in nature when he notes, "One may say that the individual remembers by placing himself in the perspective of the group, but one may also affirm that the memory of the group realizes and manifests itself in individual memories" (Halbwachs 1992: 40), especially when the events similarly affected so many over such a wide area.

It is from the memories of ordinary Palestinians made public in a variety of contexts that we draw our conclusions about the larger significance of the Nakba. We recognize that these memories have adjusted to each other, producing what Hammer (2001: 470) calls a "canonization" of some stories and symbols. We do not doubt that nationalist cultural forms, from the poetry of Mahmoud Darwish and the writings of other Palestinians to visual arts, popular music, and political slogans have helped form these narratives. We also recognize the popular and social conventions that shape memory: for example, Sayigh's chapter explores the structuring of women's personal memories by traditional storytelling conventions, even as she argues that the Nakba thrust women into historical consciousness, while Humphries and Khalili's chapter traces the roots of women's Nakba stories in gendered social experience.

We are aware that in the processes of "canonization" or social adjustment, some experiences and memories may find no place. Palestinian women's memories have rarely found a place, sometimes, as Humphries and Khalili explain, because of women's own hesitancy about the authoritativeness of their knowledge or their shame, in the case of rape. Memories of fighting that are evidence of pride, Hammer (2001:471) argues, come "in long descriptions of the military actions that Palestinian fighters carried out in 1947/48 to defend their villages and towns." Unfortunately, we have almost none of these in our collection even though they would balance the narratives of victimhood that are so common. And how many memories of betraying others are ever told? An essay by the writer Anton Shammas called "The Retreat from Galilee" and translated from Hebrew in 1988, pulls together family stories and village rumors to evoke the murky uncertainties of the Nakba, when rich tobacco merchants might intervene with Jewish commanders to give villagers a temporary reprieve from flight, or where a ruthless former political leader may have hanged himself after having turned traitor, using a burlap hood to disguise his work with the Jewish forces, and where villagers scraped together a ransom to avoid expulsion. Where are the traitor's memories, or the memories of those landowners who earlier sold their land to the Jewish colonizing agencies?

What people choose to make public, under what conditions, and with what forms of receptivity by others are central questions in social-memory studies and ones we try to explore in this book. However, what ultimately emerges from the essays about how Palestinians remember the Nakba is a strong sense of the claims social memory makes about what happened in the past and what ought, morally, to be done in the present. Palestinian memory is, at its heart, political.

How Can Those Without Lips Whistle?

The Nakba was many things at once: the uprooting of people from their homeland, the destruction of the social fabric that bound them for so long, and the frustration of national aspirations. The Nakba could also be part of an unsettling counter-history: a constant reminder of failings and of injustice.

It is a challenge to the morality of the Zionist project, as Sa'di describes in the Afterword; it is a reminder of the failures of Arab leadership and peoples; and it is a persistent question to the world about its vision of a moral and just human order.

For Palestinians, the Nakba was mostly about fear, helplessness, violent uprooting, and humiliation. It embodies the unexpected and unstoppable destruction that left them in disarray, politically, economically, and psychologically. If we agree with Nietzsche that every person's or nation's world consists of several worlds (Safranski 2002: 202), the Nakba meant the destruction in a single blow of all the worlds in which Palestinians had lived. For many, theirs was a dynamic, prosperous, and future-oriented society. The Nakba marked a new era dominated by estrangement, and often poverty. Nothing in their history or that of neighboring countries had prepared Palestinians to imagine such a catastrophe. The fact that the Nakba took place within a short period—a matter of months—made it hard to comprehend; there was little time to reflect.

Yet this shattering experience has not, until recently, found wide sympathy or acknowledgment, especially in the United States and Israel. How many people in the West know why Palestinians feel such different emotions from Israelis on their "Independence Day" on May 15? Why they continue to struggle, sometimes violently? Even why they are there, in Israeli cities and on Israel's moving borders, still provoking talk of "transfer." Their presence is the odd note in the picture of a suffering people redeemed by their new homeland, or the pioneers aspiring, like so many others before them, for national independence and a conventional state.

Some might fault the Palestinians for somehow having remained silent, for not having told enough of their story. There are, after all, surprisingly few Palestinian scholarly works on the subject of the Nakba. And many of those who experienced it have not been heard from. As part of the research for this book, one of the authors interviewed an elderly Palestinian woman in the Galilee whose Nakba story he had heard before. She had been in her early twenties when the Nakba took place. On one occasion, she recalled, "We [she and her mother] were crossing the Saffuriyya–Shafa 'Amr road. We were spotted by an armored vehicle that opened fire on us. We ran into the fields; it was harvest season. I jumped into a haystack; the bullets flew very close to my head and face. I was very frightened so I covered myself completely with the hay." She then lost touch with her mother, and was unable to locate her or the rest of her family for twenty days.

Next she talked about another disturbing experience: "Beside the village of Ilut my brother and I found a group of murdered men; two of them had once been our neighbors, slightly older than me. They were shot with a single bullet each in his forehead, may God console their mother." When asked why she had never told her Nakba stories in public, particularly since so little was known to the world about what had happened in that period, she looked astonished and retorted "How can those without lips whistle?"

What does it mean to say that Palestinians do not have lips with which to whistle? What prevented them from telling their stories? Scholars of collective memory and historians are well aware that individuals who undergo traumatic events produce belated memories; it can take victims years to be able to assimilate their experiences and give them meaning and form—a process that Kammen calls memory work (1995: 34–49). Is the paucity of narrative material on the events of the Nakba, at least until the last couple of decades, a result of this sort of response to individual trauma, a case of delayed memory syndrome? (Ibid.: 249). Or is it due to the lack of comfortable distance from which to reflect? Auerbach notes, in his analysis of Marcel Proust's *Swann's Way*, "Freed from its various earlier involvements, consciousness views its own past layers and their content in perspective; it keeps confronting them with one another, emancipating them from their exterior temporal continuity as well as from the narrow meanings they seemed to have when they were bound to a particular present" (Auerbach 1971: 542). He suggests, in other words, that narrating the past depends on having a detached perspective in the present through which one can look at one's past.

When the past is still entrenched in the present existential conditions of the individual, affecting the myriad aspects of her or his life, perhaps he or she cannot secure the conditions to narrate the past. For Palestinians, still living their dispossession, still struggling or hoping for return, many under military occupation, many still immersed in matters of survival, the past is neither distant nor over. Unlike many historical experiences discussed in the literature on trauma, such as the Blitz, the merciless bombing of Hamburg and Dresden by the Allies at the closing stage of World War II, the Holocaust, the Algerian War of Independence, or the World Trade Center attack, which lasted for a limited period of time (the longest being the Algerian war of independence, lasting eight years), the Nakba is not over yet; after almost sixty years neither the Palestinians nor Israelis have yet achieved a state of normality; the violence and uprooting of Palestinians continues. Thus many

Palestinians might find it hard to stand in a neutral place, "away from earlier involvements," from which they could explore or narrate their pasts.

Palestinian writers have symbolized this failure to narrate the Nakba in stories that themselves lack closure. Emile Habiby has perhaps portrayed the intensity and bleakness of life after the Nakba most profoundly, ending his novella, *The Secret Life of Saeed: The Pessoptimist*, with neither satisfying resolution, nor redemption. The novella tells the story of a Palestinian who has been permitted to return to his hometown of Haifa after the Nakba and becomes an Israeli citizen. His return is made possible because he has agreed to work as a collaborator with the Israelis. He is diligent but clumsy in his work, and is little appreciated by his employers. The ironies of Saeed's world—as a Palestinian and as an informer—unfold through forty-four epistolary fragments. Significantly, the first letter the narrator receives from the ill-fated "pessoptimist" (pessimist and optimist) pleads, "Please tell my story" (Habiby, 2002: 3). The narrator publishes the letters and keeps looking for their author (whom the reader learns to love, hate, ridicule, despise but eventually appreciate for his resilience). Finally he traces the letters to a mental hospital in Acre. However, when he asks the hospital director about an inmate named Saeed the Pessoptimist, he discovers that there is no such name on the register. He and the director try to identify the writer through a process of elimination: the name that comes closest belongs to an inmate who died more than a year earlier. As with the Palestinian Nakba, the storyteller or truth teller cannot be identified and his stories are open to question.

Yet unlike the woman who had stayed silent about her traumatic girlhood memories of hiding in a haystack, and perhaps other Palestinians who remained to become citizens of Israel and entered a strange limbo, many Palestinian refugees of the Nakba generation told their stories over and over, to their children and to each other. Even if "the skin enfolding the memory . . . is tough" (1990:1–1) and the talking about the past does not come from the "deep memory" of the senses (1990:1–3), as Charlotte Delbo put it so eloquently about surviving Auschwitz, they remembered and they talked.

So the problem in the Palestinian case seems to be more about collective memory than individual memory of trauma. The debilitating factor in the ability to tell their stories and make public their memories is that the powerful nations have not wanted to listen.[5] Without lips, of the political sort, Palestinians could not make themselves heard over the louder story, the one that for Europeans had been vigorously put forth for decades before the

Nakba, the one framed in terms of the powerful imagery of redemption, the one told by European Jews who stressed their alliance with the cultural and political values of the West, whether in terms of national independence, democratic organization (for Jewish citizens only), or civilizational mission, like "making the desert bloom." The Palestinians, a stateless and dispersed people, were, after the Nakba, up against a strong state with outside support, military might, and official archives. In these other hands was the apparatus of history production. What value, as Esmeir asks in her analysis of a trial in Israel about a massacre, does the halting oral testimony by the defeated have? How easy it is, as Sa'di and Slyomovics note, for historians like Benny Morris to discredit the oral testimony of the victims in favor of the official written archives of the state. As Laub (Felman and Laub 1992: 68) insists for the individual, without the empathetic listener who acts as a witness, the story is annihilated. Is this not even truer for the collective?

Palestinians find the absence of an audience to be painful. Unable to detect substantial flaws in their moral stand, they cannot comprehend why justice has not been restored. The return from exile for which they long is stalled and they are compelled to live with approximations and cheap copies of Palestine that rest in the imagination. The absence of moral reason and the seeming apathy of those who could effect some political solution have derailed Palestinians in their search for the meaning of their catastrophe and their aspiration to be "a people like others." According to the French philosopher Gilles Deleuze, this represents "a cry whose meaning [sens] is multiple; it could be a reminder or an appeal" (Deleuze and Sanbar 2001). In the absence of palliatives or moral solace, while facing the crushing demands of new lives as refugees or as second-class citizens, they sometimes have dark visions of the world and tend toward either silence or violence.

Insanity or senseless death are common themes in Palestinian literature, as in the case of Habiby's story of the pessoptimist who ended his life in a mental hospital and whose death was received with relief. A more tragic fate awaited the protagonists of Ghassan Kanafani's (1976) novel *Men in the Sun,* originally published in Arabic in 1962, before the establishment of the PLO gave political form to Palestinian aspirations. The story is about three Palestinian refugees from Lebanon who were pushed by intolerable pressures to seek work in Kuwait. They struck a deal with a Palestinian truck driver to smuggle them across the border from the southern Iraqi city of Basra in his tanker. The scheme was that the men would hide in the empty belly of the tanker when they approached the border, and get out as soon as the vehicle passed through. However, the driver is detained at the checkpoint by a bored officer who engages him in silly conversation. The three men suffocate—in the broad daylight, the reader must understand, of the world's apathy.

One question for us is whether the flood of personal memories made public around the commemoration of the fiftieth anniversary of the Nakba, and whatever private ones were triggered by these public events, can now get more of a hearing. There are many reasons why memories are solicited and noted. The proliferation of memory studies that accompanied the fiftieth anniversary of Partition on the Indian subcontinent was shaped by current events, with scholars deeply concerned about the roots of the "increasing polarization of Indian society on the basis of religion" (Butalia 2000: 276) and the communal violence that accompanied it.[6] In the same way, Palestinian attention to memory was made possible by the shaky establishment of the Palestinian National Authority in a bit of Palestine, with the signing of the Oslo accord in 1993, which symbolized some sort of recognition of Palestinian rights (while conceding most of them) and was made desperate by the demise of a liberation movement. Finding an audience for these memories may be helped by the fact that historical research on Zionism's "wordless wish" (Childers 1971) and deliberate military plans (Morris 2004a) has, as Sa'di shows in the Afterword, eroded the concocted orthodoxy that denied Israeli culpability for the Nakba even when refugee tales were so consistent and demanding that they should have been heard. Is a historical gap always necessary, as Laub (Felman and Laub 1992: 84) asks regarding the Holocaust, before witnesses' testimony is able to be heard?

Dis/placement

If the most distinctive feature of Palestinian social memory is its production under constant threat of erasure and in the shadow of a narrative and political force that silences it, one of its most characteristic qualities, as so many of the essays in this book show, is its orientation to place. For Palestinians, the places of the pre-Nakba past and the land of Palestine itself have an extraordinary charge. They are not simply sites of memory but symbols of all that has been lost and sites of longing to which return is barred. Palestinian attachments to places are both physical and imaginative.[7] Many people preserve, after more than half a century, the deeds to the land they owned and the keys to the houses they left behind. But the physicality is not just possessive but sensual, as Jayyusi explores especially well in her essay in this volume. She argues that places remembered are part of lived geographies, "mundane naturalized fields of activity and bodied interaction." The smell of cucumber, the taste of a fig, the everyday objects used for living, the embodied sociality of life lived in particular places—all attest to the bodily presence critical to selfhood and memory.

The body of place is also invoked imaginatively by Palestinians in metaphors such as the land of Palestine as a woman raped or violated, as Humphries, Khalili, and Slyomovics explore in this volume, or a beloved or mother in need of protection, gendered tropes shared with many nationalisms (e.g. Baron 1997; Najmabadi 2005; McClintock 1995). This body of place is also made real in the meticulous and compulsive mapping and cataloguing of what has happened to Palestinian habitations. Scholars like those who worked on the project organized by Walid Khalidi, *All that Remains* (1992) on the four hundred or so villages that were destroyed by Israel or, more recently, on Salman Abu-Sitta's (2004) atlas compiling demographic and statistical material on the more than six hundred villages and towns depopulated in 1948, exemplify this determined remapping and emplacement.

An emotional attachment to place is found in the memorial books ordinary people have written about their destroyed or depopulated villages. Susan Slyomovics relies on these for her essay on Qula and her book on Ein Houd/ Ein Hod (1998). But it is Rochelle Davis who makes fullest use of them for an analysis of how Palestinians map and remap the lost worlds of rural Palestine. In her essay in this volume, Davis is especially attentive to the ways these memorial books testify to the existence in and habitation by Palestinians of places that are now obliterated or inhabited by different people. These are often offered as a legacy to children and grandchildren; in addition to listing local features, they tend to paint pastoral pictures of village life in the pre-Nakba past. As she notes, there are no social rifts and no tensions in these depictions of the past, places that represent not just literally what villagers have lost but a way of life they no longer live, now that most are no longer agriculturalists (see also Swedenburg 1990 and Sawalha 1996).

The obsession with place and places, and the longing for the land, may be especially characteristic of Palestinian memory not just because of the localism of Palestinian social life in that early period (Doumani 1992) or because, as philosophers tell us, all memory is embodied, but because the Nakba was, above all, an odyssey, a mass movement of people. If by now the Nakba is the main term used to describe the cataclysmic events of 1948, this was not always so. Palestinians for a long time marked the year by the terms *sanat al-hujayj* (which in Palestinian dialect denotes both the act of escaping and its precipitant cause—an imminent grave danger) or, as Rosemary Sayigh notes in her chapter, for her Lebanese refugee friends, *sanat al-hijra* (the year of migration, a term carrying with it the heavy symbolism of the Prophet Muhammad's flight from Mecca to Medina, a migration that perhaps carried with it the promise of triumphal return).

The writer Fawaz Turki, who witnessed the mass exodus as a seven-year old child, reflected many years later on the way the Nakba would appear to him:

> Like the apocalyptic images that my mind would dredge up, out of nowhere, of our refugee exodus twenty years before, as we trekked north on the coastal road to Lebanon, where pregnant women gave birth on the wayside, screaming to heaven with labor pain, and where children walked alone, with no hands to hold.
>
> (TURKI 1998: 10)[8]

Other writers describe the emotions embodied in the movement. Elias Srouji (2003; 2004), who witnessed the expulsion of the inhabitants of the mostly Christian Galilean village of al-Rama, described their reactions when they were ordered to move:

> Meanwhile the gunfire was continuing, clearly intended to get people moving. We saw families holding their children and lugging big bags, some supporting old parents. Sobbing loudly. . . . Joining the main road leading up the steep slope of the mountain on which their village was built, they were setting off on a "trail of tears" towards the Lebanese border. The most heartrending sight was the cats and dogs, barking and carrying on, trying to follow their masters. I heard a man shout to his dog: "Go back! At least you can stay!"
>
> (SROUJI 2004: 77)

The image of pets abandoned as their owners suddenly had to leave appears in elite memoirs as well. Ghada Karmi remembers twisting to look back out of the car window as her family was departing from a tense Jerusalem in 1949 and seeing her beloved dog Rex. "And there to my horror was Rex standing in the middle of the road. We can't have closed the gate properly and he must somehow have managed to get out. He stood still, his head up, his tail stiff, staring after our receding car" (Karmi 2002: 122). She screamed to go back, but their servant reassured her that she would put him back in the house later. The same servant, Fatima, had reassured the parents that she would take care of their home until their return. There was no return from

England for the girl or her family. Nor did Ghada ever find Fatima or the dog Rex again.

If many momentous historical events are remembered through a photograph, a film, or a striking image (like the Chinese student who stopped in front of the tank in Tiananmen Square), there is no single image that represents in the public imagination the full scope of the tragedy of the Nakba. But perhaps the Palestinians' continuing flight is best captured in the spatial metaphor of the poet Mahmoud Darwish who asks, "Where should we go after the last frontier; where should the birds fly after the last sky?"[9] It is ironic, therefore, that since the desperate movements of their flight, so much of Palestinian experience has been about restrictions on movement. Not only do many remain stateless, lacking the passports that give them the legal right to move between countries, but after the Nakba, Palestine itself was divided into different areas. Movement from one region to another was controlled by others, mainly the Israelis, a theme explored richly in Elias Khoury's novel of the Nakba, *Gate of the Sun* (Khoury 2006). This even applied within regions. Between 1948 and 1966, for example, severe restrictions on movement were imposed on the Palestinian citizens of Israel; and after 1967, harsh restrictions have been imposed on the Palestinians in the West Bank and Gaza Strip, epitomized by the ubiquity of ever more elaborate checkpoints.

A tangible sense of displacement is acute for internal refugees—the Palestinians given by the Israeli authorities the legal term "present absentees" as a veneer of legality for the confiscation of their property. These Palestinians, although they have Israeli citizenship, continue to live as refugees short distances—between a quarter of a mile to a few miles—from their original homes, as is the case with the people of 'Ayn Hawd discussed in Slyomovics (1998). Most Palestinian refugees actually live short distances from their original homes. As Muhammad al-Bajirmi, a refugee in Rashidiyya refugee camp in Lebanon put it: "We are very close to northern Palestine. We see our country every day, and that strengthens our hope of return despite the duration of exile and our dispersion" (Aql 1995: 57). No wonder, then, that the places of Palestine are so central to memory.

Time and Memory

Time and memory are also closely bound. Without the passing of time there would be no memory. But the passing of time also creates distortions, fosters nostalgia, makes repression easier, and threatens us with forgetfulness.

Palestinian memory is no less bound to time than any other community's. But three aspects make for a special relationship to time.

First, as Palestinian memories of 1948 must serve as evidence of what happened in the mounting of political claims about injustice, there is a special urgency to remembering the details over time. The passing of the "generation of the Nakba," those who experienced the events of almost sixty years ago, is now being felt as a growing anxiety that the sources of memory will be lost before they have offered up their deep and irrecoverable memories (Kammen 1995: 259) to the public. Across Palestine and wherever Palestinian refugees now live, there are projects underway to interview the elderly. Particularly in and around the commemoration of the fiftieth anniversary of the Nabka, witnesses were brought forward to tell their stories.[10] They did this on *the Voice of Palestine*, the radio station of the Palestine National Authority in the West Bank; at events at the Sakakini Cultural Center in Ramallah; in interview projects sponsored by BADIL (Bethlehem) and Shaml, Palestinian Diaspora and Refugee Center (Ramallah); in oral history projects with diasporic Palestinians, such as those Rosemary Sayigh has long coordinated in the refugee camps in Lebanon (along with editing publications like *al-Jana*, whose 2002 issue contains interviews with those most active in oral history projects on Palestine), or newer projects such as the Nakba Archive, begun in 2002 and co-directed by Diana Allan and Mahmoud Zeidan, devoted to videotaping interviews with Nakba survivors living in all twelve refugee camps in Lebanon; and in the ambitious monograph project on the Palestinian destroyed villages carried out at Birzeit University's Center for the Study and Documentation of Palestinian Society, currently directed by Saleh Abdel Jawad, based on interviews with ordinary people, women included. These interviews supplement the written memoirs of intellectuals and former politicians, whether in Arabic or foreign languages, to be found in books like Masalha's *Catastrophe Remembered* and McGowan and Ellis' *Remembering Deir Yassin*; local journals like *al-Karmil*, *Masharif* and *Majallat al-Dirasat al-Filastiniyya*; or with international presses and journals like *Journal of Palestine Studies* or *Palestine-Israel Journal*. Moreover, Internet sites have proliferated, including ones whose domain names—like www.Nakba.org—indicate clearly the focus.

With the passing of time and the generation that lived the Nakba, we are threatened with forgetfulness. Salman Natour—a Palestinian novelist, essayist, playwright, and political analyst—dramatized his awakening to this danger in a play called *Memory* that was performed in many localities in Israel, including Haifa, Jaffa, Nazareth, and at Ben-Gurion University as well as abroad. The play is fashioned from a collection of Palestinian stories. They are narrated on stage as a form of traditional storytelling, allowing Nator to integrate narrative expressions that have been vanishing from everyday Palestinian language. Although the stories are from different periods—the British Mandate, the early years of Israel, and the 1982 Israeli War against Lebanon—they are narrated against the backdrop of the Nakba. The play ends with the narrator's fear of growing amnesia:

> My memory has betrayed me, and slowly I am losing it. I fear the black day when I find myself without any memory, just a body . . . that wanders in the streets and forests . . . until a hunter finds it. I, who fought the windmills, lost my memory and turned into nothing, exactly nothing. He [the hunter] will take me to the house where I was born and hand me over to my family. . . . He'll go to his family and tell them about an old man who lost his memory and pompously proclaim, "If I hadn't intervened he would have been eaten by the hyenas." We shall be eaten by the hyenas if we lose our memory. We shall be eaten by the hyenas.
>
> (NATOUR 2003: 19)

Natour's play is an urgent call to register, record, film, catalogue, and store Palestinian collective memory. The alternative is to perish as a nation, dying in the most ignoble way: eaten by scavengers. Other Palestinian plays have also used the device of storytelling to perform collective memory. Nassar (2002), for example, in an article on Palestinian theater called "The Invocation of Lost Places," discusses *The Narrow Lane* (*al-zarub*), first presented in Jerusalem in 1992. Its female narrator, Samiya al-Bakri, travels back in time, dramatizing the stories of five village women from Acre who survived 1948, invoking key places of this pre-1948 city. Such plays, along with all the technologies for eliciting and preserving memory being developed across the Palestinian diaspora, are essential to the Palestinian cause. Forgetfulness and the passage of time, as various analysts of collective memory have argued, are the enemies of causes, meaningful events, and their commemorative symbols (e.g. Huyssen 1995; Young 2001; Gross 2002), though they may be personally productive (Augé 2004).

If wanting to fight amnesia is something Palestinians share with many others, there are aspects of their experience of time that are more specific. One of the most important is that the past represented by the cataclysmic Nakba is not past. What happened in 1948 is not over, either because Palestinians are still living the consequences or because similar processes are at work in the present. "Exile," notes Janet Abu-Lughod "to the Palestinians . . .

is neither transitional nor transitory; it is an inherited state" (1988: 63). Their dispersion has continued, their status remains unresolved, and their conditions, especially in the refugee camps, can be miserable. For those with the class backgrounds or good fortune to have rebuilt decent lives elsewhere, whether in the United States, Kuwait, or Lebanon, the pain may be blunted. But for those in the vicinity of Israel, the assaults by the Zionist forces that culminated in the expulsions of the Nakba have not actually ceased. The Palestinians who remained within the borders of the new state were subjected to military rule for the first twenty years. Then in 1967, with the military occupation of the West Bank and Gaza, there was another dislocating assault. In 1982 Israel bombarded and invaded Lebanon, causing mass destruction, the routing of the PLO, and then a massacre in the refugee camps. With Palestinian resistance in the occupied territories (the two intifadas), the violence escalated. Hardly a week goes by now when Palestinians are not shelled, shot, "assassinated," arrested, taken to prison, or tortured. Not a day goes by when they are not humiliated at checkpoints or prevented from moving about by the Israeli army. The confrontation continues and with it the funerals, the house demolitions, the deportations, and the exodus. The usurping of water, the confiscation of land, the denial of legal rights, and the harassment also continue. As Jayyusi eloquently describes in her chapter, Palestinians make the connections, each major new event, like the savage bombardment of Jenin in 2002, triggering talk of the Nakba. It is, she says, the way each new event is the same but different from the last, along with their tragic cumulativity, that is finally what may be so distinctive of the Palestinian experience of time and memory.

Yet in time-reckoning, the Nakba has embodied an unbridgeable gap between two qualitatively different periods: pre and post Nakba, often experienced as generational difference. Generational time is thus a third key dimension of memory for Palestinians. There are processes of transfer from one generation to another—of stories, memories, foods, and anger; there is inheritance of the identity and burden; but there is also some resistance across the generations to the great significance of the past. For the Nakba generation, Palestine, as a birthplace, homeland, source of identity, geographical location, history, place of emotional attachment and fascination, field of imagination, and place where they want to end their lives, has dominated individuals and the collective. This is well illustrated by Ibrahim Abu-Lughod, whose attachments to Jaffa and Palestine defined his life and inspired a return of sorts (see Abu-Lughod, this volume).

Subsequent generations, though inheriting the consequences and the memories, react to this legacy in mixed ways. Many have never seen the country they have been told they belong to; they either live in its shadow or set their sights elsewhere. Some of the younger generation, as Diana Allan found in Shatila Camp in Lebanon, are impatient with the past and with their parents' and grandparents' orientation to the Nakba. They may resent the obsession, especially since it seems to be coerced by the nationalist frame and to garner so much attention now from outsiders. Because of the new assaults and the living political struggles in the camp, they are invested in their own generation's experiences. With their despair of the amelioration of their situation, and the frustration of young lives and talent, many in this new generation may even want to forget, to emigrate, to leave it all behind, as there have always been those, like Edward Said's father, who wanted to get on with their lives, given the new circumstances, as normally as possible (Said 1999: 14).

Resistance to freezing the past and focusing on the Nakba comes also from present generations of Palestinians who live within Israel. This was revealed in an important exchange between two Palestinian academics about Jaffa, the port city that was a place of intense fighting and from which almost the whole population fled in 1948, fully expecting to return once things quieted down. Instead, the city was annexed to Tel Aviv.[11] The tension in the present was sparked by the stream of diasporic Jaffans, or their children and grandchildren, recollecting Jaffa and returning—if they had the proper passports—just to have a look at what was once theirs. Salim Tamari and André Mazawi argued about their attitudes to the past—the refugees' fixation on a sharp break and the common sense, when they talked about Jaffa, of the past-ness of a pre-Nakba past. In an article about the tours of Jaffa Tamari (Tamari and Hammami 1998) had taken with various friends, he described their search for the hidden layers of Jaffa, the features of the city that, like those described in this volume by Abu-Lughod and Al-Qattan, had found a place in their parents' narratives of pre-1948 Jaffa. Mazzawi (1997) warned about bourgeois nostalgia, criticizing the appropriation of Jaffa by well-off returnees who represented Jaffa as a paradise lost and excluded from their narratives of life in Jaffa not only the working-class men and women of the past but, more painful for Mazzawi, the Palestinian residents, like himself, of the present (Diyab and Sharabi 1991; Tamari 2003). For Mazzawi, Jaffa is a living city, even if crumbling, socially conflictual, and a grim shadow of its past glory as the "bride of the sea."

Yet there is no doubt that a transfer of memories between generations has been deep and consistent. Marianne Hirsch (1997, 1999) has developed the concept of "postmemory" to capture the way in which later generations "grow up dominated by narratives that preceded their birth, whose own be-lated stories are displaced by the stories of a previous generation, shaped by traumatic events that they can neither understand nor re-create" (1999: 8). What is so powerful, she argues, about this form of memory is that "its connection to its object or source is mediated not through recollection but through an imaginative investment and creation" (1997: 22). This is true, as various chapters in this book show, for many of the children and grandchil-dren of the Nakba generation, including the two editors of this book.

However, in the Palestinian case, too many of these children and grand-children, like the intense girl in the film *Jenin, Jenin* whom Bresheeth quotes in his film analysis, have their own direct experiences of violence to make this concept useful across the board. Ongoing displacements and personal ex-periences of racism, as the American Palestinian poet Suheir Hammad points to in describing her U.S. encounters in a book of poems titled *Born Palestinian, Born Black* (1996), fire this generation to identify with the "imagined commu-nity" of Palestinians through a doubling of memory and postmemory. Key symbols, like olives, of this identity forge the connection, as in Hammad's angry rap verse, "I am the daughter / coughing up the olive branch" (quoted in Hammer 2001: 474). It is this next generation that has been making the films, organizing the collection of testimonials, trying to grasp the meaning of the Nakba, while fighting forgetfulness and making public claims on be-half of their parents' and grandparents' suffering.

The Holes of Memory

Some cynical scholars examining the "memory industry"—both academ-ic and public—that emerged in the 1980s have worried about the cloying and sacred sensibility that can infuse memory studies and the sloppy hypostatiz-ing of "Memory" that glorifies it and makes it a therapeutic alternative to historical discourse (Klein 2000). Other scholars examining colonial memory, like Stoler and Strassler (2000: 7), have warned us not to romanticize memory as "the repository of alternative histories and subaltern truths" but instead to attend to the processes of remembering, the fashioning of personal memo-ries, the strategic silences, and those experiences, like sensory recollections or itemized lists, that cannot be put into narrative form. Yet others deplore the methodological confusions of memory studies.

The essays on Palestinian memory in this book have a critical edge. Some challenge the pieties of trauma and memory studies. All are cognizant of the constructed nature of Palestinian memory, like all memory, even while they push moral and historical claims. We are forced to think especially hard when confronted with Allan's stories about the impatience, in the refugee camps, of youth with their elders for dwelling in the past; or their hostility to outside sympathizers for occluding, in their commemoration of the past and Palestinian victimhood, both the present and the future. Davis's uncovering of the idyllic past inscribed in memorial books about lost villages make us suspicious of them as historical documents, even while they testify to present longings and nostalgia born of loss. Esmeir's consideration of the inconsistencies of witness testimony in the case of the massacre at al-Tantura cautions us about the face value of memories while painting for us a clearer picture of the destructive force of fear. In the exposé, from essay to essay, of the repetitive quality of Palestinian memory, where familiar images and turns of phrase go hand in hand with a numbing iteration of similar stories across space and time, we uncover the force of convention alongside the horror of mass expulsion.

It may seem harsh to write critically about the construction and deployment of Palestinian memory because so much is at stake. Yet it is honest when Tamari faults the testimonies produced by ordinary individuals in Ramallah during the fiftieth anniversary of the Nakba for their utter localism and Mazawi criticizes visitors to Jaffa. In 1998, many Palestinian intellectuals called for critical and self-critical memory against the official commemorations of the anniversary, in part to position themselves as oppositional to the Palestine National Authority's appropriation of the Nakba story and Palestinian politics, as Hill (2005) contends. If we acknowledge the ways memory is shaped by present politics, by nationalist narratives that make the past seem more whole and identities more fixed and comfortable than they were,[12] by nostalgia for an idealized and pastoral past, by deliberate silencing of uncomfortable events (like rapes) that did happen, or by reluctance to bring forth forms of Palestinian complicity, culpability, and collaboration, do we thereby undermine the force of memory as a political tool? If we acknowledge that individual memory is just as partial, inconsistent, and subject to the ravages of time and age as collective memory, do we undermine the capacity of both to speak truth to power? Or to become the basis for claims to justice?

We do not think so. Stories heard and rumors circulated mix with stories based on personal experience—that is the nature of memory of public and shared events. Narrative forms, traditional, disciplinary, and nationalist, shape public tellings—that is the nature of social memory. Even when empirically wrong in small details, testimonies can carry deeper truths, as Esmeir argues with the survivors of the Tantura massacre, or Laub, the psychoanalyst, reveals with her subtle analysis of the deep historical truth reflected in one Auschwitz survivor's animated but inaccurate memory of how many chimneys went up in flames during the Auschwitz uprising. The truth of this woman's testimony, argues Laub, was that there had been a radical moment of resistance that completely broke the frame of daily life in the camp (Felman and Laub 1992: 59–61).

The cumulative effect of the memories we have collected and analyzed in this book is to affirm that something terrible happened to the Palestinians as a direct result of the military and political will to create the state of Israel, as described in detail in Sa'di's Afterword. The Palestinian stories must slip through the holes in the wall of the dominant story of 1948 and open it up to questioning, both factual and moral. Like the physical wall that, though declared illegal by the International Court, is now being erected to keep Palestinians out of Israel, in the process confiscating more of their land and making their lives and livelihoods on the ground even less tenable, the mythic Israeli narrative needs to be dismantled. Palestinian memories of 1948 offer a way to begin—a beginning that, through acknowledgment of what happened and what was experienced, might lead to a better future, one that is not based on hardened identities, silencings, and continuing, even escalating, violence.

NOTES

1. The figures are all highly unreliable; demographic analysis based on the British census and projections would put the proportion even higher. For the number of Arabs who remained, the figures are equally contested, inflated by adding a set figure of Bedouins first estimated in 1922 and carried over into every subsequent census intact. See J. Abu-Lughod (1971: 160–61).

2. The Nakba generation is followed by the generations of resistance (after the formation of the PLO), the generation of the first intifada, and the generation of the second intifada, among others.

3. For a discussion of different forms of time, see Melucci 1998.

4. Studies of memory and history are indebted to the abundant and complex literature on the Holocaust and German history. Among the key works that have shaped the vocabulary and themes of memory studies, besides texts cited in this introduction and elsewhere in the book, are Friedländer 1993; LaCapra 1994, 1998; Young 1993 and for Germany, Huyssen 1995. Any study of Palestinian memory finds itself in an awkward relationship to this literature because the focus on Jewish memory offers insights applicable—and rightly taken up—more widely, yet implies a sort of exceptionalism: the eloquent testimony to unspeakable horror, the minute examination of trauma, the variety of commemoration, and the justifiable accusations of world indifference implicitly block acknowledgment of Jews as anything but victims.

5. We are grateful to Gershon Shafir for insisting on this point (personal communication). For a powerful argument for the crucial importance of listeners, see Laub (in Felman and Laub 1992: 57–92).

6. Pandey (2001) explores how memories of partition construct a divided community and arise from the incomprehensibility of the collapse of lived community.

7. For an analysis of the physicality of memory in claims to Jerusalem, see Bishara 2003.

8. For a harrowing account with similar images, see Busailah 1981.

9. This line of poetry gave title to the book of photographs by Jean Mohr with an essay by Edward Said. Said 1985.

10. There had been earlier attempts to record memories, such as Abu Eishe (1982), his supported with a postface by Israel Shahak, then head of the Israeli League of Citizen's Human Rights, but the technology, support, and urgency increased in the 1990s with the commemorations and the recognition of the fast-disappearing generation of witnesses.

11. For a history of Jaffa and Tel Aviv, see Levine 2005.

12. The classic work linking Palestinian nationalism and memory is the pioneering study by Swedenburg (1995).

Part One

PLACES OF MEMORY

1 The Rape of Qula, a Destroyed Palestinian Village

Susan Slyomovics

Archives and Memory

Writing is a political act that not only represents the past, but also, within the Palestinian-Israeli context, molds the past. Words determine what is remembered and what is forgotten. To transmute individual Palestinian memories of 1948 from oral narratives into written words is an urgent task for researchers in "a race against time," according to Saleh Abdel Jawad, professor of history and political science at Birzeit University (Sayigh 2002b: 30). Given the decreasing population of Palestinians still alive from the generation of 1948, Abdel Jawad points to the history and goals of one project, the series of Birzeit University's volumes appearing under the collective rubric *Destroyed Palestinian Villages*:

> The idea to create a "memorial" monograph series about the destroyed Palestinian villages was proposed in 1979 by Dr. Kamal Abdulfattah and Dr. Sharif Kanaana. In 1983 the idea materialized, beginning with Dr. Abdulfattah's publication of the first map of the Palestinian destroyed villages. And in 1985 the [Birzeit University Research] Center began to publish its monograph series under the supervision of Dr. Kanaana. Research continued until the closure of Birzeit University on the 9th of January, 1988 by a military order which struck all Palestinian universities for years!! Work on the series resumed only in May 1993. At that time,

I was designated director and we again took up the work of documenting the destroyed villages, with a new approach. The work, focusing on the 1948 exodus, is mainly historical rather than anthropological—adding a significant number of new interviews but also grafting oral accounts with the written sources, especially Israeli archival material and secondary sources, and, finally, cross-checking the information.

(ABDEL JAWAD, forthcoming)

Each "memorial" book in the Birzeit University series memorializes a Palestinian village that no longer exists.[1] Villages are drawn from more than four hundred occupied and evacuated during the 1948 Arab-Israeli War.[2] Beginning with volume 14 dedicated to the village of Qaqun (Abdel Jawad 1994: i–iv and al-Mudawwar 1994), and in subsequent village histories, Abdel Jawad and the Birzeit University researchers enlarge the discursive domain devoted to the Nakba. Based on extensive interviews with former inhabitants that are checked against relevant written sources, scholars continue to investigate the contentious historical and historiographical issue: why did the Palestinians leave in 1948 and why is this question important? Abdel Jawad observes:

Palestine in 1948 is a typical case of a history full of holes, between a history fabricated by Israeli historiography and a history absent or lost by Arab and Palestinian historiography. Israeli historiography has adopted a denial of the Nakba, a negation of the breadth of ethnic cleansing perpetrated in Palestine. If it has always adopted a position of indifference in regards to Arab sources, Israeli historiography was particularly violent in its refusal to hear the voice of victims and their testimonies. In contrast, Arab and Palestinian historiography has never succeeded in forming a complete and solid narrative (*récit*) to confront the weight of this war of 1948, which ended with the birth of the problem of Palestinian refugees, the heart of the current Israeli-Arab conflict.

(ABDEL JAWAD 2004: 627)

To set the Palestinian narrative against the Zionist one is not an abstruse academic exercise; it is a historiographical confrontation with immediate implications and stark outcomes. Vocabulary deployed by professional historians speaks to battles about past historical events that possess powerful legal and political force in the present to influence core issues, for example, the status of Palestinian refugees, their right of return, and their claims for restitution and reparation. To debate why Palestinians left in 1948, the terms espoused by historians presuppose widely divergent ideological, and hence policy, conclusions: expulsion versus self-expulsion, abandonment, flight, exodus, evacuation, uprooting, displacement, dispersion, exile, depopulation, population transfer, ethnic cleansing, sociocide and politicide. No less than at the basic level of naming, the ways in which the respective national narratives become texts, that is, the nature and processes of text-making, are fueled by historiographical controversies that relegate Palestinian Arab testimonies to unverifiable oral, potentially self-serving, memories when measured against the weight of Jewish Israeli written discourses and archival sources.

Influenced by oral testimonies gathered as part of the *Destroyed Palestinian Villages* project, when Abdel Jawad became director of Birzeit's Centre for Research and Documentation of Palestinian Society he unearthed new facts about the 1948 period to arrive at these conclusions about the scale of Israeli killings: that there were Israeli killings of unarmed Palestinian civilians as yet not fully documented, and that accounts by his informants of specific killings in their home villages were true.

> In 1993, I worked on randomly chosen villages mainly from the central area. Why? When people left, they went as a bloc to the nearest area. People from the center of Palestine went mainly to the West Bank. So, one researcher worked on Abu Shusha, another from the north chose villagers of Tirat Haifa from a refugee camp in the north, and a third chose al-Dawayima because he himself is from there. In 1993 we knew there had been a massacre in al-Dawayima. I was astonished and shocked that in addition to al-Dawayima, there are unknown massacres in Tirat Haifa and Abu Shusha. Within days, in some cases within weeks, this led me to conclude in 1994 that we were facing a much larger scale of massacres than previously known.
>
> In 1997, the next phase of oral histories and research led us to this idea: there was a brain behind the massacres, call it a master plan, call it an outline, because there is a pattern to the killings, and a logic to this pattern. After working in different archives, my picture is that Palestine in 1948 was a theater of Israeli massacres, a continuous show of Palestinians massacred, of killings and destruction, and of psychological warfare.[3]

Individual survivor testimonies collected from exiled al-Dawayima villagers by Birzeit University researchers in the 1990s, for example, confirm an Israeli army massacre of more than eighty villagers during the 1948 war. The "slaughter"—David Ben-Gurion's term—is discussed by Israeli historian Benny Morris in his path-breaking 1987 book, *The Birth of the Palestinian*

Refugee Problem, 1947–49.[4] Morris supports his conclusions by archival sources, contemporary journalism, leaders' memoirs, and diaries.

The case of al-Dawayima exemplifies the complex interactions among historians, historiography, and oral histories. In his book *The Palestinian Catastrophe*, for example, Michael Palumbo claims accuracy for Palestinian oral memoirs when juxtaposed with Western, non-Arab sources, e.g., American, United Nations, British and Israeli (Palumbo 1987: 17). In contrast, Benny Morris explains that he "very, very, rarely" used interviews to establish facts:

> While contemporary documents might misinform, distort, omit or lie, they do so in my experience, far more rarely than interviewees recalling highly controversial events some forty years ago. My limited experience with such interviews revealed enormous gaps of memory, the ravages of aging and time, and terrible distortions or selectivity, the ravages of accepted information, prejudice and political beliefs and interests.
>
> (MORRIS 1987: 2)

Decades later in the revised 2004 edition, *The Birth of the Palestinian Refugee Problem Revisited,* Morris insists on the archives as the sole reliable window to the past, largely disregarding the role of those in power who influence the formation and content of the archive. This conceptual and methodological acceptance of the archive as the locus of unassailably authentic records excludes live witnesses as legitimate historical sources, although Morris gestures toward consulting "the essentially anthropological 'village series' produced by Birzeit University Press":

> The value of oral testimony about 1948, if anything, has diminished with the passage of the 20 years since I first researched the birth of the Palestinian refugee problem. Memories have further faded and acquired memories, ideological precepts, and political agendas have grown if anything more intractable; intifadas and counter-intifadas have done nothing for the cause of salvaging historical truth.
>
> (MORRIS 2004a: 4)

It is noteworthy that Morris's expressed concern with the unreliability of memory is occasioned by an anecdote about Israeli memory, hence a lapse or rupture not by the victims but in the perpetrator's memory. The largest single expulsion of Palestinians, some 50,000 urban-dwellers, occurred from July 9–18, 1948 after the Israeli conquest of the towns of Lydda and Ramla. Morris's decision never to rely on interviews with Jews or Arabs is clinched by a spectacular case of repressed and denied Israeli, not Palestinian, memory:

My brief forays into interviewing had persuaded me of the undesirability of relying on human memories 40–50 years after the event to illuminate the past. The
clincher came when I asked Yigal Yadin, the famous professor of archaeology
who in 1948 had served as the Haganah/IDF head of operations (and often de
facto chief of general staff) about the expulsion of the Arabs from the towns of
Lydda and Ramle. "What expulsion?" he asked—about what had been the big-
gest expulsion of the war. He did not deny that an expulsion had taken place; he
merely said that he could not remember.

(MORRIS 2004a: 6)

Morris's fidelity to the Israeli archives ensures a steady stream of revela-
tions documenting new Israeli massacres and rapes of Palestinians in 1948. In
what has since become a famous interview with journalist Ari Shavit published in Israel's *Ha'aretz* newspaper on January 9, 2004, Morris documents
statistics of a dozen cases of rapes and twenty-four instances of massacres as
supporting evidence for a pattern:

What the new material [Israel Defense Force Archives] shows is that there were
far more Israeli acts of massacre than I had previously thought. To my surprise,
there were also many cases of rape. In the months of April–May 1948, units of
the Haganah [the pre-state defense force that was the precursor of the IDF] were
given operational orders that stated explicitly that they were to uproot the villagers, expel them and destroy the villages themselves. . . .

About a dozen [rapes]. In Acre, four soldiers raped a girl and murdered her
and her father. In Jaffa, soldiers of the Kiryati Brigade raped one girl and tried
to rape several more. At Hunin, which is in the Galilee, two girls were raped
and then murdered. There were one or two cases of rape at Tantura, south of
Haifa. There was one case of rape at Qula, in the center of the country. . . . At the
village of Abu Shusha, near Kibbutz Gezer [in the Ramle area] there were four
female prisoners, one of whom was raped a number of times. And there were
other cases. Usually more than one soldier was involved. Usually there were one
or two Palestinian girls. In a large proportion of the cases the event ended with
murder. Because neither the victims nor the rapists liked to report these events,
we have to assume that the dozen cases of rape that were reported, which I found,
are not the whole story. They are just the tip of the iceberg. . . . That can't be
chance. It's a pattern. Apparently, various officers who took part in the operation
understood that the expulsion order they received permitted them to do these
deeds in order to encourage the population to take to the roads. The fact is that

no one was punished for these acts of murder. Ben-Gurion silenced the matter. He covered up for the officers who did the massacres.

(SHAVIT 2004)

Morris starkly opposes the truth of written documents in the Israeli archives against Palestinian false memory and witnessing, oppositions that help to explain both his remarkable research into, and his subsequent support of, Israel's "mass expulsion" and "population transfer" of the Palestinian population in 1948. Morris currently counts himself among the "transferists," placing himself in the company of David Ben-Gurion: "Ben-Gurion was right. If he had not done what he did, a state would not have come into being. That has to be clear. It is impossible to evade it. Without the uprooting of the Palestinians, a Jewish state would not have arisen here" (Shavit 2004).

While Morris's views about the inevitability of Israel's mass expulsion of the Palestinians have been widely debated and often condemned (Beinin 2004), it is the discipline of oral history that challenges Morris's methodological prejudices foremost by foregrounding the humanity, hence the role of the excluded Palestinian as primary witness in the face of statistics, categories, and archival documentation. When the voices of the survivor and victim are inaudible except as mere cases, the consequences for those who are the subjects of repression are political and ethical. So too, are the methodological consequences, because impeded is the creation of the secondary witness: the historian and anthropologist empathetically attentive to and informed by the full presence of Palestinians speaking and remembering. Written history, therefore, need not be opposed to witness memories; rather, memory is a source for, indeed it propels, history by instigating the inquiry into accurate, empirical facts about what happened in each destroyed Palestinian village. A different historiography, grounded in testimonial witnessing by displaced villagers, permits access to Palestinian history and narratives kept alive in no small part by Israeli attempts to expunge all traces of destruction; these attempts call the narratives of massacre into being. Archives, too, are products of their time and place, their selecting and collecting practices, often written with an eye to the future. Diplomatic, military and political documents are problematic as records of an authoritative historical understanding. Especially important here is what is absent from the Israeli archives.

These complex interactions among memory, ethical concerns, Palestinian oral history, and Israeli archives as they emerge in the aftermath of the Nakba sent me in search of the histories of one Palestinian site: the village of

Qula, depopulated and destroyed in 1948, and revived statistically in 2004 as reported in Morris's interview: "There was one case of rape at Qula, in the center of the country."

Qula's Rape

Consider Qula, a Palestinian village in the Ramla district that was destroyed in 1948, a case study in Abdel Jawad's history of the 1948 war (Figure 2). Historians Benny Morris and Walid Khalidi give crucial overviews of the hard-fought battle for the village during the war, while Abdel Jawad adds lived experience perpetuated in living memory. In the late 1990s, Abdel Jawad tape-recorded exiled Qula villagers who describe the difficult situation they faced by early June 1948, before the United Nations Security Council–mandated First Truce that resulted in a temporary cease-fire among the combatants between June 11 and July 9. Many male Qula villagers had been killed elsewhere, either defending other villages or participating in attacks. No less than fifty Palestinian fighters from the villages of Qula, al-'Abbasiyya and Kafr 'Ana died attempting to take over the British military camp at Tel Levitsky once the British departed. When Qula was attacked, villagers recount to Abdel Jawad that their main body of defenders were fighting to recapture Wilhelma, an agricultural colony founded before World War I by German Templars. None expected the Israelis, who entered from the west through the cornfields; at first, villagers expressed uncertainty about whether indeed the Israelis were attacking, since they heard only gunshots in the air. Thus, villagers' defense of Qula was minimal. Qula villagers had already paid dearly with their lives: fighters had died elsewhere, and these deaths further demoralized local defenders.

Concerning the fate of Qula, historical accounts by Khalidi and Morris concentrate on July 10, 1948, the pivotal date that fell during the ten-day period, July 9–18, between the First and Second Truces. Attempting to secure the center of the country, primarily the Lydda-Ramla plains and foothills, the 32nd infantry battalion of Israel's Alexandroni Brigade, consisting of three companies (one of which was an armored battalion), seized Qula on July 10. The Transjordanian Arab Legion, helped by inadequately armed villagers constituting a local militia, defended Qula and on July 16 they regained Qula, only to lose it the same day to Israeli units. On July 17, Arab units recaptured the village, but the following day Qula fell to two platoons and four tanks of the Alexandroni Brigade(Morris 1988: 38; Khalidi 1992: 408–9).[5]

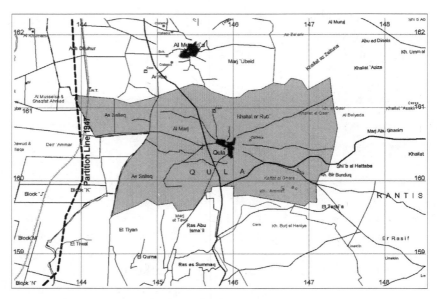

Figure 2 Qula 1947. Village land is in gray and village built-up area is black.

    Qula families fled on foot east to the Transjordanian-held West Bank, part
of an exodus that emptied Ramla district of 92,000 Palestinians. In Qula, the
elderly and paralyzed stayed behind. To convey the power of oral testimonies that live on in individuals from these villages decades later, Abdel Jawad
repeats the story of the Qula butcher, an elderly villager who refused to leave.
Family and friends remember begging him to depart. The butcher's response
burns in their memories: "No, I will stay and inherit the whole village!" According to Abdel Jawad's research, villagers from Qula assert that all those
who remained, primarily the infirm, were shot or burned to death in their
homes. In Qula, seven people were killed, six women and one man, among
them an elderly woman refugee from al-'Abbasiyya who was found burned
in the school, another old woman from Kafr 'Ana, and the butcher. Villagers
discovered their dead when they returned to Qula in search of belongings,
accompanied by a Jordanian officer, the day after the Israeli army's final takeover. One eyewitness never forgot that the Israelis used his father's kerosene
supply to burn the bodies.[6] Sometime during the attacks and counterattacks
in Qula, Morris asserts, a Palestinian woman was raped by an Israeli soldier.
Abdel Jawad, who extensively interviewed the Qula villagers, recalls no mention of the Qula rape:

Nobody talks about rape. But it is almost always present. It's there: "we left because of massacres, fear of massacres, fear of rape, rape." The men in the village
will not talk about it. At Deir Yassin, the women talked to British interrogators
about rape, that this was the worst that happened and please don't talk about it.
The society could not talk about it.[7]

Villagers frequently express fear and knowledge of rapes occurring elsewhere in 1948. For example Muhammad Mahmud Muhammad 'Abd Al-Salam
(known as Abu Faruq), formerly of the village of Ein Houd near Haifa, was
interviewed in Jenin Camp for the first monograph in the *Destroyed Palestinian Village* series. In 1985, replying to the Birzeit researchers' question about
when the villagers thought to leave, Abu Faruq insists that the villagers' only
concern was *"sharaf al-bint"* (the honor of the girls): "the first thing we left
our village for was *'ird* (honor), only *'ird*, not money, not children, just *sharaf*,
because we heard about Deir Yassin and al-Tantura next to our village where
they did things to the girls."[8] Abu Faruq refers to the most famous atrocity of
the 1948 war, which was carried out on April 9 in Deir Yassin near Jerusalem.
Approximately 105 Palestinian villagers were massacred by Jewish forces. In
Tantura on the coast south of Haifa, where villagers were expelled on May 22,
Abu Faruq's rape stories are corroborated by Morris citing the archive. Closer
to Qula, in the village of Abu Shusha in the Ramla district, Morris's book
presents the case of an attempted rape of a twenty-year-old woman prisoner
by a Hagana soldier as does the *Destroyed Palestinian Village* monograph devoted to Abu Shusha (Morris 2004: 256 and Ya'qub 1995).

From radically different perspectives, Abdel Jawad's and Morris's studies emphasize that the Israeli male perpetrator and the Palestinian female
victim do not report rape. Were Israeli soldiers out of control or were they
obeying directives to employ any means to intimidate the civilian population and force them to flee? Rape as a military tactic succeeds in many societies because it targets more than the woman; it threatens her male kin—
father, brother, husband—who cannot protect her, their *sharaf* and *'ird*. Moreover, the multiple traumas of the Nakba in general and the horrific conditions under which Qula's conquest, civilian killings, rape, flight, and exile
occurred disrupt memory and ensure silence. The rape of Qula, first publicly broached by Benny Morris in the course of an oral newspaper interview,
raises moral and representational issues. What is rape when it is not documented? Or when it is incompletely documented insofar as the Palestinian
rape victim enters a system of academic research to be transformed into a

collective category behind which Israeli soldiers are guaranteed anonymity? The story of Qula's rape, and the probability that the victim was killed to silence her, is not in any Israeli archive nor recorded on an audiocassette as part of an oral history project.

As a war crime, rape has not been specifically recognized and prosecuted, jurist Mohamed Cherif Bassiouni conjectures, because "acts which primarily harm women have not been viewed by men who make policy decisions as violations of those women's rights . . . ; rape and sexual assault are often viewed as private aberrational acts, not proper subjects for an international public forum" (Bassiouni 1996: 557–58). In the International Criminal Tribunal in The Hague, the landmark 1995 trial of *Prosecutor v. Anto Furundzija* focused on the rape and sexual assault of a Muslim woman during the armed conflict in the former Yugoslavia by the commander of a local Croatian militia. Significantly, the difficulty of relying on witness and victim memory in rape trials was understood to be inseparable from questions of how to prosecute rape when victim and witnesses were absent: many victims were killed, others feared their community's ostracism, and some were unable to identify perpetrators definitively.[9] Evidence of rape based on victim memory is open to legal disputes either as a reliable description of the perpetrators or as claims about injury and harm in ways similar to Morris's disparagement of oral history. Presumably knowledge about the rape of a Palestinian woman at Qula is the outcome of Morris's own oral exchanges with Israeli soldiers, interviews he considers inferior research tools. Moreover, such research is subject to litigation in Israeli courts, given the example of Alexandroni Brigade members who sued researcher Teddy Katz for characterizing their army practices in Tantura in 1948 as "massacres" and "war crimes" (Esmeir, this volume, and Pappé 2001). Once unspeakable past events—even a single rape as it is remembered, articulated openly in an newspaper interview, not even denied but instead noted as inevitably part of state-building projects—are rendered harmless in Morris's catalog of atrocities because there is no written archival corroboration. We only have Morris's word.

Rape takes away one's sense of oneself; it distorts the future by traumatizing the past. In rape, the cries of the victim are ignored; similarly, in the violation of history perpetrated by Morris, the voices of Palestinians have been too long ignored. For historians, the argument from silence (*argumentum ex silentio*) proposes that silence is also informative: if no confirmation exists in archival sources that something did or did not happen, such silences merely inform about a lack in the documentation and not that that the information does not exist. To undo physical rape is impossible, but critical and analytic approaches remove rape's silencing to uncover the hidden and distorted history of 1948.

The archive does recount the ways in which Qula was emptied by mid-July 1948. On September 13, 1948, David Ben-Gurion is on record in writing as requesting the destruction of a group of villages in the central region

> because of a lack of manpower to occupy the area in depth . . . there was a need to partially destroy the following villages: 1. As Safiriya, 2. Al Haditha, 3. Innaba, 4. Daniyal, 5. Jimzu, 6. Kafr Ana, 7. Al Yahudiya, 8. Barfiliya, 9. Al Barriya, 10. Qubab, 11. Beit Nabbala, 12. Deir Tarif, 13. At Tira, 14. Qula.
>
> (Morris 1987: 165)

In Ramla district, all fifty-eight Palestinian villages that came under Israeli control were depopulated in 1948, according to the 1987–90 survey geographer Ghazi Falah conducted with Birzeit University researchers. Of seven possible categories Falah employs to organize tables of "Levels of Housing Destruction" in the Ramla district, three accurately describe the fate of villages earmarked for demolition in Ben-Gurion's memorandum: (1) ten villages completely obliterated; (2) in twelve villages, complete destruction; rubble of original houses clearly identified, no walls standing; (3) in eight villages, houses are mostly demolished; rubble contains walls standing but without roofs (Falah 1996: 264). By autumn 1948, the physical destruction of Qula, following the loss of human life, was complete.

Metaphor, Memory and Material Culture

It has been a major achievement by historians of 1948 that the conditions and numbers of *actual* rape and civilian massacre of the Palestinian population are finally recognized. Paradoxically, the *metaphor* of rape to embody the loss of Palestine seems to represent an early and pervasive response to forcible exile and mass dispossession, producing the rhetorical and figurative creation of a set of cultural images about woman, the nation, and the Nakba. Repeated intertextually and circulated in literature, art, and folklore are tropes of the Palestinian woman as mother and motherland, home and homeland, lover and beloved, raped and despoiled by Zionist occupation. Metaphors of rape are used mainly by Palestinians to designate the loss of homeland and mask the experience of rape. The trope of Palestine, the virgin bride violently raped by an invading enemy, complements subsequent metaphors of

rape deployed to describe Israel's environmental spoliation and the destruction of Palestinian villages (Bardenstein 1997: 170). These Palestinian representations of collective loss and trauma as rape have elicited harsh critiques
and self-criticism as retrograde nostalgia, or alternatively are valued for mobilizing collective consciousness and political resistance. The problem with
metaphors, however, is that they annihilate history and dissolve temporality,
especially concerning the functions of memory and oral testimony with respect to Palestinian national history. The relationship between lived history
(actual rape) and texts (metaphorical rape of Palestine, the homeland) is one
of opposition, opacity, and chronological reversals.

Nonetheless, metaphoric representations of rape accomplish this: while
masking the reality of rape and while living in the margins of the Nakba,
they keep alive the memory of rape, thereby pointing the discursive toward
the real, i.e., to further archival and oral historical research about the facticity
of rapes. When collective and personal pain cannot be borne, distance and
temporary amnesis from the events of the Nakba are partially achieved by
constructing fictions and metaphors that permit us both to hide from the real
and to seek out memory. In this way, the workings of Palestinian memory
belatedly serve to delineate research topics and protocols for historians and
anthropologists. Therefore, to write oral testimony and document Palestinian material culture returns us to the everyday lived experience of Palestinians before 1948, all of which are steadily disappearing in post-1948 Israel.

In order to register this past history of destruction in significantly different ways, I offer narratives of pre-1948 and post-1948 Qula that call upon the
study of landscape and physical objects as primary historical and source data
about Palestinian rural society. Palestinian history is also embodied in material sites, land and houses, shrines and cemeteries. The study of human
interaction with the physical environment and with things, otherwise known
as the study of material culture, is defined as: "the totality of artifacts in a culture; the vast universe of objects used by humankind to cope with the physical world, to facilitate social intercourse, to delight our fancy, and to create
symbols of meaning" (Herskovits 1963: 119). What are the relations between
the history and anthropology of actual places and physical objects in general,
and in particular, to the memory of the Nakba? By studying the processes
of creating and documenting material culture, the interactions between creators and human-shaped materials are implicated in projects on oral history
such that Palestinians regain the status of historical subjects.

One declared purpose of the *Destroyed Palestinian Village* memorial monograph, the agent of this search, is to make this and other villages exist decades after their loss—to make them more than "mere names on an old map"
(*mujarrad asma' 'ala al-kharita al-qadima*). Palestinian anthropologist Sharif
Kanaana prefaces the Birzeit University project:

> Each study will attempt to the extent possible to describe the life of the people
> in the village such that the reader is able to picture it as living, inhabited and
> cultivated as it was in 1948 before it was destroyed. This portrayal will allow Pal-
> estinians, especially those who had left these villages at an early age or were born
> outside of them after 1948 to feel tied and connected to the villages, society and
> real country as if they had lived in it, rather than it just being a name on a map.
>
> (KANAANA AND KA'BI, 1987: 3 and KANAANA, 1989: 3)

In what follows, I attempt to assemble documentation for a memorial
monograph about Qula, specifically an artifactual record of Qula. By exploring the problem of relating historical understanding to the analysis of material culture, Qula stands as a concrete manifestation of Palestinian cultural
history, one that uncovers ruptures cyclically reenacted, and since 1948 re-
inforced over decades by fresh losses and destruction. I read Qula as one of
many Palestinian "memory sites," or *lieux de mémoires*, in the phrase of historian Pierre Nora (Nora 1989), invested with discourses and metaphors of
rape along with so many physical and cultural ruptures, to the point of shattering not just material traces but also efforts at representation. Consequently,
any and every reference to Qula speaks for the rich past, while pointing to the
many ways Qula was destroyed and continues to be devastated.

Kuleh

[P.n.: proper name, a word to which no meaning may be assigned][10]
Qula (also Qulah, Qulyah, Kouleh and Kuleh), rising 125 meters above
sea level, is located approximately fourteen kilometers northeast of the town
of Ramla on the site of the Crusader fortress known as Cola or Chola. On
June 7, 1873, British engineers from the London-based Palestine Exploration
Fund visited Qula while conducting a massive six-year survey project of the
Holy Land. Characterizing the local topography according to the natural
east-west division formed by Wadi Dayr Ballut, they mapped a valley steeply
descending from its eastern heights of 1,500 feet above sea level in the central

highland ridge down to the lower hills at 500 feet around Qula in the west before reaching the flat coastal plain that extends to the Mediterranean Sea (Figure 3). In Arabic, the foothills on which Qula is perched are called *arqiyat*; in Hebrew *shefelah*, the biblical name for the Judean foothills that the British surveyors describe as:

> lower hills of soft limestone, and less rugged in outline with open valleys between. . . . The low hills (or Shephelah) consists of a porous chalk, and they are supplied by wells and cisterns, the water sinking through and appearing again in the plain, as at the Ras el Ain springs which receives the whole drainage from numerous springs along the course of the Wady Deir Ballut.
>
> (*SURVEY* 1998, 2: 283).

Nineteenth-century Qula possessed houses, wells, and Crusader ruins. The surveyors note that the village is:

> of moderate size on a slope at the edge of the plain. The modern houses are principally mud, but the place has remains of medieval date. There are wells on the north-west. . . . This village includes some well-built structures. There is a large building of small well-cut masonry of mediaeval appearance; the door on the south has a pointed arch and a tunnel vaulting. South of this is a square building with walls 10 feet to 12 feet thick, and a staircase on one side leading to the roof; the corner stones are large, drafted, and with a rustic boss; there are remains of a lofty doorway. This is called Burj Kuleh. There is a birkeh, about 20 feet square, and 6 feet or 8 feet deep, lined with good cement; it is called Birket er Ribba. These remains have the appearance of Crusading work, and the name, Neby Yahyah, close by, points also to former Christian occupation of the place.
>
> (*SURVEY* 1998, 2: 358)

Crusader structures of Qula, described in Meron Benvenisti's 1970 survey, are an "example of a perfectly preserved rural depot," with a barrel-vaulted watchtower and an adjoining barrel-vaulted storehouse built of rough-hewn stones erected shortly after 1181 when the village was purchased by the Order of the Hospitallers from Hugh of Flanders (Benvenisti 1970: 227–29 and Pringle 1997: 87). From other travelers, meager details about Muslim-Arab life are gleaned despite the exclusionary focus by British and French travelers on what they perceived as their own Crusader and biblical pasts. In Victor Guérin's three-volume account of his 1863 Holy Land tour, he too describes a brief visit to Kouleh to view well-preserved Crusader structures. He alludes briefly to the presence of a small mosque, noteworthy because built

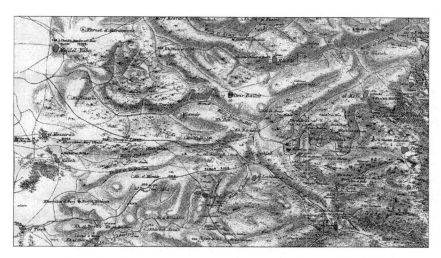

Figure 3 Qula 1878.

primarily from cannibalized ancient *(antiques)* materials, especially its orna-
mental door moldings that he dated to before the Muslim invasion. In nearby villages, for example al-Tira, he remarks on prevalent local construction
methods that incorporate ancient materials into contemporary Arab housing
(Guérin 1874, 2: 390–91).

Qula appears as a statistic during Ottoman rule over the Arab provinces.
Numbers from tax and census registers taken in 1595, note geographers Wolf-
Dieter Hütteroth and Kamal Abdulfattah, attest to its status as a revenue-gen-
erating village. The agricultural productivity by Qula villagers is carefully
measured in taxes assessed for their goats, beehives, and a press to process
olives or grapes (Hütteroth and Abdulfattah 1977).

By 1948, according to Khalidi's book and the website devoted to destroyed
Qula, the village population of 1,010 people was predominantly Muslim, lived
in approximately 172 houses, prayed in two mosques, buried their dead in the
cemetery, conducted business in several shops in the village center, and their
children attended a school established in 1919 which enrolled 134 students
(Khalidi 1992: 408–9 and www.palestineremembered.com/al-Ramla/Qula).

Post–1948 Qula: Forest, Highway and Wall

Between the years 1948—the date that Qula's population was expelled
and its homes destroyed—and the 1990s, it could be said that the physical

lineaments of the village enclave survived. A section of agricultural lands two miles to the southwest of Qula, on lands of the destroyed Palestinian village al-Tira, was allocated to the moshav (Jewish smallholders settlement) named Givat Koakh. The majority of Qula village land was given over to forests planted by the Jewish National Fund. JNF afforestation programs during the British Mandate over Palestine covered a mere 22,000 dunams. By 1997 mass-production forestry increased tracts of forestlands to 500,000 dunams (Lehn with Davis 1988: 143). Systematic afforestation of Palestinian villages and farming areas was the strategic goal of Israel's Ministry of Agriculture; forests to prove "possession of these lands, and at the same time to create a recreational element" (Cohen 1993: 112).

To interpret the State of Israel's ceaseless transformations of the landscape and geography after 1948 in relation to the current status of Palestinian villages within Israel, a useful measure is the eleven-point continuum of anthropologist Sharif Kanaana. His baseline first category is the complete obliteration of the Palestinian Arab village with a simultaneous replacement by reforestation. He concludes with an eleventh category, the only one in which Arab villages are preserved, even enlarged by the resettlement of Palestinian refugees evicted from villages enumerated in ten intervening categories. Category ten is reserved for destroyed villages that are now public parks, among them Yalu, Imwas, Kabri, Lubya, Dallata, Muzayri'a and Qula (Kanaana 1994).

A national park with monuments to the Jewish war dead occupies the land where Qula once was. So ubiquitous are memorials, plaques, stones, and sculptures throughout Israel that visitors are said to perceive them as indigenous and natural to the landscape; tourists go to site-specific, material culture displays of Israel's "state cult" in which the vocabulary of stone slabs, the wall of names, and frequently an arrangement of tanks link the 1948 war to geography and landscape (Azaryahu 1995 and Young 1993).[11] One section of former Qula village within the forest is set aside as a picnic site and children's playground. In an adjacent clearing, a smooth tall stone monument *(andarta)* on top of a rock outcropping bears the names of twenty-eight soldiers listed under the heading: "Here fell in battle on the 9th of Tammuz 1948, 28 heroes of Israel" (Figure 4). In Hebrew, a letter may function as a number permitting any word to be read simultaneously for meaning and numerical value. Thus, the letter *kaf* for twenty and *het* for eight articulate the word Koakh ("strength") that both numbers the twenty-eight Jewish dead ("Hill of the 28") and names the settlement, Givat Koakh ("Hill of Strength")

Figure 4
Qula 2004: Jewish War Memorial

instead of Qula. Names in Israel no less than material cultural objects, Nadia
Abu El-Haj reminds us, are "fetishized as *facts* . . . *rendering true* the ideological commitment that Jewish settlement in Palestine was a process, quite simply, of national return. These were not just *any* names" (Abu El Haj 2002:
54). Givat Koakh neither rewrites the past with a resurrected biblical Hebrew
name nor Hebraicizes an existing Arab one; rather, it inscribes place with
war, catastrophe, and destruction. An additional commemorative marker is
the large flat rock whose inscription narrates the 32nd battalion's history in
Hebrew to conclude:

> In the battles of Qula, twenty-eight soldiers of the Alexandroni Brigade fell and
> in their name this place is called Givat Koakh. In this case, as with Nebi Yusha,
> there is no correlation between the accepted number and the information in IDF
> history; according to this information, in Qula thirty-two soldiers of the Alexan-
> droni Brigade fell. (Ministry of Defense, Commemoration Branch).

The name of Qula has been obliterated except for the Hebrew-language sign-
post directing visitors to the park and the Alexandroni war memorial.

Qula village, with its Israeli-made ruins, retreated beneath a wide swath of forests whose eastern edges marked the boundaries of the Armistice Line between Israel and Transjordan. Israelis call this demarcation the Green Line, a name often mistakenly believed to refer to the forested green belt that covered villages like Qula. In fact, a green-colored line was drawn in 1949 on a map and transferred Qula from east of the 1947 Partition Line, thereby marking a temporary military boundary that lasted from 1948 until 1967. While the June 1967 war eliminated the 1949 Green Line as the de facto boundary between states, the establishment of illegal Israeli settlements east of the Green Line in the Occupied Territories produced new north-south annexations that continue to shift the boundaries of Israeli-controlled territory deeper to the east. Another example of the north-south boundaries shifting eastward is the "Red Line," a concept promoted by Israeli hydrologists. Citing the necessity to tap into Palestinian water resources, Israeli planners describe the 200-meter topographical contour line as the Red Line, one that underlies their claims to the aboveground geopolitical territory and to the underground water over additional Israeli-annexed territory that lies approximately six kilometers east of the Green Line and inside the West Bank (Cohen 1986).

By 2000, a "black line" had been added to the multi-layered construction of the Green Line and the Red Line. The reference is to the 300-kilometer highway that links the northern reaches of the Galilee near the Lebanese border to the region south of Beersheva. The 1949 Green Line, the post-1948 Red Line, and the 2000 black line are part of processes by which Israel re-demarcates national boundaries through territorial expansion eastward, notably due to the 1993 Oslo accords that classified the area east of Qula (from the Green Line to Rantis) as Palestinian territory Area "B" (Israeli-controlled and operated) as opposed to Area "A" (Palestinian Authority-operated areas).

From the perspective of the rights of Palestinians under Israeli occupation, the newest Road 6 is viewed as another effective component of Israel's "matrix of control" (Halper 2002), a term coined by anthropologist Jeff Halper, coordinator of the Jerusalem-based Israeli Committee Against House Demolitions:

> It's [Road 6] an attempt to move metropolitan Tel Aviv and a lot of the coastal cities eastward and in that way bring them closer to the (West Bank) border, where the settlements can then expand westward and connect up . . . to create facts on the ground that, in a sense, are immune to the ups and downs of negotiation. . . . This is one of the last holes to plug up in terms officially linking the whole net-

work of highways and settlements in the West Bank integrally into Israel itself. And once that's done, then a Palestinian state is almost impossible.

(ANDERSON 2002)

At the Rantis Junction where the Cross-Israel Highway meets road 465 (Khotse Binyamin), an access road winds eastward through the foothills to service the settlement of Beit Arye. Between the junction and moshav Givat Koakh, the highway runs right over the area comprising the agricultural lands surrounding the village of Qula pinpointed as longitude 34 degrees 57.3 minutes east and latitude 32 degrees 2.3 minutes north. Before highway construction was completed, between March–June 1995 and November 1995–February 1996, "following the clearance of the ruins of the village of Qula," Israeli archeologists "in the framework" of the Cross-Israel Highway Project and on behalf of the Antiquities Authority undertook a "salvage excavation" (Avissar and Shabo 2000: 51). Material objects that were enumerated (oil lamps, cooking pots, pottery and glass vessels), sherds and ceramics, and an extensive cemetery are variously attributed to periods ranging from the Iron Age, Persian, Hellenistic, and Early Roman to late Byzantine.

The Green Line, the Red Line, and the black line do not exhaust the borders and barriers, checkpoints and barricades, enclosures and enclaves that Israel has created to contain, constrict, and ultimately imprison Palestinians. Where stretches of the Cross-Israel Highway pass close to the former 1967 border, the highway runs parallel to Israel's latest major construction project, called either the "Security Fence" or the "Apartheid Wall." At the Kafr Qasim junction, twelve kilometers north of Qula, an eight-meter-high security barrier runs alongside Highway 6. South of Kafr Qasim the wall turns eastward, incorporating sections of the West Bank while isolating Palestinian villages. By January 2004, construction of the wall reached west of Rantis. Approximately 125 acres of Rantis agricultural land was confiscated to build a fence between seven and nine meters high surrounded by two deep ditches and two barbed wire fences on either side, another electronic fence with sensors and flanked by patrol roads and watchtowers. Rantis is one of nine Palestinian villages constricted to a 53-square-kilometer enclave that also includes the villages of Luban al-Gharbiya, Budrus, Shuqba, Qibya, Shabtin, Budrus, Midya, Na'lin and Dayr Kadis. These are the very villages where many Qula exiles settled after expulsion to be as near as possible to their former homes: across the Green Line to the east and within the post-1948 Transjordanian-controlled villages of Rantis, Lubban and 'Abud. The Qula villagers have not moved since their 1948 forced relocation, but the border has. Currently, these villages fall under the latest unilaterally annexed Israeli territory based on the serpentine route of the wall. Israel's latest boundary marches eastward up the higher reaches of the foothills, effectively annexing the Jewish settler communities of Beit Arye and Ofarim, established in 1981 and 1989 respectively.[12]

Creating walls and boundaries is the task of the bulldozer and the tank. For Jeff Halper, they are intertwined symbols for Israel's relationship with the Palestinians:

> The two deserve to be on the national flag. The tank as symbol of an Israel "fighting for its existence," and for its prowess on the battlefield. And the bulldozer for the dark underside of Israel's struggle for existence, its ongoing struggle to displace the Palestinians from the country.... The Message of the Bulldozers is: "You do not belong here. We uprooted you from your homes in 1948 and prevented your return, and now we will uproot you from all of the Land of Israel."
>
> (HALPER 2002)

The bulldozer is the weapon of choice first to demolish, then to create ruins from Palestinian houses destroyed in 1948. It has long been part of the arsenal of Jewish National Fund's tree-planting programs. Environmentalist Alon Tal's description of the Israeli afforestation program can be parsed metaphorically, not only as a cascading series of ecological disasters, but also as the foreign bulldozer's expertise in eradicating all that is Palestinian and native:

> The attack was multi-pronged. First, fires were lit to erase any remnant of indigenous bushes, trees, and brush. Next, bulldozers were brought to sweep away the debris; then plows prepared the soil for planting. Finally, pesticides ensured that the new pine seedlings would not be troubled by other undesirable biological activity. Environmentalists charged that the underlying soil inevitably suffered from the relentless onslaught, while the surrounding ecosystem was irreversibly knocked off balance. Once the trees grew their needles formed a highly acidic ground cover that decomposed very slowly. The result was a sterile forest bed inhospitable to additional undergrowth and to most animal populations. Environmentalists coined the term "the pine deserts" to describe them.
>
> (TAL 2002: 94–95)

The bulldozer excavates forests by destroying surface and upper layers; for archeological sites, it digs deeply to specific epochs, setting aside layers of Ottoman, Arab, and Palestinian life to the scrap heap. The built environment of Qula and its landscape have undergone radical transformations since 1948, depredations that are constitutive of discourses of metaphorical rape encompassing demographic, ethnic, cultural, historic, political, social, geographic, and anthropological erasures. Given the histories of mass dispossession—people, house, lands, objects, trees—how can Palestinian memorial books document the Nakba through the quality and content of Palestinian material culture? Ideal parameters for research on material culture include careful description and photographic documentation of a vast array of objects, information about how they were and are made, the skills necessary to make them, their function, and biographies of individual creators and histories of their specific communities.

The Odds-and-Ends Woman

On December 29, 1999, Saleh Abdel Jawad first visited the site of Qula. From his hometown al-Bira, the quickest route by car is over the central hills to Rantis 19 kilometers northwest, then the few kilometers due west and south to Qula. Israeli Army checkpoints enclosing Rantis forced a major detour that looped south via Jerusalem, across the checkpoint at al-Ram, then west and north on highway 444. In 1999, physical traces of 1948 Palestinian Qula were visibly scattered throughout the forested site: stone wall sections from houses, large iron door locks, horseshoes, metal dishes, broken blue glassware, and ancient fig trees. While walking around Qula to videotape village ruins, Abdel Jawad recounts his encounter with a group of Israeli excavators who waved away his camera:

> They opened up the village like a knife cutting across the belly and splitting it open to view the contents inside. It was there at Qula that the feeling was strongest for me. In my head there was a virtual scene—families gather around, people were eating, work was done, children were following each other chatting and running. There was joy. The life was there. It was amazing because there was complete silence.[13]

Individual objects salvaged were brought back to his home in Ramallah for further study and eventual placement in the planned museum and archive to Palestinian culture. Extreme mobility has been forced on Palestinian museums as with Palestinian memories. Given Israel's history of confiscating or destroying Palestinian archives,[14] much of Abdel Jawad's collection is stored for safety abroad. Beyond folkloristic salvage operations or postmodern concerns with representation and metaphors, these efforts to collect and

preserve objects return us to the object itself, to the lived experience perpetuated in things and their traditional uses. Parallel to the erasure of Qula
through war, rape, depopulation, afforestation, park, and highway projects,
the prominence we give to metaphorical and metonymic representations of
forms of historical memory that inhabit material culture overcomes a net-
work of relations in which Palestinians are collectively displaced elsewhere,
and doubly so, because never in the same vicinity as their dispersed belongings, homes, and land.

For Emile Habiby, a prominent Palestinian writer who is a citizen of Israel, memory and archival research are sustained through the contemplation
of material objects. In the short story "Umm al-Rubabikiya" (translated as
"The Odds-and-Ends Woman" or "The Junk Dealer"), Habiby tells of an old
Arab woman in Israel who collects things left behind by fleeing Palestinians in
1948, items such as "furniture and coffee cups and *kubbeh* mortars and tooth-
brushes and insect sprays and books by al-Farabi and toilet rolls" (Habiby
1992: 455). As she goes about patiently preserving artifacts, photographs and
mementos of everyday life from pre-1948 Palestine, she addresses the author
directly and urgently:

> "Go on write something! Write about the treasures from the inside of my sofa. I've
> got whole bundles of young people's treasures here: first love letters, poems hid-
> den by boys in the pages of school textbooks, bracelets, earrings, bangles, chains
> with gold-shaped pendants that you open to find two pictures inside, his and hers.
> I've got diaries in shy, delicate handwriting and others in broad, confident hands.
> They're full of questions: what does he want from me? And full of binding oaths
> for the homeland. Will you promise to write about my treasures, so the roving
> spirits can find their way to me here?"
>
> (HABIBY 1992: 459)

The junk dealer refuses to sell her things. She says she must await the true
owners whom she knows will return one day, owners she refers to as "rov-
ing spirits" (Habiby 1992: 458). The junk dealer stands for a different salvage
operation, one that squirrels away shards and remnants of a vibrant Palestinian life as hidden treasures remaining within Israel. Objects did not follow
their owners into exile. Habiby's short story unmasks one aspect of the situation of dispossession for Palestinians who live in the state of Israel, while
his literary imagination holds out several varieties of hope: the hope of return, the reunion of material culture with its human-made creators, and the
injunction to write.

In a similar fashion, research projects by Abdel Jawad and others are inseparable from memory that refuses to forget, the debt owed to the Palestinian dead, and the recovery of actual physical objects. Nonetheless, odds and ends collectors, as do investigators of Palestinian history, give proof for the memory of the Nakba, sometimes in writing, other times in material form. Methods include breaking down into component elements—for example, into individual Palestinian biographies, specific rapes and killings, patterns of massacres and sexual assaults, precise numbers of house demolitions, trees uprooted, and graves desecrated—in order to support testimonial Nakba memories as critical evidence that disturbs and makes claims on official narrated histories.

Author's Note

I am most grateful to Saleh Abdel Jawad for discussions, interviews and materials. For additional readings, maps, photographs and information, I thank Salman Abu Sitta, Hannah Nave, Dan Rabinowitz, Nettanel Slyomovics, Steven Strang, Ted Swedenburg, Heghnar Watenpaugh, and the editors of this volume. None is responsible for views expressed.

NOTES

1. See my review of the *Destroyed Palestinian Village* series (1991: 385–87); for extensive discussions on the term "memorial" books, see also "The Memory of Place" (1994: 157–68) and *The Object of Memory* (1998: 1–28).

2. The history of estimating the precise number of villages obliterated or depopulated (ranging from 290 to 472 villages) is summarized in W. Khalidi, ed. (1992: xv–xvii) especially his "Appendix IV: Palestinian Villages Depopulated in 1948: A Comparison of Sources," pp. 585–94. Mustafa Dabbagh compiled village profiles in his eleven-volume *Biladuna filastin* (1972–86). The four-volume *al-Mawsu'a al-filastiniya* (1984) is based on Dabbagh's study and presents alphabetical entries for 391 villages.

3. Interviews with Saleh Abdel Jawad, Cambridge, Massachusetts, March 31 and June 3, 2004.

4. See chapter 6 dedicated to the 1948 war in al-Adharba 1997: 195–232 with the editorial supervision of Saleh Abdel Jawad; also Morris 1988: 222–23 and W. Khalidi 1992: 215.

5. Qula figures in accounts about Jewish and Arab attempts to make peace in the months between December 1947 and March 1948. Morris quotes memos from the Jewish Hagana Intelligence Service that report that Hassan Salameh, a native son of Qula and important resistance leader, unsuccessfully tried to rouse the inhabitants in the area to mount attacks: "The Ramle National Committee told him [Hassan Salameh] that they would not attack neighboring Jewish settlements unless they were themselves attacked. Lydda's National Committee took the same line" (Morris 1987: 38).

I thank Ted Swedenburg for the following reference, a sensational account of the lives of Hassan Salameh (commander during the 1936–39 Arab Revolt) and his son, Ali Hassan Salameh (Fatah leader) that includes a village description, concocted post-1948 and noteworthy for its Orientalist tropes: "Even in its golden age, though, Kulleh, had been a desolate, miserable village. The curse of poverty and disease had always hovered over the tiny village clustered around a few brackish wells, in the narrow Lydda plain. For more than a thousand years Kulleh's inhabitants, using primitive tools, had been fighting a losing battle against its hostile soil. They lived like their ancestors before them, raising their big families in the same mud-and-straw houses, praying in the same decrepit mosque every Friday, spending their evenings in the shabby café, over tiny cups of sugary, thick *qahwah*. Nothing seemed to happen in Kulleh, except when a foreign army would roam through the village in its way from Jerusalem to the Mediterraneann coast, and their inhabitants would thus learn that Palestine had got a new master. Not that it changed anything in their way of life: Seljuks, Crusaders, Arabs, Turks, Egyptians—they all came and went, and Kulleh remained, strangely forgotten, in the shadow of the barren Samaria mountains (Bar-Zohar and Haber 1983: 17–18).

6. Interview with Saleh Abdel Jawad, Cambridge, Massachusetts, March 31, 2004.

7. Interview with Saleh Abdel Jawad, Cambridge, Massachusetts, May 6, 2004. For an excellent analysis of the rapes at Deir Yassin, see Hasso (2000: 493–500).

8. Muhammad Mahmud Muhammad 'Abd al-Salam (Abu Faruq), taped interview with Sharif Kanaana and Bassam al-Ka'bi, Jenin Camp, February 14, 1985, cassette 3; al-Ka'bi, Arabic transcription, p. 36; my translation (quoted in Slyomovics 1998: 99–101). Abu Faruq's concerns are attested to by other researchers (Warnock 1990: 23 and Sayigh 1979: 87).

9. *Prosecutor v. Furundzija*, case no. IT-95–17 transcript available at *www.un.org/icty/ furundzija/appeal/judgement*. See also Khawla Abu-Baker (in Rabinowitz and Abu-Baker 2005: 45), who recounts her aunt Nazmiya's report to her years later in which she heard the rape of a Palestinian woman neighbor at night by Israeli soldiers in 1948. While Abu Baker's account is usually inadmissible hearsay in

any courtroom, her aunt Nazmiya's presence as an "aural witness" appears in the context of the neighbor woman's immediate departure and disappearance to Lebanon.

10. P.n. was used by British surveyors to designate place names with no known biblical provenance or obvious meaning (*Survey of Western Palestine* 1998, vol. 1: v). The definition of Kuleh as a proper name is taken from the survey's "Name Lists," 8: 237.

11. For example, visible from the main Highway 6 where it meets road 444, before the turn-off to Givat Koakh is a monument to the "Egrof Varomach" Brigade with an arrangement of painted and labeled tanks, and bilingual signs recounting the Brigade's history. For Palestinian reactions to Highway 6, see Rabinowitz and Vardi (forthcoming).

12. Beit Arye was named after Arye Ben-Eliezer, a commander of ETZEL during the British Mandate who became a leader of the Herut movement now part of the Likud party.

13. Interview with Saleh Abdel Jawad, Cambridge, Massachusetts, March 17, 2004.

14. For example, after the 2002 Israeli invasion of Ramallah, see the letter to the international community by Yasser Abed Rabbo, Palestinian Minister of Culture and Information asking: "to put an end to Israel's cultural cleansing efforts against the Palestinian People. . . . The Israeli occupation army has invaded, ransacked, and destroyed every Palestinian Ministry and official building. Today alone, they raided the Ministries of Health, Social Affairs, and Supplies, and the Standards Institution. They also raided and destroyed the Khalil Sakakini Cultural Center in Ramallah, one of Palestine's most important cultural centers. During these attacks, Israeli soldiers detonated explosives to enter through the gates, exploded safes, and destroyed the buildings. However, what is far more important than this physical aggression is their systematic assault on official records, archives, historical art, crafts, and other important possessions," posted on the American Library Association website, Executive Committee June 18, 2002 Meeting Minutes.

Figure 5 Cover of the Dayr Aban memorial book.

2 Mapping the Past, Re-creating the Homeland

MEMORIES OF VILLAGE PLACES IN PRE-1948 PALESTINE

Rochelle Davis

"Are you the Canaans of Nablus or the Canaans of Jerusalem?" my mother would ask. My father, who prided himself on knowing every inch of Palestine, often joined in. But sometimes he was stumped when someone cited the name of a small village. He would worry at it until he found it. "Ah," he would suddenly say, "it's in the district of Jaffa! Why didn't you say so at first?"

For years, I thought this obsession with places and family names and who was related to whom was just a quirk of my parents. My sister and I used to imitate them in our bedroom after a particularly grueling interrogation with some hapless Palestinian visitor and laugh and shake our heads. It took me years to realize that after 1948, establishing a person's origin became for Palestinians a kind of mapping, a surrogate repopulation of Palestine in negation of the Nakba. It was their way of recreating the lost homeland, as if the families and the villages and the relations they had once known were all still there, waiting to be reclaimed.

(KARMI 1999: 40)

Ghada Karmi, in this recollection of her family's life in London, recognizes her parents' interrogation of other Palestinians as part of maintaining Palestine in the diaspora—as she says, of "recreating the lost homeland." In the face of the 1948 war, upheaval, and the destruction of communal and family ties, Palestinians have maintained these mental maps that assign Palestinians geographical locations and origins, even if those places no longer exist on the ground. The pre-1948 physical places and all that attended them have become conceptual or memorial spaces maintained and shared through many forms and forums.

Among the most intriguing forms for recreating the homeland are the books Palestinians have produced, using their own voices to describe and evoke their villages destroyed in 1948. These manuscripts are known in English as "village memorial books."[1] They are local productions by Palestinians who have independently taken on the task of collecting information about their villages of origin and publishing it for a local readership. These village memorial books, written by Palestinian refugees who have long struggled to make their voices heard, exemplify the work of a segment of the population that is seizing the opportunity to write their own history and publicize their perspectives on what happened to them in 1948, and especially what they lost. Framed within a larger national and historical Palestinian narrative, these books also compile and present information about the villages that is purely local knowledge and does not exist in any other sources.

A close look at the way places are recalled and described in the memorial books reveals that they are positioned within a national discourse of glorification of the peasant life, of living closely attached to the land. Building on Ted Swedenburg's work on the Palestinian peasant as national signifier (Swedenburg 1990), I suggest that "geographic nostalgia" characterizes the way people write about the places of the past. There are three interwined reasons for this: first, the physical destruction of the majority of the villages that these people came from makes them nostalgic for a lost place; second, the process in 1948 that turned peasant populations into landless refugees makes them associate the land with a life before catastrophic change; and third, the fact that these refugees now work in business and civil service jobs and not as peasants intensifies their idealization of what they no longer have. The village space that people recall is thus not only a place that does not exist, but also represents a lifestyle that its former inhabitants and their descendants no longer practice. I am concerned, in my study of the memorial books, with how Palestinians frame their memories of places of the pre-1948 village and the forms that their memories of places take. I will argue that in the village memorial books, despite the unique representations of village places they offer through recording detailed place names and features, the experiences and sentiments associated with those places conform to the shared experiences and sentiments expected of Palestinians as shaped by a nationalist idealization of peasant life. Thus I use the "maps of the past" that people create in the village memorial books to trace the process by which local spaces become canvases for the enactment of nationalistic visions of the pre-1948 past.

In the first part of this chapter, I offer some background on the memorial books and the events of 1948. In the second part, I present the different methods of mapping the past that are employed in the books: cartographic maps, lists, poems, and journeys. The different forms used to map the places of the past suggest a variety of ways in which these spaces are shaped and claimed as places, post-1948, through their authority of knowledge and experience. Because Palestinian maps of the pre-1948 landscape consist not only of place names—as is common in cartographic representations, but also of experiences, values, and idealizations—understanding how Palestinians represent pre-1948 spaces and places relates directly to the identities that Palestinians are actively creating in the present. The physical recording of these memories in books is inscribed by and reinscribes the history of what existed and what Palestinians experienced. I will conclude by discussing how to interpret these maps within the larger context in which they are placed in the books: that of mapping a particular past that ties the village spaces to a communal view of village life that offers a romanticized reconstruction of the places in the village to the new generations of refugees, who are no longer farmers and peasants and who do not personally know the village.

Palestinian Memorial Books and
Geohistorical Background

The Palestinian village memorial books are written about the pre-1948 villages in "historic Palestine" (British mandatory Palestine). They are written by Palestinians who today live in Lebanon, Syria, Jordan, the West Bank, Gaza, and Israel, all of whom are refugees from the 1948 war that resulted in the depopulation of over 400 Palestinian villages and numerous cities.[2] These villages, the subject of their writings, were absorbed geographically into the new Israeli state, but because of Israeli state policies during and after the 1948 war, it is estimated that 70 percent of these villages were totally destroyed, and another 22 percent were left with only a few houses or religious places standing.[3] Thus almost all of the physical places that these books describe no longer exist, or lie in ruins.

The Palestinian village memorial books begin to appear in the 1980s and 1990s. The books resemble the work of other destroyed communities such as the Armenians from Turkey, Jews from Eastern Europe, and most recently

Bosnians (Slyomovics 1998). Susan Slyomovics relies on one of these books for her study of the village of Ein Houd ['Ayn Hawd], a Palestinian village near Haifa, resettled post-1948 as an Israeli artists' colony and renamed Ein Hod. Her pioneering book *The Object of Memory* provides an overview of the memorial book genre in general as well as specific discussion of the Palestinian memorial books, in particular the Birzeit series, *al-Qura al-Filastiniyya al-Mudammara* (The Destroyed Palestinian Villages).[4] Further work on the memorial books by Laleh Khalili examined their production in Lebanon as part of grass-roots commemorations to remember the land. She views the writing of the books as both an act of salvage ethnography and of political advocacy (Khalili 2004b). My essay builds on their analyses to consider the production of these texts in all regions of the Palestinian diaspora and to discuss specifically the ways in which places are mapped and described in this genre.

The authors of the memorial books are almost always older men, many of whom wrote the books after they retired from teaching.[5] The vast majority of these men were born in the villages they write about, but left as children or young adults. The books are self-published by the author or, in a few cases, published in conjunction with village organizations, especially the ones in Amman, Jordan, or by Palestinian publishing houses, such as Dar al-Shajara in Damascus and Dar al-Jalil in Amman. To my knowledge there are at least sixty such books, different in mode of production and authorship from the Birzeit University series on the destroyed villages mentioned above and the Palestinian Cities Series published by the Cultural Department of the Palestine Liberation Organization.[6]

The books share broad categories but vary in length, how they present the material, and the amount of detail they include. On average the books are between 150 and 200 pages long, with a number of them more than 400 pages long. They contain descriptions of the geography of the village, its history, village folklore and customs, the everyday life of its residents, including photographs, maps, family trees, poetry, lists of martyrs, and reproduction of documents. The books begin with the geographic location and history of the village and its name, and then move on to more diverse subjects: crops grown; livestock raised; religious holidays celebrated; lists of the trades practiced, the vehicles owned, and the shops in the village; explanations of customs and traditions, including songs sung at circumcisions and weddings and details of material life such as how houses were built and tomato paste was made; and family genealogies. One section or chapter is usually devoted to the stories of people who witnessed the events, fighting, and fleeing of

1948. Almost all the books rely extensively, if indirectly, on oral histories the authors conducted with fellow villagers, as well as on a few other sources such as Mustafa al-Dabbagh's *Biladuna Filastin* [Our Country, Palestine] and *al-Mawsu'a al-Filastiniyya* [The Palestinian Encyclopedia] for the geographical and historical information.

For the Palestinian villagers who became refugees in 1948 and were separated completely from those places and their lands, their memorializations of the village later on in book form can be understood as an attempt both to recreate and present the village as it existed prior to 1948 and to emphasize their historical claims not only to the past, but also to the present and future. The covers of the memorial books provide one way to understand the importance of the physical space of the village through past and present, using real and imagined images of that space to define the village. The cover of one of the memorial books for Suba village is of two contemporary photographs of the village showing the mountaintop on which the village stood and, poking through the trees, the homes in various states of rubble (Rumman 2000). The cover for the 'Ayn Karim memorial book shows a contemporary picture of the pre-1948 village mosque, now locked up and defaced inside, that was built above the main village spring ('Atiyya 1992). The cover of the memorial book for the village of al-Kuwaykat contains a map of historic Palestine and a map of the 'Akka/Acre district, both of which show the location of the village; above the map is a contemporary photograph of one of the pre-1948 houses, and in the lower right corner, the stamp from the village *mukhtar* (mayor) from 1941 (al-'Ali, 2002). These contemporary images of pre-1948 places that still exist are presented as evidence of the village's existence—visual testimony from the village is supplemented with the stories and documents that are presented in the text of the books.

To the villagers in the present, however, places function differently from the other subjects recorded in the memorial books. The wedding songs, for example, are something that the villagers may still sing, or at the very least can revive, perform, or record; likewise, the lineages are part of a continual process that the villagers modify as they have children and their children have children, affected by the diaspora of 1948, but not erased. Even material practices such as embroidery and basket making are revived in forms of modern dress and home decoration. These cultural practices and material objects are tied to a notion of "tradition" that draws on a "past" but is also incorporated into the body of the "present" linked through cultural continuity, continuing social traditions, and modified material practices. The village places, however, are physically unavailable, either because people are separated by war and borders from their villages and/or the actual places have been plowed under, forested over, or allowed to fall into ruin. In the face of this physical removal and distance, the village memorial books focus on retaining place names to record and memorialize places that no longer exist, that cannot be revisited, photographed or even re-created. Pierre Nora proposes a useful way to think about how humans conceive of places in the past: as *lieux de mémoire*, realms or sites of memory, which are concrete places, objects, and gestures that symbolize a break with the past. As Nora explains, "The moment of *lieux de mémoire* occurs at the same time that an immense and intimate fund of memory disappears, surviving only as a reconstituted object beneath the gaze of critical history. This period sees, on the one hand, the decisive deepening of historical study and, on the other hand, a heritage consolidated" (Nora 1989: 12). Palestinians position the village and its physical spaces as carriers of all that was pre-1948 history. Thus, through recalling places, even ones that no longer exist, they maintain a variety of connections to the past.

In the context of their dispossession, there is no doubt that Palestinian memorial books are dossiers of evidence: land records, genealogies, photographs, and stories all aimed toward showing the villagers' relationship to the places in the village and thus proving their existence on the land, and therefore their history, even though they are no longer there and the village no longer exists. Many of the books contain extensive reproductions of land documents, such as British Mandate and Ottoman Land Deeds indicating ownership through sale and purchase of lands, and photographs of the village both from pre-1948 and the present. Yet given the local audiences, the Palestinian memorial books function most importantly as individual efforts to record the villages' histories—defined not only in terms of archaeology and geography but also in terms of the lived experiences of the villagers themselves as told to the author. Through the books, the villages become a past to be captured and maintained in textual form through stories, maps, photographs, family trees, and poems, which all seek to retain the history of the people who lived there.

Mapping the Past

The Palestinian memorial books contain numerous cartographically accurate maps, situating the village within historic Palestine and the villages

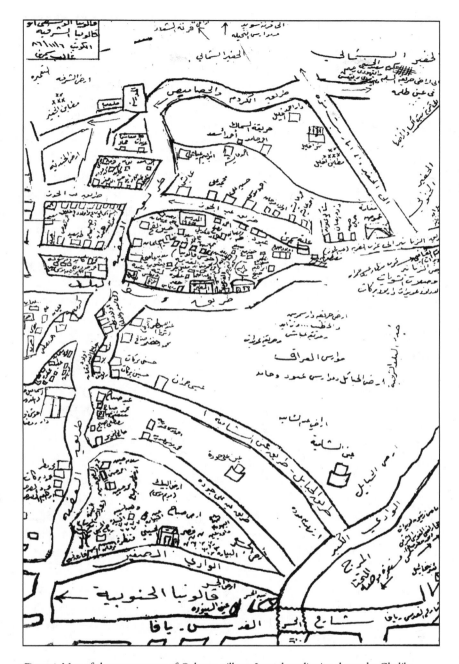

Figure 6 Map of the eastern part of Qalunya village, Jerusalem district, drawn by Ghalib Sumrayn in Kuwait, November 6, 1986. Labeled on the map are houses with owners' names, plots of land, springs, roads, antiquities, the school, the mosque, and other significant places in the village.

around it as well as providing detail about the village layout and lands. Wells, caves, valleys, hills, paths, plots of farmland, buildings, mosques, churches, trees, and stores embody this collective knowledge and are recorded, post-1948, as the essential components of the village or neighborhood or town. The Dayr Aban memorial book, for example, includes six separate maps, each with the following information marked on it: the locations of the houses in the three neighborhoods of the village; the roads and agricultural areas; the springs and valleys; the hills and mountains of the village; the landmarks and borders of the village; and the religious and archaeological sites (Abu Hadba 1990: 180, 186, 188, 192, 195, and 300). These maps, like all maps, express different ways of seeing the world, marking what is important at a particular time or place or to a particular population. Here they map physically visible spaces—roads, houses, wells, orchards—ones that were used by the villagers, creating a geography of everyday life in two-dimensional form. The maps and lists of these elements define a particular village and the intertwining relationship between geography and human habitation. Any reading of these maps suggests the close relationship of the villagers to the land.

The geography, however, has been significantly changed. The maps cannot now be used, since the intervening years have brought new places, new buildings, new people, and new farming techniques. Are they, then, just "maps of the past," or maps of memory? Given the Palestinian-Israeli struggle over land, the very act of creating the map of the past, I argue, claims an authority to know—by listing names of places, people show their knowledge of that place—and to imprint their presence on the land through this authority of knowledge. This authority serves to maintain Palestinians' ties to pre-1948 Palestinian land: by showing their intimate and familiar relationship to as well as their former dependence on the land, the maps help individuals continue to define themselves as Palestinians and as belonging to a particular village.

Lists of natural and man-made landmarks reveal the names and locations of what Palestinian villagers' conceive of as the important village places. In the memorial book for the village of al-Kababir, the author states that the natural landmarks provided the best way for people to chart their daily lives and get around. Then he provides a list of these features: the mountains [al-jibal], valleys [al-widyan], flat fields between two hills [al-khilayil], lands with a shallow creek through it [al-shi'ab], the wells [al-abar] and springs [al-'ayun]. Here is the entry for the springs:

THE SPRINGS:

'Ayn Umm al-Faraj (Wad al-Siyah), 'Ayn Risha (Wad Risha below the pool), 'Ayn 'Abdallah and 'Ayn al-Tira (al-Sira), 'Ayn al-'Aliq (Rishmiya), 'Ayn al-Suwaniya (Rishmiyya), 'Ayn al-Dalia or 'Ayn Abu Sa'id (Rishmiyya), 'Ayn al-Jawiyya (east of Rishmiyya), 'Ayn al-Sa'ada (east of Haifa), 'Ayn al-Shalala (below Bayt Oren), 'Ayn al-Hayik (west of 'Isfiyya), al-'Ayn al-Bayda' (west of 'Isfiyya) and 'Ayn Abu Dhahir (south of the mosque).

('ODEH 1980: 39–40)

The list of springs provides the geographic markers of fresh water, a crucial part of village life, since people would need to know where the springs were located for household use, watering herd animals, and irrigating crops. The list form suggests that the relationship of the peasants to the landscape is derived from knowing and harnessing its productivity, based on work and life in a particular landscape. Mapping places through lists, like cartography, retains the knowledge of names and places, even if divested of social meaning, significance, and context. Divorced from their everyday use and their history, the wells are made meaningful through the list form which quantifies them as knowledge, signifying Palestinians' relationship to the land through knowledge of it.

But for some memorial book authors, preserving the names is more than just an act of geographic nostalgia or an element in authoritative claims to knowledge. The memorial book for the village of Suhmata positions knowing names as part of the village heritage and the duty of all villagers. The following composition entitled, "So that we don't forget," is in call and response format:

CALL: *Ancestors' words to their descendants [al-aba' wa al-ajdad yaqulun lil-abna' wa al-ahfad]*: Suhmata is your village, a dear portion of your homeland, all of its land is ours, we inherited it from our fathers who inherited it from our grandfathers. . . . Our bequest to our children and grandchildren and the generations that follow us: "Remember your homeland, do not forget your village. . . . We have put before you the names of the village lands, part by part, the names of the springs and valleys, the names of the pools and wells, the names of the fruit trees and other trees, the names of the seasonal crops and we give you the responsibility, this charge, to you, the children and grandchildren, who are the trustees. . . ."

RESPONSE: *The answer of the descendants to the bequest of the ancestors:* We will retain the names and places, defend our rights, and maintain the land and stone, the crops and trees. We will maintain the bequest and fulfill our responsibility, cooperating with all who are sincere, for however long it takes and despite the hardships and difficulties, to liberate Suhmata and Palestine.

(AL-YAMANI, ET AL. nd: 160)

Even though the village itself no longer exists, this call and response piece conveys the imagined bequest of the village from the elders who lived in it prior to 1948 to their children, as their birthright and their legacy. The ancestors hand down a past but emphasize the physical places of the past—names of the springs, the wells, the crops, the village lands. This text calls on the descendants to learn these names, and thus to know the village and the location of these places, despite their absence from the contemporary landscape and despite the removal of the villagers and their descendants from that land. The composition in the Suhmata memorial book functions as a plea to both young and old: as a call to young people to know their past and to respect their history, to receive the teaching and knowledge of their elders and to continue to fight and believe that Suhmata and Palestine can be returned; and, finally, as a call to the old people, who remember their village and their village life, to ensure that their heritage and legacy are maintained. This piece illustrates one of the roles that these lists play in the village memorial books—that of preserving the names as a larger symbol of the village and as essential to claiming it and their rights to it.

Stories as Maps

Without a social context, the lists of places and maps of locations of the natural and human-built environment remain just names, teetering on the edge of becoming, as the well-known Palestinian folklorist Sharif Kanaana fears, "only names on old maps" (Kanaana and al-Ka'bi 1987: 3). They serve as a record of history but one that is removed from lived experience for those who read the books but do not know the land. But for many who lived in and remember the village, these place names also conjure up stories and experiences. Through these accounts, the places and names take on meanings beyond their role as just location markers; instead they become signifiers and ideographs of a specific past embodied in the name, and embedded in their social construction and transmission. These stories map a lived space that has depth and meaning beyond its physical cartographic presence. The social context for the place-names on maps come from stories, which Michel de

Certeau believes define how we see places. Stories endow places with specifically selected contextual meanings. Every story, he argues, is a journey through space because it projects experience onto places through the actions of historical subjects (de Certeau 1984: 118). This concept is illustrated clearly in the memorial book for the town of Majdal 'Asqalan, which includes a picture of a tree in the middle of a field. The photograph itself reveals nothing other than the tree. The caption, however, reads as follows: "Majdal 'Asqalan: 17 martyrs of the 1936 revolt, who are known as the 'Imran Shushar group, rest under this tree" (Kanaana and al-Madani 1987). It is only through the story that is told about the tree, this place, that we are able to know the significance of the tree and its history in the lives of the villagers—it is the story that gives meaning to the place.

Even some of the lists have stories attached to them that give meaning to the itemized locations. For example, in the case of the village of Qalunya, maps and descriptions provide the locations of all of the springs in the village but the author's account of the different wells tells not only where each was located but also who owned it and what role it played in the villagers' lives.

Because of the springs in our village, people didn't [need to] dig private wells in the courtyards of their homes. But there still were a number of privately dug wells in the village. The most renowned of these was the well of Isma'il Khalil Ramadan that was in the center of the courtyard of the tens of rooms he owned. He offered this well to the people of the village during the days when the Jews of the settlements of Motza and Erza[7] besieged the village. He offered a great service, providing necessary water to the families when it was impossible for the women to go either to the Upper or Lower springs where they would be targets for the Jewish snipers. Among the other notable wells in the village were the well of the Mosque of Shaykh Hamad, the well of Muhammad 'Ali Salama 'Askar, the well of Dar Khalil in al-Matayin east of al-Jifir, the well of Dar 'Isa Hamdan, and the well of al-Msawwis on the lands of al-Safha, the one that a village woman fell into when she accompanied her husband to work on the land there.

The people of the village dug a collective well on their land in the area of Dayr Nahla, near the village of al-Qubab, that everyone benefited from during the harvest and threshing. I remember perfectly the well of Mustafa Ramadan in the area of Bayt Mazza. It was the only well that had water in it year round among the seven wells found there that belonged to the clan of 'Askar in Bayt Mazza, the northernmost part of our village of Qalunya. Those wells were known as "rain-fed wells" and were known from Roman times. The winter rains would collect in them—the wells depended only on the rains and surface runoff [collected through small channels], and had no underground water source. Unfortunately, I have seen how neglect has affected these wells—they are now dry all year long.

(SUMRAYN 1993: 40)

As the stories associated with this list of wells suggest, the wells played a key role in the survival of the village when it came under assault. The wells and their stories become part of a national narrative of resistance to Zionist attempts to drive Palestinians from the land. But the villagers' knowledge of the natural resources and how best to use them—in this case, the storage of rainwater as passed down from Roman times—is also used to mark the author's knowledge of the village and to enhance the readers' familiarity and intimacy with the land. These accounts tie people, incidents, and groups to particular geographic features.

The stories in the memorial books tell of a collective history, not individual experiences. In most of the books written by people who are originally from the village, the stories told about places in the village are not framed within personal recollections or personal experiences that give meaning to a place. The stories use the collective "we" or "they" and rarely the first person "I" to talk about the village places, just as Palestinian accounts of the Nakba often do, as Jayyusi argues in this volume. I have written elsewhere that we should see the village memorial books as "collective autobiographies," the experiences of individuals and their rememberings conflated into a past that everyone in the village shares.[8] This "shared past" takes over the representation of the village in these books and smoothes over, as I will detail below, certain aspects of village life. Palestinians story the places of their past through verse, personal recollections, collective histories, maps, and artwork. Representations of people's activities transform the physical place—buildings of a neighborhood, the village square, or a tree—into meaningful spaces of village and communal life.

In the village memorial books, the stories associated with places usually center around communal places that were important at times and for events that were shared by all of the villagers. The village is divided into a variety of areas where communal activities took place, such as the village center, the empty land next to the mosque or church, the fields, wells, and springs, or the threshing floor of the village. As sites of daily activities, these communal spaces take on a particular symbolic role for the village. From the village of Qalunya, again, the author writes:

> Many memories link us emotionally to the threshing floor [of the village] that was so dear to us. The threshing floor was the ground of our youth and child- hood games. On that floor many celebrations took place. During wedding parties, women danced and girls sang, men danced the dabka, and old men danced the *sahja*. On this floor, the mats were spread, rugs laid out, and *manasif* [meat cooked in yoghurt] and big bowls of *jarisha* [wheat cooked with yoghurt] were offered for both men and women. On this floor, we took pride in showing the harvest of grains and fruits, represented in the threshing and winnowing days of each year.
>
> (SUMRAYN 1993: 40)

The threshing floor of a village is a carefully cleaned and hardened space that was out in the open and served as the functional space where people threshed and winnowed the grain. In this recreation of the space, however, it is not only invested with the memory of its useful function but also with other seminal parts of the collective village life that occurred there: celebra- tions, hosting and feeding guests, and childhood games. By presenting the account in this fashion, the author allows everyone from the village—men, women, children, and old people—to have a memory of it. The hard work of harvesting, threshing, and winnowing the grain, as well as cooking the *jari- sha* and *manasif* is absent from this account, focusing instead on the villagers' shared good times together.

In addition to highlighting the meaningful social practices and communal values evoked by certain locations, some authors use place names to sum- mon a location's known character, thus tying the place to the natural fea- tures of the landscape—the olive groves, the wildflowers, the hills of *za'tar* [thyme]. Poetic verse, as in the poem below, illustrates the specific names of village sites called on to invoke the memories of the past.

TRIP IN THE RUINS OF AL-WALAJA [RIHLA FI ATLAL AL-WALAJA]
    by Mustafa Khalil al-Sayfi

I'm thirsty. . .Where are the springs and wells?
    Nothing, only wasteland and desert,
Nothing but murky wilderness
    The earth of the fields covered in stones.

Where is "al-Dhuhur" of almond buds
    And the "Hadayif" surrounded by wildflowers
Where are the fields and birds of "al-Khalayil"
    And "Wadi Ahmad," the grounds of the partridges
Where is "al-Hina" and its flowing water
    Its shade sheltering resting travelers
Where are the guests who suddenly appear
    And in the "Quffeh" the coals are lit [to cook for them]
So that in every house the men clash
    Like a huge wave, opening the way for a tornado
As a result of their love for the guests
    They compete, young and old
And they threaten to divorce their wives if their offerings aren't touched
    They are all butchers when it comes to hospitality
[. . .]
On the "Jurun" were playgrounds
    On the "Habayil" was a house
Is there still enough in the coffeepots
    For people to stay up late and drink? . . .

(ABU KHIYARA 1993: 76)

The poem recalls various places in the village and mentions what they were known for, linking many of them closely to the generosity of the villagers toward their guests. The vestiges of the villagers' forefathers that are called upon in this poem suggest a shared ethos of hospitality embodied in the traditions of offering coffee and slaughtering an animal for a meal, rather than specific examples of visitors and the generosity shown them.

In the village memorial books, the poems about places, like the story maps, differ from the lists and the physical maps of location markers. Lists and physical maps concentrate on remembering what was in the village to perpetuate them for future generations, while the poems and stories create a direct emotional relationship between memory and the places of the past. In this poem, the author invokes *al-atlal* [the ruins], a poetic form from pre-Islamic and classical Arabic poetry, to lament the places of memory. In the *atlal* form, the poet visits the abandoned places of his past and bemoans his lost beloved.[9] This poem about the village of al-Walaja, for example, laments the lost village, merging the abandoned places and the beloved into one. The poetic journey through the spaces of the village recalls the "traditional" *atlal* poet describing the physical characteristics of his beloved, such as her eyes and hair, paralleled in the Walaja poem by the poet as he describes the physical spaces of the village and enumerates their virtues and the characteristics associated with each place, e.g. "al-Dhuhur" of almond buds, the Hina with its flowing waters. This use of an Arabic poetic form and the content of lamenting loss and celebrating generosity inserts this memorialization of the village into a larger Arab social and cultural context, idealizing and contextualizing the sentiments of attachment and longing to a known emotional expression and form. The stories and poems associated with places of the village tell of events, memories, emotions, and values that are communicated in the books as things shared by all of the villagers and as elements of village pride, thus creating a memory and a past for the village that can be collectively presented as authentic and real.

Journey Maps

The final type of mapping of the physical past is the journey map, which allows the author to reconstruct a voyeuristic visit to the village. The trip or journey through the natural and manmade landscape is a convention also found in school geography books for children, like Jordanian school textbooks of the 1950–60s.[10] Narrating the directions and locations of the village, the author takes the reader on a journey that places the names on the maps within a human relational framework embodied in the physical return to the village space. These journey maps provide the reader with the ability to traverse the village as it existed before 1948 and to experience the village through the eyes of its inhabitants, as this example from Dayr Aban suggests:[11]

> This is a trip through the lands of the village through which we will get to know the major landmarks and the location of these places in the basic structure of the village. We'll make this trip on a day in the month of June 1946, and we'll begin in Jerusalem where we will take a car from the city heading west for 23 kilometers, when we will reach Bab al-Wad at the western edge of the Jerusalem hills. Then we'll change our direction and head south; the lands of the villages of Bayt Mahsir and 'Artuf are on the left and the lands of 'Isalin, Ishwa', and Sar'a are on the right. After nine kilometers we'll reach the police station on the eastern side of the main road. . . . The private mill of Ibrahim Shuraym, and the droning of the motor as it grinds the Dayr Abani wheat, is the first landmark of the village that we pass by, located to the north after we pass the bridge over the valley of Abu

Khashaba. . . . If we face to the north, we will be pleased to see two important landmarks: Hawwuz al-Mayya [The water pool] which lies 150 meters off of the main road, and the village girls are standing in front of it—they have come to fill their containers with the water from the spring of Marjalin; and the elementary school of the village with its large garden ringing with the voices of the students in their classes and the sound of the tools working in the beautiful garden of the school.

(ABU HADBA 1990: 178)[12]

This account of the village begins from a landmark that everyone knows (Jerusalem) and takes the reader from the approach of the village into the different areas, noting their landmarks and people. Such a process could be traced on a map, and all of the significant locations are commonly represented on the village memorial book maps, including this one for Dayr Aban. But this journey account also describes more than what can be represented on a map or in statistics; it fills in for the readers the author's historical memory of the droning of the mill motor, the vision of women filling water containers at the spring, and the sounds of schoolchildren and of work. This journey map endows these spaces with a sensory element that pushes readers to imagine observing or participating in village life, as if they were standing there hearing the children at play or the grinding of the wheat.

Other journey maps, such as the one in the memorial book for the village of 'Imwas,[13] describe the setting of the village and the actions of its inhabitants as if in a folkloric tableau:

Among the famous landmarks of the village is the tomb of Shaykh 'Ubayd (Abu 'Ubayda 'Amr bin al-Jarrah) and the tomb of Shaykh Mu'ala (Mu'adh bin Jabal) and next to Shaykh 'Ubayd was a big *sidr* tree [*Zizyphus spini-christi*], as old as 'Imwas. Under its shade the village elders would sit, chatting in the evenings [*yatasamarun*] and playing *seeja* [mancala]. When the dom tree's fruit ripened you would see the village children in large numbers racing to pick the fruit. The tree was surrounded by the central cemetery of the village, and between the cemetery and the buildings of the village was a large empty square, which became the bus stop. [. . .] The street continued onto a high bridge that crossed over the Shalala valley, which collected the rainwater and the water of the spring ('Ayn Nini). The young men would go to the bridge in the evenings to chat with each other and stroll along the empty main street until reaching Dayr al-Latrun [the Latrun Monastery] or the school. While they walked, they passed by the wide gate and large walls surrounding an old church. . . . After school the boys and young men liked to go the sports field on the *awqaf* [religious trust] lands around the tomb of Shaykh Mu'ala.

(ABU GHOSHA 1990: 11)

In these journey maps, the readers can relive an idealized memory of "village life" in which the social system is orderly, people are in their places doing their appointed folkloric tasks: young women fill their containers at the well, old men sit in the village center playing a board game, the children are in school or roam freely in a large mass, and the young men claim the streets in the evening, while during the day they have their own space on the outskirts of the village away from the houses. Those doing much of the work—both women and men—are absent from the public village space, since their work keeps them either out in the fields, inside the homes, or working outside of the village. These visits are voyeuristic and yet totally controlled because the journey maps provide a unique conflation of personal and communal memories of the past. They allow the author, as the journey maker, to choose the historical time for the trip along with the elements that will be revealed to the visitor, deciding what is important to map and narrate. As such, the journey map is not only embedded in the collectively held representation of meaningful parts of the village, but it also presents the village as an object of tour with the author as guide. The journey map presents an individual understanding of the landmarks, sights, sounds, and flavors of a place in a selected image of daily life, disconnected from seasons, conflicts, weather, health, and all the other myriad unappealing or unmemorable aspects of daily life. Because these journey maps are given by individuals, they could be different depending on the author. However, they are written in similar styles and conform to a similar vision of the village as a site for the folkloric and the traditional, a place where life was pleasant, satisfying, and idyllic, marked and circumscribed by the natural world around it.

Conclusion: Mapping the Past and Memories of Place

Creating maps hinges on several issues, and what is seen and what is to be represented are central aspects of what the final map will look like. In the Palestinian case, the memorial books convey maps of a time not forgotten but of places that no longer exist. Creating maps of those places relies on the author's specific memories as well as the memories of those he solicits.

We all know that people look at a landscape and see completely different things, depending on their age, education, gender, historical knowledge, and national identity, among many other factors. The act of seeing, then, is completely tied up in the historical processes that humans create and in which they participate. The act of transferring what is seen and internalized into a representation for others pushes us to consider form, language, politics, ideology, and history—all of which are part of my analysis.

Palestinian memorial books of the villages prior to 1948 present themselves as entrusted with the task of representing the village. Thus they have produced (and continue to produce) various ways of mapping the space of the village past, whether in the form of physical maps or lists of place names, stories surrounding a particular place, poetry about the village, or re-created journeys. These maps of the geographic spaces of the village take physical places and turn them into lived spaces by providing stories of human life and experiences that are inextricably tied to those very places. These maps of the past endure, to a great extent, through forms of writing and imagery that are removed from the land as it now exists. At the same time, they map spaces that can be shared by all of the villagers—wells, springs, sentiment, journeys—in one way or another. The villages that are created in these maps of the past include landmarks of a unified society of shared values and ideals, one that is self-sufficient and free of poverty, disease, and internal strife. Village life as mapped on to these spaces is one in which everyone participates, is engaged, and plays a meaningful role.

This image of the village corresponds to the nationalized image of the Palestinian peasant—steadfast, strong, and fertile—that resounds in imagery, songs, and poems. Ted Swedenburg has argued that the Palestinian peasant has been used as a national signifier by a national movement with largely a middle-class leadership to create a nation with a unified culture and sense of authenticity (Swedenburg 1990). But this is not because Palestinians were all peasants—around 40 percent of the Palestinian population in 1948 lived in cities; rather it is an idealization of peasant practices that reinforces the land as essential to Palestinian existence and critical to defining Palestinians, thus an intrinsic part of their continued struggle. Such also is the history of the embroidered dress (*thawb*) of the peasant woman, or the black and white *kufiyyeh,* both peasant wear which have become emblematic of all Palestinians. Research done by Shelagh Weir (1989) shows the huge variety of Palestinian women's dresses that were worn in many different shapes, materials, colors, and types of embroidery (or lack thereof) up to 1948, while among village men a closely wrapped turban was more common than the *kufiyyeh* and *'iqal* now associated with peasants and which did not gain popularity until the 1930s. Urban Palestinian women in the diaspora now wear chic incarnations of the peasant embroidery tradition to weddings and other significant social and cultural occasions as markers of Palestinian-ness, while men wear the *kufiyyeh* wrapped around their neck and shoulders.[14] Artists, too, choose as symbols the steadfast, strong, and fertile peasant to symbolize Palestine and the national struggle.[15]

The emphasis on village life rather than urban life of pre-1948 Palestine, along with the focus on peasants, can be explained by Palestinian desires to claim the land lost in the wake of its appropriation by Zionists/Israelis. Yet the destruction of Palestinian village and peasant society has resulted in their romanticization and the reification of a particular type of peasant, lifestyle, and dress. The village and peasant portrayed in the village memorial books conform to this romanticized ideal. The books depict an idyllic social structure where village relations are characterized by solidarity, unity, and generosity. There is no exploitation by urban landowners. There are no tenant farmers, no moneylenders, no collaborators with authorities or Zionist agents. At the same time, the emphasis on the peasant also seeks to preserve a lost way of life. For example, names on the Dayr Aban village map include such places as Jabal Haqrus, 'Ayn Umm 'Abbus, Hariqat Aslan, Shi'b Bir al-Nahal, Shi'b al-Husayniyat, Wad Qarayqa' and al-Marj (Abu Hadba 1990: 195). These place names evoke mountains, springs, land with a creek running through it, valleys, and flatlands.[16] The book even contains a section that explains the terms used to describe land:

> *al-shaqa*: about 10 dunums
>
> *al-shi'b*: land that has a shallow creek running through it
>
> *al-maris*: long strip of level agricultural land
>
> *al-marah*: high, flat land that slants slightly
>
> *al-jisr*: smooth agricultural land that stretches between two higher places
>
> *al-jura*: agricultural land that goes up on all sides [basin]
>
> *al-marj*: flatland, plain
>
> *al-diba*: raised agricultural land that drops down all sides [opposite of *al-jura*]
>
> *al-ta'mira*: land planted with fruit trees that also is rocky
>
> *al-misha*: flat agricultural land with moist soil and wild bushes surrounding agricultural land [. . .].
>
> (ABU HADBA 1990: 207)

This key would allow someone not from the villages to read the place-names and understand that, for example, *shi'b al-husayniyat* is the "land with the shallow creek of the foxes." Since these terms refer to places that are fairly small and not on many maps, they signify the lived knowledge of this place that is intrinsic to farming and herding on the land. Not many people aside from the peasants who farm the land have much knowledge of or even use for this vocabulary, as I found when trying to decipher these place names. Since they are unvoweled in these books, I had to ask people how to pronounce them so I could transcribe them into the Latin alphabet for this chapter. I found that it was only people who had heard their parents speak of these names or agricultural terms, or were old enough to remember village life (anyone over age sixty-five), who could answer my questions. The village memorial books seek to transfer this knowledge to the coming generations, if only in written form; not for use, this time, but for memory.[17]

When peasant communities write their own histories, as they are doing in these memorial books, many academics and those in solidarity with them tend to see this process as profoundly redemptive, a popular act of reclaiming their own voices and past. And in large part Palestinians write these books to record their history from their own perspectives, since they feel that their history and memories of the past are under siege, given the continued presence of the large Palestinian refugee community in the diaspora and the absence of any settlement to the Palestine question. However, because of their refugee status and the struggle over land, and thus the powerful symbolism of the peasant within Palestinian national discourse, these village memorial books tend to map places of the past as idyllic and unified, with a view of Palestinians in harmony with nature and the land, working together. The voices that speak in these texts seek not only to reclaim their own villages, but also through discourses and images, to tie them to the Palestinian nation.

The past that is mapped consists of memories and idealizations. The books seek to re-create and reclaim the physical village imaginatively: through maps and lists of village lands and landmarks, Palestinians claim the village through knowing it; through poems about the village places they show sentiment and emotional attachment; and through journeys that take the readers on tours of a repopulated village they re-create an idyllic peasant life. While each village memorial book portrays the unique places of its past, the sentiments, emotions, activities, and associations affiliated with those places are made to correspond to a greater narrative of what it means to be Palestinian at this historical juncture. Ultimately, the geographic nostalgia for places and a peasant lifestyle is rooted both in local memories and experiences as well as in Palestinians' current status as landless and dispossessed refugees.

Author's Note

I would like to thank the various people who offered comments and suggestions on this chapter in its many configurations: Salim Tamari, Kimberly Katz, Andrew Shryock, Anton Shammas, Carol Bardenstein, Janet Hart, Lila Abu-Lughod, Ahmad Sa'di, and my colleagues in the Introduction to the Humanities Program at Stanford University. The research was conducted while on grants from Fulbright-Hays, the Social Science Research Council, and the American Center for Oriental Research in Jordan, and the writing occurred while on postdoctoral fellowships at Stanford University and the Center for Middle Eastern Studies at the University of California, Berkeley.

NOTES

1. Slyomovics (1993, 1994, 1998) has produced numerous defining works on the subject of memorial books. It is worth noting that no equivalent term for the memorial books exists in Arabic.

2. Numerous sources indicate that after 1948, the Israeli government and its affiliated bodies worked to destroy or resettle with Israelis these villages, while actively preventing the Palestinian inhabitants from returning. For the statistical breakdown, see Kanaana 1992.

3. These statistics are according to *All That Remains*, the comprehensive publication on the villages occupied and depopulated published by the Institute for Palestine Studies (Khalidi 1992: xviii–xix). Khalidi writes: "Of the 418 villages, 292 (70 percent) were totally destroyed; 90 villages (22 percent) were largely destroyed, which means that only a small percentage of the houses were left standing (20 villages in this category had only one surviving house). Eight villages (less than 2 percent) had only a small percentage of their houses destroyed, while 7 villages (less than 2 percent) survived but were taken over by Israeli settlers. [...] The level of destruction of 20 villages (5 percent) could not be determined. [...] In addition, another 69 villages and a number of towns remained with part or all of their population inside the borders of the new Israeli state."

4. Slyomovics 1993 and 1998. The Birzeit series was produced in the 1980s and 1990s at Birzeit University's Center for Research and Documentation of Palestinian Society (CRDPS). Under the leadership of Sharif Kanaana and later Saleh Abdel

Jawad, the Center published books on more than twenty different villages. I do not include them in this chapter because the majority of them were researched and written by people not from the villages, thus changing the relationship of the author of the text with the village he or she is writing about.

5. A number of books were written by younger men, again many of whom were, or are, teachers, and one woman (Sahira Dirbas) wrote three different books, starting with her family's natal village of Tirat Haifa. For the books produced in Lebanon, most of the authors were teachers in the UNRWA schools that were set up in the Palestinian refugee camps.

6. The first part of the Birzeit series was done by researchers from outside the village although the later books in the series were done by villagers themselves. The PLO series focuses primarily on cities and on known historical knowledge rather than personal and everyday life experiences.

7. I have transcribed the settlement names according to how they are read in Arabic, although the actual name of the main settlement next to Qalunya in Hebrew seems to be Mevasseret Tziyyon.

8. Rochelle Davis, "Palestinian Memorial Books as Collective Autobiographies," unpublished paper delivered at a conference on Autobiography and Social History of the Levant, December 2004, Beirut, Lebanon. The essay will appear in an Arabic translation in a publication by the Institute for Jerusalem Studies in 2007.

9. The issue of poetic form and the pre-1948 Palestinian village is dealt with more fully in Rochelle Davis 2002; see also Slyomovics (1998) for an excellent discussion of this subject. Thanks to Margaret Larkin for seeing the *atlal* elements of these poems and suggesting it to me.

10. On the subject of the contents of Jordanian school textbooks, see an unpublished paper by Kimberly Katz, "School Books and Tourism Brochures: Constructions of Identity in Jordan."

11. These journey maps also appear in Palestinian stories of returning to cities as well. See for example, Shafiq al-Hout in Jaffa (al-Hout 1998) and Abu-Lughod, this volume, who describes her father's tour of Jaffa.

12. During the British Mandate, the curriculum of the village schools included classes in agriculture; hence, the schools had gardens attached to them. See Tibawi (1956) for more on this subject.

13. 'Imwas was one of the three villages in the Latrun area that were depopulated and destroyed in 1967 during the Israeli invasion and occupation of the West Bank, Gaza, and the Golan Heights.

14. For more on the subject of the *thawb* and its deployment as a national symbol see Moors 2000. For more on the *kufiyyeh* see Swedenburg 1991 and 1992.

15. For images of Palestinian art used in posters, see http://www.liberationgraphics. com/ppp/

16. I am unaware of what a "hariqa" is, unless it denotes a fire from some past time.

17. Although it seems that without putting vowels in the texts, the authors are assuming some familiarity of the readers with the terms. My informal and limited experience shows that the younger generations in the diaspora neither know the meaning of the terms, nor know how to pronounce them. I also used 'Abd al-Latif al-Barghuthi's *al-Qamus al-'Arabi al-Sha'bi al-Filastini* [*The Dictionary of Palestinian Colloquial Arabic*] to vowel the words.

4. Palestine. Jaffa. — La Rade   Palestina. Jaffa. — De Haven

Figure 7 Postcard of Jaffa from the sea, 1930s.

3 Return to Half-Ruins

MEMORY, POSTMEMORY, AND
LIVING HISTORY IN PALESTINE

Lila Abu-Lughod

'Awda means return. For diasporic Palestinians, the charged term evokes nostalgia for the homeland they were forced to flee in 1948 and a reversal of the traumatic dispersion that sundered families, ruined livelihoods, and thrust Palestinians into humiliating refugee camps or individual adventures to rebuild lives armed with little more than birth certificates, keys to the homes left behind, and the stigma of having somehow lost their country to an alien people. The political insistence on the "right of return" is a demand for righting a moral wrong. It is also a demand that the story of that expulsion not be erased.

Not everyone fled Palestine in 1948, of course. Some Palestinians stayed on the land within the expanding territorial control of the Israeli state declared on May 15, 1948. Hanging on to their own villages or setting up near them, or staying on in their cities, they would watch their world transform before their eyes. Dislodged socially and politically but in place physically, they would learn the language of their colonizers and work among them, often in menial jobs. Those who fled to the towns of the West Bank or to Gaza would not come under direct Israeli military and administrative control until nearly twenty years later, when Israel occupied, after the 1967 war, those remaining parts of historic Palestine.

The majority of Palestinian refugees, however, found themselves cut off from their homes and their pasts. In Lebanon, Jordan, Syria, Iraq, Kuwait, the

United States, England, and even the countries of South America, they tried to make new lives. Some were successful, financially and culturally; many, generations later, still live in refugee camps that have become unsettlingly permanent. For them, memories of home were frozen.

Until 1991, my father was one of those exiles who had not been back to see what had happened to his country. His family had fled to Jordan, from where he had borrowed money for a shipboard passage to the United States, in search of an education. He had made a life there, working his way through college, marrying my mother, having children, and eventually going to Princeton to get a Ph.D. in Arab history. Eight years after his exodus he was finally able to make his first trip back to the Arab world to take a job with UNESCO in Egypt. But he could not return to Palestine. My mother tells me our family made occasional visits to the West Bank and Jerusalem. There he would gaze longingly across to his part of Palestine—coastal Jaffa. But after Israel's occupation of these areas in 1967, even this was impossible. My father was one of those who refused to go and see his former home even when, quite late, he obtained the American passport that would have entitled him to enter as a tourist what was now Israel. He tirelessly wrote, spoke publicly, and taught about Palestine. Twice, he went to live in Beirut to set up Palestinian projects. In 1982 he was driven out by Israeli firepower for a second time in his life, an experience that left him haunted and distant from us, his family, for some years. He could not imagine placing himself at the mercy of and under the authority of the state that had overrun his entire country; to come face to face with the people who continued to devastate the everyday lives of Palestinians living there and elsewhere. The military that had landed a cluster bomb on his balcony in Beirut had shattered more than his dream of setting up a Palestinian Open University.

Then something changed. After a sobering illness, he realized that he might die without ever having seen Palestine again. Recognizing a slight shift in policies that meant an easing of restrictions in the Occupied Territories, he decided he would go. I remember hearing his excited stories when he returned. On this first visit in 1991, he was nervous but curious. His first shock, he said, was arriving at what he knew as Lydda airport to find a huge sign saying "Welcome to Israel." Nevertheless, he was exhilarated. What followed was a decision in 1992 to move "back"—to return. He and my mother had already divorced. He retired from Northwestern University, where he had taught political science for twenty-five years. I could see, when he came to visit me in England after I gave birth to my twins, that he was energized by being home, as he felt it to be. As I saw much later in an undated transcript from a conference that he had left in a pile on his desk, he explained, "Most people I had spoken with [who returned] felt sadness or loss. I felt quite the opposite. I was happy to be reconnected with my land, to know that despite the changes, much of Palestinian culture survived Israel's assault. It did so through the powerful efforts of those who remained on the land, whether that of 1948 or the West Bank and Gaza."[1]

This move, I was to learn when I nervously agreed to visit him in Israel/ Palestine five months later, changed his experience of that cataclysmic and defining event known by Palestinians simply as the Nakba, "the catastrophe." He inserted his memories of Palestine directly into the present, into a living history. My father's insertion of memory into the historical present made possible a different knowledge and identification for his children as well. This essay will explore what happened to my father as well as what happened to me as a result of his 'awda. Marianne Hirsch, sensitive analyst of the transfer of traumatic memory across generations among Holocaust survivors, calls postmemory the experience of having one's everyday reality overshadowed by the memory of a much more significant past that one's parents lived through (Hirsch 1997: 22–24; 1999). But the situation she describes is of parental memories of events that have passed. The world has denounced that genocide and those horrors. What I, as the daughter of someone who lived through the Nakba learned from my father's return to Palestine, was that, for Palestinians, both memory and postmemory have a special valence because the past has not yet passed.

Storied Memories

My father was a talker and a storyteller. Because of this, there was no time when we, his children, did not know we were Palestinian. The stories I remember about his boyhood in the 1930s and early 1940s were nostalgic, both comic and bitter. Like anyone, I found it hard to imagine my grownup parent as himself a child. There was also the strangeness of a life so different from what I knew growing up in the United States, a life I could access only obliquely through some childhood years spent in Egypt and summer vacations with relatives in Jordan, and more vividly once I became an anthropologist and lived intimately with Arab communities. I loved to imagine the boy who was so excited about the new pair of shoes he got for the holidays that he slept with them under his pillow. I sympathized when he told the story about the "number zero"—the buzz-cut his father forced on him as a punishment; he would beg for at least a "number one" from the barber, which left a little more than stubble. I wondered at the amused stories he told about himself as a religious boy of eleven, twelve, and thirteen, this resolutely secular father of mine who regularly denounced the "ayatollahs," as he called them—Christian, Muslim, or Jewish—and who always excused himself from fasting during Ramadan because he was "traveling"—in exile.[2] In his zeal to outdo his brothers and win his parents' favor, he said, he had eagerly agreed to help the lazy imam by climbing up the minaret of his neighborhood mosque in Jaffa to call people to prayer. If the motivations for this show of piety were mixed, the religious idiom was also deeply personal: he told us too about how he had presided over a full Muslim burial for his pet bird, Hudhud, when it passed away while they were summering at al-Nabi Rubin.

Stories of paternal tenderness and moral training gave us glimpses into the character of his father, the grandfather we had never known, and the nature of family life in pre-1948 Palestine. My father would recount how he, as a small boy, had once gone to the bathroom in the middle of the night. In the dark, he didn't realize his father was already there. His father, an imposing man, remained silent so as not to frighten his half-asleep son, despite the indignity he suffered. But my father also told a story about the day his mother sent him out to buy salt and he gambled away the coins in a street game. When he returned home very late with no salt for the night's cooking, his mother said, "Wait 'til your father hears about this." The stern punishment was that he was not allowed to go out the next day, the big feast day. My father spent the day crying at the window, watching his friends and relatives promenade up and down the street in their new clothes, buying treats, and enjoying the holiday. The moral lesson was for us too: He never gambled again.

There were more political stories though, that began to teach us what it had meant to be Palestinian under the British Mandate. According to my father, people were barely aware that they were on the eve of disastrous events that would make them refugees. They did not realize that the Zionists, not the British, were their real adversaries. Again, I found it hard to imagine my professorial and genial father, who smoked a pipe, loved to talk on the telephone, delighted in playing with children, read voraciously, and came alive when giving public lectures (where his Zionist hecklers would fill me with stinging tears of humiliation and protective anger), as a defiant young boy having run-ins with the British Army. A version of one of his stories was preserved on tape in 2000 by Hisham Ahmed-Fararjeh, who recorded his life story. This was the well-rehearsed story of his first arrest that I myself had heard often:

> The British imposed curfews, as the Israelis do now. We were kids, aged nine or ten, and I remember we would go up to a soldier and insult him. Once my older brother was arrested by a British patrol and taken to the police station. They slapped him around and then released him. Everyone who got arrested became a hero. I wanted to be a hero too; I was competing with my older brother. So when we saw a policeman on a motorcycle, I insulted him. But the bastards came after me and my friends! We ducked into a bakery. I was so embarrassed going in there because it was shut and we had entered by a side door. One of the British soldiers came in and caught us, red-handed, as it were. Standing there doing nothing. They arrested four of us. They were on four motorcycles and they made us run in front of them. They had whips. I was dressed in robes, what we wore for ordinary street clothes, so I had to pull them up and hold them in my teeth to run. We got tired but they whipped us to keep us on the run. People called out to us from their homes, "Come in here Ibrahim! Come in here Muhammad!" But we were afraid they would come after us so went along with them.

After much crying, some genuine and some faked, he said, the police released them but not until they'd been scolded by the local collaborator and then chased all the way back by another motorcycle, the soldier whipping them again. The way my father told the story, you had to see the funny side of a scrawny kid desperate to outdo his brother running for his life with his robes in his teeth.

He would tell us that he learned more of a lesson the second time he was caught. Instead of releasing the kids this time, the British police made them work. My father and his friends were ordered to pull out by hand all the grass in a large courtyard at the police station, to turn it into a tennis court. As he told it late in life,

> There was a British police officer we called Abu-Niyab [the one with the big canines] who I now understand was a sadist. We used to fear him because he walked around with a baton in his hand. We were trying to pull out the grass, but the grass wouldn't come out. He beat us and told us to keep working. It took us two hours to finish the job. So now what could they do with us? The curfew was still on. So they told us to move the grass from one side of the garden to the other, just to keep us working. We were tired. We were being beaten continuously. I can never forget the face of Abu-Niyab, that son-of-a-bitch who beat the hell out of

me. We started crying. We didn't want to be imprisoned; what we had wanted
was to be leaders. In retrospect I think, damn that kind of nationalism. We had to
go through beating and torture to become leaders? [3]

Since then, my father said, he always used legal means—his mind, his pen,
and his gift for oratory—to struggle against colonial occupation (by Zionists
now, not the British). Enough beatings.

Yet I don't recall hearing while I was growing up his stories of 1948, the last
months before the fall of his hometown, Jaffa. Were we too young to be told?
Did it not mean anything to children who had never seen Jaffa? My mother
tells me he often told those stories to her and to others. I heard them, and I
think they took on special meaning and more regularity in telling, when he
returned to live in Palestine and was able to see Jaffa again. As Maurice Halbwachs (1992 [1914]) has argued, memory requires a social framework. But as
Halbwachs also suggested, as people get older and detach themselves from
the urgencies of professional and family life, they often become interested
guardians of an increasingly vivid past. My father was active in Palestine and
anything but detached, but the stories began to flow once he moved there.
My father's experiences of 1948 had fired his long efforts to comprehend and
publicize what had happened to the Palestinians. But the peculiar thing that
happened when my father returned to Palestine was that his memories now
became the guide to a living history and a real place.

Memory Into History: Touring Jaffa

Jaffa was the heart of my father's Palestine. On the wall of his apartment
in Ramallah, when I came to stay in 2001, was a large sepia poster: a historic
photograph of an Arab man staring wistfully out to sea with a large town in
the background. At the top, in Arabic, it said, "Jaffa 1937." Yet my father was
living in Ramallah, not Jaffa, because it was in the West Bank where Palestinian institutions were haltingly functioning in the 1990s. It was here where he
could work.

On my first visit to Palestine to see him in 1993, I sensed the thrill he
felt at having mastered the new situation. The good part was embracing and
being embraced by the community he had found, whether in the West Bank
or in various parts of pre-1948 Palestine. The anxiety of being there was betrayed by his dry mouth and the beads of sweat on his forehead as he drove
us around, approaching Israeli military checkpoints or getting lost because

he couldn't read Hebrew and was afraid to ask, a fear that rubbed off on me since I found it all so strange. The landscape was familiar from Lebanon and Jordan, which I had known well growing up. The barren highways and the cities full of Hebrew were menacing, though, especially when combined with the heavy presence of Israeli soldiers, reservists, and guns. He had become a little more accustomed to them.

He was eager to show me and my small family the whole of Palestine, from Jerusalem to Bethlehem, Nablus to Nazareth, Jericho to 'Akka. It was a hectic trip full of sights, sounds, and driving. I can barely remember my feelings or conjure images because I was a new mother managing five month old twins on the road. But I do recall that the visits to his friends across the country were warm and full of good food, even if I had that same shy feeling I often had growing up as I silently listened as talk turned to politics, or as I buried my fear of somehow embarrassing my father because, like so many of us in the diaspora, my Palestinian Arabic was not fluent and so much about me was obviously American. Though many we met had studied or worked in the United States or Britain, and all were effusively welcoming, I didn't feel I belonged effortlessly, as my father did.

He was especially keen to show off Jaffa. His tour of Jaffa was the same one, I was a little hurt to discover later, that he gave to many others. It was about claiming and reclaiming the city in which he had been born, the sea in which he had swum as a boy, and the home he had been forced to flee in 1948. On his own first visit in 1991, he'd asked friends to take him there first. Initially he was disoriented. Most of the landmarks weren't there. The neighborhood by the sea where he'd grown up had been razed by then, though twenty years earlier his brother had done what so many Palestinians have done and described: knocked on the door to find out which Jews—Russian, Moroccan, Yemeni, Polish—were now living in their old family homes.[4] Suddenly, my father said he had spotted the Hasan Bek Mosque where he had made the call to prayer as a boy. From there he had figured out where the coffee shop had been. He remembered this café because he used to hang around outside in the evenings, hoping to listen in on the storytellers and reciters of epics, only to be chased away because he didn't have the money for a glass of tea. Bit by bit, circling more widely around the mosque, he began to find his way.

It was a former student of his, someone who had become a professor of Middle East politics, who had made him rethink his refusal to go back. She often traveled to Israel and the West Bank. He recalled that she had told him once, "Ibrahim, Palestine is still there." He was happy, he said, to find this to be true. On his first visit he had asked some Arab kids on the street if they knew where King Faysal Street was. They immediately took him there, though he could see that the street sign said something altogether different. From this, he knew that Palestinian parents were still teaching their children the old names of things even as Palestine was being buried, erased, and re-written by Israel.[5]

There is an image in one of Doris Lessing's *African Stories* (1981) that has never left me. I assigned the short story in 1985 to my students in a course on colonialism. A young girl, a white settler living in southern Africa, looks out over the savanna and acacia trees and sees the large gnarled oak trees of her English fairytales. My father did the opposite. Where I, who never knew anything else, could see only the deep gouges in green hillsides made for Israeli settlements with garish red tile roofs, or miles and miles of highways criss-crossing the rocky landscape and claiming it with modern green signs in Hebrew and English, or non-native evergreen forests to hide razed villages, my father saw beyond, between and behind them to the familiar landscapes of his youth.[6]

He explained that he used to travel as a boy all around Palestine with workers from his father's foundry as they delivered, installed, and repaired water pumps and olive presses. I discovered later that he had also traveled as a politicized high school student trying to organize fellow students, worry-ing his mother sick, as my mother tells me, as he set off by bus. As my father drove us, it was clear he still knew his way around though he had been de-nied access for more than forty years and everything looked so different. He showed us the orange groves where he might have stolen a fruit or two when young. (I associate oranges with him because of the loving way he always peeled them and then, after eating a few sections, would distribute the rest to his children; I knew it was hard for him to look at Jaffa oranges in the su-permarket, with their provenance listed as Israel, when they were part of his youth.) He pointed out the stubborn cacti that still mark the boundaries of Arab fields that no longer exist. Tucked in and among the new structures that dominate the towns and cities, he would point out the arched windows of old Arab houses that had somehow escaped destruction. Half-ruins he built in his imagination, while I strained to make them out amidst the ugly concrete.

My father's tour of Jaffa actually began with the small factory on the outskirts of the city that his father founded in 1929. He remembered an old Afghani gentleman who was the guard for their foundry. With a big white mustache, he used to mesmerize them as kids by reading their palms. My father told us that this man had had a premonition that they would all have to leave Jaffa, but that he himself would not. And in fact, my father would add, he never did leave; he was hit by a car before the events of 1948. I sensed that my father considered him lucky.

We parked across the busy road, at the water fountain of Abu-Nabbut, and he pointed to the shabby industrial structure that was in his day the Palestinian Iron and Brass Foundry Company Ltd., a name imprinted on manhole covers to be found even today in Jaffa. This foundry, he proudly explained, provided a service to the Palestinian farmers by manufacturing the diesel pumps, crushes, and presses they needed for their orange and olive orchards. Though his father learned his trade first from some Germans, who left when the British seized their factory during the First World War, he then went on to work for German Jews. Later, he decided to set up his own company, with relatives as shareholders, many giving five pounds here, five pounds there. This made it possible, he explained in retrospect, for Arabs not to have to depend on foreign or Jewish industry. Over the course of its almost twenty years, the factory was shut down several times by the British. In 1936–37, the time of the Palestinian rebellion, his father was accused of secretly manufacturing arms. Nationalism, I then understood, ran in the family. One time when they sealed his factory with red wax, he surreptitiously removed all the machinery, smuggling it piece by piece through the orange groves behind the foundry and carrying it on donkey carts to a new location.

My grandfather's nationalist activities got them into trouble. My father remembers the night raids of his house by British police and soldiers. These sounded surreal to me, conjuring violent images hard to reconcile with how I had known my father, a man who rode a bike, read books, mowed suburban lawns, and taught charismatically. The British would storm in, shouting for everyone to put their hands up, then head for the kitchen to rifle through the sacks of flour and rice looking for weapons. My father and his brothers learned early to identify as cousins the many visitors they harbored from the countryside. They learned early too about lawyers and British prison guards who could be bribed to smuggle in food and bedding to his father. In and out of prison, my grandfather died in 1944, when my father was only fifteen. His factory, though, went on producing until everything collapsed with the war in 1948.

A very important stop on the tour of Jaffa was his high school, the school that he wryly explained taught him the geography of England so well that when he finally set foot in London many years later, he knew every street name. This was the school where he says he learned to use his mind, and where teachers politicized him. It now bears a plaque outside with the name Weizmann School and has bars around it. In his day it had been the 'Amiriyya Government Secondary School. He loved to talk about how one time when he went to show it to visitors, they found it guarded by young Ethiopian immigrants who knew so little history that they disbelieved that my father spoke no Hebrew, because he told them this had been his school. On his tours he would look through the gate and would try to talk his way in. He managed it once, accompanied by some friends from the United States. They had to leave their American passports with the guard. It was the same, he marveled, except that the drawings on the walls were made by Jewish kids. It was also now co-ed; they had had to climb a wall to look over at the girls' school, Al-Zahra.

Because Jaffa had been such a heterogeneous commercial city, he had no classmates from the old notable families. He and his friends were eager to learn, eager to achieve. Some of these friends were family friends now— Reja-e Busailah, the blind poet and professor of English literature who had landed in Kokomo, Indiana; Shafiq al-Hout, the smart, warm, writer who was later to head the PLO office in Beirut. They all still remember the teachers who held them to such high standards that when my father managed to get to the United States and began university, he placed out of courses in geography and European history. From the teachers, he said in an interview I read, they also learned the difference between breaking school rules and engaging in political work. The teachers spent time with them in the yard answering questions about imperialism, smiling when they went on strike, organized demonstrations, and founded the Palestinian student union. These were teachers of chemistry as well as history, so different from any I had had in high school (Ahmed-Fararjeh 2003: 37–41).

My father was incredulous when he thought back to his last year there, in 1948. Knowing that there would be trouble when they pulled out in May, the British announced that the final year examinations were going to be moved forward to March. My father and his friends studied hard. Fighting was going on across the country. It was going on right there between Jaffa and Tel Aviv. After school every day, he and his friends went to help out, telling their mothers they were going off to study together. Students were put in charge of the checkposts, he said, since they were presumed to know English and to be able to tell the difference between the British and the Jewish immigrant fighters. They didn't have a clue. Little imagining how radically their lives soon would

Figure 8 Ibrahim Abu-Lughod (fourth from right) and Reja-e Busailah (fourth from left) with classmates from Al-'Amiriyya Secondary School, Jaffa, 1947.

be changed, they felt it was critical that they pass the end of year examinations. Their future, they thought at the time, depended on it. So when Shafiq, my father's close friend, lost his brother, my father insisted that he forgo the funeral procession in order to take his exams. When they showed up to sit for their exams, they found that the roof had been blown off the school in which the Palestine matriculation exams were being administered. They carried on. By the time they heard the results on the radio several months later, it was the Jewish Education Department that announced them; there was no longer an Arab Department. My father was, by then, a refugee in Nablus, a West Bank town. He was soon to leave for Amman. He sent a telegram to Shafiq, now a refugee in Beirut. He remembers the irony: "It was such a thrill—we passed! But there we were, refugees with no future."

My father's tour of Jaffa took us down a boulevard where you passed a majestic colonial post office (where he had tried in vain to get his old postbox, just for the pleasure of being able to receive letters addressed to Jaffa); the law courts where he had dreamed of practicing law, modeling himself on Yusuf Wahbi, a star of Egyptian film whose eloquence could win people over; the spot where there had been an ice cream shop where he and his teenage friends would go, more to flirt with the European woman who worked there than to eat. They weren't used to seeing young women working, even though young girls in their section of town and women in the Christian section of the city went about unveiled. These buildings harbored meanings for him that were opaque for me, who saw only the sort of colonial buildings that looked vaguely familiar from other parts of the Middle East—other places the British and French had set themselves up to rule. I had affection for these kinds of buildings in Egypt, as I felt at home and at ease there. Here I was a stranger and my father's memories, perhaps because so caught up in defeat and hostility, were not ones I could easily embrace.

There was also a nondescript apartment building on the tour, the last in which he had lived. Jaffa and Tel Aviv bordered each other, and as the tensions intensified in the 1940s, they split Arabs and Jews. The fighting in the winter of 1947 and 1948 was near this border, and my father's neighborhood, as he explained, suddenly became too dangerous, subject to mortar and gunfire. His family took shelter with a cousin who lived downtown. But after two weeks, they realized the battles were going to be longer than anticipated and that they wouldn't be going back home soon. When the Irgun and Hagana dynamited the Palace of Justice not far from their cousin's house, killing sixty young people who had been under the care of the Social Affairs Department along with a popular soccer player who was one of the social workers in charge of them, he thought it might be best to move the family to a different neighborhood. My father, the scholar and historian with a huge library and encyclopedic knowledge of the Palestinian-Israeli dispute, insisted that although Israeli historians continue to claim that the target was the National Committee headquarters, this could not be so. The National Committee had moved two weeks earlier and he is sure that this attack was meant to terrorize the people of Jaffa, which it did.

In the book he edited in 1971, *The Transformation of Palestine*, my father would publish an article by Erskine Childers, a distinguished Irish journalist who characterized the Zionist hope from the early part of the twentieth century that the Palestinians would disappear as "the wordless wish." Based on documentary sources including Zionist, British, and Arab radio broadcasts, Childers described what had happened in Jaffa in the weeks before it was overrun—a description that I had found shocking when I first read it. Again, it was so hard to imagine that this was what my father and his family had lived through—my grandmother had never talked about it to me, her only stories from the past being about her wedding night and other fragments of magic and everyday life in Palestine. The assault, Childers noted, began on April 25 with units of the underground Irgun followed by units of the official Hagana. Although Jaffa was not part of the Jewish allocation in the UN partition plan, it was bombarded by 3-inch mortars, highly inaccurate but devastating psychologically; it was subjected to barrel bombs, described by an Israeli army-reserve officer to the U.S. Marine Corps professional magazine as especially designed for Arab towns and consisting of "barrels, casks or metal drums, filled with a mixture of explosives and petrol, and fitted with two old rubber tires containing the detonating fuse" which were rolled down the streets until they crashed into walls and doorways, bursting into flames and multiple explosions (Childers 1971: 187); its population was terrorized psychologically by loudspeaker vans with pre-recorded "horror sounds" including shrieks, wails and moans of women, sirens, fire-alarm bells and calls, in Arabic, to run for their lives (ibid. 188) and to remember the massacre at Deir Yassin; and there was even looting by Jewish forces (ibid. 191).

My father, a high school student, had volunteered for the hurriedly formed city-based National Committee to defend Jaffa. With no training, he, like the so many of the small fighting force of 1,500, was issued an old gun unfit for battle. It came in handy, he said, only once: during his search for an apartment. He knocked on doors looking for an empty apartment for his mother and sister to live in. Eventually, he heard about one. He explained politely to the agent their desperate situation. The man refused to rent it to them; the apartment belonged to a couple on their honeymoon. My father pleaded with him, assuring him that they wanted it only temporarily and would give it up as soon as the couple returned. But the man was stubborn. My father let the gun show beneath his jacket. The rental was agreed. This modern apartment with the first bathtub and upright toilet they had seen, was a place where his mother was unhappy. She didn't end up staying long because after more and more of Jaffa fell and news reached them of the massacre of the village of Deir Yassin, there was great panic.[7] It was decided that the women and children should go to Nablus to wait things out. Like the honeymooning couple, they were never to return.

My father spent his last days and nights "defending" Jaffa at the age of nineteen in various places that were also part of his tour of the city. With no sense of the geography, the streets and buildings meaning nothing to me, I again could not connect my white haired father with his black beret and his classical music playing on the car radio with this youth. I struggled to transpose those old black and white photographs of a young man with a dark mustache and bright eyes into this place. But how could I? His trauma in Palestine had lived on in me only as a wounded identification in a hostile United States where sympathy for Palestinians was scarce and aggressive lies about what had happened prevailed. My father recalled that at the end of that fateful April, food was running out, the bakeries had closed, mortar from Tel Aviv was falling on the city. The streets of most neighborhoods were by then empty. The British were escorting convoys of fleeing people. But it was dangerous for young Palestinian men to try to leave the city by land because they were vulnerable to arrest or worse; the British were unable or unwilling to protect them. There was only the sea.

On his tour, then, my father pointed to the place where he and his school friend laid down their useless guns when they left. He had lost touch with this brother, on another front; the rest of his family was gone. On the morning of May 3, the two joined a throng on a small barge that was transporting people out of the harbor to a ship that was rumored to be the last ship to carry people to safety. Sent by the Red Cross, it was going to Beirut. But then they hesitated, asking themselves what they were doing. They went back ashore. After all, they had been part of the National Committee that had been urging people not to flee, insisting the city was safe, promising that reinforcements were on the way (they weren't). But when they did return, they realized that no one was left. The shooting, my father said, was all coming from the other side. Around three o'clock in the afternoon, they saw smoke billowing from the smoke stack of the ship. It was about to leave. They put down their guns and ran to catch the last dinghy out. The words of a Belgian sailor who confronted them on board echoed in my father's ears fifty years later: "How could you leave your country?" He was to repeat to himself these words many times, even though he knew there had been no choice.

The tour of Jaffa always ended with the sea. My father ignored the Hebrew being spoken all around him, the young couples in tight jeans flirting and laughing, the downmarket Oriental Jewish families having picnics. He refused to go to the Israeli beach café. Instead, he made himself a place on the sand and went in for his swim. As I held my infants, with their silly sun hats, I knew he wanted me to admire this glorious place. I had always known he loved the sea because he had grown up swimming. I found it interesting that he told a colleague in 1999, "Growing up by the sea, I was not confined to the city, I was not confined to my community but was part of a world that was really large; I dreamt about going out to see it" (Ahmed-Fararjeh 2003: 22). As it turned out, he had been forced to go out and see that world.

All my life I had watched him gaze out to sea—from Alexandria, from Beirut, from Spain, Morocco, New Jersey, and the Caribbean. I had seen him swim out, stretching his long fingers with his wedding band glinting in the sun, his broad shoulders breaking out of the water when he did the butterfly stroke he liked best. He had made us all love the sea. Yet here, in Jaffa, like the man in his sepia poster, he looked out from the place he somehow stubbornly considered home, even though I felt we were vulnerable intruders. His blue American passport allowed him to sit on the beach where he swam as a boy with dolphins and turtles, the beach his mother could see from her window as she drank her coffee. It was his unthreatening white hair and turtleneck shirts that allowed him to pass as a foreigner, not a dangerous or despised Arab "native." The yellow license plates that identified his car as Israeli and thus gave him freedom of movement allowed him to pull up unnoticed alongside the others in the parking lot at the beach. (Cars sold to temporary visitors who need not pay taxes always have this color license plates, like other Israeli cars, distinguishing them from the cars of the West Bank or Gaza.) These, not the sepia of his poster, were the vivid colors of his return to Jaffa.

Memories as History

As a scholar obsessed with Palestine, my father had long thought it critical to gather people's recollections of the forced exodus of 1948. His introduction to the extraordinary memoir he solicited from his old friend and high school classmate Reja-e Busailah began with a comment on the Nakba. "Powerful and shattering as it was," he wrote, "and although it constitutes an important aspect of the Palestinian legacy, it is the one event in Palestinian history that has gone essentially unrecorded from the standpoint of the victim."[8] An understanding of the exodus had to be obtained, "even at this late date," he wrote in 1981, to understand the Palestinian experience, to bear witness to a silenced history, and to reconstruct the event in its complexity. Always concerned with the wider picture, he wrote, "We know that the circumstances of the exodus differed considerably from one region of Palestine to another and from one social class to another." (Busailah 1981: 123)

Busailah's harrowing memoir of the exodus from Lydda in July 1948 is different from my father's stories of the doomed fight for Jaffa and the flight by sea. It brings together the political understandings of a young high school radical with vivid aural and physical descriptions of the bombardment, the city overrun by Zionist fighters, the rumors of massacres, and the forced march of the whole bewildered population of this town that had believed itself so permanent. Lydda had not been within the borders of the area allocated to the Zionists under the UN Partition Plan. It was attacked and its inhabitants driven out in the second of the two short wars with Arab forces that the newly declared Israeli state fought. Busailah describes their expulsion in the summer and their long march into the unknown in Biblical terms—into the wilderness. At the end of that march on the terrible day turned out to be an Arab village called Niʻlin, fifteen miles away including the detours to avoid hostile areas. His recollections include moments of intense fear before the departure, as when he hid, shaking, behind a rolled up mat as the Jewish forces burst into houses, their shots accompanied by women's screams. They are haunted too by incidents of his own hard-hearted denial of others, as when after he had made it to Niʻlin, he pushed his way back through the stragglers to bring a little water to a close friend and his mother, hiding it from all those pitifully begging.

Busailah recalls events as he experienced them and as he heard about them from others. Being blind, the mingling of experience and hearsay that forms all our memories is perhaps more acute for him. His memoir describes the sun beating down, the clawing for water at muddy wells, the talk of grandfathers left behind because they could not go on, of "bodies that might have been without life," and of babies abandoned in ditches. "I was made aware," he writes, "slowly, by piecemeal, through exclamations or incoherent phrases, that some of those who lay dead had their tongues sticking out, covered with dust and down. I did not see. And that perhaps frightened me the more." Finally he writes, "Someone talked later—I think when we reached Ni'lin—of having seen a baby still alive on the bosom of a dead woman, apparently the mother. . . . (Mother and baby are not unlike the reverse of what was related later about the Deir Yassin mother seen in Jerusalem with her killed baby on her bosom.)"

Struggling for the right voice, later he would turn terse description into poetic image. He reworked this last story into a poem called "Remembering After Forty Years in the Wilderness," the wilderness now signifying not just the road to Niʻlin along which he stumbled, but his lifetime of exile in Kuwait, Jordan, and the United States.

> *Over Europe there hung a strange mist,*
> *America was at the tree-breaking age,*
> *and God was ordering that there be light*
>
> *and when there was*
> *there was paraded on the road to Ni'leen*

as the wind played possum
a pair of two dead breasts
and a baby his face buried between them
waiting to be nursed

the July sun was pitiless then
citing and reciting the incident when God that spring
went merciful and ordered that there be light

and when there was
there was paraded from Deir Yaseen
in the breath of the orange blossom
in the view of God's City a baby lying on his tummy
dead between two breasts that yearned to nurse.[9]

My father did not worry, as do the academic analysts of collective or so-cial memory today, about the fragmentary outlines of personal memory, the silences, and the bending of memory by the present or by the mingling of the lived and the heard. He saw individual memoirs such as his friend's as the stuff of a history of the Palestinian experience. He encouraged people to write and recount, even if he focused more on his intellectual friends than on the former villagers who contributed to memorial books such as the ones discussed by Davis and Slyomovics or the women in refugee camps who gave their stories to researchers like Rosemary Sayigh, Diana Allan, or Laleh Khalili (all in this volume). He offered his own stories not just to his children but to newspapers, journals, and interviewers including Hisham Ahmed-Fe-rarjeh, who compiled them into a book. Some of his memory production, like that of other Palestinians, was heightened by projects undertaken on the occasion of the fiftieth anniversary of the Nakba. In the twilight of his life, he also worked on a proposal for a Palestinian Memory Museum, a proj-ect that seems even more quixotic now that Israeli tanks can drive by his old apartment and the waves of Israeli offensives since 2001 have destroyed what fragile hope there was when my father was alive for even moderate Palestinian sovereignty and calm. He wanted the museum's ethnographic, ar-chaeological, and art exhibits to show the dynamic and continuous history of Palestinians. This was definitely not to be a Holocaust museum, he insisted. The Nakba was deliberately consigned a small space. These exhibits were to be complemented by an archive of the basic documents needed for research on Palestinian history.[10]

Memorializing Material Remains

For a daughter, a father's death is always hard. But when he is someone whose life has been tied up with something much larger than family, his death takes on much more than a merely personal meaning. My father died on May 23, 2001, surrounded by family and friends. For me, the first aftermath was intensely personal and fixated on objects. Draped over the back of the black wheelchair with its shiny red wheels were his khaki "bair of bants," as he used to joke, in his self-mocking caricature of an Arab accent. The belt dangled limply. On the bathroom counter was the untouched shaving mug, its water gone cold. Everywhere in his Ramallah apartment were the abandoned signs of his life. His Vivaldi CDs that my sisters and I would insist on playing rather than Qur'anic recitation, as one pious distant relative urged. The oxygen tanks, two big ones by the bed, four small ones lined up in the hall, the one on the trolley with a stenciled Star of David marking it as from "the other side." My father's room held so many small objects that would make a daughter cry: his watch, his glasses, his wallet, his sandals, his dried fruit, his piles of scholarly papers.

It had all stopped now, the routine of taking care of him. My aunt wasn't going to bring him his Arab coffee in the hand-painted aquamarine mug and hear his praise. My sisters and I, having left our families and jobs to come to Ramallah, weren't going to help him get dressed for the day. Encourage him to eat his breakfast. Open the door for his many visitors. Scold him for having so many guests. Tell him it wasn't time yet for his painkiller. Take directions on how to make correct chicken soup. We weren't going to get him the newspapers, Arabic and English, he insisted on having even though he didn't have the energy to read them.

We were now to be swept into an even more public world, as his friend Suheil had warned us, sitting us down and explaining seriously, as if we knew nothing about the Arab world, that there were certain customs that had to be followed. While we, his children with various levels of familiarity with Palestinian society but almost no experience in Palestine, grieved, my father's friends indeed took care of everything. They had to negotiate the complex world of a Palestinian community steeped in the political during an intifada, a world we were hardly prepared for. His death certificate was written; his burial certificate was obtained from the appropriate Israeli ministries. Plans for the funeral in Jaffa were made. Arrangements for the three days of condolence visits in Ramallah were made. Plastic chairs arrived at the apartment and were set up in rows along the walls of the living room, dining room, and terrace. Counters were cleared and bitter coffee made. Posters with his photo on them appeared. Arab coffee, cases of water, and boxes of Kleenex were piled in the kitchen, compliments, I was surprised to learn, of the Palestine National Authority. Arafat would come straight from the airport among a flurry of bodyguards and commotion to offer brief condolences to this Palestinian academic who had given so much to the cause. Announcements were placed, newspaper interviews were done, and the speakers list for the memorial was drawn up. People came and went, dignitaries and neighbors, journalists and politicos, acquaintances and cultured friends. When my uncle and cousin arrived from Jordan, they relieved us from the duties of receiving condolences so we could escape into our father's bedroom, feeling for his presence, feeling the emptiness.

The next time we saw my father was on the day of the funeral. He was a frail body lying in a little concrete room with green metal doors set behind Maqasid Islamic Hospital in Jerusalem, ritually prepared for burial. Wrapped in white sheets and bound, he looked small and thin. When I went to look at his face, only a small bit of it uncovered, I had to turn away. He was lifeless—the finality so physical.

But he was at the same time now becoming a symbol for others. Already shrouded as a Muslim, he was also going to be a national hero of sorts. We began the long wait as people gathered for the drive to Jaffa, a very public affair. We were watching tensely for any unusual movement, wondering if "they" were going to prevent us from taking him. A man filmed us with a video camera. It was a relief to find out that he was from Al-Jazeera Television, the Arab satellite channel, not then well-known outside the Arab world because this was still May, a few months before the events of 9/11 thrust this news station into Western consciousness. The evening before, with the house full of mourners, we had received an unnerving phone call. The man spoke Arabic; after offering ritual condolences, he demanded to talk with the person in charge of the funeral arrangements. He identified himself as from Israeli intelligence, Shin Bet. My legs were weak and I could only think how glad I was that we were in an area under the Palestinian Authority. All this officer could do was telephone, not come knocking on/down the door. I could never think of Israelis without the sharp black and white images of the French colonial commandos in Pontecorvo's brilliant film *Battle of Algiers* kicking down doors. Had it been a few months later when Israeli tanks reoccupied Ramallah, he would indeed have been able to invade our private grief.

I had quickly passed the phone to my father's friends. I could hear heated discussion in the back bedroom. They were being told that they would not be permitted to bury my father in Jaffa. How had Israeli security known? It was all over Radio Palestine and in the local newspapers: the first Palestinian refugee to be buried back in his hometown. My father's colleagues insisted that we had all the proper documents: the death certificate from Jerusalem and the burial permit from the appropriate Israeli Ministry, thanks to our "Israeli Arab" friends who had grown up in the system. But the security officer was insistent. He said he would call back. We were agitated. The men went over possible scenarios, all terrible to me: of being halted as we tried to take the body from the hospital, or as we were on the road to Jaffa, or as we approached the cemetery. Could we really have a confrontation with the Israeli army while my father's body lay in the hot sun? What should we do? Someone suggested that I should call the U.S. consul general in Jerusalem. There was no other way. So I telephoned and explained that we had a problem. My father's wish had been to be buried in Jaffa and we had all the proper papers. The consul said some kind words about my father and assured me that he would call the ambassador in Tel Aviv. When we didn't hear back from the Shin Bet officer that night, we thought it was a good sign. I wanted what was best for my father; others were ready to use this occasion to assert their rights in the face of Israeli challenge.

So it was a relief that nothing was happening that Friday morning behind Maqasid Hospital except that people were milling about. More and more people. There were the familiar faces of his friends and those we knew, people we had seen at the house over the last months. I was glad to see a few people I considered friends, academics of the younger generation who spoke to us in English. There were many others we didn't know. People came to shake hands with us. Friends hugged each other. The men stood outside the emergency room entrance. Whispering started up when particular dignitaries or controversial figures arrived. We sat with some inside the hospital, under the bare cement ceilings with trailing wires. I couldn't help feeling sad about how different this tired underfunded Arab hospital was from the bustling corporate professionalism of Hadassah Hospital where my father had gone for his last difficult appointments with the smart pulmonologist and the unsympathetic oncologist.

Eventually it was time to move. An unmarked white van pulled up in front of the morgue and the coffin was loaded. My sisters and I clung to each other as we peered through the van window at that plain, lonely box.

The crowd got into cars and the bus that had come from Ramallah, forming a long cortege. Slowly we drove, looking right and left for Israeli army
jeeps or police. But the road was clear. We had heard that the U.S. ambassador this morning had reassured someone that they would be monitoring
the situation. I felt the irony—my father protected, as a citizen, by the same
government that he always berated for supporting and arming the killers of
his people. But I was grateful.

It was a long drive, on highways and through a back route into the industrial sector that led to the Arab part of Jaffa. In a crowded neighborhood, we
parked and got out. Plastered on the walls were bills with newspaper articles
about my father and his curriculum vitae. A professor, I realized, is a respected figure in this community. And he was special because of the way he'd come
in fresh, breaking through the inertia of strikes, ignoring curfews, refusing all
the borders between Palestinians—diasporic, in the occupied territories, and
within Israel—and, as he had done in his years in the U.S., willing communities
to take action.[11] We were at the center of the Jaffa Arab Association, a place
where my father had spoken many times to a community he was exceedingly
fond of, these remnants in what had been a Palestinian city. The association
was headed by some men who had gone out of their way to help arrange
for the burial. For them, my father's support and concern for their activities
(squatting in condemned buildings, clearing paths to houses whose access had
been blocked by the dumping of garbage for a Tel Aviv landfill, advocacy and
social services for the downtrodden Arabs of a rundown neighborhood so different from the gentrified areas where Jews lived) had meant a lot.

The coffin was laid out on a large table in a small room to the left. There
were wreaths of flowers. Now draped with the Palestinian flag, the coffin suddenly looked vibrant. My father was no longer the frail mummy we'd seen
earlier. His death was being given great meaning. Eulogies I barely heard
stopped in time for afternoon prayer. Everyone spilled out the doors and followed the coffin. Men carried it down the side streets to the 'Ajami mosque,
jostling to take their turns. My nephew was among them, the only one with
a ponytail, but the one who loved him best, having himself lived with him for
two years in Ramallah. In the front of the procession some young men held
the Palestinian flag as a banner. People looked out from the windows above.

At the mosque, they carried him upstairs. I wondered how long it had been
since he had been in a mosque, but this was the way. He was being absorbed
into a society and community. All the women stayed outside but I also noticed
that there were many more men waiting outside the mosque than had gone

inside. I asked a colleague of his from Birzeit University, "Are all these Christians?" "No," he answered with a smile, "I see a lot of Marxist-Leninists!"

We stood around. The sun was strong but we were beginning to feel good now that we could see the sea. A young teenager with long hair, doe eyes, and a tee shirt and jeans struck up a friendship with my sister. She didn't know our father, she admitted. "But," she added, "for the first time in my life I feel proud to be from Jaffa." In fact, I suspect there were many people there who didn't know him. Those who did came from all corners of Palestine, but especially from the part of Palestine taken in 1948. There were a few Israeli Jews as well—anti-Zionists for whom my father was an important bridge. On the other hand, I came to understand there were many more people who couldn't be there: all those with West Bank or Gaza identity cards. None were permitted to cross the checkpoints into "Israel." Even a close friend of my father's, a professor who had been elected to the Palestinian legislature, had been refused a permit to leave Gaza for the occasion, though his American ex-wife had tried to intervene.

When prayers were over, we began to move. Carried on the shoulders of waves of men, the coffin swayed wildly. Far in front was a Palestinian flag, now defiantly waving. A large procession of people walked together up the hill, holding hands, talking, feeling part of the group. We passed the fish restaurants that my father liked to take people to. Like oranges, fish were for him part of the cherished tastes of home in Jaffa. Stronger tastes than Proust's famed madeleines. Bystanders watched, perplexed. Some children waved, thinking perhaps this was a parade. Many Israelis now live in the Arab neighborhoods of Jaffa, some enjoying tastefully restored houses with Arab tiles and arches, as my aunt would be devastated to discover when we returned to Jaffa a week later. The sea shimmered to our right below, the afternoon sun catching the windsurfers who were out enjoying the gentle breeze. The sense of exhilaration was intense—so many people walking together, following a coffin draped in the flag. Miraculously, it seemed, we were not being prevented from burying him as he wished, in the cemetery overlooking the sea in his hometown of Jaffa.

I had fallen behind but when I caught up I saw, in the cemetery, a cluster of men high up, to the right of three trees. I hurried up, my feet in their open heeled shoes catching on crumbled graves and twigs. My sisters and aunt stood at the edge of the crowd of men. We watched my father, wrapped in a flag, his small face now uncovered so we would see him for the last time, being hauled out of the coffin and dropped into the freshly dug earth. His material remains put back into his land in the most beautiful of spots (save for the decaying houses, the empty lots, and the construction work on the "Peres Peace Center"), this bluff next to his favorite beach.

As we made our way down through the cemetery, a close friend of my father's asked, "Do you want to see your grandfather's grave?" My uncle had remembered where it was because he had, as a boy, gone every week to visit it. It was large and looked still new, standing out amongst the crumbling stones. The sea air is hard on most kinds of stone but it must have been of amazing quality. On the side was a poem carved in ornate calligraphy. Near the bottom we could see his name, 'Ali Khamis Abu-Lughod. He had died shortly after being released without charges from the last of his imprisonments by the British. Just nearby was the grave of my father's brother who had been killed by the British a year or so before they had to flee in 1948. We learned later that no one had been buried in this cemetery for twenty years.

When we emerged from the gate, stepping through the dust and rubble, people came, one by one, to shake our hands in condolence. How many people were there? It was overwhelming. Did all these people know my father? Or was he just a symbol—a son of Jaffa, a prominent Palestinian, a lover of Palestine, exercising, in the end, his right to return?

Memorializing my father a few days after his death, Mahmoud Darwish, Palestine's great poet, would say, "Every death is a first death—sudden as a thunderbolt, not familiar, not known." And yet my father's death was saturated with stories already known. He himself had surprised me by resorting in his illness to odd expressions with religious referents, likening the pain in his side to a kick by angels and half-jokingly remarking, as he stoically suffered the pain of cancer, "We [Palestinians] were born to suffer . . . like Jesus." Others were now bolder in their metaphors, Palestine and Jaffa offering particularly resonant "sites of memory" (Nora 1989). Darwish (2001) likened my father's Palestine to "heaven and hell entwined because the eternal tree of Paradise grows in the city of Jaffa." He described my father's presence in "the caravan of expulsion" from Jaffa as the original sin, not because he had approached the forbidden tree of knowledge but because he had been too far from it: this explained his lifelong commitment to research and intellectual pursuits. Darwish ended, as did so many, by talking about my father's return to Palestine. "He returned," he said, "to plant in it the tree of knowledge, and he was that tree." Playing on the Qur'anic language of return in death, he said, "He was born in Jaffa and to Jaffa he returned, to remain, there for eternity, close to the tree of Paradise."

A few years later I was struck by the passionate remarks of an old Jaffa refugee living in Gaza who also brought heaven and Jaffa together. Captured in Omar Al-Qattan's 1995 documentary film about the fall of Jaffa, *Going Home . . . A British Veteran in Palestine*, the old man argues with his son that he cannot and will not accept what happened. Almost blasphemously he insists, "On Judgment Day when God asks me to choose, saying, 'I want you to enter heaven, what do you say?' I'll say, 'No, return me to my country instead so I can go live in Jaffa.' You see, I would refuse heaven and say 'Please let me go live in Jaffa because it's my hometown (baladi).'"

The more common story to enfold my father in death was the one told by the Palestinian flag with which they covered him. My father was not a flag waver; he was dedicated to justice, he loved Palestine and its people, but he was not a crude nationalist and remained always critical, always scholarly, always independent politically. Yet they draped his coffin with the Palestinian flag as it lay in the Jaffa Arab Community Center Hall awaiting burial. I had never waved a flag either and found the politicization overbearing. Yet I felt that the flag charged the coffin with a strange charisma. Young men held high the Palestinian flag at the head of the funeral procession to the cemetery, a defiant gesture in a country where people have long been imprisoned for showing that flag, although also a trite move in a land of so many funerals of young "martyrs." Two days later a fiery speaker would commend my father for his decision to return to Palestine, leaving the comforts and advantages of life in America, because he had not set conditions for this return. "The nation," he approved, "is to be loved unconditionally."

Edward Said, brilliant scholar and close friend of my father's, who would outlive him by less than three years, was less romantic about the nation. At the same memorial service in Ramallah he countered this imposed image of the nationalist, the image that was carried also by hundreds of posters that appeared, in the name of the Palestine Liberation Organization, the Palestine National Authority, and the Liberation Movement of Fatah, in what has become a tradition for marking the martyrs of the struggle for Palestine, by talk of my father's cosmopolitanism. He described my father's openness to the people and culture of the country in which he'd spent forty years, the United States, despite his opposition to its policies. He described his curiosity and wide travels—to China, Peru, India, and the countries of Africa. His was a subtle critique of the provincialism that can dog nationalism. To temper the megalomania that can also accompany patriotism, he quoted my father's latest bittersweet refrain, "We are a mediocre people. A good people, but mediocre." Later Said would write about how, despite his return, my father "was still unfulfilled and unsettled." He noted, "The return didn't change him, though he was more contented at home than he had been in exile. For him, Palestine was an interrogation that is never answered completely—or even articulated adequately." But even Said could not help reading my father's life and death in terms of a larger story. Noting the swings from "his gregariousness to his moody introspection, from his optimism and energy to the immobilizing sense of powerlessness" he concluded: "His life simultaneously expresses defeat and triumph, abjection and attainment, resignation and resolve. In short, it was a version of Palestine, lived in all its complexity."[12]

What no one failed to mention was that he had made his *'awda*—his return, finally, to Jaffa.

The Past in the Present

For my father, return meant the insertion of honed stories into the roughness of history and a genuine confrontation with the present. Surprisingly, he had taken this on with enthusiasm. He who had for so long refused to come began encouraging every Palestinian to return, even if they had to suffer the offensive interrogations of Israeli authorities at the airport and the bridge, the shoes taken off for inspection, the notebooks confiscated, the suitcases emptied, the body searched, even the diaper bags and toiletries opened. When an interviewer on Al-Jazeera Television asked him if he wasn't bitter that his dream of return had brought him into a situation where Palestinians were faced with daily problems and herded into zones called A, B, and C, separated by Israeli military checkpoints, he answered, "I do not feel bitterness at all. I feel, rather, that the Israeli presence is a challenge to us. And it is impossible to meet that challenge with bitterness. It is a barrier—I struggle with it; I call for equality; I call for the removal of all these checkpoints. . . . Our task is to struggle together, in order to change this reality. My coming here, a big part of it, was in order to change this reality. Because I cannot fight far away from the field of struggle." He felt strongly at the end that the Palestinians had made a major mistake in 1948 when they fled in fear, though he, more than many, knew they could hardly have done otherwise. He had spent his life researching this history. But still he said, "It was incumbent on us to remain on the land, even if the Israelis arrived. It was incumbent upon us to stay, because the struggle requires confrontation by the resistors."[13]

I saw for myself that confrontation on the ground. I saw the armed riot soldiers facing the young boys throwing stones. But I also saw my father as he approached the Israeli checkpoints steeling himself nervously for the charade and forced smile of this gentleman flashing his American passport to get through. Later I experienced Israel through his illness and death. Through the inability to get anywhere on the West Bank the painkillers prescribed by the Israeli doctor. The unavailability of morphine patches, not to mention his favorite foods of broccoli and salmon, except on the "other side." The need to take an ambulance to go to doctors' appointments for fear his oxygen tank would run out while the car overheated at a slow checkpoint. The fear on his lively friend's face, an Israeli Palestinian from the north who knew Hebrew and came along to help him negotiate the hospital, as we approached a checkpoint. She was not technically allowed to cross into the West Bank, with her Israeli identity card, even though she and her husband and children lived there. And the telephone call from Israeli security, in the midst of grief, threatening our arrangements for the funeral.

The physical reality of my father's death was for me inseparable from the details of Israeli domination: from his blue fingertips to the Palestinian medics who rushed him down the stairs to the ambulance but couldn't guarantee that they'd be allowed to pass quickly, from the intrusive phone call of an Israeli officer to the inert flag draped over the coffin in the Jaffa Community Center, from the anxiety about surveillance to the inexpressible generosity of his community, from the fears about the fate of the lecture notes we had to throw into the dumpster as we cleaned out his apartment to the panic we felt the eerie day none of his friends came to visit—because they'd gathered their children early from school and were intently watching the news to find out whether, or where, Ariel Sharon would bomb in "retaliation" for some incident.

I had heard my father's stories all my life, but it is different to walk, orphaned, through a hot dusty checkpoint dragging your suitcases because they won't allow any Palestinian vehicles to cross. It is different to be held up by arrogant soldiers with reflective sunglasses and burnished muscles who willfully delay you. It is different to go to the airport in an Arab taxi. On your way to catch your plane they slowly search the car and disappear for a long time with the driver's identity card, humiliating you with their power to make you sit silent though you know you are perfectly innocent. Stories of the underground railroad and the smuggling of slaves to freedom, images of displaced refugees from the second world war trudging with their bundles of possessions—these came to me as I crossed over, out of the West Bank to the safety of Jerusalem, then to catch my plane. But they can't capture this particular reality with its growling Hebrew arrogantly proclaiming ownership. With its guns and soldiers everywhere you turn. With its utter separation of Arab and Jew. These experiences, more than my father's stories, have made me want to write about the Nakba. For the Palestinian catastrophe is not just something of the past. It continues into the present in every house demolished by an Israeli bulldozer, with every firing from an Apache helicopter, with every stillbirth at a military checkpoint, with every village divided from its fields by the "separation" wall, and with every Palestinian who still longs to return to a home that is no more.

Author's Note

For comments and other help with this essay, I am grateful to Janet Abu-Lughod, Lori Allen, Susan Crane, Vicky de Grazia, Farah Griffin, Saidiya Hartman, Marianne Hirsch, Jean Howard, Martha Howell, Alice Kessler-Harris, Timothy Mitchell, Susan Pederson, Ahmad Sa'di, Carol Sanger, Julia Seton, Susan Sturm, Janet Wolff, and the participants in the workshop on "Al-Nakba in Palestinian Collective Memory" in Montecatini Terme, Italy. An early version of part of this essay was published in the *Jerusalem File Quarterly* 11–12 (2001) just after my father's death. See www.jqf-jerusalem.org/journal/2001/jqf11–12/. I am deeply grateful to Hisham Ahmed-Fararjeh for having shared with me and my family, and then put into print, his interviews with my father.

NOTES

1. Answer to Leila Fannous. I do not know the occasion.
2. This secularism extended to his minimization of religion and religious education in his controversial plan for a Palestinian national curriculum, a plan that was overturned. See Hovsepian 2004, ch.7.
3. All quotations from my father's stories are based on taped interviews conducted in English by Hisham Ahmed-Fararjeh. Where these were included in the publication by Ahmed-Fararjeh (2003), I indicate page numbers. Some other stories and sentiments can be found in a two-part interview by Zakariya Muhammad (1995). In this interview my father says he left Jaffa by boat on May 1, not May 3.
4. For descriptions of such visits, see Karmi 2002, Tamari and Hammami 1998, and Al-Qattan (this volume). For Edward Said's return to his family home, see the

documentary by Charles Bruce 1998. For an insightful discussion of films, including "In Search of Palestine" about claims to houses and homes in Jerusalem, see Bishara 2003 and Sa'di 2002.

5. For some of the ways this erasure and rewriting takes place, see Abu El-Haj 2001 and Benvenisti 2000.

6. For more on the forests, see Bardenstein 1999 and Bresheeth, Davis, and Slyomovics in this volume.

7. Deir Yassin was a village whose inhabitants had a nonaggression pact with the Hagana but was attacked by a joint Irgun-LEHI force that by conservative estimates slaughtered about 115 men, women, and children and stuffed their bodies down wells (Smith 2004: 194). Publicity about the massacre through Irgun and Hagana mobile loudspeaker units in cities such as Jaffa and Haifa and through Arab radio created enormous fear. For an account of the impact of the massacre in Deir Yassin on Palestinians, based on interviews with refugees, see Nazzal 1978. As Benny Morris (2004a) has shown, this was not the only massacre conducted by Jewish forces; see also Abdel Jawad (2007) for documentation of sixty-eight massacres of Palestinians conducted in 1948 by Zionist and Israeli forces. A memorial sculpture commemorating the victims of Deir Yassin by the Algerian-American artist Khalil Bendib was erected in Geneva, New York in 2003. See also McGowan and Ellis 1998.

8. Here he was perhaps echoing the title of his friend Edward Said's watershed essay "Zionism from the Standpoint of its Victims" included in Said 1979.

9. Busailah explains matter of factly in a footnote to the poem that Ni'lin is a Palestinian village to which some 60,000 Palestinians were marched by the Israelis in July 1948.

10. A full outline of what they had planned for the Memory Museum can be found in Mu'assasat al-Ta'awun 2000.

11. I am grateful to Roger Heacock for clarifying my father's role in Palestine in his moving remarks at the workshop on "Al-Nakba in Palestinian Collective Memory" at the Sixth Mediterranean Social and Political Research Meeting of the Mediterranean Program of the Robert Schuman Centre for Advanced Studies at the European University Institute, Montecatini Terme, Italy, March 2005.

12. Said 2001. For more on their friendship, see L. Abu-Lughod 2005.

13. My father gave me an unlabeled videorecording of the interview, which I believe is with Muhammad Khrayshat on the program, *Dayf wa Qadiyya* (Guest and Issue), Al-Jazeera Television, probably in 1999. Thanks to Lori Allen for transcribing.

Part Two

MODES OF MEMORY

4 Iterability, Cumulativity, and Presence

THE RELATIONAL FIGURES OF PALESTINIAN MEMORY

Lena Jayyusi

There are perhaps few concepts that, like "memory," offer a fundamentally problematic conceptual terrain, the possibility of a basic fracture within, or confusion of, registers. The concept itself implicates the notion of an "objective" character, an exogenous facticity to the social biographical world, *at the same time as* it is precisely the site where the very idea of that facticity being available in a pristine unmodified way is systematically questioned. Whilst "memory" suggests that there was something real outside persons' subjectivities to be "remembered," "re-called," "re-collected," and "re-presented," it is precisely that facet of "memory work" that must come under increasing scrutiny, interrogation, and contestation. In contemporary work on the subject, "memory" is understood as articulating a past condition, a biographical event, a historical facticity, always *from the point of view of the present* (Bal 1999), that is, from the perspective of present interests, particular current relevances, viewpoints, and subjective (even also subjunctive) modalities. But parallel concerns can also, to some extent, be raised about "history," which can be said to be subject to similar fractures and contestations, based as it partially always is, on the accounts, notations, and annotations of particular persons in the situated conduct of practical concerns and life tasks.

When one ventures into the terrain of "'memory," then, several different terms are mobilized and several kinds of relationship are rendered salient: there is the relationship between "past" and "present," the very heart of what we address when we talk of "memory" and "memory work"; then there is the relationship between "memory" and "history," the latter also always organizing our understanding of the "past" and thus unavoidably conjuring the relationship of "past" to "present," as well as the relationship between "fact" and "artifact," "event" and "narrative"; and there is, of course, the thorny relationship between "individual" memory and that which has come to be called "collective" memory (sometimes appearing as "social" memory, at times as "cultural" memory, and yet at other times as "historical memory," even "myth," and so on). My concern is to locate some of the specific features and modalities of Palestinian memory, memories, and rememberings as articulated around the Nakba of 1948. In the process, facets of these conceptual issues and relationships will themselves be addressed so that they can throw light on the Palestinian "moment" and, in turn, be further illuminated by it.

The Palestinian Nakba

In less than eight months, Palestinian society in its entirety was suddenly and violently extracted from its moorings in time and place, fractured along multiple axes, expelled and undone. Within lived collective Palestinian consciousness this can be likened to the "world undone" by the catastrophic invasion and erasure captured in the narratives of Noah's flood. Yet, albeit catastrophic for Palestinians, ejecting them onto multiple trajectories that continued to heave beneath their feet, it was for some others (Israelis and their various allies) a productive turning point with a dramatic outcome whose *process of production* was to be excised, to a greater or lesser extent, from public discourse and official accounts, to be worked into a "fold" in history. Its site, its location, its space always mutely present in the body of recognized history, in the tales of "in-gathering" of the Jews, in the talk of the Israeli state's security, in the multiple advertisements for authentic Arab houses in the Israeli press, was nevertheless a site, a location always tucked away, under and within the folds of history, a lesion within memory. It is, in part, in this radical disjuncture where the poetics and agonistics of Palestinian memory of the Nakba arise.

For at least nineteen years after the Nakba, the different politico-existential or practico-moral zones in which Palestinians lived were such that the most visible, intelligible, and emblematic constituency was the population that had suffered outright expulsion from their homes, lands and towns or villages: the refugees clustered in the remaining areas of Palestine and in a number of adjoining countries. And of course, it was indeed that population, and the cataclysmic moment that had produced it, that formed the very spine and scaffolding of the Palestinian problem. Had there not been a *massive* dispossession, if *more* Palestinians had been able to remain in their land, the visibility of the Palestinian *collectivity*, and its rights, might not have been so easy to "fold" away, and would not eventually have constituted such a deep fault-line in the terra-firma of contemporary global politics. Palestinians perhaps could not have been so easily dismissed, treated simply as a population of refugees, persons with merely survival needs.

The Nakba of 1948, accompanied as it was by the establishment of a Jewish Israeli state in two thirds of what used to be Palestine, created a rupture within Palestinian collective life that produced three distinct populations: the refugees, the Palestinians inside Israel, and those in the West Bank and Gaza. They constituted three differentiated sites of collective experience and memory work. The shape of one's day, and the ways in which it might configure the features of the next, were distinct in each case. While the refugees were the most visible constituency, the one that embodied the experience and fact of rupture and dispossession,[1] the Palestinians within the state of Israel remained for long years, at least to many Palestinians and other Arabs outside, *opaque* (for the most part), even *invisible*, not merely as actual persons, but as intelligible moral beings, except for the specific members of now divided families who would send heart-breaking greetings and news across airwaves which, unlike telephone lines, would never be able to carry back a direct response, or even a certainty of reception at the other end.[2] This only began to change slowly when the resistance poetry of Palestinians within Israel, like Mahmoud Darwish, Samih al-Qasim and Tawfiq Zayyad began to filter through to the other side of the border, most visibly after 1967, when Israel occupied the remaining parts of Palestine, in what came to be known as *the Naksa*. Palestinians from then on began to reconnect their accounts and memories in relation to each other in their different sites and were able to mediate their own experiences through the different ones of other subgroups within the larger collectivity. Therefore, 1967 was the point when a mutual orientation to, and connection between, different Palestinian communities of quotidian experience began to be radically reconstituted and refashioned.

The unfolding trajectory of continuous dispossession and upheaval experienced at the hands of the Israeli state was to reshape the space of the collective narrative over time. It was to become obvious that the Nakba was not the last collective site of trauma, but what came later to be seen, through the prism of repeated dispossessions and upheavals, as the foundational station in an unfolding and continuing saga of dispossession, negations, and erasure. This enabled Palestinians to reinsert each new episode in relation to the intent, vision, and objective of the original rupture. Sites of experience and temporal events were reconnected into a living narrative, which continues to reconstitute the salience of the past in the fabric of the present. Palestinian memory and its narratives, then, have to be located *relationally* in this unfolding context where the cumulativity of the experiences which re-present the intent, vision, objective, and valency of the original one, come to be reconnected to it, and to the diversity of sites of the continuing figure of erasure and denial that marks the contemporary Palestinian condition.

Iterability and Cumulativity:
Individual Experience, Collective Landscape

Stories of the catastrophe of 1948, of the dispossession and expulsion experienced and crystallized within that constitutive historical moment, come from multiple sites, a plurality of voices, and in a diversity of forms and modes. Although some Palestinians have said that they have found their elders reluctant to speak and tell, betraying a sense of shame and guilt or a closely guarded pain, this may be a function of particular settings and persons or relationships. For the most part, Palestinians have been keen to narrate if and when asked: as a child, I grew up listening to these tales of the exodus, not so much from parents and grandparents as much as from others around. In later life, no sooner did I ask for an account than I got a long and detailed narrative. The will to narrate, and to tell, is everywhere evident, and evident too in various practices and forms, from poetry to graphics and posters, from film to theater.[3] And it is in the repeated tales, *similar* but *different*, that the collective space and dimensions of the catastrophe and the predicament that ensued from it are figured and made present. It is in and through the iteration of similar tales, similar stories of attack, death, and expulsion, like tales of loss, that the character of the catastrophe is shaped and understood. Each new tale is an echo within the echo, focusing and conjuring the collective predicament through the individual, and ramifying the significances and symbolic meanings of the individual experience through the collective. Iteration of the same yet different, difference within the same, is a feature of collective identity, and it is a feature of the work of constituting, shaping and apprehending collective fate and experience. The iterability of same/different tales and trajectories provides the glue of what can be proposed and constituted as a collective tragedy. However, it is not iterability on its own, but a further feature which together with it is significant here: this is the *simultaneity* of the iterable narrativized event, present *within* the narrative itself, and iterated endlessly in one narrative after another.

Writing about public memory with respect to the World Trade Center tragedy, Edward Casey (2004) points to the poignant expressions of public remembrance that flowed in profusion during those painful days in the immediate aftermath—the photographs hung on lines between trees, the bouquets on railings, and the messages from family members affixed to walls. What strikes one about these messages, and about the texture of emotional expression, grief, and remembrance in other tragedies of like magnitude, is that their public character not only reaffirms the bond tying the bereaved family members to the one lost, but that it is in and through this public affirmation that the bond is more deeply reaffirmed, expressed, and thus felt. This is made possible by the *shared character* of the bereavement, the fact of the simultaneity of loss experienced by other members of the larger community. The grief is "public" in *both* senses of the term: that meaning it is visible, declared, or witnessed, and that suggesting a "for all" character, a sphere in which, in principle, membership is generalized, open to anyone within the collectivity, with no special qualifications for entry.[4] The grief is public because it is shared. This adds a layer to the individual's grief, the putatively private sphere of feeling and remembrance, which can enhance its sharpness, its associated sense of the tragic, and the potentiality for continued remembrance through its entry into a public register and what Casey (2004) termed "public memory." Here, the simultaneity of the tragic loss, its iterability, *and* its simultaneous onset, refigures the loss as not merely one of a personal contingency but one that also implicates the very *identity* of the bereaved. It is this which shifts the sense of loss from the level of personal grief to that of collective trauma. It recasts the personal experience of each from the "hers" or "yours" (the third and/or second person voice respectively) to "ours": the collective first-person voice.

This same feature is present in the Palestinian narratives of the Nakba—of the expulsion and uprooting. These accounts are always in the collective first-person voice, the communal voice.[5] And it is the sheer repetition of like stories that articulate differences of specific *local* outcomes and dynamics—cast as *simultaneously lived*—and of different stories bespeaking a shared generalized impact on the coherence of collective subjectivity and on the integrity of the communal fabric, on the taken for granted condition of being-

in-place—recounted as *simultaneously experienced*—that provides the powerful emotional valency of the cataclysm. In numerous stories, for example,
people tell of moving from place to place, and meeting up with relations,
acquaintances from other places caught up in the same kind of trajectory.
There are warnings mutually given, tales mutually told, indexed *within* the
individual account, an awareness of, and orientation to, the shared tempo-
rally collocated character of the experience. The iterability and simultaneity
are not merely encountered by the later recipient of the tales but are present
within many of these accounts themselves.

The iterability of the experience itself, the story repeated across multiple
others, individuals and families, and the iterability of the experience and story
for *the same person*, in 1948, are both intimately bound together in the tale of
massive and sudden communal displacement, as the following account shows.
This is from an interview broadcast over the *Voice of Palestine* on the fifthieth
commemoration of the Nakba. The interviewee, Hajja Safiyya Husni Hasan,
is a woman from the village of Surif, who describes how the expulsion from
her village was followed by expulsion from locale after locale, village after
village, where she and her family tried to take refuge.[6]

> We took with us our clothes, a mattress and cover, and the clothes we were wear-
> ing, and we took the little kids and left. . . . We went to Bayt Mahsir.

In response to a question about their condition at the time, she adds:

> Woe betide me, they met us in Bayt Mahsir and brought us things and sheltered
> us, God spare you our condition. And then we stayed in Bayt Mahsir nearly a
> week and then again it went, Bayt Mahsir, they took it . . . they attacked it from
> our town.

And recounting how they had then taken refuge in the caves around Bayt
Mahsir, she continues:

> . . . and in the morning—the things which we had taken from Surif stayed in
> Bayt Mahsir—in the morning we went to Bayt Mahsir we found them. They had
> expelled everyone and the one who enters Bayt Mahsir dies, the one who enters
> dies, . . .

Yet again:

> . . . we again left. Where? We went to 'Allar—a town they called 'Allar—we went
> up to 'Allar, we stayed almost a month, we were in 'Allar the Jews followed us. We

left and went out where? We went on walking to a town, who knows what they call it. . . . We then went to Bethlehem. From Bethlehem we went to 'Izariyya, from al-'Izariyya we went to 'Akabat Jabir, and from 'Akabat Jabir we went and we settled in Nabi Ya'qub. We stayed a year or two. And in Nabi Ya'qub[7] it snowed on us and the tents fell down over us, God spare you our fate. And then we came here to Ramallah.

This tale, spoken in the first person plural, the communal voice, tells of the same fate being encountered in various locales by her and her family over time, and by other villagers, in an increasingly wider arc of dispossession. Indeed, if we look through a corpus of other narratives about the 1948 events, such as those that appear in Nazzal (1978), a similar structure emerges, as it does in a corpus of oral history interviews conducted with refugees from Lifta.[8] The same kind of story is repeated; the details sometimes different, often similar; the local outcome occasionally variable, as between those who survived and those who were killed, those who managed to return and those who ended up as refugees. But in all, a shared collective fate: the loss of community, the disaster of collective dispossession and radical displacement.

The iterability is also produced across time. Whether in narratives of the Nakba itself, or in narratives of more contemporaneous events marked specifically as Palestinian, such as the assault on Jenin in 2002, this continuity, again of like but different, is indexed, oriented to, and explicitly noted. In the oral history interviews conducted with the refugees from the village of Lifta (on the outskirts of Jerusalem), we encounter the *cumulative iterability through time* of the similar experiences, assaults, and outcomes. In these interviews, a number of the interviewees move easily between various emblematic dates: 1936, 1948, 1967. In some of the accounts, the transition between dates and streams of events is not always explicit, not always marked as such.[9]

M., for example, describes in his narrative the events of 1948. Toward the end, he moves on to describe the events of 1967, drawing a horizon of experience, loss, and trauma that unfolds in stage after stage. Y. starts with a very short narrative of leaving for Ramallah in 1948, eventually building a house there. Then he goes on to describe the arrest of his daughter by Israeli occupation forces after 1967. R. describes how his home was demolished time after time—and as a response to this, he moves on to assert his claim to the land, to the country, and to return ('awda). Here the *cumulativity is both temporal and chronological, as well as horizontal and networked*—i.e., it is both *synchronic*, across the population as in the iteration of similar experiences in the moment of the Nakba, and *diachronic,* as in the iteration of similar/different experiences and outcomes over time (the Naksa, arrests, house demolitions).

In *Searching Jenin* (Baroud 2003), a number of the narrators of the attack on the camp frame their account, and the trajectories made visible from "within-the-attack," in relation to 1948. The book, a collection of first-person testimonials of the invasion and destruction of the Jenin camp in April 2002, reveals an orientation based on a sense of past-within-the-present, the present as a continuation of the past, and 1948 as a focal date. But in this continuing history, new focal dates and experiences emerge, and Jenin is one of them. In addition to survivor testimonies and the accounts of camp residents, the book also includes testimonies by others who had either visited the camp straight after or who had witnessed the battle from another spot, itself also under siege and curfew. One of those testimonies (given by Sam Bahour) says:

> Today, Jenin, the city and the refugee camp, is embodied in every Palestinian. Jenin, the latest collective memory milestone in our struggle to end Israeli occupation, joins the ranks of Deir Yassin, Kufr Kassem [massacre 1956], Qibya [destroyed 1953], 'Emmwas [destroyed 1967], Yalo [destroyed 1967], Sabra and Shatila [massacre 1982]. This time the world watched Jenin scream for help and was silent. . . . Rest assured that the children of Jenin, those who made it out of the rubble of their homes will never forget. Never remain silent. How can they while Jenin continues screaming for help?
>
> (BAROUD 2003: 235)

In narrative after narrative, the braiding and indexing of various particular sites of new trauma, injustice, and loss are evidenced: marking a trajectory of what Rosemary Sayigh has called the "continuing Nakba." New narratives revisit the more distal yet formative moment of the Nakba, spoken from the site of the *active* present, seen and constituted as emerging from that past. *Time* here, post-1948, is *continuous*, rather than discontinuous as in other possible modes of remembering, despite the discontinuity of locales and routines. It is precisely this accumulation of particular events which nevertheless weave into a *narrative of continuity*, the logic of a constantly *re-engendered condition*, that marks the texture of both Palestinian history-as-remembered and experienced, and Palestinian memory as an existentially felt relationship of the past to the present, one potentially unfolding itself into a future. A narrative of continuity that marks not only the past within the present, as legacy, scar, outcome, wound, etc., but also the past *still at work* within the present, still actively re-engendering it in its own shape, the past potentially therefore

within the future about to unfold unless consciously confronted and defied.
It has been a consistent issue of discussion, for example, as to whether Israel
would create an opportunity to "complete" the work of conquest and uprooting accomplished in 1948 (and furthered in 1967), and whether, regardless
of the measure of force and violence used, Palestinians would this time flee
or stay fast to their homes and lands. It is in a sense precisely this imaginary
of a "fate," a dispossession still planned and worked for, still an active agenda,
that gave rise to the language and conception of *sumud* (staying fast). In Sam
Bahour's testimony below, this is precisely the point: that what was different
in the battle of Jenin was that the Palestinians stayed and resisted, and Palestinians elsewhere did not panic.[10]

> Huddled around the television between the electrical outages to witness this
> atrocity unravel, my only thought was that this dose of colonist shock by Israel
> was different than those of 1948 and 1967. *This time no one fled,* no one moved, no
> one panicked. We only wept with anger and internalized a vow that Jenin would
> never be forgotten.
>
> (BAROUD 2003: 235; italics added)

Thus the accounts of the Nakba itself, the events of 1948, as seen from
within a *new*, different, yet *like* present, get reinserted into a narrative that
is larger, filled with the full signification of the Nakba, which includes and
involves a continued assault. This was also one of the constituent features
of reporting on the *Voice of Palestine* (the official Palestinian radio) at various critical junctures throughout the Oslo years. In the commemoration
of the Nakba's fifty years, for example, the *Voice of Palestine* carried many
on-air interviews with individuals (Khadija Abu 'Ali, and Mustafa al-Bar-
ghouthi are two examples) who specifically spoke of the *series* of crimes, *repeated* dispossessions and assaults, and used them as grounds for affirming
strength, fortitude, and agency. In poetry, (Darwish and Zayyad for example),
in personal accounts and other forms of literature, in speeches, in interviews
with ordinary people, there is this constant orientation to a potentially unfinished trajectory of fatality, sometimes implicit, often explicit, reference to
a repeated series of assaults and dispossessions, experienced as a result of
a constantly escalated conflict, and ever-rising stakes of survival. It is here,
I suspect, that the expressions many ordinary Palestinians engage in "that
nothing like this has happened to anyone," or that "the Jews are doing to
us worse than what was done to them" take their intelligibility. This repeatedly encountered expression of singularity—from refugees, villagers, and

ordinary professionals—who clearly are not even acquainted with the actual details of what collective others have experienced (Africans taken into slavery; Native Americans being destroyed wholesale and herded into reservations), or what the Nazi death camps really were, simply embodies and embeds the sense of the actively widening abyss into which they sense they are falling. It expresses their perception of the cumulative and ramifying character of the ultimately deadly attacks on every aspect of their ordinary lives, including life itself, rather than a minimization of others' traumas about which they are not genuinely knowledgeable.[11]

Even outsiders to the collectivity, as they come to see events from the stance of Palestinians or in solidarity with them, do so from the grounds of the constantly re-engendered condition: the synchronic iterability and the diachronic cumulativity of like/different events, all of which contribute to a reproduction and amplification of the original condition. The term "Deir Yassinization" was coined by Jules Rabin, to mark and point to both the repetition of like/different events, and their cumulative valency for Palestinian life.[12]

The complex figure of iteration, repetition of the *same/different*, produces the pattern of ramifiability of a condition that reproduces itself within every dimension of individual and collective life. This is, of course, not singular to the Palestinian experience, although it is a distinct marker of it—it is in the very nature of colonial regimes that every existential register and every register of subjectivity is marked by the violence and disruption, the will to erasure and coercive reshaping, that a predatory formation (the colonial) imposes and works on the body of the colonized. It is here that the relationship between individual fatality and collective condition is visible at its most acute and in its most transparent mode. The Palestinians may perhaps, however, be singular in their *narrative awareness* and rendition of this, a marker perhaps of *the consciousness of its still unfolding character* and the collective need to hold fast: memory as resistance. It is this trajectory of still active cumulativity that opens up the space for collective action. "Remembrance" and "collective memory" produce the figures and grounds for *collective agency*.

It is perhaps necessary here to unpack some of the terms critical to the different phenomenological modalities of "memory work": one of these is the nature of the *agent* of the trauma. In the work of Palestinian memory narratives, narratives of cumulativity and iteration, the practico-moral historical agent can be located as consistent: sometimes *the very same persons*, certainly the same institutions which have persisted, the same state (or prior to that the proto-state). Hourani (2004: 48) writes in his short memoir on returning to Palestine: "Oh, homeland, to which we have no alternative homeland; departure from you was painful and the return to you has become painful. And the cause and agent is one and the same in both cases." Moreover, the recipients are also characterizable in some modality of concrete existential contiguity: often *members of the same families*, routinely co-located in space and time (or would have been had one or other of the tragedies not engulfed them). The relational networks, intra-generational and inter-generational, can be traced through different narratives given by different people in various times and places. This is memory-work, in other words, whose spatio-temporal phenomenal object is still consistent, unified and concretely present, not abstracted as might happen over generations; a contiguous body of agency, experience, consequence and practico-moral responsibility. This is perhaps the critical dimension within this narrative of cumulativity that makes the nature of Palestinian memory work a little different from certain other instances of putatively collective memory.

Writing on France, a very different example, Pierre Nora (2001), talks of the *divergence* between history and memory during the 1930s. In the Palestinian case, however, it is the *convergence* between the two that is clearly in evidence. This is perhaps so for two reasons. First, it is precisely because the nature of the Palestinian experience and condition is that of excision from space and time, from the manifold of social being, from the very dimension of history. Memory-work was/is directed at the reclamation of history, and indeed of *national history*. Second, it is the *acceleration* of history that is increasingly the Palestinian experience of time and place, but in terms that are very different, again, than those delineated by Nora (2001) in the case of France. This acceleration of history for Palestinians both grounds the turn to memory and transforms it into history's ally, its daily archive, conscience and redeemer. It is precisely this acceleration, by specifiable consistent agents, and not the depersonalized machinery of modernity, that makes *the memory of the present*, not merely the past, achieve urgency as well. The immediate testimony, in the service of leaving the trace, the image, and the knowledge of what is in the here-and-now, what it came out of, what it proceeds toward. The unwinding trajectory of current events instigates past memories and *future* visions that are used to keep faith, stand witness, and gird for change. And they *write history*. Thus, the project of a national history, as acknowledged, recorded, written, preserved, enshrined, and transmitted, is palpably embedded in the work of memory, and in the instigation, production and co-location of narratives. In the case of France, as both Nora (1998) and

Aymard (2004) effectively indicate, national history (as centered and sanctioned by a strong state) is, in contrast, subject to the contestations of, and
erosions worked by, various group memories, the narratives of collectivities
within the "national body" who have been silent/ced, re/oppressed and otherwise marginal/ized.

Looking Back, Looking Forward: Memory in the Subjunctive Mode

All memory work involves a critical relationship between past and present, and between those and the future: what will be, what is to come, what
is expected and/or willed. Most writers on memory have emphasized the
particular relationship to the past from the point of view of the present: the
significance of the "retrieval" of the past to present needs and stances, and
thus of memory in the service of the present (Nora, 1998, 2001; Halbwachs
1980; Bal 1999 and others). Casey (2004: 31) aptly talks about the "inherent
bi-directionality" of public memory: its inherent relationship to both past
and future. But this relationship is not docile or one-dimensional, nor does it
work in one given modality. The relationship of past to present, of "memory"
to the "contemporary," and *both* to the future, can be wrought, inscribed,
and deployed within a range of different modalities that have differing relationships to subjectivity, lived experience, and agency. This bi-directionality
can be laminated onto, or interwoven with, the subjunctive mood in which
memory is often (although not always) cast to produce different inflections
of the relationship of the past to the present and the future, and distinct inflections of the subjunctive mood itself within memory, as between the voice
of *nostalgia*, that of *critique*, and that of *agency* or *justice*.[13]

The subjunctive mode in Palestinian memory of the Nakba is a recurrent-
ly structuring trope directly linked to the here-and-now stance; to a know-
ing-now-what-it-all-was-going-to-amount-to, and a not-knowing-then-what
it-was-to-become; the tensing within the past tense: future past. This is not
merely the past viewed through the present, but the present experienced as
given, shaped through and by the past, the latter still working its way, its
consequences into the present. The past as unfinished. This is a particularly social conception of time, not time abstractly moving us forward, ever
away from the past, but rather the time of social agents working their plans,
visions, and desires, appending the present to the past, potentially mortgag-
ing the future.

Hajja F. from Lifta tells in her account of her own family's departure from the village that some of the villagers of Deir Yassin had come to them in al-Bira and chided them for having left: they had left before the famed café attack[14] and before the massacre of Deir Yassin, the village situated next to them (in some accounts perched "above them"). The Deir Yassinis had chided them for leaving and declared that the Jews had told them that if they were peaceful they would be okay. And "here we are," they had said to them, "nothing has happened to us." And then the Deir Yassin massacre had happened. There is a double irony embedded in her account here. The people of Deir Yassin were proved, very shortly, to have been wrong, to have miscalculated. They would not be spared, even though they had kept out of the "troubles" (to borrow a term from Northern Ireland). Had they then known what was to happen a week or more later, they would not have spoken thus. Yet, despite that, Hajja F. says of herself and the people from Lifta:

> We left before the café was hit. . . . they say a month a week, two weeks, it is all talk within talk. . . . Everyone left after us, but we turn out to have been wrong. I wish we had stayed there and had lost a thousand. We would afterwards have brought forth (i.e. given birth to) two thousand. Am I right or wrong? . . . Finish, that was our fate, God wanted it like this.

Note how the subjunctive mood encompasses both past and present. There is here a tale of innocence betrayed, for both the people of Deir Yassin and the people of Lifta—a distinct sense of an avoidable trauma, betrayal, but also *self*-critique. Both past and present tenses merge into each other and blur into a constituent of a present state directly experienced as an outcome of the past.

Hajja F.'s words are echoed in the words of others. What comes through clearly in these accounts of the pre-cataclysmic moment, these narratives of the days before the 1948 Nakba, is the sense of a collective lack of awareness of the *valency of actions then for the future that has become now,* their future potentiality as only later to have been realized in full and concrete detail. There is a looking at past events from the point of view of the present-as-having-been absent-in-that-past-moment, *opaque,* the past's blindness to the future, the present now as having been an unforeseen future of that past. This blindness to the future is, of course, a recurrent element in narratives of individual loss and trauma; however, in this case it picks out the irremediable blindness that inheres in the *natural attitude,*[15] which cannot conceive of the corporeal world as-known-and taken-for-granted itself turned upside down, inside out, erased and negated, and then folded aside and forgotten. There is, structuring all these renditions of the past, a sense of the taken-for-granted character of the world-as-given: tragedies could occur *within* this world—killings, losses, even massacres—but not *to* this world *as a whole*.

M. (quoted earlier) has this to say:

> And the Arab Higher Committee was not aware of their methods. It would call on people and work with simple tactics and not a process, for example, like organizing the members of the Scouts with respect to arms and teaching them the rights of citizenship and other things. They used to consider that these things are simple and that *we are present in strength and it is not possible for anyone to expel us from our properties and our lands*. And the Jews were weak in our eyes. . . . *so our exodus from the country in the year 1948 was a great surprise to us*.

Here the cataclysmic character of the Nakba is clearly marked. In a sense, it is presented as something that had been inconceivable: presence was in the very nature of life itself as known. Presence was in the nature of things.

Presence:
The Self-Body in Place; the Bodied-Self Displaced

Much of the literature on memory ties memory and memory-work to the self, narrative, and identity. Take, for example, the argument offered by D. Walker (2003) on the importance of the recollection of place. He notes the shift in conceptions of subjectivity and the self from the Cartesian model to one where the subject is constituted *within and by language*, and in turn, the way that the coherence and continuity of the self is thus located by various scholars within memory and narrative.[16] Walker goes on to suggest a critical inflection in the ways that these two (memory and narrative) impart a sense of continuity to the sense of self: ". . . within this broad theme of the relationship among sense of self, memory and narrative, it is possible to distinguish a subset in which continuity is imparted to the sense of self not just by narrative . . . *but more particularly by the narrative recollection of place*" (p. 22. Italics added). He tries to demonstrate this through an analysis of a section in Proust's *Swann's Way* and Edward Said's *After the Last Sky* (1985). His main point is that "Our narratives of the self, both in casual conversation and in written autobiography, are dominated by narratives of place" (p. 25). This point is well taken, yet the problem is that Walker's analysis (as indeed much work in this area) fails properly to locate what it is about place that makes it significant. This may be a function of the focus on literary texts and narratives rather than immediate personal accounts or oral testimonies, which may bring home much more sharply the lived character of the concepts and relations that theory takes as its object. Although Walker goes some way to capturing the significance of place to self and memory, he nevertheless ultimately projects these relationships as *textual relations*, or as though they were between observer and observed, effectively a structure similar to the Cartesian one.

> The self that is recollected and re-collected is thus the creation of memory, of the act of gathering and assemblage. It is held within language and inscribed in narrative by an insistence on place (earth and land).
>
> (WALKER 2003: 28)

Indeed even as he also refers to the body's relationship to space, he ultimately misses its deeply *lived character*. In this he also misses the *lived character of place* itself—i.e., the relationship of the lived self/body to place, which the French philosopher Merleau-Ponty addresses at some length in his work.

Merleau-Ponty's phenomenological analysis is taken up and elaborated by Edward Casey (1997: 232) in his own work on place. Casey observes that Merleau-Ponty's is a conception of place as "an ambiguous scene of things-to-be-done rather than of items-already-established." The other side of this is that, as Casey puts it, "my lived body is said to be 'the potentiality of [responding to] this or that region of the world' " (Merleau-Ponty 1962: 106: as quoted in Casey 1997: 233). He goes on: "Merleau-Ponty teaches us not just that the human body is never without a place or that place is never without . . . body; he also shows that the lived body . . . *constitutes place*, brings it into being" (Casey 1997: 235).

The continuity of the self has, therefore, to be located in the continuity of the body in time, and both *in* place and *with* place. The body is the locus from *within* which we always *are*, *act* and *do*, even if it does not alone (or exhaustively) determine our sense of self. Merleau-Ponty notes: "We have no idea of a mind that would not be *doubled* with a body . . . established on this *ground* anchored in it" (Merleau-Ponty 1968: 259. Italics in the original). Thus, we can say that it is *in* and *through* this (mindful) body that we are *in* "place," and navigate through it, make bonds with others, work the land, converse and tell stories. And it is in and through the body that place is therefore experienced, shaped, and navigated; and it is through this relationship to the body that it is remembered and narrated. The notion of "place" itself, however, needs to be further unpacked here: as both Merleau-Ponty and Casey show, it is clearly not just an amorphous or featureless homogeneous location. Rather, it is constituted differentially in terms of *objects, relationalities,* and *trajectories of possible action*: hence, not only is "place" relative to body and self, but place is constituted, in part, by what I/we can do here. It is in this way that it reflexively constitutes and shapes our sense of self, of ordinary quotidian agency, which is so fundamental to the experience and reproduction of mundane living in the world.

In many of the refugee recollections of the period of the Nakba, they talk of trips back to the village, or the house, or the land, to bring back needed utensils, objects, clothes for living, etc. These narratives, and the trips they speak of, demonstrate the ways that "places" are constituted as *environments for living*, filled with the elements needed for the sustenance of daily life and already shaped by action as particular environments of living, of activity, use and interaction. Accordingly, "place" is organized by a lived *moral geography* which distinguishes it from the moral geography of "space" (Jayyusi 1995). In one Lifta family, who had made and screened a video showing them revisiting their old village and home, the son talks of numerous trips back to retrieve various *objects* from the old house. One of these was the old metal bed. He showed it to us, resting against the outer wall of the house, not actually in use, yet a significant object within that environment, bearing a visible emotional valency. From the storeroom he brought a series of other old objects: most of them kitchen utensils, pans, ladles, metal bowls, etc. As I have indicated elsewhere (Jayyusi 1988), objects are constituted, encountered, oriented to and read as "activity-objects." They are treatable and function within our practices as telescoped or *collapsed trajectories of activity/action*: a nexus between present and future time and circumstance. Vehicles of lived presence and activity, they "thicken" with usage, acquiring the sense of "habit" and shared contexts. Available to us always in the here-and-now, in the present, objects become markers both of the past (usage, accomplished tasks, lived moments, a life habitually engaged) and the future (potentiality). Actuality and potentiality.[17] As such they are transformed by our activities into nodes of our life and of our biography—both corporeal and emotionally laden, mundane and imagined/desired, actual and virtual. They can become symbols and emerge as memory-objects, encapsulating and telescoping past times as corporeally lived, and the relationships in and through which they were lived.[18] This applies both to produced (human-made or manufactured) objects, such as furniture, items of clothing, instruments, as well as to naturally-occurring objects, such as plants, and animals. Bardenstein (1999), for example talks of trees as potent symbols in Palestinian (and Israeli) collective memory. She suggests that in some of the visions of the olive tree, as in Darwish's poem "The Earth is Closing in on Us," "only olive trees will remain as a living, fragmented replacement for collective Palestinian existence in Palestine" (p. 155). But why the tree, why the olive, what is it about these that endows them with the power to become symbols of this kind and potential carriers of memory? Is it the longevity of the tree? Or the tree's properties that have made it a living constituent of the quotidian, habitual rhythm, fabric and performance of bodied life? "Trees are activated as sites of Palestinian collective memory at different points of dislocation and disruption of the Palestinian bond between land and people—refugees, exile, occupation—being grasped at, as it were, on the way 'out' of Palestine" (p. 157). This "bond," however, is engendered, in part, through the ways that trees had functioned within the weave of daily life, providing the bodied means and pathways for reproducing life "naturally," the life of the *in-vivo* subject, and the bodied field of *in-vivo* subjectivity and agency, and thus for weaving the links of community.[19]

On one of the April 8, 2004, newscasts on the Arabiyya satellite channel, a time when Israeli construction of the Wall in Palestine was at a peak, there was a segment about the clearing of a particular tract of land by the Israelis to open the route for the Wall. This involved the cutting down of the olive trees belonging to a Palestinian family. The segment shows the Israeli cutter springing between the trees vigorously, cutting them with his machine saw, soldiers all around, whilst the owner follows him in wild grief, literally doubled over and beating his head in pain as he laments: "The olives, the olives" (meaning the olive trees), as though his own children were being herded off. It is precisely in and through his bodily movements, and expressions, that we can see the very solidity of his grief, the extremity of his loss, its pulse, its congealed trace and effect. Here the cutting of the olives is like a visceral blow to him, something extracted and uprooted from his very own life and body. The olive, nurtured in various ways, courted, sung about and then received as nurture in return, constitutes a corporeal bond of living, of need and sustenance. It is in this that it becomes possible to carry the image or idea of the olive tree farther into other contexts as a symbol of that very life: it begins to function metonymically *as* life itself.

The coordinates of "the land" as a place are just such objects that sustain, protect, and contain communal bonds of living: trees and vegetation, houses, the water well. In one of the Lifta interviews, R. talks repeatedly of the smell of the cucumber from their land as he affirms his claim to land and return. The cucumber's smell (and thus his claim) is located in the body's memory, in perceptual memory. This is tied simultaneously to the body both of the *rememberer* and that of the object (or other) *remembered*.

In most Lifta testimonies the names of people are imbricated with places, places with each other, including houses, stretches of land, and villages. These places appear as mundane naturalized *fields of activity and bodied interaction*. The moral claim is always intertwined with a sensory, object-ified or concrete description. Indeed, throughout the Lifta interviews, as in the memorial books analyzed by Davis in this volume, the description of land and of events is always given by reference not merely to particular places but to *particular relationships of place: lived geographies* as opposed to the imaginative geographies that Said (1994b) analyzes so powerfully.

In 'Aysha 'Odeh's (2004) memoir of her imprisonment in 1969, she describes the moments when her Israeli army captors go through her house, searching for weapons, knowing all the while that her arrest was going to mean the demolition of the family home. She describes the house and its details, such as the concealed square opening in the upper section they used to call "the secret," details tied to particular events remembered and communicated from the past: "My mother would tell us about the importance of 'the secret' when Anis 'Abd al-Fattah escaped through it when the British soldiers broke into the house to arrest him, as he was under pursuit and sentenced to execution" (p. 30). These details both produce the house as lived relational space and reproduce the sense of iterability and cumulativity that make for a continuity in the Palestinians' experience and perception of their history. 'Aysha continues:

> Here am I narrating the details of the old house to discover the extent of its intimacy for me, wondering whether all that is connected to childhood is intimate, or whether intimacy springs from the house itself, or from the nature of the relationship with it. . . . here am I discovering in a better way the philosophy of parents and grandparents through their relationship with their places and themselves and with life. . . . I feel now as I write about the house as though it is the waters of a warm river engulfing me and I do not wish to emerge from it!
>
> ('ODEH 2004: 30)

In one woman's second-generation account, her father-in-law had, at a crucial juncture in 1948, urged *his* father-in-law to leave with him for fear of the Jewish attack on their respective towns. His father-in-law refuses and says to him, with expressive gestures (reproduced by the narrator) "You can carry your degree with you and work anywhere, but how will I carry my land in my hands?" The "degree" and the "land" are both, along one dimension, potentialities for the future. Like "place," both traverse and describe expected and possible (as well as accomplished) modes of living, courses of action, horizons of activity, which also implicitly describe the possibilities of the *agent* or *actor*. [20] In this account, which was repeatedly transmitted vertically and transversely through familial networks and thence to others like myself, the point about carrying the land is its organic link to identity-as-courses-of-enactment of the *in-vivo* subject: the ways in which he/she could and would, in actuality and prospect, conduct his/her routine activities-as-place-within-the-world, as various ways of reproducing one's life. The organic bodily relationship with the land is located in this reversible nexus between identity/self/body as courses of action and interaction on the one hand, and place as trajectories of action and potentialities of action on the other. Both "self" and "place" are mutually constitutive and experienced through their enactment and potentiality: as trajectories of prospective-retrospective action and interaction.

It is here too that Rosemary Sayigh's point (1979: 107) about the descriptions the refugees gave of the early post-Nakba period, referred to by Bowman (1994), has its salience: the self-descriptions which used notions such as "death," "paralysis," "burial," and "non-existence." This bespeaks the destruction of the corporeal lived geography that subsists within and sustains a quotidian moral geography, always present in the conduct of daily life, and even when radically disrupted, sustaining itself *in* and *as* a set of fundamental reference points.

Memory, History and Agency

Everywhere, as Palestinians became further embattled at the hands of both Israelis and various Arabs, in Jordan, Lebanon, and the West Bank and Gaza, there was always the spoken appeal and injunction: tell them, let them know what is happening. The "them" was the rest of the world, somehow deemed innocent of what was being perpetrated by dint of simple ignorance, "knowledge" being able to redeem both Palestinians from their plight and others from their complicity of silence. But the conscious recording of Palestinian memory—the will to reach back, retrieve and represent, voluntarily to communicate the details of events, to record the here and now, to reach out visibly and persistently—is a relatively new phenomenon. This awareness of the valency of past/present events for future understanding and for future consequence perhaps started during the civil war in Lebanon, mostly within literary genres, and began to come to maturity during the Israeli invasion of that country. As more and more people came to see and report, as the media became more and more central in the global negotiation of meaning and political action, as clearly the trajectory of tragedies, losses, and further dispossessions continued, yet at the same time other parties were always the ones to command the stage of international discourse, more and more Palestinians turned to documenting their own and their people's experiences.

This was to intensify visibly during the post-Oslo period, as two dynamics distinctly unfolded, both arguably as a consequence of Oslo: one was the movement to foreground the issue of the right of return, after an initial yet marked backgrounding of the refugees and their issues. This became a concretized demand, a pivot of discourse, after the early post-Oslo years, arising from diverse directions simultaneously. On the one hand it arose within official discourses, especially during and after the fiftieth anniversary of the Nakba, when it became mobilized in the pursuit of the project of statehood that began to seem more elusive. On the other hand it came from grass-roots constituencies and organizations, most particularly refugee camp groups, as the shadow of Final Status negotiations began to loom.

The second dynamic was the development of a stronger Palestinian identity *within* the 1948 boundaries of the Israeli state. There too, the battle for equality and against the continued appropriation of land began to consolidate its position, grounded implicitly in the de facto "recognition" attributed to Oslo. This had a counterpart in the logging of the past, the documenting, slow and piecemeal, by Palestinians within Israel, of the displacements of 1948 and *after.*[21]

However, a further development could be seen in the practices of memory-work that Palestinians engaged in, particularly after the Intifada of 2000, and that have become accelerated and widespread at the same time: *the documentation of the present as it unfolds. Writing the history of the present.* In part this too may paradoxically be due to the Oslo process itself, as Palestinians experienced their lives, and the social processes in which they became enmeshed, in two ways: one was, as indicated above, the hope, the dream, in their eyes become a realizable horizon after Oslo, of an independent State. This itself provided an impetus for the attempt to develop the kind of institutions that are deeply entangled with the authority and the claims of the sovereign nation-state, one of which is to be the guardian of national history and memory. For Palestinians this was no mere mechanism of institutional politics, however; it would index both the movement toward, and phased accomplishment of, the national state. At the same time it was a way to affirm and invite public acknowledgment of the trauma of national history and the just cause of the national project. It is in this context that plans for a national museum of memory were discussed and drawn up, and in this context too that various institutions went about the pursuit of documentation, record keeping, and oral history projects. But in all this there was another way in which Palestinians, in the West Bank and Gaza specifically, experienced life during this period: the existential sense that they were *making* history, or that they were at least enfolded and living within the very visceral mechanisms of history-in-the-making. Thus, when the invasions of the Palestinian Authority areas were carried out in 2002, unleashing the intensified brutality of the Israeli occupation (as experienced particularly in the refugee camps and Gaza), it was perhaps this sense of being part of history-in-process that accounts for the immediate and widespread phenomenon of writing diaries, testimonies, day-by-day accounts of events, and shooting films and videos. The destruction in the refugee camp of al-Amʿari in al-Bira, for example, and the accounts of residents of the first attack on the camp in early March 2002, were immediately documented on video by members of the Ministry of Culture and broadcast on Palestinian television. It is specifically a sense of agency which is being interpellated in these various sorts of testaments, documents, and testimonies. "Bearing witness" becomes an active trope. Even in the coverage of the destruction to the fabric of daily life and of its *persistence nevertheless*, agency is still precisely the focus, although here it is the agency of the *ordinary in-vivo subject*, as distinct from politicized transformative agency which is the emerging figure in more active resistance.

Perhaps the most potent embodiment of the sense of agency, and its relationship to memory and remembering, can be located in the aftermath of the invasion of the Jenin refugee camp in April 2002. The battle/massacre of Jenin both revealed and engendered a specific articulation of past, present, and future, and the memory/agency nexus. In the aftermath of the invasion, when the massive destruction in the heart of the camp had forced many camp inhabitants to seek temporary shelter elsewhere, the

discourses and activities around the camp began to address these very issues. The camp became an intense scene of recording, witnessing, filming,
screenings, oral histories, and other activities connected with memory, but
connected with it in such a way as to shift memory from the figure of recollection to that of reconstruction, so that the very relationship of the past
to the present and the future became inflected with the voice of "agency."
Here, the past is not nostalgic but held as a resource and landscape to be
revisited in a re-envisioned future. Almost immediately after the end of the
battle, there was talk of establishing a memorial in Jenin to the battle and its
martyrs. One of the proposals was to keep the destruction at the heart of the
camp (specifically the central and obliterated Hawashin neighborhood) as it
was, so it would remain a potent reminder, testament, and memorial to the
people, the struggle, and the sacrifice. The camp population itself, however,
felt differently: instead of the destroyed camp being left as it was, which would
mean people rebuilding their lives and places of residence in a *radically different
configuration from their camp life*, the camp becoming simply a "memory," they
insisted on rebuilding the camp in the same location and *as it had been*, with
minor modifications. Instead of the camp becoming a memorial, a silent site
of memory (*lieux de mémoire*) and in the process undoing its own existential
significance and vitality, a museum of memory would be established in one of
the old buildings within the reconstructed neighborhood, a building related to
the pre-Nakba time: the old Hijaz railroad building. In an interview (Al-Qalqili,
2004) with one of the active camp residents, Jamal al-Shati, who was also head
of the Committee for Refugees in the Legislative Council, the researcher asks
why the camp's emergency committee rejected the first proposal. Al-Shati re-
sponds that everyone rejected it and goes on to talk about the Israeli housing
minister's announcement that they planned to repair the damage to the camp
by building housing units *nearby* and enlarging the camp's roads. He saw this
as simply part of the continuous policy against the refugee camps "because
the Israeli objective is to finish . . . to erase the camps from existence, because
these camps *as a political reality* constitute living testaments to the Nakba of
the Palestinian people. Consequently, their removal is necessary. . . their removal could take many forms" (p. 126. Italics added). This point about the plan
to "target the Palestinian camps" and the Palestinian response to it, is repeated
throughout the interview and produced as an affirmation of the camp as an
existential and political site, a lived bodied place that was a locus of agency. Al-
Shati goes on: "So the Palestinian response in the camp was that we shall build
the camp as it was, with its alleys and its [passages?] and we shall not allow the

Israeli army or the Israeli government to attain its goal. . . . through enlarging the roads"(127). He said that people wanted to return their houses to what they were; new construction should not differ significantly so it "becomes a different reality to the reality of the camp." "We are demanding the rebuilding of the houses which were destroyed . . . as they were, based on the wishes of the camp community" (p. 128). The message of the "national" museum in Jenin

> is . . . the message of those who fought until the last minute defending their existence, defending their community, *defending the political reality of the camp*, defending the right of return and the insistence on it.
>
> (AL-QALQILI, 2004: 127. Italics added)

In this, as in other Jenin testimonies, the condition of refugeeness is a positively valued emblematic identity. But it is positively valued only as a trajectory toward its own overcoming by restitution and return. It is affirmed as a political condition, now able to connect the in-vivo-subject (the ordinary actor) with the political agent. Refugeedom is now able to reshape and telescope history, to telescope the trajectory of past dispossession with that of future justice. *Memory here is a technology of the self.* It is in this way that, although Palestinian memory has had to be registered in the context of the Israeli master narrative, the latter becomes increasingly caught in the shadow of Palestinian memory, in a negative dialectic between attempted erasure and the confirmation and conscious reconfirmation of presence that attempt reproduces. Al-Shati ends his testimony with:

> The issue of refugeedom [being a refugee] is not just through a house being in the camp; even if one dwelled in a palace the feeling remains that one is a refugee, refugeedom is an indivisible part of the psychological, moral, economic, social constitution of the Palestinian refugee person. . . . consequently . . . the refugees inside the camp . . . have come to form a social cultural administrative unit which has its own understandings, so from this it is difficult after 54 years of the voyage of suffering and refugeedom to adapt oneself to a new reality outside the camp. . . . Those who moved out of the camp and whose houses were destroyed, I feel through seeing their looks and expressions and words that despite the fact that they are living in stone houses and apartments, . . . the feeling does not differ from the feeling of the Nakba of '48, . . . In the final analysis, for us as refugees, the camp is not our final destination. The camp is a waiting station on the road of return to our lands and our properties in Palestine, which was occupied in 1948.
>
> (AL-QALQILI, 2004: 129)

The camp itself, as a site, is constituted as a moral architecture that embodies the two trajectories of past and future *simultaneously* (i.e., therefore of potentiality). Not merely the past in the present and potentially in the future, or the present as the future of the past, but past and future as co-embedded trajectories, simultaneously co-present: memory and agency. And in this we can detect two forms of the present, the "double present": the everyday and the historic, each recoverable from the other.

For Palestinians, the acceleration of history means that they know exactly where they come from, but not necessarily *where they will end up*. Memory/history is a preparation for that future, a mode of selection, an activism of agency—it is oriented, in part, to telling the outside world where, what, and to where. Acknowledgment becomes paramount in this—it is in the face of a hostile, amnesiac, or recalcitrant world that memory/history become important: giving notice, laying claim, affirming right and presence, declaring choice/refusal. It is precisely because of the continuity of the past in the present that the possibility of agency emerges. This is not nostalgia pure and simple, something lost, like a love lost and now irredeemable. This continuity is simultaneously historical, figurative, and biographically bodied. Thus, the weight of Palestinian memory-work is not so much involved in a fixing of the past, a construction of timeless symbols attesting to history (as perhaps one may sense in the construction of French "realms of memory"), "time out of time" so to speak, but in the reverse: documenting and indexing the vicissitudes of time, the work of others, indexing the presence and agency of the historical subject (on both sides of the Palestinian/Israeli divide), the concern with what happened and what is happening. This is "'time within time": the pocket or fold of time unfolded, opened up. And in that, it provides the dynamic and power of that agency. It offers not merely a vision of, but a project for, the future.

NOTES

1. But one can, of course, discriminate a further constituency of Palestinian: the Palestinians dispossessed were not all to remain refugees, although they continued to be exiles.
2. Based on personal communications as well as childhood observations/memory.
3. This does not mean that the stories and the narratives of the Nakba itself were consistently or densely passed on to younger generations. In fact, arriving to work in Ramallah in 1995, after the Oslo Accords, it was a big surprise to me to

discover that many young people were unaware of the significance of May 15, the day which had been designated many years earlier, by the PLO, as the Day of Palestinian Struggle (*Yawm al-nidal al-filastini*), and a day that in the Diaspora had always been very actively marked. The disjuncture (or gap) between the consciousness or knowledge of younger people and the responsiveness and willingness to tell among the older generation needs some interrogation (see Allan, this volume). The will to narrate, however, expressed itself often in telling and talking of the most *recent* events, crises and confrontations, and of the multiple forms of organization in response, all of which, perhaps, displaced the telling and narrating of the Nakba itself.

4. And indeed, at such times, exhibiting one's membership in the collectivity comes to be through the expressions of public grief, through visibly "sharing" in the orientation to the trauma.

5. Although there would be accounts later on, in other circumstances, in which Palestinians in one constituency would speak of other Palestinians in the third person.

6. The interview is drawn from a large corpus of taped broadcasts from the Voice of Palestine made under the auspices of a research project, initially funded by an SSRC Fellowship and a Ford Foundation individual grant, and pursued while the author was a Senior Research Fellow at Muwatin: The Palestinian Institute for the Study of Democracy, in Ramallah, Palestine. Thanks are due to the project's research assistant, Bassam al-Mohr, for his extensive and meticulous work in recording and transcribing programs from the Voice of Palestine.

7. These places, of course, were occupied in 1967. Nabi Ya'qub is now the site of a substantial Jewish settlement in East Jerusalem.

8. The Lifta interviews (about eighteen of them, each at least one hour long) were conducted by Ahmad al-Adharba of the Jalazoun camp, some with the help of the author, and all with the support of BADIL (Bethlehem), where the materials are currently resourced.

9. The interviewer himself brings them up at times, but what is obvious is that the interviewee usually has a ready account. The dates are woven into the interview in relation to each other and in relation to the topic at hand, not always explicitly spoken but always present: the Palestinian condition, the Palestinian trajectory, the Palestinian place in, and share of, history.

10. The debate as to whether a new opportunity would present itself to complete the work of 1948 (the unfinished "War of Independence") has also surfaced as a significant debate in Israeli Jewish society (see Sa'di's Afterword, this volume).

11. Most ordinary Palestinians only know of the Holocaust in the context of developments and pronouncements (often by U.S. and other Western figures) encoun-

tered in the news and routinely used in a context of justification of official Israeli needs and positions and/or neglect of their own predicament.

12. This was in a lecture delivered at a memorial commemorating the fifty-fifth anniversary of the massacre at Deir Yassin on April 9, 1948. The occasion was organized by *Deir Yassin Remembered* and held at the Ascension Lutheran Church in Burlington Vermont. *Deir Yassin Remembered* was founded by Dan McGowan, professor of economics at Hobart and William Smith Colleges in Geneva, New York. The massacre at Deir Yassin was frequently cited in the Lifta accounts as having been a landmark, a focal point in the events of the Nakba itself. On Deir Yassin, see McGowan and Ellis (1998).

13. The "subjunctive" is a grammatical mood which expresses a conditional, hypothetical, or contingent act or state of affairs that is not fact or actuality. It can thus express doubts, wishes, and possibilities, as well as desired or feared states and outcomes.

14. The attack on the Lifta café, as the assault later on Deir Yassin, seemed to have been the critical turning points for the Lifta villagers; the local transformative event constitutive, with multiple like others, of the overall collective cataclysm that was the final outcome.

15. Alfred Schutz, drawing on Husserlian phenomenology, first introduced this concept into sociological/cultural analysis. See Schutz 1962 in particular.

16. The Cartesian model is based on the idea of mind/body dualism developed by the French philosopher René Descartes (1596–1650). Cartesian dualism is the principle involving the separation of mind and body as well as mind and matter. It suggests that mind and body interact in a causal manner, and involves a clearcut distinction between the mind that observes, and the world that is observed.

17. If one thinks of a hunting rifle, a matchbox, or a car here, one can see the very different actions that are afforded, and thus the very distinct trajectories, imaginaries, and narratives that may be built around them.

18. Producing objects such as kitchen utensils, as the Lifta family does, is different from producing objects such as title deeds, which many refugees also do: although deeds are also collapsed trajectories of action and telescoped relationships-in-the-world, they are interactionally produced in the register of moral and legal claim-making, rather than as memory-objects, or indices of presence. Refugees also produce photographs and receipts: signs, traces of lived presence. Each kind of phenomenal object has distinct interactional parameters and experiential registers, and any proper analysis needs to attend to these specificities

19. By the *in-vivo* subject I mean the ordinary actor within the *endogenously produced* world of everyday life. *In-vivo* subjectivity thus describes the self as constituted *within* ordinary mundane agency.

20. Identities themselves describe and represent possible and expected activities that are conventionally bound to, and embedded within, the category-identity of the actor (mother, peasant, artist, doctor). See the work of Harvey Sacks (1972) and L. Jayyusi (1984).

21. See for example *Majallat al-Dirasat al-Filastiniyya* (the Arabic edition of the *Journal of Palestine Studies*) 45/46 (Winter/Spring 2001), especially Wakim, pp. 90–104.

Figure 9 Ghost Girl, Burj al-Barajna Camp, Beirut Lebanon, 2004.

5 Women's Nakba Stories

BETWEEN BEING AND KNOWING

Rosemary Sayigh

[In the beginning] men and women worked. We worked to buy blankets, quilts, beds, saucepans, frying pans . . . Every time we worked we bought something . . . From the time we left Palestine until now, this has been our life . . . Whenever we save a bit of money, or build a home, or do anything, it all goes, nothing is left for us.

(UMM KHALID, born 1938, Shatila camp, recorded July 20, 1992)[1]

Getting out of the text enables us also to get out of the tyranny of the facts. The realization that historical production is itself historical is the only way out of the false dilemmas posed by positivist empiricism and extreme formalism.

(TROUILLOT 1995: 145)

The Nakba (catastrophe) of 1948 has indeed formed "a constitutive element of Palestinian identity," a site of Palestinian collective memory that "connects all Palestinians to a specific point in time that has become for them an 'eternal present'" (Sa'di 2002: 177). But, paradoxically, the unifying and identity-creating effect that Sa'di describes has taken root before the Nakba as historical event has even been fully chronicled, let alone written into world knowledge.[2] Missing from all accounts so far is the experience of Palestinians during the period of expulsions. While the causes of the Nakba can be adequately explained through an analysis of a number of external, regional and internal political factors, the absence of Palestinian voices from most such accounts parallels on the textual level the discounting of Palestine's indigenous population by imperialists and colonizers alike. While this silencing of popular Palestinian experience of the events of 1947–1949 needs to be rectified, this task, however central to our understanding of the aftermath, needs to be part of a recognition that not all Palestinians experienced the Nakba in the same way, or with the same consequences. On the one side unifying, since it left all Arab Palestinians stateless, the Nakba experience differed widely depending on class, sect, region, locality, and period of attack. It differed for men and women, old and young, rich and poor, those who left and those who stayed. It also differentiated between people in terms of subsequent fate and life chances—where and how they would live, under what regime, with what degree of acceptance or rejection. Truly to challenge the silencing of the Palestinian narrative that Edward Said so tirelessly criticized, internal differences need to be written into the unwritten collective story.

Calling for a fresh start in Palestinian history writing, social historian Beshara Doumani notes the lack of theoretical works in the field of Middle East history, attributing this to assumptions of modernization theory (Doumani 1992). Non-theorized history writing tends to be shaped by a common-sense idea of history as "political events, personalities, and administrative structures" to the neglect of everything else, including the native population: "the major lacuna in the historiography of Palestine during the Ottoman period is the absence of a live portrait of the Palestinian people, especially the historically 'silent' majority of peasants, workers, women, merchants and Bedouin" (Doumani 1992: 6). Particularly when narratives of the past arise out of anticolonial struggles, they are bound to reflect ideals of national unity forged during military and political struggle. Projected into national scholarship, the "unified nation" concept becomes a source of weakness, since it hides (to some extent intentionally) many kinds of inequality that may be maintained and even increased by post-independence regimes. Disparities of power or status between classes, sects and ethnicities, city and rural residents, the educated and uneducated, men and women: all are glossed over in nationalisms that lead to, and follow, the establishment of a state. Historians of the Palestinian people need to reflect on whether the predominant model of "history"—with its focus on "facts" and the "public domain"—is inclusive enough to match the full reality of a uniquely difficult struggle.

E. Valentine Daniel's distinction between two basic forms of orientation toward the past, "history" and "heritage," may be helpful here.[3] Daniel proposes that "history" as orientation is built around "events," requires archaeological and documentary evidence to validate itself, is chronological and epistemic, and separates subject and object. "Heritage," on the other hand, is ontic rather than epistemic. It is a way of "being in" the world rather than "knowing" the world, and it often takes the form of ritual or myth, has no beginning or end, and is open toward the future—"a sign of possibility that needs no actualization to be real and that no number of actualizations can exhaust" (Daniel 1996: 28). Daniel defines the Euro-American mode of history writing as aimed at "knowing" or "seeing the world," and he suggests that with the global spread of imperialist influence this mode of history has influenced other world cultures, marginalizing the "heritage" mode as ethnic or premodern. Through its requirement of knowledge of "facts" and chronology, "history" tends by its nature to exclude marginal groups such as women and rural populations, whether as narrators or topic.[4]

But women in many cultures—and this is certainly true of Palestinian rural women—are the transmitters of kinds of narrative and cultural performance that fit within the "heritage" paradigm. Hilma Granqvist's studies of the village of Artas in the 1920s and 1930s show that the songs and dances that celebrated the central peasant institution of marriage were part of women's repertoires, "owned" and transmitted by them.[5] Most village storytellers were women, according to Muhawi and Kanaana, who recorded two hundred folk tales between 1978 and 1980 in the Galilee, West Bank, and Gaza. They note that Palestinian Arabic differentiates between the *hikaya* (fable, folk tale), and the *qissa*, an account of a real happening, either in history or in the speaker's experience. The telling of hikayat, defined by men as *kizb* (lies), is traditionally the specialty of women, the qissa of men (Muhawi and Kanaana 1989: 2–3).[6] Discussing gender in a context of exile, Slyomovics notes: "al tarikh (history) [is] a discourse usually identified with a male teller" (Slyomovics 1998: 207). But uprooting, exile, schooling, employment opportunities, and national movement mobilization have changed life conditions for women in particular, partially creating a "new" Palestinian woman and disrupting gender boundaries.

In this chapter I hope to show how life stories recorded with refugee women from Shatila camp between 1989 and 1992 display different narrative structures linked to generation, locality of origin, and degree of national mobilization. We find both "heritage" and "history" combined in these narratives in different degrees, forming a gender-specific mode with its own historical value: as expanding "history," and as giving evidence of cultural change in exile. Women's narratives of the past may in this sense be more complete than men's.

Their structural subordination through men's authority to speak and represent has not prevented some Palestinian women from becoming articulate since early in the twentieth century. This presence in the public sphere has been achieved even as women have been constrained by family and community gender norms, and re-inscribed as women by the national movement through gender-specific tasks. Yet because their national activism symbolically represents Palestinian "modernity," women as a collectivity have achieved a voice and a visibility not shared by other marginalized Palestinians. There are other levels of subordination and suffering that remain hidden from view and debate. I do not wish to be understood as making a special case for women as a silenced group within (backward) Palestinian society; rather I present women's narratives to challenge all narrative exclusions, and as compelling a wider notion of what Palestinian national history should be and do.

Learning About Gender in Refugee Camps

The exclusion of women from those qualified to tell Palestinian history was first brought home to me in the early 1970s, when I was doing a study of Palestinian refugee experience in Burj al-Barajna camp in Lebanon.[7] Kamil, a young UNRWA teacher, was helping me to find people to record. His first list consisted entirely of men the age of his father, a bias he defended by explaining that these were the only people in Burj camp able to tell me Palestinian history. I tried to explain the difference between "history" and "experience." Though unconvinced, Kamil revised the sample so that it balanced equally between men and women, and included speakers between the ages of seventeen and sixty. One of the questions I asked was about sources from which respondents had first felt their identity as Palestinian: from family members, teachers, friends, books, encounters with others? A girl student of about seventeen replied to this question, "My mother told me most, but she didn't know the plots."[8] It appeared that it was generally mothers or grandmothers who described villages of origin—dwellings, landscape, neighbors, work, celebrations, fruits, and other products. Mothers were often cited as expressing, and therefore transmitting, rural Palestine through turns of phrase, songs, food preparation, home cures, idioms of raising children, stories of the past, and local dialect.[9]

The phrase "the plots" used by the Burj al-Barajna student is a good way of characterizing "history" defined as knowledge of events, from which experience, especially women's experience, is rigorously excluded by most Palestinians of whatever educational level. In 2003, a Palestinian student in the United States wanted to record with Palestinian refugee women in Lebanon, but a male colleague had advised her against this on the grounds that women are generally too ignorant of history to be worth recording. As proof, he cited a recent oral history project among Palestinians in Jordan:

> Every time we used to ask who lived in the town, the major road in and out of the town, health clinics, sanitation, water, electricity, transportation, major wadis, etc., they [women] used to give us very limited information. On the other hand, educated people gave us a wealth of information, much more, and very detailed. . . . I believe it all has to do with education. . . . women at the time were not encouraged to go to school. . . . Initially we thought there was something wrong, but when we asked one of the women she answered, "We women did not have the same rights as the women of today. We used to sit at home, except when we went out to get water or when harvesting the crops. Other than this we sat at home.[10]

The criterion of a respondent's value is assumed by this (male) researcher to be an ability to give "facts" about water, electricity, and transportation in a pre-Nakba town. I would argue that to evaluate so highly the ability to describe an urban infrastructure betrays a restricted notion of history.[11] It seems that some Palestinians who want their national history to be written are not ready to give women "permission to narrate."[12]

My own interest in the different ways that women express and transmit history in its fullest sense, by which I mean inclusive of the "domestic," the "personal," as well as the marginal and the deviant, has developed through a series of research experiences from camps in Lebanon to areas of historic Palestine. To do this is necessarily to become sensitive to the awkward relation between nationalism and feminism, both of them "strong languages" (Asad 1986: 158), the first claiming to be indigenous, the second often accused of being Western. It was partly to see how this contradiction would play out in the (spoken) lives of refugee women of different generations that I recorded the eighteen life stories that form the empirical basis of this paper. The work was carried out between 1989 and 1992 (before the Oslo Accords) with refugee women, all of whom had lived some part of their lives in Shatila camp, in the southern suburbs of Beirut.[13] As a site of many Resistance offices and projects, Shatila had been the target of attack by Israeli and Rightist Lebanese forces in 1982; by Amal militia and parts of the Lebanese Army in the mid-1980s; and by Fateh Dissidents allied with the Syrian Army in 1987. This had led to the almost total physical destruction of the camp and the scattering of its inhabitants. At the time of recording, most of the speakers were living in derelict or unfinished buildings in West Beirut.[14] All but five had lost members of their close family in war. They ranged in age from twenty-six to ninety, with fairly even distribution between the three main generations distinguished in camp speech as "the Generation of Palestine," "the Generation of the Disaster," and the "Generation of the Revolution."[15]

The recordings were done in "public," usually in homes with family and neighbors present, occasionally in Resistance offices in the presence of comrades. I believe this was justified by the way it "naturalized" the social atmosphere around narrations. The questions and occasional critiques raised by audiences both prompted and disrupted narrative sequence, and had the value of showing common ideas of what constitutes Palestinian history, what is important to tell, and what is not. One elderly speaker's description of her wedding in a Galilean village in 1930 was interrupted by a daughter-in-law saying, "*That's* not history." Earlier in the session a male neighbor had advised the speaker, "Tell her about the land you owned." The presence of men during most recording sessions was valuable in revealing privileged themes of collective memory, as formed in camps in the shadow of the Resistance. That Palestinian "history" should include land ownership but exclude women's experience of marriage is illustrated not only by the remark just quoted, but also by village memory books where (male) heads of clans are the usual compilers and providers of data.[16] Not only women are left out of such histories but also those who did not own land, or were marginal in other ways.

Women's Nakba Stories

A striking feature of the life stories is the primordiality of expulsion from Palestine, displacing more usual beginnings such as birth or first memories. Most speakers already adult in 1948 began with it, as did many of the "Generation of Disaster," too young in 1948 to have personal recollections. Only with the "Generation of the Revolution" did this narrative take other forms, in recollections of camp conditions as experienced by a child, or of national commemoration days in school, or in declarations of Palestinian identity. The degree of detail of that terrible journey preserved in memory over four and a half decades expresses not only the significance assigned to it retrospectively—as rupture in space and time, as beginning of exile and precursor of other tragedies, as historic mistake — it also suggests processes of collective memory formation as individual stories were told and re-told in refugee gatherings.[17]

Hajja Badriyya, already married and mother of children in 1948, began her story with the *hijra*: [18]

> We were all staying in our village, nothing was happening.[19] They were fighting Israel, we were staying. At the end, we were sleeping, it was night. My sister-in-law came and woke me, "Get up!" I said, "What's happening?" She said, "The Army has retreated."[20] "How could it retreat?" "It has." Israel was threatening Majd al-Krum a lot. Because our village has mountains on each side and there's only one road. . . . [Israel] closed the road but they couldn't enter our village. . . . Perhaps there was some agreement with the Army, God only knows. Nothing was happening and then at nine o'clock we woke up and people were all leaving. The men were all scattered in the mountains, fighting. They caught the leader of the Army, they asked him, "Where are our men?" He said," Your men are in the mountains, and I'm crying for you. I got the order to retreat at two o'clock but I refused to retreat. . . . You have no choice but to surrender to Israel." The young women all got up and left because they had been frightened ever since Deir Yassin. They left immediately, men and young women all left. We walked from Majd al-Krum until we reached Rmaysh [Lebanon].[21]

Other older speakers gave the briefest of introductions before reaching the *hijra*. For example Umm Ghassan, born in a small Galilean village in 1930, and married in 1945, began: [22]

> I am sixty years old. I had a son, Ghassan, and a daughter, Zuhayra. We left and came to Lebanon. There were planes and cannons shelling us. We ran away. The man stayed at home, he refused to leave. Just I and the kids left. And we came [sighs] to Lebanon. I wish we had died rather than come here.

A detailed *hijra* story comes from Umm Mahmud, born in 1933 in the outskirts of Jaffa, married one year before the war: [23]

> We left Palestine from the Port. My father came and said, "Yallah! You mustn't stay here. The Jews are attacking us." We were afraid about honor, because of Deir Yassin. So my father took me. [RS: What about your husband?] I didn't even leave him a note. He used to say, "I won't leave even if the house is destroyed over my head." But my parents . . . took me and we left for the Port. There was shelling over our heads while we were at the Port. We stayed there waiting for our turn to go. We went in a rowing boat, not a ship. It was full. Many people were with us. We set off. My son was only one month old. We hadn't gone far when rain and wind started, we felt that the boat was going to overturn with us

on board. . . . When we were in the middle of the sea, halfway to Beirut, we had a pregnant woman on board, she was in labor. Who was going to help her? "Oh people! Wake up! We need help, in God's name!" So my aunt, God have mercy on her soul, told her, "Come over here" and made her squat. And a baby was born and it was a boy. They had nothing to wrap him in. I had a bundle of things for my son, so I undid it and gave her some. There wasn't anything to cut the umbilical cord. My younger brother . . . had a piece of iron in his pocket. They took it from him and cut the cord.

The detailed, reportorial style in which these speakers from the "Generation of Palestine" describe the *hijra* suggests that for them this event was an entry into "history." This is so even though their subsequent life stories do not follow chronology or recount other events of national or regional importance. For them the *hijra* of 1948 was *"The* Event" that meant the beginning of a destiny of victimhood, and of tragedy to be repeated through further displacements and losses. Umm Nayif, born in Sha'b in 1912, married in 1930, summarized this history in her opening sentences: "Our life in Palestine was very good, everything was fine. The Jews came and threw people out of their villages. We came to Lebanon, and we stayed here. At the beginning people respected us, but now everyone is against us. We ask help from God."[24] Umm Ghassan (quoted above), aged eighteen at the time of the *hijra*, gave a similar summary condensing the *hijra* with victimhood in Lebanon as narrative beginning. While linked to a particular event in "history," the *hijra* of 1948 takes on in some women's narratives the status of a destiny to be played out over a large time cycle, mingling history with cosmology. An echo of sacred literature can be heard here, with certain historical events—such as the prophet Muhammad's birth—raised by connection with divinity to an extra-temporal level. Born in 1941, hence a member of the "Generation of the Nakba," Umm Subhi began her life story with these words:

We suffered tragedies, it was very hard. We were made homeless; we found difficulties in being homeless. We were victims of a catastrophe. Our children went [were killed], our home went [was destroyed], we didn't find people to look after us. Even so, we thank God, because this is what God wants. . . . I also thank God, and ask him to unite the Muslim word and the Arab word. [25]

Too young in 1948 to remember clearly either Palestine or the *hijra*, Umm Subhi nonetheless produces a statement about Palestinian "history" that amalgamates the Nakba with more recent tragedies, the collective "we" with the personal "I," and the sacred (God's will) with the secular (national politics). A cyclical rather than linear concept of history is foundational to expressions such as these: Only God moves history, not men; it is He who will eventually restore Palestinians to Palestine. Yet endowing God with supreme history-making power does not turn believers into passive witnesses. Daily life stories told me by Umm Subhi when I visited her revealed a *munadila* (struggler), as ready to visit Palestinians in prison as to lobby political leaders for funds to rebuild her house. Her daughters and friends in the camp confirmed this image.

After the beginning quoted earlier, Umm Nayif from Sha'b told an anecdote describing her *hijra*. Like most rural women, she left Palestine in a group of other women and children from her village, without their husbands. Men often stayed behind to help defend villages, joining families in Lebanon later. The core of Umm Nayif's *hijra* account was an anecdote about arriving in Rmaysh (Lebanon) with four children, drenched from rain, to seek shelter with a woman she knew only by her familiar name ("Umm Ilyas"), and how hard it was to find her because so many Rmaysh women had the same name. This anecdote, too long to be quoted in its entirety, has several points of interest, particularly its similarity in both form and style to the *hikaya* or folk-tale, complete with ordeal, suspense, and happy ending.[26] I had the good fortune to record this anecdote again in a second session with Umm Nayif, when she repeated the story using the same sequencing of episodes, quotations of her own and others' speech, set phrases, injections of humor, and tones of voice. It was evident that this story had been crafted through repetition in family and neighborhood settings into the form in which I heard it. Umm Nayif was unschooled, like most rural women of the "Generation of Palestine" and, as with the *hikaya*, structure and style worked in her story as aesthetic devices to aid memory and hold audience attention. But, unlike the *hikaya*, what she narrated was a real-life experience.

It was striking that women already adult in 1948 did not begin their life stories with their early life but began with the Nakba.[27] Older speakers recalled their lives in Palestine only after questions from the researcher and audience. Other speakers too young to have remembered the Nakba also began with it, showing how strongly it was imprinted on their memories through family transmission. For example, Nozira said: "I am a Palestinian woman, born in Palestine. I came with my family when I was about seven days old. We came to Lebanon. My family used to say that we came for a week or two and then we'd go back."[28] It was as if the Nakba had replaced personal birth as "beginning" for the refugees, a moment of total rupture between life in Palestine and life in exile.[29] Much younger speakers, those of the "Generation of the Revolution," chose other beginnings—usually the camp in which they had grown up—but reverted to the Nakba when speaking of their parents, and its effects on them.

The Nakba as Force That Historicizes Women's Life Stories

Reviewing the life stories as a set of texts, I was able to establish two quite different formats, focusing on narrative structure, style, and degree of autonomy and coherence—qualities that I found were correlated in most cases with their initial response when asked to tell the stories of their lives, either hesitation or readiness. My notes show that some speakers responded very readily to this request, giving sustained and autonomous stories that also tended to be closely referenced to national history while others were unsure what was expected of them; by appealing to me for specific questions, they made clear the difficulty for them of speech autonomy, and the absence of a "life story" concept.[30]

This group would begin their "stories," but depended on prompts and questions from the audience to proceed; their stories were nonlinear, structured thematically rather than chronologically. The Nakba for them was the end of history as "being," and the beginning of another kind of history they named "tragedy," or "destiny," or "God's will." The Nakba was the only national event they referred to, whereas the second set of speakers produced stories of the "self" that were closely linked to national events, whether in Lebanon or in the larger Palestinian *saha* (public sphere). National history offered these mainly younger women both topic and narrative structure, with personal "events" positioned in their narratives through association with "events" of history. Stories about the "self" thus became "factual," and the style of telling them reportorial, sequenced by chronology.

The hesitancy of the first, mainly older, set of speakers could have been linked to contextual as well as demographic factors—older age, low levels of education, or fears of "mis-speaking" in a period of Syrian arrests.[31] Such speakers became fluent once questions aroused particular memories, for example, leaving Palestine in 1948, life before 1948, hardship in the first tented camps, labor in the fields or in homes. But each story or episode stood alone; "history" did not supply them with a move to a new subject or episode.

Another common characteristic of this set of speakers was that they used the pronoun "we" more often than "I" and emphasized the collective Palestinian tragedy rather than personal details. If they identified themselves at all, it was in terms of their relationships to others—parents, brothers, and children—rather than by personal name or self-descriptions. In terms of narrative structure, their life stories were accumulated rather than composed, a non-chronological sequence of anecdotes that often, as in the case of Umm Nayif cited above, possessed aesthetic qualities similar to those of folktales. To give an example of this pattern I return to Umm Subhi. She gave me a brief recitation that was not a "life story" in the sense of a narrative constructed about the "self," but rather a testimonial to collective Palestinian tragedy in which personal episodes are given to illustrate and *prove* a collective case of marginality.[32] After the opening, which is quoted above, she spoke of Palestinians as "people who spend the summer in the Ghor," thus likening them to bedouin who, in peasant eyes, are deprived of the normality of fixed, family-owned homes.[33]

The public nature of her discourse is clear not only from its evocation of collective disaster but also from the appeals to God that mark its transitions. The sequence of her testimonial is not chronological, but moves as one episode reminds her of another: an evocation of Palestinian homelessness; her loss of home, sons, sons-in-law, and nephews in the recent "Battle of the Camps" (1985–87); an allusion to a daughter's imprisonment; an invocation to God to allow all wanderers to return to their homes; her recent operation, with none of her children near her; her husband's disablement which prevented him from providing a new home; a story about being hit by a Lebanese Army soldier in 1983; the chance visit of a Japanese journalist, a "stranger" like me, who had helped one of her daughters pay college fees (implicitly contrasted with Palestinian, Lebanese and other Arab authorities who do nothing to help); and a conclusion, "This is our life, this is our destiny. We always say, 'Thank God!'" The transitions of this structure are thematic rather than chronological, and express Umm Subhi's sense of oneness between her fate and that of the Palestinian people—for both God has "written" lives of dispossession and loss. This tragic collective destiny that her life *represents* eclipses other characteristics and episodes through which Umm Subhi might have narrated a "self."

The main structural feature of the life stories of speakers like Umm Subhi was a preference for bounded anecdotes that were encysted in a multivocal narrative sustained as much by audience participation as by the speaker. A figurative description for this format could be "beads on a string," where the "beads" are anecdotes crafted through frequent retelling, while the "string" is the haphazard product of quasi-natural interaction between those present during the recording session.[34] The anecdotes are only haphazardly linked to national history, with the outstanding exception of the *hijra* which, as noted before, figured in almost all the narratives. Connection between the anecdotes was a product of interaction, or in some cases it was thematic, referring back to the original tragedy, exemplifying it with incidents, or recalling later episodes that mirrored it. An anecdote told by Umm Subhi at our first meeting illustrates this thematic linking, following an allusion to her sadness at being without her children around her during a serious operation: [35]

> People came and said that the Lebanese Army were hitting one of the sisters [i.e., a Resistance cadre]. It was the time of the Army. I was washing clothes. When I got outside, I found it was true. One of the soldiers had got her in an alley, and was pressing his baton against her stomach. No one in the camp dared to approach except me. . . . I approached and said, "Why are you doing this? She's a girl not a man." He said, "You're from the camp?" I said, "I'm a daughter of the camp, like those kids you are arresting." He said, "Are your children among them?" I said, "All of them are my children." "And this girl, how is she related to you?" "She also is my daughter. Every Palestinian girl is my daughter and every Palestinian boy is my son."

As a result of this intervention, Umm Subhi was struck on the back with a rifle butt, arrested, and taken before the Army district commander. She gave no date for the anecdote beyond, "It was the time of the Army," a typical peasant/camp formula for marking historic epochs.[36]

As a final remark about the thematic, interactional narrative format, I propose a second look at Umm Nayif's *hijra* story, referred to above. Though in the form of a self-contained anecdote, unlinked to a before and after, it connects thematically with the beginning of her "life story," when she said, "Our life in Palestine was very good. . . . We came to Lebanon. . . . At the beginning people respected us. Now everyone is against us." Her story of the *hijra* dramatically contrasts her arrival in the Lebanese village of Rmaysh with five rain-soaked, shivering children with the warm welcome given them by Umm Ilyas: [37]

> All the people who had left Sha'b with me were with her. She lit a fire in the *mawqada*; she lit a fire in the *kanun*; she lit a fire in the *mastaba*.[38] She wanted to

warm these people up. She dressed the children in her grandchildren's clothes; and she took off her own clothes for me. We slept that night in her house.

Being both Lebanese and Christian, Umm Ilyas's welcome echoes the opening words of Umm Nayif's story, "At the beginning people respected us." But now, following the long Lebanese Civil War with its sectarian roots, "everyone is against us." I suggest that history is being told here through anecdotes that follow an originally *hikaya* form. In other words, elements of rural women's verbal culture should be re-viewed as the mode of history that Daniel provisionally calls "heritage" (Daniel 1996: 25–28). But though they retain the *hikaya* form, these anecdotes are no longer fiction but tell of real events located in a specific time, even if the speaker does not know the "history" of the time as professionals would tell it. We may read in these fragmentary "life stories" evidence that the Nakba forced many refugee women of rural and poor city origin in exile to make the cultural jump toward history as "knowledge."

Narrating the Self in "History"

The other main pattern, distinct from the first to the point of dichotomy, was linked to those speakers who responded readily to my request for their life story. They appeared at ease with this request, and did not ask questions such as, "Where shall I begin?" or "What do you want me to say?" They used "I" rather than "we" and identified themselves through personal names and nationality, sometimes also specifying place of birth, gender, and class (e.g., "from a poor family"). To describe themselves, they selected personal rather than relational attributes and included personal desires and ambitions as well as those related to family or community. But the most striking feature of this set of narratives is their composition as a continuous, reportorial narrative, chronological in sequencing, beginning with earliest memories (or date of birth or family provenance), moving on to school days, university studies if any, employment, travel, and war experiences to reach the present day. Even though others were present during these recording sessions, the narrators did not require them as prompts; rather they were reduced to passive listeners, as if attending a lecture. Though these speakers also told anecdotes, these do not have the same self-contained structure or aesthetic qualities (suspense, reported speech, irony) that characterized those told by the first set of speakers. Instead they are flattened by, and subordinated to, the overall narrative, and do not interrupt its flow.

More important for the light it sheds on the radical rupture created in Palestinians' historical consciousness by the expulsion of 1948, this second set of narrators adopted a chronological sequence that was closely referenced to national history. In the case of two of the speakers, actively affiliated with the Resistance movement, concern for national events expunged all personal details from their life stories, or reduced them to a minimum.[39] Others in this set referred to national events that affected their personal lives; yet even so, the national reference is much more clearly present as narrative structure than in the first set of life stories. Since space does not allow quotation of an entire narrative, I shall try to illustrate this point by offering a summary of Umm 'Imad's life story.

Umm 'Imad begins her narrative with her *ism al-haraka* (party name), then the *hijra* and first refuge in Sidon city.[40] From here she proceeds to: transfer to 'Ayn al-Hilwa camp; description of her home and family; childhood and schooling in 'Ayn al-Hilwa camp; post-school travel to a Gulf country to work with a wealthy family; meeting with the man she eventually married, story of the engagement, the move to Shatila camp; the Israeli attack on Beirut airport (1973); birth of first child; the beginning of "struggle work" (national activism); births of two other children; the "Two Year War" (1975–76); purchase of land in the *hursh* (forest) outside the camp, and the building of a home; the Israeli invasion of 1982 and massacre of Sabra/Shatila; postwar activism with the Red Cross and Palestinian Women's Union; the Lebanese Forces' attack on 'Ayn al-Hilwa camp (April 1984) in which her parents were killed; a trip to the Gulf to stay with her husband and recover from the shock; beginning of the "Battle of the Camps" (May 1985); her return to Shatila; birth of youngest child during the siege; experiences of the five months' siege of Shatila (November 1986–April 1987) and destruction of the family home; the move to the unfinished building in West Beirut where the recording took place; and conclusion appealing to the world for justice for the Palestinians.

Because Umm 'Imad possessed an unusually rich memory and enjoyed describing life in 'Ayn al-Hilwa camp as it had been in her childhood, I returned to her often. In later recording sessions, freed of the obligation to produce a "life story," she told many anecdotes similar to the *qussas* referred to earlier, including stories of Palestine that her mother had told her. But I would argue that the structure of Umm 'Imad's life story reveals her conscious intention to fashion it as a reflection of national history. Personal happenings (marriage, births of children, the death of parents) are integrated into the narrative flow as "events" similar to "events" of history in being "factual" and sequenced by chronology. Others in this set of speakers adopted a similar chronology of national events, with stronger national referencing in the case of speakers who were, or had been, Resistance cadres and members.

I would argue that the Nakba has been translated into most younger refugee women's cultural stock as consciousness of "history" in Daniel's definition, and more by activist women than others. The difference in structure and style between the two sets of life stories is not after all a dichotomy; rather it represents a moment of transition in women's experience between rootedness in Palestine and exile in Lebanon. The more fragmented, nonchronological narratives preserve a heritage of women's *hikaya* that has been ruptured by a cataclysmic event, while the historical narratives are testimonials that use personal histories to illustrate and enrich the collective tragedy of expulsion, transforming narratives of "being" into narratives of "knowing." Yet to describe the second set as merely reproducing knowledge of national history would be to overlook their richness of inclusion, the way they interweave the personal with the collective, conveying a sense of "being in history" as well as of "knowing history."

How to account for these distinct formats for telling stories about the self? One might be forgiven for looking no further than age and educational level, so strong is the association at first sight between these demographic factors and pattern of narrative structure. The hesitancy/plural subject/discontinuity pattern was manifested mainly by older, unschooled speakers, while the second pattern—readiness to speak, the singular subject, and autonomous narratives referenced to national history—came mainly from younger and literate speakers. Employment histories reinforce the impression of a dichotomy based in age and schooling: of the first set none had worked outside the home except in occasional agriculture. Speakers of the second kind had either held salaried employment or worked as regular volunteers with the Resistance movement. The clearly marked contrast between the two sets of speakers could be taken as pointing to processes of "modernization" as cause of difference; the production of an autonomous "life story" could be seen as based in education, employment, and other situational changes that may create a sense of a self located in a specific group history.

Such a conclusion is invalidated, I suggest, by speakers whose demographic characteristics should have made them conform to one of the two main patterns, but who did not. Two of the younger, literate speakers showed the same hesitance and need for prompting as older ones, and made little reference to national history.[41] More challenging to a "modernization" explanation was the narrative of Umm Ghassan, who was among the five oldest speakers, the "Generation of Palestine," all unschooled; her life story was autonomous and coherent, using "I" never "we," and relating her "self" to "history" as both victim and active participant.

Umm Ghassan, Paradigm-Breaker

Umm Ghassan was one of the few speakers I did not know at all before the recording sessions.[42] Friends in Shatila spoke of her as having a gift for oral poetry, and strong recollections of the early days of refugeedom; she was also respected as a "mother of martyrs." The two recordings made with her were memorable, most of all for the frankness of her critiques of her husband—present throughout—for his excessive sexuality, for having procreated thirteen children while leaving all the labor of raising them to her, and for having failed to support his family above a level of abject poverty. Open sexual allusions are repressed in camps by norms of respectability, and such expression at that moment (mid-1992) gave rise to questions about the conditions of its possibility, and whether these were interactive (my identity as foreigner), or historical (post-PLO evacuation), or some other, less obvious reason. Her life story also depicts Umm Ghassan's "self" as nashita (politically active), not in the sense of Resistance group membership but as wa'ia (politically aware) and wataniyya (patriotic). She had stood up to Israelis and Lebanese to try to save her sons, and stayed in Shatila camp throughout the sieges of 1985–87. Her oral poetry, recorded in a second session, expressed the wounds of exile and loss.

The structure of Umm Ghassan's narrative reveals its close national linkage: the hijra (quoted above); suffering cold and hunger with small children in early refugeedom; poverty and her husband's difficulty in earning a living; her frequent pregnancies and childbirths; her husband's imprisonment; oppression by the Lebanese authorities, eviction from the Hursh (next to Shatila camp), the army's prevention of repairs to homes; the uprisings of 1969, when the camps were liberated from army control; the arrival of the fighters from Jordan (1970); the shelling of Shatila during the war of 1975–76; the five-month Amal/Lebanese Army siege of 1986–87; the Sabra/Shatila massacres (1982); death of a son; the disappearance of another son taken by Lebanese Army Intelligence in 1983; caring for her orphaned grandchildren; a more detailed description of the terrors of the siege of 1986/87 and the destruction of their home; the Syrian/Fateh Dissidents' attack of summer 1987, and evacuation to Sidon.

Umm Ghassan's narrative also displays the story-telling artistry characteristic of the "Generation of Palestine." This example set in the immediate post-expulsion period shows several features of the traditional *hikaya*, while graphically conveying the new reality of refugeedom:

> He [husband] needed to work; we had spent the money we brought with us. I had my jewelry. According to our custom, when a girl gets married she takes her *mahr* [marriage endowment] and buys gold jewelry with it. I had with me two bracelets, four rings, and some earrings. I gave him the bracelets and told him to sell them. He sold them for 15 Lebanese pounds. Ah! It was too cheap; they were gold, real gold. He sold them and we spent it. I gave him the rings. He took them and went to Beirut, and worked selling coffee in the city center. He stayed a week. . . . He came back and told me, "I spent the money." I took my earrings and gave them to him, and said, "Sell them. Try again, be patient!" He took the earrings, and went back to Beirut, he worked, he persevered. He was away for ten days, then he came and gave me five pounds.[43] Hamdillah! (Thank God!)

This anecdote follows the three-fold narrative structure of many *hikayat* (Abu Ghassan takes his wife's gold three times, and only succeeds the third time in making a profit). An additional *hikaya* feature is the way the woman takes the initiative, and uses an attribute of gender (her gold) to save the situation. The husband appears foolish by contrast, unable to earn a living in a strange city (Muhawi and Kanaana 1989: 18, 36).

What differentiated Umm Ghassan from other speakers with whom she shared age, rural origin, illiteracy and never-employed housewife status? Her self-assertiveness may have derived partly from the role of economic provider she was forced to undertake during her husband's two-year imprisonment. In addition, she came from a "weak" village and possibly this lack of status within the camp community freed her tongue from the norms of silence about sexuality.[44] But what most distinguishes her from the other speakers of her generation is the richness of her national references. Even if too old to be a member, she had clearly been a friend of the Resistance movement, bringing up her sons to be patriotic, and probably was herself involved in vital support activities such as attending martyrs' funerals, visiting the fighters in the bases, and cooking for them.[45] Her narrative is deeply "historical," not just by beginning with the Nakba—as others of her generation did—but in drawing out the consequences of the Nakba as refugees in camps in Lebanon experienced them, in a coherent, historically sequenced personal and collective history. I would argue that Umm Ghassan's experience of national, class, and gender suffering as a Nakba victim made her respond to the message of the Resistance movement with an intensity that pushed her toward activism, in the belief that the Resistance was the "answer" to the Nakba.[46] Not suffering alone, but political activism is, I suggest, the factor that gives Umm Ghassan's life story its structure, style, and status as an authentic "testimonio" (Beverley 1992: 94–95). Such an interpretation situates change, not as modernization theory does, in a macro factorial framework but within the subject as member of a collectivity.

Conclusion

Refugees in camps in Lebanon often say, "*Tarikhna majhul*" (our history is unknown), unconsciously echoing Doumani, whose reflections on the gaps in histories of Palestine I quoted at the beginning of this paper. Palestinian absence from history can largely be explained by the power of the victors in 1948, as well as separation after 1948 from national archives and monuments, and the dispersion of scholars and cultural institutions. However, I would argue that some obstacles have been self-imposed, that sources for Palestinian history-writing were and are available in the form of people who "lived the events"; and that if this pool of potential historians has been neglected it is due in part to a theory of history that undervalues human experience and memory. Though oral histories of survivors of the Nakba have begun to be recorded, gender discrimination as well as other kinds of exclusion linger on among practitioners. A certain view of women as "ignorant" because in general not highly educated still permeates certain strata of Palestinian society, and can be found among refugees, whether of rural or urban origin.[47] The prevalence of concepts of history as chronicle of "facts" carries the danger of history-writing that reinforces already existing hierarchies of class and gender, silencing women and social strata left behind in the race for education.

The speakers from Shatila who began their life stories with the Nakba, whatever their age at the time, convey their understanding of the dimensions of this event as historical marker, the termination of one kind of history in Palestine, and beginning of another as stateless refugees in Lebanon. Their Nakba stories have been well preserved over time through constant retelling; as both "heritage" and "history," they offer a valuable source for a still-to-be

written account of the expulsions from a Palestinian perspective. The form
of women's stories is as historical as their contents. The Shatila speakers did
not tell the Nakba as a "fact" in history, or as an international conspiracy, but
rather as an "experience" that they have crafted into the form of a *hikaya*,
using a fictional form to convey a real-life happening. It was characteristic of
most of the older speakers, those born in Palestine and already adults in 1948,
that they did not set their "life stories" in a chronicle of Palestinian history
but assembled them from recollections stimulated by questions, or through
thematic links. The single exception was the Nakba, which they translated
from an "event" to a personal and collective catastrophe of cosmic dimensions. Other mainly younger speakers wove personal and collective histories
seamlessly together, conforming to Beverley's description of the genre of
"testimonio." The self-contained anecdote tends to disappear from the life stories of the more "historical" speakers, absorbed into the smooth flow of a descriptive account. I suggest that the Nakba constituted a historic rupture that
shifted women's narratives from the *hikaya*, a gender-specific, rural mode
of cultural heritage, towards the *qissa*, the reportorial story about events
in the "real" world, or in Daniel's formulation, from "heritage" to "history."
The Nakba is thus doubly historicized in the life stories, first as cataclysmic
experience, second as bringing about cultural change in modes of women's
speech and locating of "self." Such change needs to be recognized and registered because national discourse denies post-Nakba change in the interest of
preserving selected elements of the pre-Nakba past. Preserving the past as a
fixed reality has a stabilizing effect on class and gender relations, with its bent
to silence both women and marginal or junior men.

   The Nakba became a constituent of Palestinians' sense of identity not
only because of the scale of their loss, but also because it generates new catastrophes that scar each succeeding generation afresh. It cannot be separated
from what happened afterward; to view it as an event, recorded and classified,
would be to mask its meaning as a continuing predicament. In Lebanon, the
Nakba was followed by the Lebanese civil wars (1956–58; 1975–89); Israeli air
attacks, mostly against camps; the Israeli invasion of 1982; the "Battle of the
Camps" (1985–87) and the Fateh Intifada (1988). Violence invaded homes, destroying shelters, killing loved ones, displacing Palestinians yet again. This
meant that speakers such as Umm Subhi, who did not tell coherent or historicized stories about the "self," had in the real world expanded their gendered
identity as "housewife" into political actions and words, as when she told the
Lebanese soldier that she was a daughter of the camp, and mother of all the

children he was arresting. These stories speak to us as audience about how the Nakba was experienced by refugee women as personal stories of suffering and loss, and as testimonials of a larger collective tragedy.

There has been some tendency among feminist historians to research women's history as a form of addition, or "writing in." Yet new historical facts have a limited anecdotal interest if they do not shift our understanding of what happened in the past, and engage us in the present. Trouillot questions the usefulness of accumulating facts: "The turn towards hitherto neglected sources (e.g. diaries, images, bodies) and the emphasis on unused facts (e.g. facts of gender, race and class, facts of the life cycle, facts of resistance) are path-breaking developments . . . [yet] when these tactical gains are made to dictate strategy they lead, at worst, to a neo-empiricist enterprise and, at best, to an unnecessary restriction of the battleground for historical power" (Trouillot 1995: 49). It is in this battleground that we need to situate these Palestinian women's narratives, and ourselves as listeners: first as challenging the silencing of Palestinian history, second as challenging colonialist (Western-Christian-Zionist) constructions of Arab/Muslim women that are part of a larger enterprise to dominate and exclude; and third, as challenging a social structure and attitude that would limit their speech and agency.

NOTES

1. Umm Khalid, born in 1938 in a small village near Haifa, married in 1957. Recorded July 20, 1992, Beirut. All names are fictional.
2. This is still true in spite of the revisionist work of Israeli scholars such as Flapan (1987), Morris (1987; 2004a), Shlaim (1988), Pappé (1988), T. Katz (1998); and Palestinian scholars such as Nazzal (1978), Kanaana (1992), Masalha (1992), Dirbas (1993), Farah (1997), Abu-Sitta (2000) and Abdel Jawad (forthcoming). Among Western scholars, Palumbo (1987) is exceptional in using Palestinians' oral testimonies.
3. See Daniel 1996, 25–29, 43–47. The context is Sinhalese-Tamil violence in Sri Lanka.
4. In Palestine, the European concept of history penetrated through mission schools, the education of many of the local elite in Western universities, the spread of literacy, and the adoption of "modernity." From the elite this concept spread to men of the urban upper and middle classes, to reach rural populations later, and women last. The provision of schooling under the Mandate was highly unequal between urban and rural areas, and between men and women (Fleischmann 1996: 62, 64 [fn 63]).

5. Granqvist (1931, 1935), presents a wealth of transliterated cultural material.

6. They say, "The Palestinian folktale is a highly developed art form" that relies on "verbal mannerisms and language flourishes not used in ordinary conversation, especially by men. Women were largely responsible for developing this style, and they carry on the tradition" (Muhawi and Kanaana 1989: 3)

7. Influenced by the Chicago school of Symbolic Interactionism, this study attempted to examine Palestinian experiences in Lebanon as "socialization into identity."

8. The Arabic word used was *mu'amarat*, conspiracies or plots, a term widely used by Palestinian refugees to mean the externally produced causes of the Nakba.

9. Rarely heard today, the use of *Filastini makht* ("pure Palestinian") is a cultural attribute mainly of older rural women.

10. Personal communication, M.S., October 30, 2003.

11. A second point of interest here is the quotation from a woman confirming women's ignorance; it demonstrates the way an existing gender hierarchy is reconstituted from new values as they enter a cultural system.

12. Edward Said first used this expression as the title of an article in the *London Review of Books*, February, 1984, reprinted in Said (1994a). He often deplored "the crucial absence of women" from Palestinian discourse, assimilating their silencing to that of the Palestinians as a people, as in this passage: "Unless we are able to perceive at the interior of our life the statements women make—concrete, watchful, compassionate, immensely poignant, strangely invulnerable—we will never fully understand our experience of dispossession" (Said 1985: 77).

13. Subjects from a single camp were chosen to explore differences within a category, "women," too often homogenized in Western feminist approaches, even when belonging to the same social milieu. The speakers were diverse in class/status background, marital status, and employment experience, as well as age and education. Like most Palestinian refugees in Lebanon, they came originally from Galilean villages or cities of the coast (Acre, Haifa, Jaffa).

14. Four speakers were recorded outside Beirut: two in Sidon (Lebanon), one in London, another in Tunis. For the story of the "Battles of the Camps" as told by those who experienced it, see Sayigh 1994.

15. I do not know if this way of naming generations was used in other regions of the Palestinian diaspora, and by other social strata. It may well be a product of people of rural origin, and of Lebanon as diaspora region.

16. See Slyomovics 1998: 1–31 on memory books. Palestinian "memory books" have been written mainly about villages. A series has been produced by the Arab Research Centre at Birzeit University, and another by Al-Shajara publishers, Yarmuk,

Syria. Others have been the work of individuals, usually those expelled from the village they record. See the bibliographies in Al-Jana, 2002; more recent ones are cited by Khalili, 2004b and Davis, this volume.

17. First-generation refugees were blamed by their children and blamed themselves for leaving Palestine, possibly as a reflection of Lebanese accusations of cowardice. A common formula for expressing this guilt and anger was, "If only we had died in our country rather than come here!"

18. *Hijra* (migration) is used by older refugees for the exodus from Palestine, perhaps with reference to the Prophet Muhammad's flight from Mecca to Medina.

19. For "village," the speaker uses *beledna*, which also means "our country."

20. The Arab Salvation Army, *al-jaysh al-inqadh*, was a pan-Arab militia led by Fawzi al-Qawukji that participated in the 1948 conflict. Mainly stationed in the north of Palestine, it was widely blamed by Palestinian refugees in Lebanon, as well as Palestinians who remained in Galilee, for incompetence and desertion. Many of the testimonies recorded by Nafez Nazzal (1978) in his *The Palestinian Exodus from Galilee,1948,* tell the same story.

21. Hajja Badriyya was born in 1926, married in 1943, unschooled, never employed, not politically active. Insecurity at the time of recording meant that some speakers omitted any connection with the Resistance movement. Recorded July 6, 1992.

22. Umm Ghassan, born in 1939 in a small village near Acre, married in 1945, unschooled, never employed, two sons dead or missing. Recorded May 22, May 25, 1992.

23. Umm Mahmud was unschooled, never employed, probably not active politically. Recorded December 2, 1992.

24. Umm Nayif was unschooled, never employed, probably not "active." Recorded May 17, 1992.

25. Umm Subhi, unschooled, never employed, voluntary activism. Recorded January 29, 1991.

26. The story appears in *Al-Jana* 1998: 54.

27. The only exception was Umm Muhammad, born at the beginning of the twentieth century, who began her narrative with stories of British Army raids and searches.

28. Nozira, born in 1948 in 'Akka, unmarried, a worker in a Palestinian health service. Recorded July 11, 1992.

29. Though the Nakba marked a beginning, it was even more an end, both of Palestine and of pre-expulsion lives. Many older refugees described life after 1948 as "death," "non-existence," and "burial."

30. Asking in-camp refugee women for their "life story" may have been culturally inappropriate. Lila Abu-Lughod writes about Egyptian Bedouin women that "the life story may contribute to a sense of the person at its center as an isolated individual. The women whose stories are told here neither live that way nor think of themselves as such" (Abu-Lughod 1993: 31). Yet the fact that about half the Shatila speakers did give self-sustained narratives about the "self" raises questions about differences within a group sharing a milieu and similar life conditions.

31. 1989–1992 was a period of Syrian control of the camps in West Beirut, with many arrests of Palestinians considered to be "pro-Arafat."

32. Defining the testimonio, Beverley writes, "The situation of narration in testimonio has to involve an urgency to communicate, a problem of repression, poverty, subalternity, imprisonment, struggle for survival ... unlike the novel, testimonio promises by definition to be primarily concerned with sincerity." Further, it must be "a representation of a social class or group" (Beverley 1992: 94, 95).

33. The Ghor is a flat, semi-desert region running along the west bank of the River Jordan. Villagers tended to cultivate it but did not build solid houses there because of the heat and mosquitoes. Bedouins used it to pasture their flocks, though Umm Subhi may have mis-remembered when she says that they went there in summer.

34. One speaker's daughter was eager to hear stories about home in Jaffa; another reminded her mother about stories she had told before. Younger family members are the best prompts because they are familiar, and evoke a sense of parental duty to transmit a heritage.

35. "I had an operation about three months ago. I didn't cry because I was ill, but because if I died, there was no son, no daughter beside me" (Umm Subhi, January 29, 1991).

36. Compare with the common identification of periods of Palestinian history as "the time of the Turks" or "the time of the British." "The time of the Army" in a Lebanese context indicates periods when the camps were under Lebanese Army control, either from the early 1950s until the liberation of the camps in 1969; or after the Israeli invasion of 1982, when Army control was reinstalled until February 1985 when Maronite-dominated army battalions were expelled from West Beirut.

37. Umm Ilyas's name indicates that she is Christian.

38. Note Umm Nayif's rhythmic triple repetition of the different receptacles in which Umm Ilyas lit fires, again reminiscent of the *hikaya*.

39. Exclusion of the personal was so extreme with one PLO cadre that when I asked about her marriage, after she had finished speaking, she expressed surprise that I

could be interested in this. For a good discussion of why politicized speakers edit out the personal, see Stanley 1996.

40. Umm 'Imad born in 1946 in Acre, married in 1968; completed UNRWA schooling, worked briefly in the Gulf before marriage; a voluntary activist and Resistance supporter. First interviewed December 13, 1990.

41. Avoiding political references could be explained by the fear and suspicion that reigned at the time of the recordings. Two of these nonconforming cases came from higher class/status levels of the Shatila community. A third, university educated, and an ex-Resistance cadre, used her "story" to ask questions about a conflicted and lost "self." See Sayigh 1999.

42. See endnote 22.

43. Nearly $2.00 in those days.

44. The researcher in a marginal community is often slow to perceive status differences between its members, homogenized as "poor" in relation to the outside society. Refugee marginality in Lebanon did not prevent status distinctions in the camps, a complex mix of pre-1948 origins (urban/rural, large village/small village, strong clan/small clan) with new bases such as occupation, income, ownership of home, education, and occupations of children. Having sons working abroad—as in Umm Ghassan's case—was one of the few avenues to social promotion.

45. Support from the women of the camps was far more essential to the Resistance movement than could be guessed by the occasional and auxiliary nature of their activities. There was also a wide range of active roles through which women could be involved. See Peteet 1991: 143–52.

46. "The meaning of return in the Palestinian collective consciousness is the very opposite of the Nakbah of refuge and of exile" (Suleiman 2001: 87).

47. While Palestinian women of peasant origin are widely seen as ignorant of history—since history is assumed to be "known" through books rather than through experience—Slyomovics notes truly that they have—and are recognized to have—an alternative discourse: "an authoritative male voice projects the correct, official history which is challenged by a reactive, female one. Women ... are associated with a domestic, oral history rather than a written, political history" (Slyomovics 1998: 207). Yet it needs to be added that "speech" (orality) and "women" are equally depreciated in this close association.

Figure 10 Still from *Jenin, Jenin*. Directed by Muhammad Bakri, 2002.

6 The Continuity of Trauma and Struggle

RECENT CINEMATIC REPRESENTATIONS
OF THE NAKBA

Haim Bresheeth

In recent Palestinian cinema, narratives of loss and trauma centered around the 1948 Nakba have a strong relationship to the continuing traumas of occupation and oppression by the Israeli forces. The prevalence of Nakba themes in recent Palestinian films, always connected to the second *intifada*, suggests that the Nakba is not mere memory or a trauma of the past; instead, these films seem to point to both a *continuity of pain and trauma*, reaching from the past into the heart of the present, as well as a *continuity of struggle*. The losses of the Nakba, they suggest, fire the continued resistance to Israeli occupation and subjugation. The resolution of trauma is the struggle itself. This chapter will examine the links across memory, trauma, and identity in the context of the Nakba, arguing that recent Palestinian film has been engaged in a storytelling project that is tied to trauma, reliving it and thus perhaps turning melancholia into mourning work. The turning from the pathology of melancholia to the normalcy of the work of mourning is not a simple or straightforward social process, but it is this very process, through recent Palestinian films, which is the focus of this chapter.

The Economy of Pain: From Freud's *Mourning and Melancholia* to Caruth's Trauma Writings

Memory is at the root cause of trauma, Freud tells us, but is also the source of its resolution. In one of his later works he outlines how the pain of reliving the events leading to the trauma may in turn hold the key for a gradual return to normality (Freud 1991 [1920]). Mourning, and the work of mourning, he tells us in a piece written some years before, is crucial for the return to the normal life (Freud 1991 [1917]). Those who are not able, or not allowed to mourn, may well lapse into a pathological state, such as melancholia. Mourning the dead is an essential need of human society, and of the individual within it. Freud writes of "the economics of pain" when designating mourning as a reaction "to a loss of a loved person, or to the loss of some abstraction which has taken the place of one, such as one's country, liberty, an ideal, and so on" (ibid.: 252). The link made here by Freud between the self, a loved person, and "one's country" and "liberty" is of special interest to us when examining films that also juxtapose such entities in their narrative structure.

Freud clearly distinguishes between mourning—a normal process that duly ends, and melancholia—a pathology that may destroy the subject. One of the most interesting differences between the mourning process and the pathological loops of melancholia is that the latter may well be triggered by a loss of what he calls an "ideal kind": "one can recognize that there is a loss of a more ideal kind. The object has not perhaps actually died, but has been lost as an object of love" (Freud 1991 [1917]: 253). Hence, the loss that may trigger the melancholia is not necessarily a death, or total loss, but something like the loss of one's country. Real as it is, this loss is different from death. After all, the country is still there. Thus the loss continues, gets fixated, cannot be mourned and done with, as in the case of death. The loss of one's country *never ends*. It must be even more pronounced when the loss is experienced *in situ*—while living in the lost country. Freud reminds us that melancholia contains "something more than normal mourning. In melancholia the relation to the object is no simple one; it is complicated by the conflict due to ambivalence" (ibid.: 266).

So what would become of whole societies where mourning is prevented? Where coming to terms with the loss is not an option? What of societies whose loss and catastrophe have been covered up, hidden away, and systematically erased? One such example is Palestinian society; it has been reeling from its great loss of country and autonomy ever since 1948—since the formative event of the Nakba, or the great catastrophe. In this chapter, I examine the Nakba and its construction in, and of, Palestinian memory and identity, through some cinematic representations in recent Palestinian films. The rereading of Freud's work on trauma offered by Cathy Caruth's writings, which link it to life, play, and storytelling, applies particularly well to situations and people within a number of films I have chosen for close study.[1]

Recent Palestinian Cinema and the Memory of the Nakba

The choice of films was made with the fiftieth anniversary of the Nakba in mind. It is no accident that this painful anniversary, happening as it did concurrently with Israel's fiftieth anniversary as an independent state, produced reworkings of the memories and history of the 1948 disaster. Palestinian films that emerged around this important date have some common characteristics: they tell and retell the history of the Nakba. I shall examine six films produced by three Palestinian filmmakers, all Israeli citizens,[2] that deal with recent history, memory and narrative. The films discussed are *Ustura* (Israel, 1998), *1948* (Israel, 1998) *Chronicle of a Disappearance,* (Europe and Palestine, 1996), *Jenin, Jenin* (Israel/Palestine 2002), *Egteyah* (Israel/Palestine, 2002) and *Divine Intervention* (Palestine, 2002). The films represent a special interest in the Nakba and in cinematic storytelling, which they use as a unifying device while still operating roughly within the boundaries of documentary cinema. Even films dealing with contemporary events invoke and reference the Nakba in various ways. Many other Palestinian films have similar concerns but this small number of better known films represent well the gamut of expression on this topic.

For many years, the Nakba in Palestinian or Arab films was noticeable by its absence.[3] This is far from surprising; the images of loss and destruction meted out by the Zionist forces to the many hundreds of thousands of Palestinian refugees are far from easy for Arabs, especially Palestinians to confront. A long time had to pass until the Nakba could become a live topic within Palestinian cultural life, serving both the need to purge the trauma as well as to construct identity. A whole generation of Palestinians had to grow up with hardly any cinematic representations of the great catastrophe of 1948 as well as the acts of resistance that were part of their history. This reminds us of the similar attitude (though for different reasons) in Israel toward the Holocaust during the 1950s. The images of Jews led to the slaughter were an abomination for the Zionists of post–World War II Palestine—the Old Jew of Europe has always been seen as an embarrassment for Zionism, a motivating negativity that propelled it to construct the *New Jew*, the Israeli Zionist.[4] Thus, visual representations of the Holocaust, and especially cinematic representations, were very rare in this formative period of Israel.[5]

The important exceptions to this demeaning condition of European Jewry, are, in Zionist eyes and texts, the Warsaw Ghetto uprising, other smaller uprisings, and the struggle by Jewish partisans against the Nazis. Such armed resistance is seen and hailed as the precursor to the activities and existence of the IDF, the armed forces of Israel. Thus, Israel managed to capitalize on the few important acts of armed resistance by Jews in Nazi-controlled Europe, and to make them, ipso facto, a justification and raison d'être for its own actions in 1948 and afterward. It is therefore interesting to note that Palestinians also have seen the Warsaw Ghetto struggle as iconic. At many points Palestinian organizations and individuals have made reference to the Holocaust events. One such reference was the visit in 1983 of a PLO delegate to the Warsaw Ghetto monument, at which he laid a wreath and pronounced: "As the Jews were then justified to rise up against their Nazi murderers, so now are the Palestinians justified in their own struggle with the Zionists."[6] While this fact, like some other instances of Palestinian references to Holocaust events, is mentioned in James Young's (1993) illuminating book, he manages to overlook, in a work on the texture of memory, some interesting facts about the memorial sites he discusses. When describing Zionist memorializing projects, such as the forests planted to commemorate Holocaust victims, Young does not mention that most of these forests formed part of the active destruction and erasure of hundreds of Palestinian villages and towns taken over in 1948. Most of these villages were bulldozed in the 1950s and planted with trees so as to remove all signs of earlier habitation that would tie past occupants to the land (see Slyomovics, this volume). The trees, like those who planted them, are in the main foreign. The trees were firs of European origin, not native to Palestine; they covered up the evidence of an earlier Mediterranean ground cover, removing even the memory of the natural environment. Such forests cover the location of the town of Saffuriyya, which some of the films dealing with the Nakba feature.[7]

The great injustice meted out to the Palestinians by the Israeli state is thus covered up and camouflaged by commemorating another, unconnected injustice. The story of Palestinian ruin and expulsion is turned into a positive narrative of Zionist rebirth, with the European fir tree as its potent symbol.

While Israel has planted millions of those trees, as well as setting up thousands of stone, concrete, and metal memorials, it has consistently refused to allow the Palestinians to commemorate their own history. Power is not only exercised over the land and its people, it also controls the story, its point of view, and the meta-narrative of *truth* and *memory*.

Ethnographic Film and Ethnotopia: Who is Telling the Story?

So how is *truth* established? Is documentary cinema a vehicle in such a historical process, or could it be? The history of documentary cinema is consistent in one thing: it concentrates on identity, on the struggle between images of *selfhood* and *otherness*. In Russell's words: "One of the most important cultural ramifications of early cinema was the exchange of images made possible by traveling cameramen and exhibitors" (Russell 1999: 76). Such a division of identities, necessary for the process of identity formation to function culturally, is obviously problematic—the filmmaker is helping to define self by gazing at others. Russell outlines a safer and more complex perspective, which she calls *Ethnotopia*, after Bill Nichols' use of the term (Nichols 1991: 218). In her own use of this term, the documentarist/ethnographer assumes a more dynamic position than that occupied by his or her predecessors; the term combines *Utopia* and *Ethnos*—suggesting that the story changes depending upon the positioning or *topos*. In the Palestinian films I discuss in this chapter, the *Ethnotopic* impulse is directed away from the oppositional self–other binary precisely because the filmmaker is presenting his or her own *ethnos*, dramatically altering the equations used by these analysts of documentary. However, one can apply the notions Russell develops, and especially that of the "return of the colonial repressed," to a selection of recent Palestinian films.

All the films to be discussed here use storytelling as an *Ethnotopic* device in order to deal with the tragedy of the lost *Heimat* or homeland, Palestine. The stories told within the films not only function as devices for delivering historical detail and personal memory but also revive and reclaim for Palestinian memory the experiences of the Nakba and the expelled inhabitants, convey the enormity of loss, and offer empathy to the exiled. More importantly, they offer a voice to the unsung and unheard continuing tragedy of Palestine, constructing a possible space for national and individual existence and identity today. In telling the story of Palestine, they counter the enormously powerful narrative of Zionism that occupied center stage for most of the second half of the twentieth century.

A Tale of Two Towns: Saffuriyya (1948) and Jenin (2002)

The practice of using a storyline in documentary is as old as the genre itself. What I want to discuss here is the unique relationship between storytelling *within* a film, and the story *told by* the film. This relationship is especially germane to documentary cinema as a discourse of identity-formation—a discourse that represents the social and cultural *Self* and *Other*.[8] This argument could quite justifiably be extended to fiction film, and definitely to the fiction films under discussion here.

It is perhaps not entirely coincidental, considering the centrality of the Palestinian town of Saffuriyya in Palestinian accounts of the Nakba, that three of them feature the town, which was forcibly evacuated in 1948 and later destroyed by the IDF, as a means of exploring the loss of *Heimat*. Arguably, Saffuriyya has become symbolic of the Nakba, an icon of the totality of its loss. In at least two of the films, *Ustura* and *1948*, Saffuriyya's story stands for the story of Palestine itself. Elia Suleiman's film, *Chronicle of a Disappearance*, also features the famous Palestinian writer and native of Saffuriyya, Taha Muhammad 'Ali, who appears also in *1948*, where he speaks of his hometown.

Behind *1948* hides another Palestinian storyteller, the late Emile Habiby, a writer, intellectual, and leftist politician. Habiby's ironic, harsh, and humorous novel, *The Pessoptimist* (also called the *Opssimist* or *Optipessimist*) has served Muhammad Bakri, director of *1948*, as the reference and starting-point for a rambling theatrical production by the same name. This show, which Bakri, also an accomplished actor, has delivered many times in Arabic and Hebrew to packed audiences, tells the story of the invisible Palestinian minority of Israel, its Nakba, its subsequent marginalization, oppression, and mistreatment in the newly formed state of Israel, and its aspirations for freedom, equality and development, all dashed by the harsh realities of the Zionist entity. This bittersweet story of human suffering, survival, and hope in the face of the immovable object of Zionism, is the source of the novel's name—a blend of optimism and pessimism.

Of the three newer films, all completed in 2002, two deal with an iconic event during the second *intifada*: the destruction by the IDF of the center of the Jenin Refugee camp, an event of such brutality as to still command international anger. Both *Jenin, Jenin,* by Bakri, and *Egteyah* directed by Hassan—two documentaries that explore the Israeli invasion in revealing (though very different) visual discourses and have led to complex debates in Israel[9] and abroad—use the framework of the Nakba and its remembered/memorialized acts of destruction as a referent. Arguably, Jenin has become, like Saffuriyya before it, symbolic of the terrifying wanton destruction that has become so normalized across Palestine. While *Jenin, Jenin* leaves the telling of the destruction to the inmates of the camp, and especially to a young and impressive girl (fig. 10) and a deafmute man, the film *Egteyah* (which means Invasion) tells the story mainly through the eyes of one of the Israeli D9 bulldozer operators, whose narrative is that it is a "difficult job that has to be done." Both films expose an Israeli soldiery of a kind that most Israelis continue to deny; they are presented with a clear image of a society that has brutalized itself and then gone on to brutalize and devastate the Palestinians.

The newest of these films, Elia Suleiman's *Divine Intervention* (Palestine, 2002) is, like his earlier film discussed here, a heady combination of fiction, documentary, and agitprop, moving freely between formats and even building in a fantasy musical scene that combines the Hong Kong action movie with a musical agitprop. While this film does not deal with the Jenin incident specifically, it does deal with the second *intifada* in general. The film is set, like his earlier *A Chronicle of a Disappearance* (1996), in his native Nazareth, as well as in the liminal spaces between the Israeli and Palestinian entities. This grey zone in which Palestinians now exist is his main interest, and he sets the most remarkable parts of the film in the parking lot of the A-Ram checkpoint near Jerusalem.[10] The enigmatic Suleiman, silent throughout the film, as in his last one, is seen with his girlfriend. She comes from the Occupied Territories, while he lives on the Israeli side of Palestine. The only place they can meet with relative impunity is in the no-man's-land of the checkpoint.[11]

The two help us remember that the Nakba has separated the Palestinians since 1948 and continues to do so now. The film was shot after Ariel Sharon's calamitous visit to the Haram al-Sharif (Dome of the Rock) in September 2000, a visit that triggered the second *intifada*. It starts with poor Santa Claus pursued up a steep hill by a gang of kids, losing all his colorful baggage on the way and finally suffering a mortal wound, just outside a hilltop church. In one scene Suleiman blows up a red balloon with the effigy of Yasir Arafat on it and sends it flying across Jerusalem, past the checkpoints, until it reaches the same golden dome and lands on it. In this pastiche of Arafat on a pumped-up balloon, he connects the hopes of Palestine to the symbol of its identity,

Figure 11 Still from *Divine Intervention*. Directed by Elia Suleiman, 2002.

the Al-Aqsa mosque. The film becomes almost a child's fable, with its red balloons, and an indestructible flying superwoman who defies her enemies with kung fu action and stops bullets with her bare hands. It ends in a marvelous scene of a female, victorious Christ, crucified by Israeli bullets, but to no avail, as she survives all their attacks, even one by an army helicopter, using a metal shield of Palestine as her only armor. Arafat, Suleiman, his Superwoman girlfriend, the musical and action extravaganza, Christ's crown of thorns, the *intifada*—all become elements in a mélange rich with cinematic references.

At this point, it is useful to return to Freud, through the creative agency of Cathy Caruth, in order to illuminate some of the devices in the films discussed. In a recent piece, Caruth (2001) discusses the famous *fort/da* episode in Freud's *Beyond the Pleasure Principle*, and draws out of his article some hidden meanings crucial for discussing trauma and representation. Caruth charts Freud's advances in this seminal piece, from the description of World War I traumas in surviving soldiers, through the *fort/da* story of the little boy, to the deep implications of this theoretical notion, not just for trauma studies, but for our culture as a whole, and especially for history and memory, and their social functions.

In this rereading, Caruth parallels the form and content of Freud's famous essay, showing that the interplay (*spiel*) between the death drive and the life energy is at the heart of the little *fort/da* story and gives the whole piece its structure. By rephrasing Freud's questions in his piece, she manages to reframe his work to bring it up to date and make it useful again. She talks of transforming "the original questions of trauma—*what does it mean for life to bear witness to death? And what is the nature of a life that continues beyond trauma?*—into an ultimately more fundamental and elusive concern: *what is the language of the life drive?*" (Caruth 2001: 14). In Bakri's film, *Jenin, Jenin,* another child, this time a young girl, takes us through her traumatic experiences of the invasion. At one point in her account, she says to the filmmaker, and through him, to us: "The Israelis can kill and maim, but they cannot win. . . . all the mothers will have more children . . . and we will continue the struggle."

The movement charted in this sentence, from death and the trauma of destruction to the new life that will bloom and bring salvation, is exactly what Caruth unearths in Freud's article—the constant seesawing between the polarities of the death drive and the life drive, between utmost despair and new hope. Both are actually inseparable in the girl's story, as they are in Freud's story, or in Caruth's account of the trauma suffered by the friends of a murdered boy in Atlanta; the font of hope lies in the obsessive return to the "scene of crime," to the locus of pain. Representing the trauma in a story, a *spiel* (*game,* but also *play* in German) is the mechanism chosen by all to deal with the various traumas they are facing—death, parting, loss, devastation.

This throws new light on the many stories of woe told in the films under examination, and on the whole practice of storytelling of the Nakba—a tradition richly represented by the films selected for examination. Even the structure of the films is deeply affected by the storytelling function. Like his earlier film, Suleiman's *Divine Intervention* is divided into chapter-like scenes, as is the film *Egteyah* by Nizar Hassan, who even names the chapters: for example, *The Dream, The Passage, The Guest House.* Such storytelling strategies are just part of a wide variety of storytelling techniques integral to the films discussed in this chapter. Two of the films even start as a children's fable would—*1948* starts with the director/actor, Muhammad Bakri, playing the role of Habibi's central character, Sa'id Abu al-Nahs, telling the story on stage: "Every folk tale begins: 'Once upon a time, a long time ago.' . . . Shall I tell the story, or go to sleep ?" (this is said against the background of four black and white images, gradually filling the screen, of Palestinian families in flight during 1948), "But Papa knew that Churchill[12] did not intend to stay here very long, so Papa befriended Yaakov Safsarchik."

While the voiceover recounts this, we see archival footage of the British forces leaving Palestine. At the point of the voice reaching Yaakov Safsarchik [based on the Hebrew *safsar*, for illegal peddler or black marketeer] we see the archive footage of Ben Gurion and his wife on the occasion of the transfer of power from the British mandatory forces. The scene ends with the British flag being lowered, and the Israeli flag being hoisted on the same pole. Bakri tells us, in Habibi's words: "Before dying, Papa told me: 'If life is bad, Sa'id, Safsarchik will fix things!' So he fixed me."

This is obviously, as the title suggests, the story, or stories, of the Nakba. The framing device of the many stories of Palestinians who were driven out of their homes, never to return, is indeed a fable about the betrayed Palestinian whose father/leader trusted Israeli double-dealing, or at best, false promises. That the stories are not just about houses, wells, and trees, is beautifully clarified by Taha Muhammad 'Ali, speaking later in the film about what Saffuriyya means to him:

> Saffuriyya is a mysterious symbol. My longing for it is not a yearning for stone and paths alone, but for a mysterious blend of feelings, relatives, people, animals, birds, brooks, stories and deeds. . . . When I visit Saffuriyya I become excited and burst out crying, but when I think about Saffuriyya the picture that forms in my mind is virtually imaginary, mysterious, hard to explain.

Like Freud's little boy, with his game of *fort/da*, the writer returns to Saffuriyya—the town that lies perfect in his memories but is totally destroyed in reality. Telling the stories is his way of dealing with the unimaginable—the totality of destruction and loss. What was lost during the Nakba, then, is not just houses and stones but a whole life of a nation—the country, the people, their homes and gardens, their animals and birds. Showing the stones that are left cannot provide the picture; neither can the black and white photograph of Saffuriyya on the writer's wall.

Story follows story in 1948, interposed by Bakri riding a broomstick on stage, interpreting, contradicting, and complementing the tales. The storytelling is disarming—both Palestinian Arabs and Israeli Jews in the audience fall into the trap: disarmed, they listen with compassion, understanding, even anger. The stories in 1948 are not limited to Palestinians telling of their fate. Some Israelis were also chosen to tell their stories. One of them is Dov Yermiya,[13] who was the IDF officer responsible for the conquest of Saffuriyya. His story confirms most of the facts given by the inhabitants who fled and describe the background for the battle. But later he tells us of the atrocities committed, clearly siding with the Palestinians, speaking with anger and grief about his "side of the fence." His story, told in Arabic, is an obvious deviation from the Zionist narrative about 1948 and reinforces the Nakba narrative.

Nizar Hassan's *Ustura* also starts with the director's voiceover, telling us the story of Saffuriyya. This is another fable, told with irony, humor, but mostly with pain: "In 1948, there was a town called Saffuriyya. In one of its houses lived Grandfather Musa al-Khalil, and his wife, Grandmother Amna al-Qasim." (This takes place with a background of archive stills of Saffuriyya and the family photographs of the Nijim clan pasted on the wall of their living room. We see the photographs of Musa and Amna, marked by time and by the journeys they endured.)

> One Ramadan evening in 1948, everyone was breaking the fast. Suddenly the Jewish planes began bombing; people got up and fled. They say that when people ran away, they locked their houses and took the keys, positive that they'd only be away for a short time.[14] That's what they thought. Amna al-Qasim did not take the key, but she took her grandson Salim. . . . And the Jews took Saffuriyya, and named it Zippori, and that's when Israel was established. "That was it for Palestine," as we say. Thus begun the journey of Umm Salim and Abu Salim's family. [15]

Hassan is not only telling us this "fable"; he also partakes in it in the prologue. Later in the film, he is seen seated with the three sons of Fatma, facing her in the large family room in which the whole family is seated, listening to the mother's story. Hassan relates to this story personally—his own mother told him a similar story when he was a young child (Ben-Zvi 1999: 80). By sitting in line with the sons, Hassan becomes a son too, and his presence (and the presence of his camera crew) transforms the private event into a public one.

Factually, *Ustura* narrates the story of a Palestinian family, the Nijim clan, from the Galilee. When the film begins, the family is living in a town called Saffuriyya before 1948 and is expelled by the Israeli forces. Some of the family members stay behind in Palestine, trying to get back to their home town. Others are trapped in Lebanon and not allowed back by the Israeli authorities, now in control of the whole Galilee, then as now mainly populated by Palestinians. The family is never to reunite again. As the Lebanese exile gives birth to other exiles—Jordan, Syria, Europe, the United States—the family is dispersed over the whole exilic spectrum of the Palestinian diaspora. It must be clear even from this limited description that the film is iconic, because the family experiences chosen here are representative of the Palestinian people, and their continuing plight after the Nakba. The Nakba in these films is the *beginning of the story*[16] of Palestine, and in some sense, also its tragic end.

But nothing becomes truly universal before it is specifically particular, and this is a film about the specificity of a particular family. The family flees from Saffuriyya after a bombardment by the Israeli forces and starts on the well-known refugee trail, first to the Lebanese border, then to Ba'albak, where they stay for a couple of years. Only the old patriarch, Grandfather Musa al-Khalil, stays behind, while his wife, Amna al-Qasim,[17] flees with the rest of the family—her son Muhammad Musa, his pregnant wife Fatma, their son Salim and daughter Khadra, and the aunt Khadija, daughter of old Amna. During their stay, Grandmother Amna decides to return home. Taking with her her grandson Salim and her daughter Khadija, the three steal across the border back into Palestine, now called Israel, intent on returning to their home town, Saffuriyya. The town, however, has since become the Israeli Zippori. Most of the houses have been destroyed by the Israeli army, but some of the remaining houses have been populated by new immigrants. Since there is no way for the family to go back home, they settle clandestinely in the local convent and Amna, whose husband still lives in the town, registers her small grandson Salim as her own son, on her Israeli ID. Thus does the family become exiles in their own *Heimat*, illegal infiltrators into Israel. Thus their story becomes the iconic Nakba story, combining the loss of home, town, and country in one powerful narrative.

In returning to her town, although "she didn't take her keys," as the director so pointedly reminds us in the prologue to the film, Amna al-Qasim displays not nostalgia, but resolution to survive in her homeland. There is disagreement on the reading of the gesture of "taking keys" to the abandoned home in refugee narratives, and Hassan relates to this in his own narrative in *Ustura*, quoted below. Patricia Seed (1999: 91) argues that the keeping of the key to the old house is not a nostalgic gesture but a gesture meant to prompt the memorizing of the old home as a story to be told. History becomes a story. But Amna al-Qasim has another key to her homeland. It is not a key made of metal, but her grandson Salim. The boy Salim will become the key to reuniting the family in Palestine. Salim, growing up away from his parents, with two adoptive mothers—his grandmother and his aunt—is sent to a prestigious Jewish preparatory school numbering many Israeli elite as former students. In the 1960s, through trying to get his family back from Jordan where they had settled in the meantime, he finds out that his brothers, Mahmud and Yusuf, who were born since the separation from the family, are the reason his application for family reunification is rejected. He is then advised by the Israeli security forces to remove the names of his brothers from the application. After ten years, and with the assistance of Shimon Peres, he succeeds in reuniting with most of his family, except his brothers. During the Israeli invasion of Lebanon in the early 1980s, Salim thinks that the PLO fighter interviewing an Israeli pilot who was shot down in Lebanon is his brother Mahmud (who he had seen in Lebanon thirty years earlier). He reports this to the Israeli authorities, who try to recruit him and to trap his brother through him.

The first meaningful reunion of most of the family takes place because of the shooting for Hassan's film, and a very painful event it is. By that time, the family is anywhere but in Saffuriyya—the new patriarch, Salim, now lives with his family and mother and aunt in Nazareth; his brother Mahmud lives in Germany, where he has married a German woman; and his brother Yusuf and sister Khadra live in Irbid, Jordan. Saffuriyya itself is no more—it suffered the same fate as hundreds of Palestinian villages and towns eradicated by the Israeli authorities. For all intents and purposes, it had never existed.

Here is the place to ponder an unusual quality of *Ustura*. Although all information regarding the characters and their travails is presented, the film does not yield this information easily—one could even say it is unwilling to part with it. To use a phrase coined by Jeffrey K. Rouff (1998: 287), it is a "text at war with itself." This form of narrative unclarity is an important departure from normative documentary practices and a clear indication of its exilic and "interstitial" structure, to use Hamid Naficy's term (1999: 125–50). The film opens with a prologue, lasting a mere three minutes, cramming into this short period a number of seemingly unconnected utterances by yet-to-be-identified characters of the drama and a high-speed argument. By the end of the prologue we are clear about one feature—the family that lost its home in Saffuriyya has also lost its *Heimat*—Palestine. It is the story of the Nakba in microcosm.

The film's title, *Ustura* (fable or story), appearing after the prologue, presages the stories that the film tells. This mode of storytelling is not just a product of the Palestinian/Arab oral tradition of storytelling but also a substitute for the lost *Heimat*. If we recall Steiner's (1985: 26) reference to the *text* as the "homeland of the Jew," then the story told to the family is the homeland of the Palestinian. Hassan, in an interview published in an arts and media journal (Ben-Zvi, 1999: 80) says:

Reality turned into a catch, and this catch is our fate. . . . I had only one choice left: grasp my fate and construct an order for myself. This I could do only through a mythical story. One cannot undermine a mythical story, a legend. It cannot be challenged, and I don't want anybody challenging my existence.

When asked about the rationale for telling a political story as a myth, Hassan takes us back to his childhood and, more specifically, to his mother. Mothers are the family storytellers in his and other Palestinian films (Ben-Zvi, 1999: 80) as the Nakba becomes an inseparable part of his cultural heritage:

My clearest meeting with Palestinian history as a story, a narrative, and not as a collage of isolated incidents, I owe to my mother. . . . I was six or seven years old—and my mother took us to our bedroom. She sat on the bed and we three sat in a circle around her (which is what gave me the idea for the central scene in *Ustura*, in which Umm Salim tells her story). I only remember her telling the story without any tragic note, without victimhood, but with a dramatic sense of survival. She was full of anger, a strong will, and much hope. . . . We went to bed, and for the first time in my life I felt *grown up*, not just "a big boy," but grown up, like kids think about grown ups. I understood that I live in my homeland, Palestine, that I belong; I am Palestinian, and no one can take that away from me.[18]

Here as in the other films analyzed, the story is the anchor for identity—personal and national. The story of family meets and overlaps the story of nation. The story includes secret coding: Hassan describes himself as wishing to "discover the hidden codes of Palestinian discourse" (Ben-Zvi 1999: 76) when speaking of one of his earlier films, *Istiqlal* (Israel, 1994). By discovering the codes, interiorizing them, one internalizes the identity of Palestine, of the Palestinian. The story is the secret of making sense as a person, as part of a larger unit. Narrative and myth are here seen as the "organizers of reality and of the past," what Grierson terms "the creative treatment of actuality" (cited in Rotha, 1952, p. 70). The stories of the Nijim clan and Hassan's own family history are closely related and intertwined. Hassan succeeds in relating this through engaging the social actors very intimately: As documentary theorists Anderson and Benson (1991: 151) note, "Without the participation of social actors, the documentary form known as direct or observational cinema could not exist. Without the informed consent of the subjects, the form lacks ethical integrity."

The stories that start *Ustura* and *1948* act as framing devices, offering irony, a sense of humor, a perspective from which to view. In both, it is the filmmaker who directs our attention to details. This colors the documentary material that follows, affording and dictating a Brechtian positioning for the viewer—a spectatorship that is active, in which judgments are to be made by the viewer, who is not allowed to passively consume the film.

The third film that involves Saffuriyya, Elia Suleiman's *Chronicle of a Disappearance*, is peppered through with storytelling, coming to a high point with a story *about* storytelling, told by the same writer we see talking about Saffuriyya in 1948, Taha Muhammad 'Ali. The film's stories remind one of Walter Benjamin's *Angel of History* ([1966] 1968: 257) who, looking backward over history, can see only the piles of rubble and destruction, a cacophony of massacres and privations. But the stories here go somewhat further. They seem to indicate that memory is the material of myth, and myth is the foundation of the identity of nations. Benedict Anderson has pointed out that the conditions for the growth of national narratives are traumatic: "All profound changes in consciousness, by their very nature, bring with them characteristic amnesias. Out of such oblivions, in specific historical circumstances, spring narratives" (Anderson, 1983: 204). While it is impossible to assume amnesia in the case of Palestinians living in Israel after 1948, a sort of forced *public* amnesia was experienced for a number of decades within the Palestinian community in Israel: the conditions for remembering and commemoration did not exist because Israeli rule prohibited any such activity. Only gradually, with the ending of military rule and the establishment of the Palestine Liberation Organization in 1964, and especially after the shock of the 1967 war, did a narrative begin to develop and grow to its open manifestations of the last three decades.

If the first two films discussed perform the task of unearthing evidence, making visible that which was erased and hidden by Zionist occupation, Suleiman's *Chronicle of a Disappearance* tells the actual story of a disappearance—that of Palestine as an entity. A series of stories outline the situation. A story told by a Russian Orthodox priest, with the Sea of Galilee in the background, clarifies the process of disappearance by encirclement:

> I'm encircled by giant buildings and kibbutzes. As if that's not enough, my collar's choking me. An odd bond unites me to those people, like an arranged marriage, with this lake as a wedding ring. Not long ago, those hills were deserted. At night, when I gazed at the hills from the monastery, I contemplated a particular spot, the darkest on the hills. Fear would grab me, a fear with a religious feeling, as if this black spot were the source of my faith. . . .

Then, they settled on those hills, and illuminated the whole place; that was
the end for me. I began losing faith. . . . I feared nothing any longer. Now my
world is small. . . . They have expanded their world, and mine has shrunk. There
is no longer a spot of darkness over there.[19]

The two entwined worlds, that of the priest, representing the disappearing
old pre-Nakba Palestine, and the kibbutzes, representing the growing sphere
of Zionism, are a graphic representation of the conflict. This undoubtedly is
not documentary footage but a staged scene; yet it frames the documentary
footage with which the film plays. Toward the middle of the film, the weight
of the scenes, autonomous in a true Brechtian fashion, starts adding up to
a critical mass. We begin reading the absent *other* into the collapse of realities. The absent other is Elia Suleiman, coming from exile in New York to a
double exile at home in Nazareth and ending up in a worse exile yet—that of
life in Jerusalem under occupation. Instead of finding an old and cherished
self, Suleiman is gradually and painfully disappearing—a simile of the disappearance of Palestine, and of the Palestinians. This disappearing act is everywhere—in his endless and aimless sitting by his cousin's souvenir shop, waiting, waiting . . . then not even waiting anymore; in the slowness and frailty of
his parents, who, in the last scene, fall asleep in front of the television, while
the Israeli TV channel is broadcasting the closing item of the day—the Israeli
flag waving, as the national anthem plays in the background; in the Jericho
scene, in which Elia sits alone in a Palestinian cafe on a fine evening in liberated Jericho, with a flag of Palestine beside him, in a further attempt to find
the missing Palestine; when the café lights, put on to mark the passage of day
into night, keep arcing away as he looks at the darkening town, they cause
him to appear then disappear. In a similar scene, the lights also fail in the
rooms he rented in Jerusalem. But instead of going out, they keep on blink-
ing with a will and rhythm of their own. At the end of the film, the exiled
director chooses to disappear, with a proverbial suitcase, reminiscent of the
famous poem by Mahmoud Darwish, in which home is a suitcase.

Suleiman's alter-ego in the film, the young Adan, a Palestinian woman
choosing to fight the occupation, represents, like his parents, *sumud*, adher-
ence to the land, resistance, and survival. If the struggle of the old generation is by powerful inertia, Adan chooses the active road. To fight an enemy
like hers, one must adopt some of its tactics and methods, use some of its
machinery. She thus operates through the ether, broadcasting in Hebrew to
the enemy, using a found army radio to send her messages, coded in the

nonsensical fashion so beloved by the IDF. As an ultimate weapon, she uses *Hatikvah*—the Israeli national anthem, which speaks of the hope residing in every Jew for a return to Jerusalem, read in its original sense as an anthem of the oppressed who have lost Jerusalem, who have lost the land, who have disappeared. Only this time, it is the Palestinians who hope for return and liberation. Those without means, deprived of everything, have to use the power of their oppressors in order to survive, in order not to disappear.

The Al-Aqsa *Intifada* Films

The films that have appeared since the start of the second *intifada* have built on the same principle and used similar strategies, with one crucial difference: if the films before 2000 are still treating the 1948 Nakba as the ultimate catastrophe, some of the people speaking in the recent films see the events unfolding before them as an even worse turn. In Bakri's *Jenin, Jenin* (2002) we hear the story of an old man who has followed the orders given by the IDF soldiers to vacate his house, only to be shot at close range in his hand and foot in an apparent attempt to disable him. Speaking from his hospital bed, waving his mutilated, bandaged arm, he weeps and says:

> In 1948 we tasted the same pain, but nothing like this! All that we have achieved—
> we built a house, had children—all gone in a single hour! So Bush can be really
> satisfied, him and his friend the murderer, Abu Sabra and Shatila.[20]

The mention of the Nakba in earlier films, including in Bakri's *1948*, is normally used in order to recall the greatest catastrophe of all; but in this new crisis, the residents of Jenin who, like this old man, have experienced the Nakba, realize that what they are now going through is even worse. In most of the films, memory of life after the Nakba has been one long tale of pain and suffering for the people interviewed. Nizar Hassan's *Egteyah* starts with reminding us in the opening titles, that the fourteen thousand residents of the Jenin refugee camp are actually refugees from fifty-six different towns and villages in 1948 Palestine. Some of them, like the old woman telling her story in the ruins of her home, were refugees for the second or third time, before settling in Jenin. Losing the Jenin camp epitomizes despair, a Nakba that continues for a whole lifetime, only getting worse with time. The woman, originally a resident of Zirin, a village long gone and erased by the IDF in the 1950s, has ended up in Jenin, thinking she may have some respite there. But of the intervening years she says: "Since 48 . . . I haven't had one good day, only fear and horror [. . .] Our story with the Jews is a long one. . . . Since they arrived we have lived in suffering and bitterness." The links to the now long-gone villages is evident in most stories. A man who had suffered enormously during the Jenin events in 2002 tells Hassan:

> Since my childhood I had dreamt of building a big house in my original village, Al-Ghazal near Haifa, a house with curtains, windows, chandeliers. . . . When I had money, I was forced to build it here [Jenin refugee camp] on the camp's slope. It's the highest house.

Which is, of course, why the house was taken over by the IDF, causing its residents to suffer. The stories all go back to that great catastrophe of 1948, the event after which all others seem secondary.

But if the old people had experienced some peace and quiet before the 1948 disaster, the young residents of the camp know only its dusty alleyways and rickety shacks, now all destroyed by the U.S.-made, mammoth D9 bulldozers of the IDF. A young girl, the main speaker for the camp in Bakri's *Jenin, Jenin*, amazes us with her concise logic and unfailing commitment to the camp and its inhabitants. She tells the viewer that the Israelis cannot win: that Palestinian women will bring other babies to replace the dead ones, that the camp will be rebuilt, and that she can never have peace with those who have done this to her people, her country, her camp, and her family. She notes that while the Israelis may well be able to shoot, kill and maim, destroy houses and whole neighborhoods, their deeds reek of fear rather than bravery, of weakness rather than strength. The moral fiber she instills in her story is the foundation of a redemption narrative. As Hassan has told us, being able to control your story is the fountain of strength of the dispossessed.

Storytelling as Defensive Practice:
Stories of Palestine vs. the Story of Zionism

In the period following the Oslo Accord of 1993, until the start of the second *intifada* in 2000, the main struggle between the dominance of Zionism and the emerging nationhood of Palestine passed from the arena of armed struggle to that of culture and memory. The narratives of Zionism, annulling Palestine, denying its oppression by Israel, and telling the one-sided story of Zionism as a liberation movement, decimated the space for Palestinian cultural work after decimating the physical space that was Palestine. First it conquered and subdued the physical space. Then it renamed and reassigned it, thus erasing its past, its history, its story. Fighting the injustice of such narratives has to take place in the cultural arena—not as a replacement for the arena of the physical, but as its complement.

In each of the films mentioned, characters tell stories—mostly stories of the family that are inseparable from the story of Palestine itself. These stories form the films' idiom and structure. Hence the "documents" in these documentaries are really the oral stories told. This raises the most important typological observation about the films: they deal with the story of Palestine as a strategic defensive move, a move designed to recapture ground lost to Zionism and its dominant narrative.

The narrative of Palestine in the cultural arena carved by Zionism is, first and foremost, a story of erasure, denial, and active silencing by historians and intellectuals. The first casualty was the very word Palestine itself. After 1967, when the whole of Palestine was occupied by Israel, it became *de rigueur* to replace the historical term Palestine with the nationalist and expansionist Hebrew phrase *Eretz Israel*. The use of the Hebrew phrase acted as a hidden marker of ideology. It denoted the very absence of Palestine—the country, the people, the language, and its history. The phrase provided a virtual (and false) connection between the biblical existence of the land, and its current occupation by the Israeli state. Here also we can clearly see in action the type of historical amnesia noted by Anderson for nationalisms (1983). This erasure is applied not only in the case of texts that deal with the area and its recent history, but also as a blanket term, even when nonsensical.[21] The use of the term *Eretz Israel* to replace and erase Palestine is not peculiar to the right wing of Israeli politics. It has become a test of conformity and political correctness. Similar codes embedded in Israeli public discourse are the terms used to describe the wars in the Middle East: the 1948 war is referred to only as the *War of Independence;* the 1956 war *The Sinai Offensive;* the 1967 war *The Six Day War;* 1973 is called the *Yom Kippur War;* and the invasion of Lebanon in 1982 is quaintly called *Operation Peace in the Galilee*. Any departure from such terminology is understood as a dangerous deviation, opening the door to arguments about the moral justification for any or all of those military campaigns, and ultimately, to justifications for Zionism itself.[22] The daily papers, whatever their political leanings, have accepted and adopted such terminology without question, as have the various broadcast institutions.

In the face of such thorough suppression, erasure, and socialized forget-fulness, it is not surprising that the Palestinian response seems to be centered around unearthing the story, telling it first to the Palestinians themselves, al-ways in danger of losing their story, but also to Israelis who may listen. This telling of the suppressed story is not only crucial for Palestinian identity, but may also serve as a way of bridging the aspirations of both communities, by trying to bring understanding and compassion through recognizing the other's pain.[23]

The erasure and eradication practiced by Zionism in Palestine are mul-tilayered, and affect each Palestinian on at least four distinct levels, all refer-enced in *Ustura*. The first level is that of the nation/country—the level most responsible for the production of melancholia. The second level is much less abstract and even more traumatic—that of the locale. This is the town or village occupied, destroyed, and erased from memory, as if the *self* itself was erased. The third layer is that of the family—each family in Palestine has suf-fered directly, in many ways, during and since the 1948 Nakba. The family has, in many cases, been dismantled as the basic unit of social organization—it has been disbanded, fragmented both mentally and geographically, and has lost its cohesion and efficacy. This is conveyed by the central role attributed to the family and the mother in Hassan's work (Ben-Zvi, 1999: 80). The last and most complex layer, affected by all the others, is the individual Pales-tinian—Salim, in *Ustura*, for example, or for that matter filmmaker Hassan himself—real people who have had to continue and to fight mental as well as military occupation by the forces of Zionist myth and army.

Hence the dispossession brought about by conquest is even deeper and more painful than just losing home and country. The ultimate loss is that of one's story, losing the right to tell one's own story and history. In *Ustura* we find out that this happened to Salim, who became the hero of a Hebrew short story for children about a little Arab boy. But the retelling of one's own story, which brought tears to Odysseus's eyes, is here barren and distant. In the scene with the author, Salim is so disturbed by the written (Hebrew and Zionist) version of his life story that he departs, leaving filmmaker Has-san alone with the author reading aloud. His story has been appropriated, as were his land and country before.

So Hassan, Suleiman, Bakri, and their colleagues in Palestine fight for the right to at least tell their own story, and history, in their own way. Con-ceptually and ideologically, they must operate in the interstitial space be-tween cultures: the Israeli and Palestinian, the Palestinian in Israel and the

Palestinian in the occupied territories, the Palestinian in Palestine and the Palestinian in the diaspora, Palestine and the Arab world, and Western versus Oriental discourse. This interstitial mode of production is forced and justified by the normative state of Palestinians in Israel—living on the seams of Israeli society: they always are situated between two other points, Israeli and Hebrew points, on the virtual map of Palestine. The names of their habitations are missing from the road signs, as is their language, an official language of Israel noticeable by its absence. Some of their habitations are not even midway between Israeli named places because no road leads to them, and they are not connected to the electricity grid. They are termed "unrecognized settlements" and receive no assistance from any government agency.[24] They simply do not exist, however large and populous they may be. But of course the Palestinians see this relationship in reverse. All the Jewish settlements are either built on the remains of Arab settlements or lie between such remains, however difficult to discern. When Hassan takes the family back to Saffuriyya, trying to locate the old house, all that Salim can find are some foundation stones of his birthplace. Significantly, the map he uses to draw the route of the refugees in 1948, early in the film, is a map showing the Arab names of the Palestinian habitations, totally disregarding the Hebrew names of Jewish settlements. So there are two virtual countries within the same space, two parallel universes disregarding each other yet totally bound to each other.

The deeper irony is that the victorious newcomers are also refugees, claiming this as the justification for that which cannot be justified.[25] In one scene Hassan discusses with Salim's Jewish ex-headmaster the fact that it is their homeland that the Israelis occupy. The headmaster says he has a very short answer to this accusation: "Auschwitz." Here Hassan is heard saying "cut," ending the scene abruptly. Not only are there two parallel universes superimposed on this landscape, but the powerful occupiers also project a third—that different planet of Auschwitz and the Holocaust, so that the Palestinian interstitial existence is now situated on the space between two universes of Judaism, rather than in their own country. They are also situated on another interstice—that of the space between the Jewish distant past in Palestine and their current control of it. Hassan refers to this in the interview quoted above (Ben-Zvi 1999: 80–81). The normal use of language in Israel, as well as its dominant ideology, connects both instances into a continuum, despite the two thousand years that gape between them, filled by nonexistent people whose nonexistent settlements have filled the nonexistent gap.

Recurrent Dreams, Nightmares, and Stories

The six films and their representation of trauma should remind us of Freud's question in the beginning of *Beyond the Pleasure Principle* (Freud 1920). Cathy Caruth sums up Freud's question thus: "What does it mean for the reality of war to appear in the fiction of the dream? What does it mean for life to bear witness to death? And what is the surprise that is encountered in this witness?" (Caruth 2001: 8). One can make the case that all the films discussed here are trauma agencies, the trauma-resolution social mechanisms of Palestinian society. It is hardly surprising, then, that all films are marked by trauma and melancholia. In *Ustura*, in a deserted park in Germany, the director Nizar Hassan is offered "the only fig in Germany" by Mahmud—a token of the lost *Heimat* and also a biblical token of home—"under your vine and fig tree." Yet the only fig is a barren fig—not to be eaten, never to be continued, like the exile Mahmud who has no children himself. And while he talks of his existence in Germany as merely temporary, he is destined to die in exile, under someone else's fig. In one of the film's last scenes, Hassan discovers Salim sitting high on the branches of a carob tree, the tree of his lost childhood in the convent. Sitting in the tree, he talks of his childhood with no parents, without his siblings, without his people, a childhood spent in exile within the Jewish Israeli community, away from Palestine, while in it.

In a terrifying end to Bakri's *Jenin, Jenin,* the little girl who is the main commentator throughout the film, together with the deafmute who leads Bakri though the ruins, says this of her life, whilst holding a large, twisted metal casing from an Israeli bomb which has destroyed her home and her community: "I saw dead bodies, I saw houses destroyed, I saw sights which cannot be described. . .and now, after they ruined all my dreams and hopes— I have no life left!" So the girl, who claims to have no fear of Sharon and his tanks, like another boy described in the film by his father, may not be fearful, but is frighteningly mature enough to utter such sentiments, which more than any physical damage ever could, damn the continued occupation and its inhumanity.[26] So, melancholia is not the only disturbance which mars the Palestinian social landscape. The film, and through it the little girl, who, one must assume, is *also dreaming* of what she speaks of, is a kind of psycho-social equivalent of dreaming, of dealing with the trauma encountered. The girl's repetitive return to the trauma, like that of others in the film—the deafmute man, the children playing in the devastated landscape (in this film as well as in Hassan's *Egteyah*) are all reliving moments of trauma, in a desperate search for relief, obviously unavailable, as the trauma continues and intensifies. This is true of the many people telling their stories in the other films—*1948*, *Chronicle of a Disappearance*, and *Ustura*.

Another common factor in the Palestinian films under discussion is that all six were made by Palestinians who are citizens of Israel, and hence enjoy greater freedom of movement and expression (though not equal to Israeli Jews) than that experienced by Palestinians in the Occupied Territories of Palestine. The three directors are hence sensitized to the very fracture lying at the heart of Palestinian existence since the Nakba—the division of their people into three distinct groups, and maybe even four. Edward Said has enumerated (Said 1979: 116–18) the various parts of the Palestinian nation, separated by the Nakba: The "1948" Palestinians (those who stayed and ended up as Israeli subjects), the rest living in Palestine (the West Bank and Gaza Strip), and the many others living in the Arab countries as refugees (mostly in Jordan and Lebanon). To those one needs to add the many Palestinians living in the larger diaspora that sprang out of the Nakba: the Gulf countries, Europe, North and South America, and elsewhere. If the events of 1948 brought Jews from all over the world to live in Palestine/Israel, the same events have dispersed Palestinians into a diaspora similar to that left by the Jews emigrating to Israel. One immediately is reminded of this separation forced by Israeli occupation in the many scenes in Suleiman's *Divine Intervention*, when the two protagonists, divided by the Israeli checkpoints, can meet only at the checkpoint car park, or in Hassan's *Ustura*, in the vast, green and peaceful German park strewn with *Sans Souci* sculptures, where the "only fig in Germany" is discovered by Mahmud. All the films deal with the various parts of Palestinian existence, and, in a sense, are among the most powerful means of bringing the distinct groups together to work through the collective memory of the Nakba and the atrocities that followed in its wake. The very act of making such films is an active reclaiming of Palestinian identity by the directors, an act of sharing the fate of the divided nation and community, and of bridging and combining memory.

How does one make a film about people and places that "do not exist" or whose lives have been destroyed? Whose hopes and dreams have been desecrated, their eyes exposed to taboo sights and to inhuman suffering? Memory is not enough. The foundation of *Heimat* must be fortified by story and storytelling. The place of home is now taken by narrative icons of the Nakba and the lost *Heimat*, re-created for and by film. Palestinian cinema exists in an exilic interstice—between fact and fiction, between narrative and narration, between the story and its telling, between *documentary* and *fiction*, not to mention between Israel and Palestine, and between life and death. Insofar as it parallels the existence afforded by most Palestinians, facts are not enough, these films seem to tell us. In order to create a space to live in, to bring an end to personal and political trauma and melancholia, one must employ fiction, one must play (*spiel*) in the Freudian sense—one must tell stories.

NOTES

1. Though Caruth's oeuvre in its great richness informs my analysis, I shall use one of her recent articles (Caruth 2001) to anchor my main observations about the films.

2. Not by choice, of course, but by dint of being born in the Israeli-controlled part of Palestine before 1967. Some of the films actually appear as Israeli films in various catalogues, including the website of the Israeli Film Fund. This is obviously misleading, as the proper denomination would be Palestine. I have used the current denominations, but found it useful to explain here the travesty behind such a system of definition.

3. It is important to remember that until at least the first *intifada*, the ability of Palestinians to produce films independently was almost nonexistent. Film production is one of the hallmarks of a developed, independent society. The Israeli occupation made this almost impossible for many years. Only the Oslo process in its early stages, and some important technical innovations in video production and especially post-production, made it possible for Palestinians to produce films of quality in great numbers.

4. This New Jew was a creature of a modernist grand narrative, the result of deliberate cultural identity construction, a synthetic projection denoting the very opposite of the Ghetto Jew. Hence, military and physical prowess are seen as essential for this New Jew, as essential as intellectual qualities and commercial acumen have been for the old Jew. As the Zionist project and its official (and unofficial) mythology has depended on, and has contributed to a process of controlling the land of Palestine, connections to the land and to tilling the land have also become crucial elements of this new ideological projection. If the Old Jew was landless and demilitarized, as argued by Boyarin, living and existing not on the land, but in the word, as Steiner has put it (Steiner, 1985), then the new Jew was living on and in the land, depending on his military might. The myths and realities of Zionist existence in Palestine, and later in Israel, would, it was argued by Zionist polemicists, somehow purge the New Jew not only of the shame and

humiliation of the Holocaust, but also of the whole period of living in the Di-aspora, rootless and lacking a national identity and a land base. Zionism is thus seen as a massive national therapeutic project, a social-engineering of national identity in a people which is deemed to have lost it, and must regain it.

5. I have dealt with this in detail elsewhere (Bresheeth 2001).

6. Quoted in Young (1993: 180).

7. One such forest in the center of Israel, Britannia Park, financed by the British Jews according to the plaque welcoming visitors, is actually planted over the re-mains of at least five villages, one of which is still easy to decipher as one walks through the former streets and orchards. It seems the construction of Zionist memory requires erasures of earlier memories: it is actually built on such era-sure and denial. This can be easily learnt from the 1947 Ordnance Survey maps. The detailed story of the destruction of Arab Palestine after 1948 can be found in Khalidi (1991 and 1992) or in Said (1979), among others.

8. I have dealt with this issue elsewhere (Bresheeth 2001: 25–26).

9. *Jenin, Jenin* was banned by Israeli censorship a short while after its release, and this banning was contested at the Israeli Supreme Court. This film has caused enor-mous disquiet in Israel, with the brutality of the invasion fully exposed in graphic terms, and with powerful montage. The banning followed action taken by some of the soldiers who took part in the invasion, and claimed the film has desecrated the memory of soldiers who were killed during the operation. Such banning is a most unusual act of political censorship, almost unthinkable until quite recently, and bearing witness to the deep decline in the Israeli political scene.

10. Obviously, he was not allowed to film there, and had to reconstruct it as a set elsewhere.

11. This is no longer the case—Israeli soldiers no longer allow such meetings to take place.

12. Churchill was obviously out of government by 1948, having lost the elections in 1945. Habiby uses Churchill generically, as the icon of the British Empire.

13. Also the author of *My War Diary: Lebanon, June 5-July 1, 1982* (1984). Yermiya who was a high-ranking officer in the IDF, broke his silence rather earlier than many, and exposed a number of atrocities committed by the IDF in 1948–49.

14. See Patricia Seed's analysis of "taking the key to the house" narratives in her article in Naficy (1999: 87–94).

15. Another perfect example of the fort / da model: "now you see it, now you don't"—one moment they had a home, sat down to break the fast, and then, in a moment, all was gone. The impossibility of preparing for the inevitable is the source of trauma, as Freud and Caruth remind us (Caruth 2001: 10).

16. Those are the very words used by two of the filmmakers at the start of their films!

17. Arab women keep their family names when they marry.

18. Indeed, the achievement of a widely recognized national identity despite all odds is presented as the main achievement of the Palestinian liberation movement by Rashid Khalidi (Khalidi 1997: 201–9) in the concluding chapter of his exacting work on the topic.

19. The text is quoted verbatim from the English version subtitles—it is spoken in Russian.

20. Abu Sabra and Shatila—a reference to Ariel Sharon, the one responsible for the Sabra and Shatila massacres, even according to the official commission of inquiry which forced his sacking as Minister of Defense in 1983.

21. One such recent case of replacement of the English Palestine with the Hebrew *Eretz Israel* occurred in the translation of Eric Hobsbawm's *Century of Extremes* into Hebrew, and pointed out by Yitzhak Laor in *Ha'aretz*, May 12, 2000.

22. See the discussion of naming in Rashid Khalidi's book, where he looks especially at the naming of Al-Quds/Jerusalem and Haram Al-Sharif (the Temple Mount) (Khalidi, 1997: 16).

23. This need was first pointed out by Azmi Bishara, the philosopher and political scientist turned politician, in an article on the Holocaust and the Arabs (Bishara 1995: 54–71). The importance of understanding the suffering of Jews during the Holocaust, and the importance of empathizing with such suffering, as a precondition to the demand and expectation of the same consideration offered by Israeli Jews to the Nakba, was an important departure from the more usual denial or indifference displayed by Arab intellectuals. Bishara argues for a mutual empathy that one may develop through familiarity with the story of the other as a precondition for a long-term relationship of neighborhood and equality. In a sense, what is argued here is a reversal of historical/political amnesias on both sides as a precondition for a common future.

24. There are more than one hundred of those. Many of them are settlements of Bedouins, but others also are termed and treated in this way. This is a brutal mechanism for removing people from their land, which they have settled for many generations, even centuries. There is an ongoing struggle by the communities but to date it has not been successful. One of the early innovations by Sharon when commanding the Southern Command was the use of military force, and, together with another general, Yaffeh, the setting up of the so-called "Green Patrol," supposedly there to protect the environment but in reality serving as a force against the "unrecognized settlements" of the Bedouins.

25. On the same topic, see Bresheeth (2003).

26. Again, Freud and Caruth illuminate this point—it is exactly the lack of fear and the lack of preparation (the impossibility of preparation) for what they have experienced that causes the trauma in the first place. Not being fearful does not protect from trauma, but causes it (Caruth 2001: 10).

Part Three

FAULTLINES OF MEMORY

7 The Secret Visitations of Memory

Omar Al-Qattan

> Go back where you started, or as far back as you can, examine all of it, travel your road again and tell the truth about it. Sing or shout or testify or keep it to yourself: but know whence you came.
>
> —JAMES BALDWIN[1]

There is no single Palestinian memory—rather, there are many tangled memories. A collective memory or experience is in its nature complex and elusive, constantly changing with time. It is not lived by hundreds of thousands of people together or in the same way. Thus to remember is essentially to be on your own, even if sometimes you have the illusion of sharing your memories with others. And however hard you try, telling or retelling a collective experience, even in the hands of the most eloquent poets, is always unsatisfactory. Ultimately, only a description of a crossroads will do—how it happened that your own journey crossed that of so many others.

There is surprise, anxiety, and suspicion about these coincidental encounters. There is also guilt about those who have been left behind by the passing of time, the dead and the voiceless, or about those to whom you may not have the opportunity to bequeath your stories, like the children of your exile who never learned to understand your language.

What is certain is that we cannot escape memory. When the individual narratives of pain accumulate, they become not only inescapable, but also impossible to dispel, at least for a few generations. Nowhere is this truer than in the memories of the Palestinians.

Nonetheless, if we are facing an accumulation of losses and defeats, as we certainly are, the exercise of constantly remembering can be both irritating and frustrating. It is acceptable if our memories of injustice mobilize us and give us hope and a future to look forward to, but when they don't, they become a burden, empty and hollow, and overwhelm us with a renewed bitterness.

IT TOOK HIM a long while to finally decide to go. Ever pragmatic, he had prepared a very busy schedule, in which he was to visit several development projects that he had either directly or indirectly helped to fund. He was also to be granted an honorary degree by Palestine's leading university, Birzeit, for his work as one the most prominent Palestinian philanthropists living in exile. I wondered, however, whether much of this overcharged program was but a shield against the emotional shocks that he anticipated.

My father's last stay in his birthplace, Jaffa, had been in late 1947, when he left it to study at the American University in Beirut. When the city surrendered to the Jewish Forces on May 13, 1948, he lost all contact with members of his family, and decided to return to find them. However, the military situation and the Jewish Forces' refusal to allow Palestinians to return to their towns and villages cut short his trip, and he ended up in the nearby town of Lydda, which would remain in Palestinian hands until the summer of that year. Fortunately, his mother and seven siblings had taken refuge at the house of one of his maternal uncles, who lived in Lydda. But by now, the military situation was increasingly alarming so the family decided to leave for the relative security of Amman in neighboring Jordan until the end of hostilities. It was a time when they could still hope to be able to go home.

Before its surrender, Jaffa had been one of Palestine's largest and wealthiest cities, with a population in excess of 100,000. Indeed, in the 1947 UN Partition Plan for Palestine the city had been given to the Palestinians even though it lay at the heart of the planned Jewish State. As soon as the British Government had announced its intention to pull out of Palestine, Jaffa became the scene of some of the most vicious fighting between the poorly armed Palestinian irregulars and the Hagana and, more particularly, the Irgun militias.[2] By the time Jaffa surrendered on May 13, 1948, it had become a city of ghosts, its inhabitants dwindling to a mere three or four thousand. The Hagana— which two days later would become the official Israeli army—ordered all the remaining Palestinians to assemble in one neighborhood, 'Ajami, where for

more than a year they were surrounded with barbed wire fences and forbidden to leave. Until as recently as the late 1990s, Tel Aviv Municipality would
very rarely issue a Palestinian a building permit to erect or refurbish his or
her house. To add insult to injury, only the meanest of public services were
granted to the city's Palestinians.

Jaffa soon turned into the impoverished, drug-infested prostitution capital
of Israel, its beautiful mix of Ottoman and European architecture fast wilt-
ing into a shabby and dilapidated mess. In a poem named after the city, the
Palestinian poet Rashid Husayn (1936–1977) writes:

> Chimneys of hashish spreading stupor
> Its barren streets pregnant with flies, and boredom
> And Jaffa's heart silenced with a stone
> The streets of its skies mourning the moon . . .

(HUSAYN 1968: 51)

Thousands of homes—previously owned by those the Israelis now called
"absentees"—were either confiscated by Amidar, the Israeli body in charge of
property belonging to the Palestinian refugees, and handed over to new Jewish immigrants, or simply bulldozed. The old port city was also emptied and
converted into an ugly tourist sprawl of cheap restaurants and cafés, with
large information panels telling of a mythical Jewish history of the city in
which the Arabs figure, at best, as mere passers-by.

Yet despite these efforts to eliminate the Arab character of the city, those
who stayed (and who today number more than twenty thousand) persist in
their efforts to defend Jaffa's identity and their existence in it. Despite municipal fines, they nonetheless managed to preserve some of the mosques
and churches, and a few houses and schools. When one enters Jaffa after
coming out of Tel Aviv's noisy, ugly modernity, one is surprised by the tenacious Arabness of the city and its peculiar mix of melancholy and defiant
elegance.

My father's immediate wish, on arriving there, was to go and look for the
house he had last lived in. His expression conveyed a mixture of childish ex-
citement and anxious sorrow. We were accompanied by several people from
Jaffa whom he knew either by name or through correspondence, as well as a
couple of friends who had come along for the ride. After a short discussion in
which the Jaffites tried to locate where the house would be from my father's
recollections, we set off for the Jabaliyya neighborhood where, my father explained, the house had stood near a little mosque and close to the Ayyubiyya

School (which still exists). He also remembered that in front of it there used to stand a sycamore tree.

Astonishingly, we had no sooner approached the first few streets of Jabaliyya than he immediately and without the slightest hesitation recognized the house: "This is it. I'm certain. We lived on the second floor. This is our house, where my father died. Here is the sycamore tree, here is the school, there the mosque, and that's the road which leads to the 'Shabab Beach' where we would swim. It's extraordinary. Here I am, as if I were looking at it fifty years ago. But where are the other houses? The street used to be full of houses." When we looked in the direction he was pointing to, a whole side of the street stood empty of buildings.

This is Jaffa today: patches here and patches there where once there stood houses and shops. It seemed like an old, moth-eaten but beautiful dress, patched up with black cloth, desperately clinging to its fading beauty. My father's beautiful Ottoman house, for example, had recently been bought at an "auction" by the brother of the ex-Israeli Minister of Absorption—the absorption, that is, of new Jewish immigrants to Israel. (Auctions are regularly held to sell "absentee property," though bribery and clever maneuvering by the authorities ensure that these houses are rarely sold "back" to a Palestinian).

I am not sure why my father chose that moment to speak to us of his own father's death in this house, how he had been called back from boarding school in Jerusalem to bid him farewell, how he had brought the doctor from the Municipal Hospital (which has also been razed) to examine my grandfather for the last time. On our way back to Jerusalem, where we were staying, I wondered why I had been surprised and somewhat shocked by this almost incantatory reminder of my grandfather's death. When I tried to analyze this rationally, I was soon filled with a feeling of failure and guilt. Had my father perhaps felt the same? Was it because we had both failed to secure our continuous existence on this land? Or was it something altogether more complex, where a father's death is at once a moment of terrifying loss but also the source of a new courage, and of that elated feeling that pertains to all new beginnings?

I know that every father hides secrets from his children, particularly those mixed feelings of love and anger, sympathy and resentment, pride and disappointment. Perhaps fathers do this more than mothers, or perhaps this is simply a matter of character, but I often wonder how much my own children can read my mind, how well they feel the doubts I try so hard to hide from them. There is something profoundly cruel about the nature of communication between generations, in the sense that parents must constantly try to "clean up" the confusions of their thoughts and simplify them for the benefit of their children, with the frequent result that an idea is transmitted only partially or inadequately. Something of this cruelty pertains to the transmission of memories, which in cases where loss or bereavement are involved, are even harder to transmit in anything but very partial form. From the point of view of the older generation, part of the reason why in every feeling of love or joy or pride lurk doubts and anxiety is that we have no way of ensuring that we or our memories are remembered the way we want them to be. It is an anxiety children feel when they grow up but are helpless to do much about. Indeed, it may be that with the sorrow of losing a parent there is also a sense of relief from these emotional burdens. Otherwise, I am unsure why my father became so fixated on his father's death.

Yet, as we returned from visiting the house where my grandfather died, I was filled with the old childish fear of my parents' disappearance. I remembered as a child, in Beirut, the lullaby of fear and anxiety that would finally overwhelm my resistance to sleep, the fear that anything should happen to either of them, and then the delight of morning summoning back their voices and their smiles. Now that he had spoken of his own father's death, this old fear came back again. For it is true that the sycamore is still there and that nothing will ever move the sea from its place. Yet what will remain, I asked myself, when they have both left us?

OVER THE YEARS of their long exile and dispersal, the Palestinians experienced a series of profound changes in the very nature of their society. These changes were often brutal and rapid, and led a relatively simple and poor society to become a strange mixture of individuals who are best described, I think, as deeply complex and filled with extreme contradictions. You can find in Palestine, as in exile, not only an astonishing array of achievements, but also great backwardness; refreshing, even defiant openness to the world, as well as tenacious conservatism. These contradictions have not been attenuated by the return, since the Oslo Accords, of several thousand exiled Palestinians.

My father's more precise remark during our visit was that Palestine seems to be a sad combination of generous, brave individuals and a society that so far has been unable to build modern, democratic structures for itself, where the current Authority is no more than a poor reflection of this failure. In other words, we have failed to substitute our nostalgia for a past long gone with anything more than a patchy national project.

In 1990, my father had resigned as a member of the Palestinian National Council, primarily to voice his objection to Yasir Arafat's support of the Iraqi invasion and occupation of Kuwait, not able to understand or accept how the PLO could possibly support one occupation while suffering from another. This led to an almost total rupture in his previously cordial relationship with Arafat. Nonetheless, soon after his arrival in Palestine in the spring of 1999, he received an invitation to lunch from the Palestinian president. Arafat welcomed us at his Ramallah headquarters with his usual theatrical warmth, surrounded by his entourage of guards and aides. We were then invited to eat at a very long table and joined by at least twenty of his men (there were no women), Arafat insisting, to honor my father, that I should sit next to him, although he did not address a single word to me throughout the meal.

Over lunch, the conversation was rather formal and general. It covered, naturally, the political situation and the "peace" process. As I listened, I was struck by the naïveté of Arafat's men. Two of them in particular took it upon themselves to convince us that Israel was not the powerful country the "media" claimed it was; that things, God willing, would turn out fine eventually, and that thorny questions such as the removal of Israeli settlements from the West Bank and Gaza were a minor issue that would easily be resolved. As this foolhardy analysis proceeded, I noticed Arafat's hands and was amazed at how small and white they were and how strongly they contrasted with his paternal authority. Throughout the conversation, he had remained mostly silent, too wily perhaps to agree or disagree with his over-sanguine retinue.

There was, though, something disturbing in the faces of his men: a combination of naïve goodness and nervous obsequiousness. I now realize what it was: they were all in awe of their political father, Arafat, fearing his anger yet—like a group of disgruntled adolescents—resentful and hateful of his authority.

Is the whole of Palestinian society, I wondered, a prisoner of its "father's" secretive and whimsical authority? It was a strange thought, not least because Arafat's small white hands, and his famously twitching knee, conveyed something uncertain, perhaps even feminine and youthful. Perhaps this is the nature of all power, in that it is ambiguous, arbitrary and yet essentially vulnerable. In this case, though, there was something of a heroic caricature about this president with his authority over an infantile, mildly corrupt and naïve bureaucracy governing a nonexistent state. And it is a situation that has produced one of the paradoxes of contemporary Palestinian politics, where a population that was fully aware of the shortcomings of its president, was nonetheless quick to defend him against Israeli aggression.

LATER, AFTER THE LUNCH was over, I recalled something that had happened the night before during our trip to Jaffa. A group of Jaffites had kindly invited us to tea after our walkabout near my father's house and had eagerly listened to his views on the political situation. Then, suddenly, someone interrupted this discussion and called on the man sitting next to him to give a short "performance." It transpired that this man was famous for his imitations of the voices of Arab political leaders and this was confirmed when he proceeded to "do" a Nasser, then a Sadat and then, finally, Arafat.

As this was going on, I was suddenly filled with a terrible feeling of helplessness and sorrow. It was not only that the performance was slightly embarrassing and quaint. It seemed to me, rather, that for these Jaffites who had for so long been cut off from the rest of the Arab world, this imitation game was one of their ways of maintaining contact with it. Ghosts imitating ghosts, I thought. It reminded me of a moving passage in Jean Genet's masterpiece on the Palestinians, Un Captif Amoureux,[3] where he describes a group of young commandos stationed in a camp in Jordan during the 1970 September War against the Jordanian Army. Genet sits among the group after their commander has gone to bed, having forbidden them to play poker, this "bourgeois game for bourgeois people."[4] The description of the game that ensues has the entire book's extraordinary detail and its sensual irreverence which is yet full of love and sympathy. As the game ends, Genet remembers the Japanese feast of Obon, where once a year the dead return for a short sojourn among the living who light up candles to help them find their way, treat them with courtesy and then escort them back to the world of the dead. But throughout the feast, the living exaggerate their hospitality with clumsy gestures. It is as if, remarks Genet, the living were saying: "We are alive, we laugh at our dead, they cannot even be offended and they will remain skeletons at the bottom of a hole."[5] And then, with an ingenious nonchalance, he tells us that in fact the game of cards had only existed in the commandos' "scandalously realistic movements. They had played at cards, without cards . . . and the game had reminded me that all the activities of the Palestinians resembled the Feast of

Obon where the only absentee is he who must not appear and who imposes a solemnity even on the way you can smile."[6]

The tension here is, on one level, between the absent commander and the players, but also between the dead—"who must not appear"—and the living, between the real and the illusory. Yet it is also a fitting metaphor for the tension between the past and the present in Palestinian consciousness. What has previously existed is not the same as what exists today and what may exist. This truism may seem simple and clear, but for a people dispossessed of their whole existence and now forced to build a new one, it is not. The commandos are disenchanted because "to play a game of gestures only, when through their hands should have passed kings, queens and knaves, in other words all the figures symbolizing power, gives a sense of deceit, something very close to schizophrenia. To play cards without cards, every night: a sort of dry masturbation."[7] In other words, this game, in which you engage in make-believe, where the past is immanent, but the present as it were absent, cannot carry on without the danger of madness.

SHE HAD ALWAYS described the large family home as brimming with watermelons: under the beds, in the loft, everywhere! So much so in fact that she came to hate the fruit and never touched it in her adult life. As a child, I could not understand how one could possibly dislike the sweet, juicy, thirst-quenching fruit, or resist its lovely crunch and the deep red of its center which always heralded the coming of early summer. There had been so many watermelons in the house, it seems, that her elder brothers would play at cracking them open on a pointed stone and eat their delicious cores, dispensing with the rest.

It is curious how differently we remember things. My mother's memories of her childhood, bereaved and heart-breaking as it often was, are vivid and dramatic, full of eccentric characters and delicious detail. How ironic then that she has always claimed to have a very poor memory, at least for names and dates and events. My father always teases her about it, he who never forgets anything and who has always carried a sheet of paper with notes and reminders just in case his memory should falter. Indeed, the blind and cruel aunt who brought her and her siblings up after their mother's early death from tuberculosis and their father's imprisonment by the British would thrash her severely for her lapses of memory.[8] In contrast, my father has an unerring memory, which has served him well in his long career as a businessman.

Despite this, it is my mother's memories of Palestine that are the more colorful and detailed, his more limited to specific facts and dates, even though she left at a younger age. I am not sure whether this is to do with the different ways in which men and women of their generation were brought up to think about themselves, or whether it is simply a question of character. It may also have to do with the fact that my mother's house in Tulkarem still stands today and is lived in by distant cousins of hers, and that Tulkarem remains a Palestinian town, though when we visited it together, accompanied by my aunt Rufaida, a year or so after my father's first visit to Jaffa, she too had not been back since 1948. And the experience of that visit—or should one call these journeys visitations rather, such is their ghostly character—was altogether different too.

It is almost as if the quality of light enveloping the house was warmer, more redolent with life, more contemporary, than the melancholy haze in which I remember the journey to Jaffa. The inside of my great-grandfather's old house had been modified and modernized, but even so, both my mother and her sister were alive to the place, their curiosity stirred like that of a child who is returning to her home after a long absence and decides to explore every room and every corner anew. Looking at them both, I could almost imagine them as children, standing in the sun-drenched courtyard, arguing and laughing and screaming at each other, just as they were doing now.

With the benefit of hindsight and passage of almost seven years since that visit, it seems to me now that the two separate experiences that I shared with my mother and father revealed two contrasting ways of remembering. In neither case did they accompany each other, which has always struck me as telling of the essential loneliness of these journeys, a loneliness you can perhaps share with your children, but not with your closest companion. And these two types of remembering permeate the many varied ways in which Palestine has been sung, eulogized, missed, symbolized—in other words, to use a fashionable term, the ways it has been "represented." For example, the literature about 1948 and pre-1948 was for a very long time rhetorical, political—one could perhaps call it a highly masculine response to catastrophe. Much later, particularly after the 1967 War and the recoil of Palestine even further from our reach, more personal, detailed accounts began to emerge, more "feminine" recollections if you wish, though these were by no means confined to women writers, even if I am certain that much of our oral heritage is carried by our mothers and grandmothers.

Writers like Ghassan Kanafani and Emile Habiby created vulnerable, doubting, profoundly nostalgic characters evoked through laconic and, in the latter's case, profoundly ironic narratives. In poetry too, the need to recount, to preserve in living detail the life that was lost (and that could perhaps still be retrieved) became highly popular, particularly through Mahmoud Darwish's early mixture of nostalgia, lyricism, and defiance. In the early 1980s, the cinema, that most revelatory of forms, offered up a similarly nuanced, vibrant, and sensuous narrative—indeed, cinema allowed Palestinians, particularly those in exile, to *visually* re-discover for the first time their lost homeland. And it is no wonder that the first film made by a Palestinian inside post-1948 Palestine was a portrait of two women entitled *Fertile Memory*,[9] directed by Michel Khleifi.

The central tension in this ravishing film, as in so much of our literature of that period, is between a tenacious attachment to the past and the need to militate—against the Israeli occupation of the West Bank and Gaza Strip, but also against Israel's racist abuse of its Palestinian citizens, and the oppression of our own society. There are two women in the film, an older, working-class factory worker whose central drama is her refusal to relinquish the rights to her land, even though it had been confiscated by a Kibbutz; and the younger Sahar Khalifeh, a divorced, radical and feminist novelist who is acutely conscious of the need to act for change.

In other words, the 1967 War created a new, relentless tension between what we desire to retrieve of the past and what we are able to achieve for ourselves in the present and in the future. The ramifications of this tension in the political sphere are not difficult to spot—the debates, which continue to rage today, between the "realists" who assert that we need to accept what we are able to get, even if this means giving up most of Palestine, and those who continue to cling to the right of return to all of historic Palestine, are only one expression of this tension. And I believe that they will not be resolved easily or quickly, unless of course justice is achieved. In the meantime, there is no question that our relationship to our memory is treacherous. In 1983, the great Russian film-maker Andrei Tarkovsky called nostalgia a Russian national disease.[10] The same may perhaps be said of Palestine. Sometimes it seems to me that we become prisoners of an angry, stubborn and bitter tenacity to return—to the past, to the land that has been taken away, to a sort

Figure 12 Two generations of Palestinian refugees from Jaffa in Shati' Camp, Gaza Strip. From *Going Home* (Al-'Awda). Directed by Omar Al-Qattan, 1995.

of national childhood from which none of us wishes to awaken. But the daily struggles for survival we must engage in—immediate ones in the face of an Israeli bulldozer or checkpoint, a Jordanian or Egyptian immigration officer, or a Lebanese bureaucrat refusing us permissions to work; or political ones, where we seem hardly to exist on the map of international consideration—these struggles impose a break with this embittered nostalgia.

I have noticed how in several instances of my own film work, there are discussions between the young and the old that vividly express this tension: a dying refugee in Gaza refuses to accept his son's "realism" at the onset of the Oslo Accords and tells him that he will never give up his desire to return to Jaffa[11]; a middle-aged refugee stands on the Jordanian side of the Dead Sea and tells her son: "People have been to the moon and we can't go back home?! No! Of course we will."[12] Yet all the way through these films, the continuing *contemporary* struggles reimpose themselves, pointing up the absolute necessity of reinvesting our anger, bitterness and nostalgia with a new defiance and a new vision for the future. In other words, to borrow Michel Khleifi's phrase, to make our memories fertile.

DURING OUR TRIP to Palestine, my father and I were invited to a fundrais-
ing dinner in aid of the Palestinian hospitals in East Jerusalem. I mention this
dinner because the guest speaker was Dr. Pauline Cutting, the courageous
British surgeon who braved the brutal siege of the Palestinian refugee camps
in Beirut by the Amal militia and remained in one of them from 1985 until
the end of the various sieges in 1987,[13] by which time the inhabitants of the
camps had suffered hundreds of casualties, while much of their poorly built
neighborhoods had been leveled to the ground.

Cutting rose to speak of the heroism of the people in the camps and their
immense generosity toward her. Explaining her decision to stay, she mentioned, as an example of what she described as a far greater courage than her
own, the story of a little girl whose leg had had to be amputated after she
was hit by a shell while her little brother, who had been standing next to her,
was also injured. When Cutting asked the girl one day why she never cried
when her bandage was being changed, the girl told her that if she cried, her
brother would cry too and she did not want this to happen.

This brought back, in the painful way that memories have of coalescing at
unexpected moments and revealing themselves in a new light, another trip to
the past—my own this time. A few months before our trip to Jaffa, after more
than twenty years, I had myself visited our old flat in Beirut where I had lived
as a child until the outbreak of the Lebanese Civil War.

There is nothing special about this kind of return anymore, for many have
done it, and in much worse circumstances than mine. But this visit was in a
way harsher than my father's, though I am certain that one pain can never really be compared with another. Our flat was in a four-story building near the
camps where Cutting had spent those horrific three years under siege. After
the Civil War, my parents had lent it to a Lebanese charity on condition that
the charity repair any damage done during the intervening twenty years of
our absence.

When the charity's director showed us around, I was amazed at how faithfully they had restored the flat: the door handles, the bathroom tiles, everything but the furniture of course, was the same, except for the size, which in
my child's recollection had been far bigger than it turned out to be.

We were then led down to the basement of the building. I know this well
because as children we would play hide-and-seek here and dare each other to
stay more than a few minutes in its eerie darkness. During the first months

of the Civil War in 1975, we had also spent many a night here. The charity's director explained that this had been used as a prison by the Amal militia during their siege of the camps. He paused a little, and then added that when the contractor had excavated it in order to lay a new floor, he had found not only the desperate writings of the Palestinian prisoners etched on the walls but also human remains.

EVERY PALESTINIAN MUST have asked his or her parents the same question: why did you leave? I imagine that the answer comes always in two stages: first, there are the obvious explanations, the threats, the bombs, the rumors of massacres, the death of close ones, as well as the great fear of rape, the traditional Palestinian man and woman's paramount anxiety about the loss of honor. Then, after a moment's silence, there comes the doubt as he or she examines his or her memories, which have, perhaps, begun to fade. Guilt then sets in, embarrassment, a whispering, nagging skepticism: what if I had been cowardly, what if. . . . But then, like waves on a sandy beach, the memories disappear, the questions evaporate, and life returns to its normal ebb and flow.

I too asked my parents this same question about our leaving Beirut. Of course, the answer was always simple and matter-of-fact—the Civil War made it too dangerous, though I always noticed a profound regret clouding over their eyes when they would finish answering. It always made me angry, even if I knew that it was done with the best of intentions. In fact, I am certain now that I would probably do the same if such a situation were to face my own children. Moreover, I have now come to understand that the indignity and humiliation of forced exile and loss is at the root of my parents' determination never to experience it again, and certainly not in the same way, even if they have sadly experienced it three times in their lifetimes—from Palestine, in 1948, Beirut in 1975, and finally from Kuwait in 1990 where, unlike most of the Palestinian community which had lived in Kuwait, they were at least able to return after the end of the first Gulf War.

But the image of the corpse in the basement of our Beirut home returns to me. Here is the corpse of a dead man to which I have no way of posing the thousand and one questions which I would want to ask of him. A corpse without memories, certainly not my own, but which has attached itself to me because it has crossed my journey just as it has unintentionally inhabited the space of my childhood. Who is his father, or mourning mother? What corner of Palestine had they left behind in their angry, fading memories? What was he hoping or dreaming, what hurt him most as he began to realize his end? Perhaps he died of negligence, of a minor disease, or perhaps he was shot when his jailer lost patience then felt intolerably guilty about the extermination of a body so young. I have no way of telling or retelling his story except in the refuge of my imagination, with the tools of fiction at my disposal. Whatever I write of him, it will not be a memory or a secret, but an invention born of sympathy, of an imagined love. Almost twenty years after his death, I am only capable of reinventing his faded, buried memory. Yet I am also capable of preserving the anger he must have wanted to shout as he lay dying. I am even tempted to think that he might have heard the echoes of our childish screams in the darkness. But I am uncertain.

AS WE TRAVELED along the coast while returning from our trip to Jaffa and turned east toward Jerusalem, another thing occurred to me too: an Arabic saying my father mentioned, almost casually, during his trip to Palestine: the child is his father's secret. It took me time to understand the paradoxical nature of this saying. The Arabic word for secret, *sir*, shares the same root verb with the word for joy, *surur*, conveying the sense of elation that secrets generate. But even if secrets are a source of complicit pleasure between people, they are, like memories, weighty things that we often carry around with a sense of guilt, or shame or regret. It is as if the act of inheriting, of preserving and taking pride in what is left to you, is also a heavy burden from which we somehow must liberate ourselves. If we think of this process collectively, particularly as time is passing us by and the past slipping further and further away, we need to think of memory no longer simply as assertion and testimony, but as the point of a new departure.

It is clearly impossible to return to point zero, to eliminate everything that has happened and retrieve the illusory moment of purity which every adolescent dreams of at the height of his oedipal crisis, for this would amount to no less than a vain attempt to cancel the past. But it is also impossible for any Palestinian to honestly pretend that the trauma of 1948, or of the subsequent dispossessions and forced exiles which have afflicted us and continue to do so, are no longer central to our lives. Nothing makes much sense without those memories and that history.

AUTHOR'S NOTE

This article has been translated into French by Omar al-Qattan and Sabria Yahia Cherif under the title "Les visitations secrètes de la mémoire." In *De L'Autre Côté*, no. 1 (Spring 2006): 90-103. Published by L'Union Juive pour la Paix.

NOTES

1. James Baldwin, interviewed in *The Price of the Ticket*, a film by Karen Thorse (1990).
2. The Hagana, meaning defense in Hebrew, was the largest Jewish military organization operating in Mandate Palestine and later became the Tzva Hagana le-Yisrae'l or Israel Defense Force when the State of Israel was established. The Irgun Zvai Leumi, or National Military Organization, was a right-wing group that split from the Hagana in 1939 but was later forced to disband when the State was created. A museum was later created in memory of Irgun fighters who fell attacking Jaffa. In an act as cruel as it is ironic, the museum's glass structure was built inside the shell of a destroyed Arab house in the old Jaffa neighborhood of Manshiyya. The rest of the neighborhood was razed and is now a park.
3. Genet 1986. The English translations of the original French are my own.
4. "Jeux bourgeois et de bourgeois," Genet 1986: 39.
5. "Nous sommes vivants, nous rions de nos morts, ils ne peuvent s'en offusquer, ils resteront squelettes au fond d'un trou," Ibid. 40.
6. "Le jeu de cartes, qui n'avait existé que par les gestes scandaleusement réalistes des feddayin—ils avaient joué à jouer, sans cartes ... le jeu de cartes me rappelait que toutes les activités des Palestiniens ressemblaient à la fête d'Obon où seul manquait, exigeant cette solennité—fût-elle dans le sourire—celui qui ne doit pas apparaître." Ibid. 40.
7. "car jouer avec les gestes seuls, alors que dans les mains auraient dû passer des rois, des reines, des valets, enfin toutes les figures symbolisant le pouvoir, donne le sentiment de truquer, d'approcher très près de la schizophrénie. Jouer aux cartes sans cartes, chaque nuit: une masturbation sèche." Ibid. 45.
8. My maternal grandfather, Darwish Miqdadi, was a schoolteacher and politically active nationalist. In 1924, he was fired from his job for refusing to integrate his class into the (British) Baden-Powell boy-scout system, preferring to create an alternative, Arab one. Two years later, he immigrated to Iraq to look for work. In June 1941, he was accused of taking part in the failed nationalist coup led by

the Iraqi general Rashid A'ali al-Kilani and imprisoned there until the end of the Second World War, when he was able to return to Palestine for a few precious years before his final exile in 1948.

9. Produced in 1980, the film was originally entitled *Suwar min thikrayat khasba* (*Images from Fertile Memories*), but was finally named *Athakira al-Khasba* (Fertile Memory).

10. In *Tempo di Viaggio* (1984), directed by Andrei Tarkosky and Tonino Guerra, a short film made by the director and the eminent screenwriter about the making of Tarkovsky's *Nostalguia* (1984).

11. In Al-Qattan 1995.

12. In Al-Qattan 1991.

13. See also Rosemary Sayigh's (1994) harrowing but brilliant narrative of the siege.

8 Gender of Nakba Memory

Isabelle Humphries & Laleh Khalili

"I can't say I know all this history. Others know it better. What I know, I heard
from my grandmother and mother and my aunts and mother-in-law."

— UMM KHALED[1]

If the written record of the Nakba is often the history of battles,
exile, and dispossession, painted with the broad brush of geopolitics, the "history-telling" (Portelli 1997) of Palestinian women—all those grandmothers,
mothers, aunts, and mothers-in-law—has quietly imbued generation after
generation of Palestinians with concrete, tangible, and colorful details of life
and loss in ways not always recognized or understood. The specificities of
women's memories, and the ways in which their narratives are affected and
shaped by gender relations have only in the last fifteen years been opened to
scrutiny and analysis (Hirsch and Smith 2002), and while Palestinian wom-
en's changing social and political roles and milieu have been studied, their experience and memories of the Nakba have not always been acknowledged.[2]
Nevertheless, if we are to extend and complicate memories of the Nakba
by including the multitudes of neglected and silenced voices, it is necessary
to analyze the ways in which gender relations and Nakba memories refract
through one another.

Memory is an "act of transfer" (Connerton 1989: 39), an active, ongoing,
and relational process through which meaning is created, and seemingly dis-
parate events of the past are collated as coherent and whole narratives (Giles
2002; Halbwachs 1992; Malkki 1995; Olick 1999; Popular Memory Group 1982;

Portelli 1997; Zerubavel 1995). To remember is not simply to retrieve stories and images out of the storehouse of memory, but rather to reconstruct, reinterpret, and represent events for specific audiences and in specific contexts (Hirsch and Smith 2002: 5). Furthermore, collective, cultural, or social memories "emerge out of a complex dynamic between past and present, individual and collective, public and private, recall and forgetting, power and powerlessness, history and myth, trauma and nostalgia, conscious and unconscious fears and desires" (ibid.).[3] While memory is always "the product of fragmentary personal and collective experiences" (ibid.), experience itself is not a neutral or given category (Scott 1988: 1992). As feminist scholars have shown, experience is itself a complex amalgam of the lived, the imposed, and the attributed (Riley 1988: 100) and is deeply shaped by the web of social relations that contextualize it.

What women experience is wrought in the crucible of gender, class, race, and colonialism; and women's memories—like any other—are permeated with and mediated by relations of power and domination. To understand women's memories of the Nakba, the role of gender in successive layers of remembering has to be excavated. First, relations of gender influence whether women are allowed at all to speak publicly about their memories. Rosemary Sayigh (1998b: 42) has written persuasively of how women's narratives are seldom "recognized as history, either by themselves or others." Portelli (1997: 7) similarly points to the primacy of men's "battle tales" over women's "hospital tales." Secondly, gender authorizes—or disallows—women to speak of particular topics. Thus, in the passage quoted above, Umm Khaled, an articulate woman and an eloquent history-teller, can apologetically claim that "I can't say I know all this history; others know it better." Finally, the details of women's remembered experiences, the very narrative contents of their memories, are themselves shaped by gender relations. The gendered division of labor, the sexual identities and roles of women, and their position in their complex social context all influence the particularities of women's memories. Gender relations also influence the nationalist discourse in both tacit and explicit ways, further complicating the act of remembering and the content of women's Nakba memories.

Our goal in this essay is to excavate the role of gender in Nakba memories, and to examine both *how* the Nakba is remembered by women, and *what* women remember about it. Drawing from our fieldwork among Palestinians in Israel and Lebanon, extant oral histories, and secondary sources, we argue that through an exploration of the gendered themes present in the Nakba memory, we not only come to new understandings of how Palestinian women's experience of the catastrophe may have differed from—or indeed, been similar to—the more familiar male story, but also how these very experiences and women's memories of them were imbricated by both the nationalist discourse and the same patriarchal values and practices that also shape men's lives and their memories. In this essay, we first examine the gender of remembering. We explore the ways in which women's voices are often silenced, and the extent to which women feel themselves authorized to speak about the Nakba. We then examine the recurring themes of women's Nakba memories—rape, loss of gold jewelry, and loss of families and communities—in order to show the specific foci of women's stories and the continuities and ruptures with men's memories of the Nakba.

The Gender of Remembering

While Palestinian memory as a whole has been pushed to the backstage by the Zionist narrative, Palestinian women's voices have been doubly marginalized (Hammami 2003). Sometimes, women's memories are silenced because the histories they tell destabilize and complicate established nationalist narratives (Hasso 2000; Khalili 2004a: ch. 8). Often, women are not considered reliable conduits of histories of dispossession. Rosemary Sayigh recalls a politicized teenager's claim that "my mother told us about Palestine, but she didn't know the plots" (Sayigh 1998b: 42), where the plots (mu'amarat) designated larger political forces causing the catastrophe. In the nationalist milieu, elite Palestinian voices belonging to politicians, military leaders, and those with Western education are given priority, and these voices are usually masculine. Those women who tell their histories and memories tend to belong to more affluent classes and are not typically representative of ordinary women residing in camps and villages (Sayigh 2002c).

Even within the oral history framework, where the voice of the subaltern and women is privileged, there are difficulties in gathering women's testimony. Social norms dictate that when a visitor arrives at a Palestinian home, the woman will withdraw to make coffee (Gorkin 1991: 67). Sometimes women will defer to what they claim is the better memory of their husbands, even if the men are a few years older. Others feel intimidated by and less free to talk in the presence of a tape recorder. If a researcher wants to visit a destroyed village, the chances are it will be the man who drives him/her there, as the woman has to attend to food and children in the home.[4]

Women themselves reproduce the gendering of remembrance, indicating their absence of authority to speak about certain aspects of it. In trying to explain what happened in 1948, women sometimes apologetically would say, "But you have to ask the men why this all happened."[5] Umm Mahmud similarly states that she cannot explain why the Nakba occurred:

> Me, I hardly had any idea what was happening. We didn't have a television, I couldn't read, my husband couldn't read—what did I know? I was busy with the children all the time, I didn't have time to sit and talk with people.
>
> (GORKIN AND OTHMAN 1996: 30)

Umm Mahmud emphasizes her own role as a mother and her primary concern of caring for her children as the reasons behind her supposed lack of knowledge about the events. She believes that while men could speculate about larger historical events, her immediate task was the protection and survival of the family. In recounting the division of labor as something "natural," even necessary, Umm Mahmud perpetuates ascribed and imposed gender roles, even in remembrance. In thus essentializing the experience of womanhood (see also Scott 1988; 1992), Umm Mahmud does not necessarily prioritize women's role behind that of men's. Not entirely approvingly, she later talks of her husband as taking on a passive role in the war: "He sat through most of the war with me." In fact, by taking the ascribed gender norms as given, she provides a discursive space in which she recognizes the importance of her own role in maintaining the family's health and safety in extreme circumstances, and contrasts herself to her husband who could not fulfill his ascribed role as financial provider, or as fighter and protector during the war.

Gender has been used in complicated ways to critique the Palestinian decision-making during the Nakba. Frances Hasso (2000) has shown that within some strands of nationalist Palestinian discourse, a primary cause of flight in 1948 is critically construed as the very existence of gendered definitions of honor and shame, which compelled many men to move their families away from danger. Thus, nationalism itself authorized particular manifestations of women's stories, or at least stories about women. Outside the nationalist framework, existing gender norms can also be utilized to encourage critiques of the Nakba. With the advantage of hindsight, many women reflect with bitterness that things could have been different if they had fought to remain. They often do so not as a manifestation of their nationalist credentials but in direct response to the hardships they endured in the aftermath of the Nakba. To do so, women apportion blame for the Nakba to men as the sole decision-makers:

"That's what the men decided. . . . Oh God, what a mistake! I swear, we should have stayed" (Umm Abdullah in Gorkin and Othman 1996: 107). Interestingly, gender provides the Palestinian women a critical—though not autonomous—space for examination of historical events, even if this examination ultimately ends in assignation of blame to an essentialized category of men.

The Gender of Nakba Narratives

Where women are in fact sanctioned to speak of the Nakba, recurrence of certain themes in narratives of—or about women during—the Nakba is striking and significant. These themes point to the catastrophic dispossession that the Nakba wrought in the lives of so many Palestinian women and men. But also significantly, these themes illustrate the ways in which women's re-membered *experiences* were themselves structured by gender relations. In the following sections, we examine how rape and the fear of it are remembered. We also explore women's stories about their loss of bridal jewelry as both a material and symbolic index of dispossession. We analyze the emphasis women place on the loss of communities and livelihoods, and on their domestic and family role as mothers or daughters. In doing so, we interrogate the gendered division of labor often remembered as authentic experiences of our history-tellers.

RAPE AND THE LOSS OF HONOR

In a great many narratives about the Nakba, the fear of rape of Palestinian women has played a pivotal role in articulating the catastrophe of 1948. As Benny Morris writes, the regular and irregular military forces of the Yishuv had employed rape in "several dozen cases" (Morris 2004a: 592) and the news of the rape, though subsequently silenced by both perpetrators and victims, spread as quickly as the news of massacres, aided by the fear and horror of the Palestinians and the "whispering campaign" of the Yishuv military commanders. Even for those who had not fallen victim to rape themselves, its threat precipitated flight. Morris continues: "The fear of rape . . . may in part account for the despatch (sic) of women and girls out of active or potential combat zones, and in some measure, for the headlong flight of villages and urban neighborhoods from April [1948] on" (ibid.).

Years later, for many of those who remembered the massacres at Deir Yassin (or Safsaf or a number of other villages and towns), these rapes were one of the more devastating components of Hagana assaults and perhaps the primary explanation behind the decision of many of the refugees to flee.[6] Abu Mansur, an elderly refugee in Lebanon, explained, "We had to leave Palestine, we had heard what they had done to the people of Deir Yassin, especially to their women."[7] Umm Jamal similarly remembered how horrified Palestinian women and girls were about "what could happen" to them.[8] A woman who was in her teens in 1948 recalled, "we were afraid about honor, because of Deir Yassin" (quoted in Sayigh 1998b: 46). Another woman remembered how her father had chosen to leave rather than encounter the rape of his daughters, and tried to convince his son to leave also by reminding him of "honour and his sisters" (Sayigh 1979: 87).

In Palestine, as elsewhere, men's honor was bound up with "the possession of land and the maintenance of kin women's virginity (when unmarried) or exclusive sexual availability (when married)" (Hasso 2000: 495). This notion of honor—and fears of loss thereof—silenced narratives about rape for a great many victims. In the aftermath of Deir Yassin, a British investigating officer wrote in his report that "the majority of those women [survivors of the massacre] were very shy and reluctant to relate their experiences especially in matters concerning sexual assault" (quoted in Collins and Lapierre 1972: 276fn.). Despite the use of rape as an instrument of expulsion, however, direct descriptions of the circumstances of rapes have never been incorporated into narratives of Nakba atrocities, and raped women have rarely—if ever—been named.[9] For many women and their families, having been raped meant a lifetime of shame that could hamper their chances of marriage. For example, Nafez Nazzal (1978: 95 fn.122) recounts a story about a refugee in 'Ain al-Hilwa who when asked for his daughter's hand in marriage "did not object, [but] he made it clear that his daughter was not a virgin because she had been raped by the Jews at Safsaf in 1948." Only in the context of an impending marriage, where a woman's lack of virginity could become a potential source of future conflict, could the name of rape be spoken. Where fear of rape compelled the families to leave, this fear is always named in a euphemized way. Those who left, men and women, speak of "honor" or loss thereof, of "what they did to women," and "what could happen to women," and less frequently—if ever—of rape (ightisab). Rape reflects so powerfully on men's honor that neither men nor women feel authorized to speak of it openly or directly, though it is so central to the Nakba narrative that it is alluded to almost universally.[10]

Another dimension of rape during the Nakba complicates narratives about it; perhaps even silencing memories of rape. While the rapes were certainly acts of bodily violence upon the Palestinian women's bodies and men's honors, they were also seen by nationalists as symbolic performances of Israeli superiority and domination over the Palestinian nation (Massad 1995: 471; Peteet 1991: 59; Warnock 1990: 23). In fact, *ightisab* and its derivations were often—and continue to be—used to refer to the expropriation of national territory during the Nakba.[11] For many of the male refugees, particularly those mobilized by the nationalist movement, the rapes were not only a wholesale negation of their manhood, they were also construed as assaults on their political identities. "The familiar image of the nation as a female body" (Slyomovics 1998: 200–201) is so powerfully inscribed in nationalist discourse that colonial domination and usurpation of territory is often seen by nationalists as a rape perpetrated upon this female body (Enloe 2000: ch. 4). The elision between the rape of the nation and the rape of womenfolk underwrites and strengthens the dreadfulness of each violation. Rape as a metaphor for colonialization gains a great deal of its resonance from being made personal and tangible through accounts of physical rape against women. Similarly, the rape of women is made the concern of the wider community, thus in a sense "nationalizing" women's experiences and memories of the catastrophe. In Palestinian society, the metaphorical equivalencies between land and women's sexual exclusivity, prevalent in the pre-1948 gender discourses, was thus preserved in nationalist discourse, but the relative importance of each was reversed. Where before the advent of nationalism, for many men, defending women against rape was "more important than defending their homes or showing personal bravery and defiance" (Warnock 1990: 23), thereafter, the nationalist movement chose the slogan "land before honor" (*al-ard qabl al-'ird*) to indicate the importance of the preservation of national territory at any cost.[12] Because of this prioritization within nationalist discourse, then, narratives of rape and fear of it are associated with the guilt of losing the land, once again encouraging silencing of memories of atrocities against women.

LOSS OF GOLD JEWELRY

Although rapes are one of the most extreme modes of violence obliquely remembered, other elements of Palestinian women's Nakba memories reflect the devastation of both material and social security and safety. In many of the stories we heard, refugee women spoke wistfully of bridal jewelry they had lost or had been forced to sell during their exodus. Umm Nizar told us,

When my father and his sisters heard about the Deir Yassin massacre, they decided to leave Palestine. My father told his sisters to bury their gold and jewelry under an olive tree near the house, and covered it in earth, so they wouldn't be robbed on the way to Lebanon. And he said to them—he promised to them—that they will be coming back so they can retrieve the gold. But then months went by and months went by, and they were stuck in Lebanon, and had nothing to eat and nowhere to sleep, and my aunts looked at my father and said, "That wasn't very clever. If it weren't for you, we would have our gold now!" Oof, they were really upset. Until my father died, they still blamed him for leaving the gold![13]

Others risked their lives for their jewelry. Umm Jamal, for example, spoke about how her grandmother, who had also buried her jewelry near their house, was forced to return to retrieve it in order to ensure her children would not starve in Lebanon. While attempting to dig up the gold, she was fatally shot by Israeli soldiers who considered her an infiltrator. Her fate became known to her family only decades later when they met with a cousin—now a Palestinian citizen of Israel—who had witnessed her death in her village Kabri.[14]

Because the nationalist narratives of the Nakba invariably incorporate material loss of (men's) land as a central element of the narrative, women feel authorized to speak of their equivalent loss of their jewelry. More than a few women spoke of being robbed by Hagana fighters of their jewelry (Nazzal 1974: 70). Those who did not lose their jewelry to flight or robbery were forced to sell all their valuables to support themselves in the uncertain times following the war. Sayigh (1998b: 51) recounts the story of Umm Ghassan whose husband sold all her bridal jewelry piece by piece in order to ensure the survival of the family in exile. A prominent female activist from the West Bank, who, as a result of the war was trapped in Gaza for four years, recalled how she had to sell her wedding jewelry for food, and how she found other women suffering the same predicament:

> Every day, young women, like flowers, would knock on the door. They would say, "Aunt would you buy this bracelet, take it for thirty—it would be expensive—take it for twenty, take it for ten. We need milk, we need bread for the children." That began a boiling in my heart.
>
> (SAMIHA KHALIL quoted in Kawar 1996: 9)

The loss of their bridal jewelry was a devastating blow for all these women. The jewelry is never merely decorative or aesthetic, but rather it is considered an emotional symbol of a transformative moment—marriage—in women's lives. More practically, jewelry has been an accessible and portable means of financial savings for uncertain futures (Moors 1995: ch. 5). Where men's livelihoods and source of future savings lay in the land in their possession, women's financial assets were much more mobile, thus much more liquid, and were almost entirely vested in their bridal jewelry. Furthermore, being stripped of a valuable symbol of marriage and family life brought on a great deal of guilt and loss. For women to emphasize their loss of jewelry was to stress that women had suffered material and symbolic losses comparable to those of the men in the Nakba: if the men had lost land (and the honor therein vested), women had also been divested of a crucial material good (and the values therein contained). This double loss of property often guaranteed a devastating erosion of the life-conditions of women, their being forced into jobs they considered undignified (such as house-cleaning), and an increase in their uncertainties about the future (see Moors 1995: 39–45). However, paradoxically, in those instances where the sale of bridal jewelry ensured the survival of the family, women's recounting of this narrative justifiably highlighted their proud role in reproducing the family in times of danger and uncertainty (Sayigh 1998b: 51), while simultaneously underlining the shame and regret of losing an important index of familial and community cohesiveness.

THE LOSS OF COMMUNITIES

Being stripped of symbolically rich material possessions, however, was not the only way in which Palestinian women recounted the losses of the Nakba. The breakdown of village and neighborhood community bonds, with all the support which these provided, is a recurring theme in women's stories about the Nakba. Gender practices in the Palestinian peasant community were structured in such a way that—although patrilineal kinship was crucial in organizing living arrangements—women's community networks included both their natal and marital families. This gendering of the experience of community translated into fond—and idealized—recollections of pre-1948 Arcadian life and correspondingly horrific loss of community during the Nakba.

Many of the refugees spoke of families torn asunder by hurried escapes, while others lost family members, attempting to return to their homes, to the new Israeli state's policy of killing or imprisoning "infiltrators" (Morris 1997). More than a few women were widowed in this way. Others recounted being refused water for their children, or having to beg for food from strangers, indicating the breakdown of communal support. Some remembered walking for hours from village to village and only being allowed to shelter under olive trees, "there in the fields, with no place to go" (Umm Abdullah in Gorkin and Othman 1996: 107). In remembering their losses, some idealized a utopian past where

> no one would say you are a *gharib* (stranger), no! Everyone was brothers. If I made oil, you would come and get it from me, and if I wanted to get milk from a cow for the children, then I would come to you. We lived in a natural way. The whole village was like a single family.
>
> (UMM JAMAL)[15]

Umm Jamal's recollection of idyllic village life also contains clues to the ways in which the community was structured and to the reflection of gender relations therein: while the ties of community were affirmed through women's tasks (borrowing milk for the children or oil for cooking), and although the whole of the village was "like a single family," nevertheless, everyone was like "brothers." The past thus structured by gender was retrospectively idealized because its effacement by dispossession, poverty, and privation was so abrupt and radical as to cause a profound sense of dislocation, loss and even nostalgia.

In women's memories of the Nakba, the experience of loss of community also extended to those institutions which provided a space for interaction within the community, such as schools and places of worship. Forced to flee from Haifa under night fire, Umm Muhammad's family went to the village of Sulam, south of Nazareth. Despite her father's birth and kin in the village, she felt like a stranger there, isolated and alone, the refugee town girl from Haifa. In the first days of exile, Umm Muhammad's father was given a brief opportunity by a Jewish former colleague to return one last time to their home in Haifa to collect some belongings. So Umm Muhammad's father went back to the house from which they had stumbled away in the dark. He gathered clothes and some possessions,

> and for me he brought my book, *The Little Red Hen*. I was so astonished that I had this book back in my hands. It was a library book, from the school which I loved so much. . . . In a village it was amazing to see such things, an English story book. Everyone wanted to see it. One day another child grabbed it too roughly and

tore a page. I was distraught because I knew I had to give it back [to the school library]. I went running and crying to my mother, "but I have to give it back to the school!" My mother became hysterical, "Don't you know we are never going back? Not your book, not us, nothing," she screamed. "What did you think? We have nothing left!" For the first time someone had told it to me straight. My mother had told it to me in such a brutal way, "You've finished with Haifa and the school forever."[16]

In wistfully remembering a past in which *The Little Red Hen* was an ordinary element of life rather than an anomaly, Umm Muhammad pointed to losing schools as a crucial node of community interaction. Young girls who had been able to partake of education before the Nakba found their opportunities curtailed in its immediate aftermath.[17] While young men also experienced similar privations, women's education was in many instances considered secondary to men's, and prioritized behind fulfillment of more urgent financial needs.[18]

THE LOSS OF LIVELIHOODS

The transformation in women's ability to contribute to the family economy as a result of the Nakba is also noteworthy. Palestinian *fallahin,* whether exiled in Lebanese camps or in towns in the Israeli occupied Galilee, were cut off from their land. Prior to the Nakba, women, old and young, would take an active part in the agricultural tasks of the season, often spending from dawn till dusk far from home in the fields. Some were also involved in selling their agricultural products in nearby towns and villages. Umm Abdullah recalls,

> Oh yes, my mother was some worker! On market days she'd take a basket of vegetable in each hand, fifteen kilograms each, and she'd carry a small child on her back. Down the hill she'd go when it was still pitch dark. She'd catch the "Train"—that's what we called it, in English—it went by near the streambed, and in ten minutes or so she'd be in Jerusalem. She'd spend the day there selling and then return at night with good money. She was a clever merchant, very clever.
>
> (GORKIN AND OTHMAN 1996: 108–109)

Many younger Palestinians speak of life in their ancestral villages and cities, "remembering" those elements of prelapsarian life which were central to women's lives.[19] Fruit-bearing trees and plentiful orchards, rich and sweet water sources (springs, rivers, and streams), and comfortable and beautiful homes figure heavily in the younger generations' imagining of the life lost during the Nakba (Khalili 2004b). Younger Palestinians often covet the "oranges that taste so much better than anything you can buy," "herbs we don't even know today," and "the beautiful stone houses in which we lived back there."[20] They "know" that food tasted better in that Arcadian life, that vegetables, fruits, and trees were abundant and bountiful, and that the bread that was cooked in home ovens nourished one so much more wholesomely than store-bought bread.[21] All these elements point to the role of women in history-telling, since carrying water from streams and springs was the job of women, as were making bread and tending the orchards that abutted houses and villages in Palestine (see Rogers 1989 [(1862]: 49). As Amna Sulayman tells her story of life in the village of Saffuriyya, her daughters interrupt with anecdotes about their mother from their childhood, the food she taught them to make, and the songs they used to sing. Unlike the skills of working the land, domestic tasks have continued to transfer from mother to daughter as they had been before the Nakba (Sayigh 2002c).[22] Amna believes that she has brought up her daughters the way her own mother brought her up in the now destroyed village of Saffuriyya. These retold memories and partially reproduced family practices also illuminate the crucial role women played in the family economy and the loss of livelihoods resulting from the Nakba.

In the post-Nakba world, unemployment was high, and any work available was taken by men trying to fulfill their primary role as family breadwinners. Women were relegated solely to maintaining the household. Even there, however, tasks that had been routine—such as bringing water to the house from a well or a stream—became quite complicated and exhausting. Umm Abdullah recalls that after their internal displacement in Bayt Sahur, "we had no water and were forced to go all over looking for some, and when we found any, clean or dirty, we'd take it" (Gorkin and Othman 1996: 113). No longer able to tend their orchards, or interact with others in the market, and often isolated in their home, women recall the difference between the Edenic paradise in the sun—irrespective of how physically exhausting and economically exploitative the work actually was—and a life of dispossession spent between the four walls of a dark home in crowded camps and city neighborhoods. Many women complained of depression and feelings of worthlessness trapped inside their homes. Where, once, women had been contributors to the family and community economies, exile and their loss of livelihoods circumscribed and transformed this role severely.

MOTHERHOOD AND FAMILY

A significant aspect of women's Nakba memories is their focus on the family and the domestic space of the home. Since caring for the family has been the primary role of Palestinian women, their memories of the Nakba are often inseparable from family life and their identity as daughters or mothers. In her research on Chinese women's memories of the 1950s, Gail Hershatter (2002: 68) writes that particular narratives "remain effective in memory" only to the extent that they are authorized by "local notions of female virtue, domestic arrangement, and gendered narrative practices" (Hershatter 2002: 68). Because of the "gendered division of labor whereby women would remain primarily responsible for housework or childcare" (Hasso 2000: 503), women's stories of the Nakba similarly privilege women's roles as mothers and protectors of the family. In their narratives, women mark time with the birth of children, refer to domestic routines in describing the conflict, and allow their role as mothers to authorize their narratives of the Nakba. Wrenching familial separations and losses appear with greater frequency and immediacy in their recollections.

Both before and after the Nakba, Palestinian social norms deemed that upon marriage a woman would join her husband's family household, and rarely vice versa. While undoubtedly many men suffered the pain of familial separation, gendered social patterns led specifically to a large number of women being separated from their natal family—mother, father, sisters, and brothers. Amna Sulayman was only fourteen years old when the Hagana airplanes attacked Saffuriyya. She hid in the olive groves with her family and many other villagers. After the planes left, the family set off by foot in search of a refuge. Flight was not simply proceeding to one final place of refuge, but rather a winding journey from village to village, dictated by external circumstances such as Hagana advances, the reception of the locals in the host village, or in later months, Israeli creation of military zones (Bokae'e 2003; Cohen 2003; Sayigh 1979). Passing through 'Arraba in Palestine and Bint Jubayl in southern Lebanon, the Sulayman family finally found themselves in 'Ain al-Hilwa camp, on the outskirts of Sidon. Some three years before the Nakba, aged eleven, Amna had become engaged to be married, and after the Nakba, her fiancé's family had remained in the Galilee. After two and half years in 'Ain al-Hilwa, Salah Shihada came with his father to claim his bride in Lebanon, and Amna chose to go back to the Galilee with him. In the early years, while the Lebanese–Galilee border remained fairly porous, the trip was fraught with dangers, as the Israelis fought ferociously against returning refugees. Those caught faced expulsion, detention, or even being killed as "infiltrators" (Morris 1997). Those who managed to return would also have to find some way of securing an ID card—not an easy process—issued to those Arabs allowed to stay. Now an old woman, Amna was able to meet with her natal family only a few times again in the whole of her life:

> In the early days it was possible to cross via Syria and Jordan, or Ra's al-Naqura from Lebanon. But after I married I could never go to meet with them again.[23]

Amna's story is one of thousands of tales of sisters, daughters and mothers separated on either side of the border. In Shatila refugee camp, Najwa tells the story of her mother:

> My mother succeeded in staying in her home village of Nahaf, close to Haifa, but her fiancé (my father), and his family had fled to southern Lebanon. He tried again and again to return home to my mother but he couldn't find a way. My mother had been given an Israeli identity card, but he had no papers. . . . She had to choose between staying in her village with her family, or going to join him in Lebanon and to be a refugee. After four years of hoping he would return she left her family and went alone to find her fiancé. When she crossed the border she tore up her Israeli papers. She could never go back and see her family.[24]

These two women, alongside many others, could have little or no contact with their kinfolk for the rest of their lives. In losing contact with their natal families, women lost their primary networks of personal support, modes of transmission of domestic and local knowledge and skill, and reinforcement in possible conflicts with demanding in-laws.

Women's role as mothers also influenced their memories of the past. Since motherhood was so central to their sense of time and personhood, many punctuated their narratives, dating the events by the birth of children— "It was shortly after the twins came that the war broke out. That was 1948. We had six children then" (Umm Mahmud in Gorkin and Othman 1996: 30). Umm Khaled from Abu Ghosh recalled the most frightening event of the war as giving birth to her son alone in her empty house, when everyone else was in hiding in the nearby monastery (Gorkin and Othman 1996: 173).[25]

Women's narratives showed their keen sense of responsibility for holding the family together, and women were justifiably proud if their foresight and preparation provided some measure of protection for their families. Women's protective role was due not only to social expectation, but also to the circumstances, which often led to the separation of adult men from women and children. Some men were away fighting, or seeking work, or forcibly separated from women and children. In many cases, as Israeli forces entered the villages, people were separated by religion, Christian from Muslim from Druze, but in other cases, people were divided by gender, children being sent with the women (Esmeir 2003: 42). Umm Ibrahim, newly married with a young child at the time of the Nakba, was exiled from Tiberias to Nazareth. She recalls the lengths her mother went to protect her younger brothers and sisters, among the more than five hundred refugees from Tiberias in Nazareth and the surrounding areas (Kamen 1988: 79):

> We didn't know what was happening and so we didn't bring anything with us. We got to Nazareth and saw all the other refugees and my mother did not even have a blanket to cover the children in. She pleaded and begged the British soldiers to let her go back home just to fetch some possessions.[26]

Umm Ibrahim describes that when the British officers refused to let her return, her mother crept onto an empty bus returning for more refugees, without the officials seeing her. "She hid between the back seats and was able to reach our home to get just a few blankets. And then she got the last bus out of the city to Nazareth."[27] Her mother faced unknown risks just to get blankets to warm her children. In her work in China, Hershatter (2002: 64) has drawn attention to the ways in which women emphasize "their enduring virtues [and] their important achievements" when recounting their memories. In Palestinian society, as with other societies in times of national crisis, women's ascribed role—especially in the nationalist discourse—is as the reproducer and protector of children (Bardenstein 1997; Bock and Thane [eds.] 1994; Massad 1995; Peteet 1997; Sharoni 1997). This ascription of roles shaped not only women's experience of the Nakba, but also what they considered worthy of recall with some sense of satisfaction. For Umm Mahmud, preparation was the key to safeguarding her family, and she was justifiably proud that her gathering of supplies for a siege or flight, following the news of what had happened in Deir Yassin, allowed her family to survive (Gorkin and Othman 1996: 31). While she recounted these preparatory works with pride, she was more perfunctory about the times she herself was nearly killed while performing domestic tasks, once as she did the laundry under a tree, and another time as she made bread outside (ibid.).

To illustrate the catastrophic rupture that the Nakba wrought on ordinary lives, those who remember the exodus sometimes illustrate the horror of that experience by recounting stories about women who accidentally left children behind. Umm Muhammad was nine years old at the time of the Nakba, in the third grade at school in Haifa. Her family was forced to flee when, following the withdrawal of British forces from the city on April 21, 1948, the Hagana launched a full-scale assault against the Palestinian population (Morris 1987: 73):

> We all thought somebody else was carrying my sister. . . . But no one realized that we had left the baby under the cushions. She was put there to shield her from the bullets flying through the window.[28]

The baby was remembered in time, and someone returned to fetch her from under the cushions. Similarly, in his memoir of 1948, the late Fatah leader, Abu Iyad (1981: 3–4), recalls,

> The boat [leaving Jaffa] had scarcely lifted anchor when a woman started shrieking. One of her four children wasn't on board and she implored us to put back to port to look for him. Caught under the heavy fire of the Jewish guns, we couldn't turn back without risking the lives of the several hundred people, many of them children, crushed together in the small craft. The piercing cries of the poor woman went unanswered. . . . Her nerves finally cracked and she straddled the rail, throwing herself into the sea. In an apparent effort to save her, her husband jumped in after her, it soon became clear that neither knew how to swim. The angry waves finally swallowed them up under our very eyes.

This devastating "forgetfulness" is remembered as a disruption of what is considered to be the most primary and ordinary human bond—that between mother and child. The "unnaturalness" of mothers forgetting their children is invoked not only as another example of the terror of the Nakba, but also as a symbol of the breakdown of human ties, community, and ordinary sentiments at the time of such catastrophe. In fact, Ghassan Kanafani's famous novella, Returning to Haifa, fictionalizes such an event—a mother unintentionally leaving a child behind in the melee of eviction from Haifa—as an allegory for the social losses and transformations wrought by the Nakba. Remembering this loss affirms at once the horror of the catastrophe and the enduring ways in which gender structures social roles and identities, foremost among them that of motherhood.

Conclusion

Women have had a seldom-acknowledged role as conduits of Nakba memory. Though often silenced and circumscribed by multiple dominant discourses, they have promulgated concrete narratives and details about life in Palestine and the dislocation and losses of the Nakba across generations. Their narratives, at the very least, complicate and extend better-known histories and memories about the Nakba. Highlighting recurring themes within women's Nakba narratives—rape, loss of gold jewelry, and loss of family, communities, and livelihoods—we have demonstrated the specificities of women's Nakba memories and analyzed the interplay of gender and colonialism that shape these narratives. We have explored the ways in which patriarchal or nationalist practices and discourses have authorized some narratives and silenced others.

Rape, as both brutal violation of women's bodies and as an assault on men's honor, is often invoked as a primary cause of refugee flight during the Nakba. While within the nationalist discourse, the loss of territory is often construed as "rape" of the nation, rape as the practice of violence against women's bodies is often euphemized, and stories about this violence are silenced. Few women—or indeed men—feel authorized to speak about the experience of rape in 1948, since recounting rape is inextricably linked to shame and lost honor. However, many implicitly explain their flight by referring to "what could have happened to women" had they stayed behind. Because within the nationalist discourse, fear of rape has been construed as detrimental to nationalist mobilization (Hasso 2000; Warnock 1990), recounting the fear of rape is bound up with feelings of guilt and shame about leaving the nation behind. Thus an important and devastating element of women's experiences and memories of the Nakba is often made abstract and placed in the foreground of the nationalist discourse, while its concrete details and personal horrors are pushed to the background by both relations of gender and discourses of nationalism.

Women's loss of gold jewelry, on the other hand, can be spoken about as an index of material and symbolic loss during the Nakba. Women usually bought gold jewelry with their bridal dowry, and as such, these ornaments symbolically represented home and family life, while also marking gender divisions in property ownership, where women's financial savings were often wholly vested in their bridal jewelry. Because material expropriation has been such a central and sanctioned element of Nakba narratives, women have felt authorized to speak freely of their loss of valued jewelry, or alternatively of their ability to make an active economic contribution to family survival through the sale of their most precious belongings during the period of hardship after their exile.

Finally, since in dominant gender and nationalist discourses women feature so centrally as mothers, in Palestinian women's Nakba memories, motherhood, reproduction of the family, and its care in times of danger are similarly emphasized. Because women's experiences have been shaped by the gendered division of labor, their narratives are punctuated by memories of childbirth. Those events which explicitly show women's role in protecting their families, or highlight women's fear for the survival of their families, often take center stage in women's narratives. Similarly, women's stories of dispossession highlight their loss of livelihoods, destruction of ties to their natal families, and decline of communal norms of behavior as central to the understanding of the meaning of the Nakba. Gender is inflected in remembering the Nakba in such a way that women often foreground those stories which best showcase their maternal and feminine virtues; thus, women most proudly recount their ability to protect their own children as their singular accomplishment during the catastrophe. If a story is recounted about the breakage of maternal bonds in times of hardship, it is often meant as a concrete example of the horror of an event that can even undermine "natural" ties between mother and child. Thus motherhood and communal and kinship ties are remembered in such a way as to make tangible and concretize the terrible devastation of the Nakba and the location of women as actors in the events.

Listening to women's narratives of the Nakba draws attention to the details of women's everyday experience of the catastrophe often marginalized by dominant narratives centering around male activities and memories. Nonetheless, our findings do not take us to some autonomous cultural space beyond patriarchy. On the contrary, this study shows that women's experience and reproduction of memory are shaped by the values and discourses of patriarchy—the association of women's sexual exclusivity with family honor, the differentials of property ownership, the norms and customs of marriage, and the gendered division of labor. Marked silences surrounding rape heavily underline memory-making through the lens of patriarchy. Nationalist discourses and practices further construct remembering, through silencing some narratives and authorizing others. Yet even within such constraints, women's Nakba narratives elucidate not only the multivocality of the memo-

ries of the Nakba, but also the crucial relevance of women's experiences and
their memories to our understanding of various and complex devastations
the Nakba has wrought in the lives of ordinary Palestinians.

NOTES

1. Gorkin and Othman 1996: 161.
2. A notable exception is of course the work of Rosemary Sayigh (especially 1979;
   1994; 1998b; this volume) who has long worked with and written about Palestinian
   women and their history-telling practices, including and especially with references
   to the Nakba. But also see Hammami 2003; Katz 2003. On women's changing social sphere see Kanaaneh 2002; Moors 1995; Warnock 1990; on their more overtly
   political role in the national movement see Abdo and Lentin (eds.) 2002; Antonius
   1979; Augustin (ed.) 1993; Fleischmann 2003; Jammal 1985; Najjar 1992; Peteet 1991;
   1997; Kawar 1996; Sabbagh 1998; Sharoni 1995. This list is of course partial.
3. The term collective memory is used extensively by a large number of scholars
   (Halbwachs 1992; Gedi and Elam 1996; Nora 1996; 1997; 1998; Schwartz 1982; 1991;
   Zerubavel 1995), but so are social memory (Collard 1989, Connerton 1989; Fentress and Wickham 1992; Tonkin 1992), and cultural memory (Sturken 1997).
4. For example, despite the interviews with women in the films of Michel Khleifi's
   Ma'loul Celebrates Its Destruction and Rachel Leah Jones's *500 Dunam on the Moon*,
   men are the main protagonists. For a researcher from outside the community,
   even if acutely aware of the gender dynamics, insistence on addressing the im-
   balance could be construed as inappropriate.
5. Zahra M., personal interview with Laleh Khalili, Nahr al-Barid camp, Lebanon,
   March 18, 2002.
6. On rapes in Deir Yassin and Safsaf respectively, see Collins and Lapierre 1972: 275;
   Nazzal 1978: 95.
7. Personal interview with Laleh Khalili, Burj al-Barajna camp, Lebanon, February
   12, 2002.
8. Personal interview with Laleh Khalili, Burj al-Barajna camp, Lebanon, March 4,
   2002.
9. In her account of rapes of Bosniak women by Serbs in the Balkan wars of the
   1990s, Boose (2002: 72–73) writes that the shame associated with rape which pre-
   vents speaking about it "hands the invader a useful weapon for destroying the
   invaded community and may in fact encourage him to rape."
10. Diana Allan states that during the recordings of Nakba memories in the refugee
    camps of Lebanon as part of the Nakba Memories Project, only two women

were willing to come forward and recount their memories of being raped by Yishuv fighters in 1948. In one instance, after the interview, the family of one woman approached Allan and asked that the segments of testimony having to do with the rape be struck from the record (private conversation with Allan, August 16, 2004).

11. As recently as August 2004, a banner at the entrance of Burj al-Barajna camp in Beirut commemorated May 15, 1948 as "ightisab filastin."

12. Warnock (1990: 23) defines the aversion to rape among ordinary Palestinians as the "Achilles heel of national resistance."

13. Personal interview with Laleh Khalili, Burj al-Barajna camp, Lebanon, February 5, 2002.

14. Personal interview with Laleh Khalili, Burj al-Barajna camp, Lebanon, March 4, 2002.

15. Personal interview with Laleh Khalili, Burj al-Barajna camp, Lebanon, March 4, 2002.

16. Personal interview with Isabelle Humphries, Nazareth, September 13, 2003.

17. It is worth noting that in most villages, girls were not able to go to schools as were their counterparts in the cities. Even village boys did not necessarily have 'schools,' but rather attended Qur'anic lessons (see Gorkin and Othman 1996: 110).

18. In remembering the losses of the Nakba, Abu Walid recounted how his joyous school days and exhilarating secret escapes from the school were replaced by a backbreaking job of a porter in exile as a nine-year-old, in order to help feed the family (Personal interview with Laleh Khalili, Nahr al-Barid Camp, Tripoli, Lebanon, March 19, 2002).

19. It is a trope of Palestinian memory-work that the older generations transmit their memories and stories to their children and grandchildren. In fact, institutionalized ceremonies, publications, and electronic media play an increasingly meaningful role in promulgating memories of the Nakba, as does the work of political activists –both "inside" and in the diaspora– who are engaged in memory-work.

20. The first two statements are from Fatin I., personal interview with Laleh Khalili, Burj al-Barajna camp, Lebanon, January 22, 2002. The latter quote comes from Zina S., personal interview with Laleh Khalili, Burj al-Barajna camp, Lebanon, January 17, 2002.

21. The appearance of roots, plants, trees, and seeds (not to mention land) in titles and contents of Palestinian books, stories, essays, poetry and songs is frequent and widespread. See for example *Scattered Like Seeds*, *Wild Thorns*, "The Land of Sad Oranges," '*Abbad al-Shams (Sunflowers)*; "A Land of Rock and Thyme," and

countless others. For an examination of the importance of trees in Palestinian poetry and their symbolic importance in Palestinian protests in the Occupied Territories see Bardenstein 1999: 148–57.

22. By contrast, with the forced urbanization and proletarianization of the refugees, many who hailed from villages were unable to transmit their agricultural skills to subsequent generations. In Khleifi's *Ma'loul Celebrates Its Destruction*, one woman says, "Every harvest we say to ourselves: 'In Ma'loul we'd be shaking the olive trees.' Our children don't know how to sow wheat. They would if we were still in Ma'loul. These days no one knows the wheat from the straw."

23. Personal interview with Isabelle Humphries, Saffafri neighborhood, Nazareth, March 25, 2004.

24. Personal interview with Isabelle Humphries, Shatila Camp, Beirut, April 2, 2002.

25. Also see Umm Mahmud's narrative about a woman giving birth on a boat leaving Jaffa (Sayigh 1998b: 46).

26. Personal interview with Isabelle Humphries, Nazareth, October 29, 2000.

27. Ibid.

28. Personal interview with Isabelle Humphries, Nazareth, September 13, 2003.

Figure 13 Section of a map showing Palestinian villages and cities depopulated in 1948. The total number is 672.

Memories of Conquest: Witnessing Death in Tantura

Samera Esmeir

The year of the Nakba, 1948, was a year of conquest. It was a year in which death and destruction were imposed, though not to a perfection, on what had previously existed. The year of conquest, in its inherent incompletion, was constitutive of the new sovereign state on the land of Palestine. Absent the year of conquest accompanied by destruction, Israel, or what has come to be Israel, could not have existed. Hence, the need to deny that year, to turn away from it, and the impossibility of such a denial. This denial is equally impossible because the 1948 death was not total; it left behind, in the scene of destruction, some witnesses, and later they would remember.

This essay is about some of these Palestinian witnesses, their acts of witnessing, their memories and the challenges to the memories' truth-value. It examines the testimonies of the inhabitants of the Palestinian village of Tantura, who witnessed and remembered one specific atrocity during the year of conquest: the destructive occupation of their village by Zionist forces, which was followed, or accompanied, by what Theodore Katz (1998) coined "exceptional acts of killing," and others defined as a "massacre."

The challenges to the memories about the Tantura atrocity rested on the argument that they were incoherent and contradictory. They lacked a narrative closure, and as such could not establish a historical truth. Instead of responding to the denial claims on their own terms, and arguing for the existence of a narrative closure, this essay argues for the necessity of examining the conditions under which these memories were generated. It does so in an attempt to gain a different understanding of the truth regime governing these memories, one not organized around closures, uniformity, and finality.

To understand the conditions under which these memories about Tantura were produced, an examination of their two constitutive moments is required. One is the moment of witnessing an atrocity during the year of conquest; another is becoming a witness of that moment and recalling it. These are two separate acts that take place in two distinct temporal spaces. The first takes place at the scene of the crime simultaneously with the occurrence of the event (Mona witnessed her sister being taken away by the soldiers). The second takes place immediately, or not immediately, after the occurrence of the event (Mona acted as a witness and gave a testimony as to what the soldiers did to her sister). These two moments in the past and the present, I argue, produce memories that belong neither to the past nor to the present; rather, they are memories that defy this flow of time.

The separation between past and present is central to positivist law and historiography. In them, the two moments in time, and the two acts of witnessing, are to be distinguished if an objective truth is to be produced. The witness narrating her past to the historian, or recollecting her past for the lawyer, is expected to describe her story from a distance. The time separating past and present offers this measure of distance. Although the lapse of time might generate forgetfulness, its significance lies elsewhere. The passing of time externalizes the witness in the present from the event she witnessed in the past. It allows for witnessing from outside.

Accordingly, and in addition to understanding the truth regimes governing the memories of witnesses from Tantura, this essay traces the career of these memories in both the fields of Israeli positivist law and historiography. It examines legal attempts at presenting the witnesses from Tantura as incapable of coherent or objective memory. It also probes the fate of these memories when they were incorporated into a historical narrative that failed to comprehend their truth-value about past and present. The essay concludes with a different reading of these memories. This reading connects the two moments of witnessing, of the past and the present, and investigates an alternative story emerging out of them—a story about the death of the past alive in the present.

Witnesses and Deniers

The case of Tantura involved a disputed historical account of the seizure of the Palestinian village of Tantura by Zionist forces during the 1948 war and what were called the "exceptional acts of killing" that followed the village's surrender. Theodore Katz, an Israeli Jewish graduate student in history at Haifa University, wrote a master's thesis in March 1998 about the exodus of Arabs from five Palestinian villages in 1948 (Katz 1998). The thesis received an exceptionally high grade. It was a product of microhistorical research on five Palestinian villages located on the Mediterranean coast between Haifa and Hedera, with a special focus on two villages: Umm al-Zaynat and Tantura. For the chapter on Tantura, Katz wove the stories of the Tantura refugees with those of the veterans of the Alexandaroni Brigade, the unit of the Israeli army that captured the village, and the official records he located in various Israeli archives. The testimonies included reports concerning the killing, or massacring, of the village's inhabitants by Alexandaroni fighters on the night of May 22, 1948, after the inhabitants had surrendered.

Amir Gilat, a journalist, read the thesis and published an article outlining the conclusions of the chapter on Tantura in the widely read Hebrew newspaper Ma'ariv (Gilat 2000). Gilat interviewed some of Katz's witnesses, both Tantura refugees and Alexandaroni veterans. The Palestinians talked about the massacre that took place after the occupation of the village, while the Alexandaroni fighters denied it. Gilat also solicited the opinion of several academics, some of whom praised the thesis while others dismissed it as a work of fabrication. However, what the thesis labeled as "exceptional acts of killing" after the occupation of the village were transformed in the media discussion that followed into talk about a massacre, partly drawing on the vocabulary of the Palestinian survivors and of the Israeli academics who praised the thesis.

Following the public debate about the thesis, the Alexandaroni Brigade veterans' association sued Katz for libel, seeking NIS (New Israeli Shekels) 1.1 million ($250,000) in damages (Alexandaroni Society v. Theodore Katz, 2000). Katz was understood to have argued that after the fall of Tantura and its inhabitants' surrender, Zionist soldiers entered the village, deported the women, old men, and children to the nearby village of Furaydis, killed some 200 to 250 men, and took the remaining men as prisoners. Some of the killed were executed in groups on the shore. Others were killed in a rampage unleashed by soldiers' rage at shots fired (with lethal results for one, two, or eight of them) after the village had officially surrendered. The imprisoned men were held for a year and a half. After their detention, most of them were expelled to what became the West Bank, where they were joined by their families. The other inhabitants of Tantura fled east to Syria. The Alexandaroni veterans denied killing the village's inhabitants after its surrender.

To win the case, Katz had to choose between one of two arguments in his defense: either that he had told the truth or that he had acted in good faith. The second defense argues that even if he did not speak the truth, he had no intention to libel and acted in the subjective belief that his statements were true. Five lawyers represented him. One attorney, a cousin of the defendant, argued for minimizing the political nature of the case by adopting the good-faith defense. The other lawyers wished to prove that Katz spoke the truth by bringing Palestinian witnesses to talk about the massacre. This legal strategy would have enabled them to turn the trial into a case about the denial of the Nakba. They wanted to transform the courtroom into a stage for a dramatization of historical pain and a public telling of the story of the ethnic cleansing of Palestinians[1]—a story, in their view, that the institutions of the Israeli state have suppressed.[2]

Katz was the first witness to take the stand. His testimony lasted two days. Despite the conversations that Katz had with the legal team advocating the defense that he spoke the truth, he ended up adopting the good-faith argument. Katz stated several times that all he did was present the different stories about the war. "I don't know if there was a massacre in Tantura," he insisted. After an adjournment, Ilan Pappé, an Israeli historian, was scheduled to present evidence supporting Katz's research methods. A number of Palestinian survivors of the massacre whom Katz had interviewed were due to follow Pappé. Instead, thirty-six hours before the resumption of the hearings, Katz signed an out-of-court settlement in which the Alexandaroni veterans dropped the suit in exchange for his retracting accusations that they had massacred Palestinians. The cousin-lawyer was with him, while the other lawyers were not informed of the settlement. As part of the settlement, Katz agreed to publish an apology in a half-page advertisement in two Israeli daily newspapers. The text of the apology reads as follows:

> I would like to clarify, that after re-examining the matter, it has become clear to me, beyond any doubt, that there is no basis to the argument that the Alexandaroni fighters, or any other force of the Hebraic Yishuv, conducted acts of killing

after the surrender of the village. I ask to clarify that what I have written was apparently misunderstood, as I did not mean to suggest that there was a massacre in Tantura and today I say that there was no massacre in Tantura. I believe the Alexandaroni veterans who completely denied the occurrence of a massacre. I retreat from any implicit conclusion in the thesis as to the occurrence of a massacre or the killing of people with no weapons or means of defense.

(CENSOR 2000)

Judge Drora Pilpel of the Tel Aviv District Court approved the agreement and gave it the force of a court ruling. Meanwhile, Katz decided that he had made a terrible mistake and asked the court to allow him to rescind his agreement to the settlement and his promise to publish an apology. The judge rejected his request, noting that when two mature parties reach a settlement and ask the court to give it the force of a court ruling, they are expected to understand the implications of what they are doing. Katz appealed to the Supreme Court, but his appeal was rejected.

Following the libel case, Haifa University formed a committee to investigate the accuracy of the thesis. The committee included one historian who had previously studied the 1948 war, one biographer of Saddam Hussein, and two experts in Arabic grammar and classical Islamic poetry. What brought them together was their knowledge of Arabic—a knowledge deemed necessary to understand the testimonies of the Tantura refugees. The committee reexamined the quotations whose accuracy the plaintiffs had challenged and decided that in four out of the six instances there were gross inaccuracies (Pappé 2002: 191). In June 2001, the committee published its conclusion regarding the major defects in the thesis, and in November 2001, the Council for Higher Education in Haifa University revoked the master's degree that Katz had received and requested that he write a new thesis. The university rector ordered the removal of the original thesis from the library's shelves (Pappé 2002: 194).

Legal Challenges to the Memories

The Tantura case was concluded without hearing the testimonies of the village's survivors. The court, following the settlement, did not need to decide whether or not a massacre took place, and so arguably it never issued its final verdict on the matter. Nevertheless, the legal procedures that preceded Katz's decision to reach a compromise with the plaintiffs should not be understood, I suggest, as external to Katz's decision. They indeed had a significant effect. The two-day cross-examination of Katz, as with any effective cross-examination, destroyed the witness's credibility. In addition, the cross-examination was successful not simply because the plaintiffs' lawyer was good or because Katz, as a witness, was weak. No less important were the mechanisms that Israeli law provided, within the framework of the rules of evidence, that in turn structured the interrogation.

Evidence is legally evaluated according to four criteria: relevance, admissibility, reliability, and weight. In the course of the cross-examination, the evidence provided in Katz's thesis was questioned on the basis of its admissibility or its reliability. To win the libel case, the plaintiffs' lawyer, Giora Ardinest, had to prove one or both of the following: to challenge the defense that Katz spoke the truth, he had to establish that there was no admissible or reliable evidence proving the fact of the massacre; to challenge the good-faith defense, he had to demonstrate that Katz fabricated the evidence. Ardinest employed both strategies. The first aimed at demonstrating that the testimonies of the survivors did not prove the fact of the massacre. Both the admissibility and reliability of the evidence provided by the survivors were questioned. Some witnesses were shown to have not directly witnessed the supposed massacre, some were shown to be confused, some were old and no longer capable of accurate memory, while others were shown to have a "political" interest in the case.

Once the survivors' testimonies, as recorded by Katz, were proven defective, Ardinest turned to the second strategy. He tried to establish that Katz had fabricated the evidence about the massacre by revealing a lack of congruence between Katz's thesis and the testimonies of the survivors he had tape-recorded. The plaintiffs presented six instances in which Katz misquoted or misinterpreted the witnesses' words, demanding from Katz an acknowledgment that he had led the Tantura witnesses into stating that a massacre had taken place, that he had preferred the information presented by the Palestinians over that presented by the Alexandaroni Brigade fighters,[3] and that he had chosen to ignore the testimonies of the latter that denied the massacre. My concern is with the attempts to disqualify the testimonies of the Tantura survivors rather than to disqualify Katz's academic work. I therefore focus on the first strategy of the plaintiffs, which aimed at refuting the fact of the massacre.

Hearsay and the Hearsay of the State

Ardinest opened the case by objecting to the transcripts of some of the interviews Katz had conducted, submitted to the court as appendices to Katz's affidavit, on the grounds that they constituted hearsay evidence and as such were inadmissible (court protocols: 8). Ardinest would later argue that some of the Tantura refugees that Katz interviewed, some of whom were due to testify in court, had not witnessed the exceptional killing. They heard about it from others, or learned about its occurrence in an indirect way. Such was the case with Abu Nayif's testimony, for example. Referring to the arrival of "the Zikhronites," people from the nearby Jewish settlement of Zikhron Ya'kov, he said: "We were lucky that they showed up, otherwise the soldiers would have continued" (court protocols: 17; Katz 1998: 121). However, Abu Nayif also said that he did not see the killing. Ardinest asked Katz why he had failed to mention that Abu Nayif was not an eyewitness to the killing. The reason, answered Katz, was that Abu Nayif also said that "aside from this instance, I had three other cousins who collected the bodies." "I am not asking you about what Abu Nayif heard; I am asking about what he saw," replied Ardinest (court protocols, December 13: 18).

Hearsay evidence, following the common law system, is not admissible according to the Israeli rules of evidence. A witness who did not directly experience the event about which he or she is testifying cannot assert or refute the content of that evidence. It is also commonly argued that hearsay evidence opens the door for the fabrication of facts about the event in question. Direct evidence is considered to be more reliable; there is less of a threat of it being fabricated (Yehezka'el 2001). Note that under the Rome Statute, the rules of evidence operative in the International Criminal Court do not exclude hearsay evidence or indirect evidence (Prosecutor v. Tadic 1997: para. 555). The Rome Statute follows the tradition of international criminal tribunals by allowing the admission of all relevant and necessary evidence (Schabas 2001).

Ardinest asked Katz more than once whether he had reached a conclusion as to what happened on that day. Upon his insistence that all he had done was gather the different stories as they had been shaped and reshaped during the forty-nine years that had since passed, Ardinest asked Katz whether his thesis was in fact a collection of gossip, which ignored the written documents (court protocols December 13: 36). Ardinest further suggested that contemporary newspapers, for example, which Katz included in his thesis, did not refer to a massacre in Tantura, and that should have alerted him, for how could it be that nobody reported it? (court protocols, December 14: 43).

Among other things, it was the lack of written documents that undermined Katz's argument that some exceptionally violent acts might have taken place in Tantura after its occupation. But not any written document would have sufficed. Written documents, according to the rules of evidence, also constitute hearsay. For unless the author of the document is available to testify, he or she cannot be subjected to cross-examination aimed at asserting or refuting the content of the document. State documents, however, are an exception to this rule. Article 36 of the Evidence Ordinance states that an "institutional record" of an event is admissible, provided that first, "the institution normally conducts a recording of such an event as a matter of course and soon after its occurrence"; and second, "the way in which the data is collected for the purpose of recording the event and the production of the record testify to the true content of the record." An "institutional record," according to Article 35 of the Evidence Ordinance, is a document produced by an institution during its regular activity. An "institution," according to the same article, is a "state, municipality, a business or anybody who provides a service to the public."

The power to generate evidence about the occupation of Tantura was an important factor in this case. One event can give rise to very different amounts and types of evidence. But the social and political process by which events are transformed into legally relevant information is not inscrutable (Coony 1994). Within the framework of hearsay evidence, the state is privileged twice: by allowing for the admissibility of its written documents despite their hearsay characteristics, and by being endowed with institutional capacities facilitating the very generation of documents, reports, and written accounts.

The centrality of the state in modern positive legal systems has generated considerable scholarship. But of importance here is the centrality of Israel as a Zionist state in the production of evidence about the 1948 war. Israel, in its official story, denies the very occurrence of the Nakba; it denies that it was established on the ruins of the Palestinian people and suppresses attempts to expose the oppressive realities of the 1948 war. In the declaration of the establishment of the state and in its basic laws, Israel defines itself as a Jewish state, resulting in the exclusion of some 20 percent of its population from its definition—the Palestinian citizens of the state. For Israel, Palestine, if granted any reality, is an entity that can be located in the future next to Israel, in the West

Bank and Gaza, and not one that existed on the very land of Israel before its establishment.

The establishment of Israel is not recorded by revealing the victimization of the Palestinians. It is addressed through exposing the victimization of the Jews in Europe in the Holocaust. For example, Idit Zertal argues that the State of Israel has appropriated the Holocaust and transformed it into a powerful instrument, both for the building of the nation and for negating the national aspirations of the Palestinians. Because the Holocaust threatened the existence of the Jews, any other embitterment of the lives of the Jews in Israel is haunted by the shadow of the Nazis (Zertal 2002). To account for the suffering of Palestinians during the war is to negate this project and to depict the Palestinians as victims, not as perpetrators. It follows that the absence of state documents reporting on the atrocities against the Palestinians during the 1948 war stems from the very project of the state. This absence makes it difficult to find "good" written evidence about violence against Palestinians during the war. What remain are the memories of those who survived the war.

The Lack of a Grid

Even if it is admissible, not all evidence is legally reliable. Memory-based narratives have to manifest a certain order when admitted to modern law, Israeli law in particular. Describing modern law as a Faustian-Cartesian dream of order, Seyla Benhabib calls it "transparent, precise, planned, symmetric, organized and functional." It stands in opposition to the "traditional, chaotic, unclear, lacking symmetry and overgrowing" system (Benhabib 1999). Patricia Ewick and Susan Silbey notice the historic absence of the narrative from legal scholarship as a self-conscious achievement designed to ground such work in the realm of scientific authority (Ewick and Silbey 1995). Ronen Shamir, in his discussion of the property rights of Palestinian Bedouins in Israel, extends Ewick and Silbey's argument to Israeli law and judicial discourse more generally in its treatment of the Palestinian Bedouins' narratives (Shamir, 1996). He argues that the "conceptualist framework" of modern Israeli law enables the denial of Bedouins' claims to land. It also permits judges to deny "history, culture and context to a constructed Other" (ibid: 253).

Inaccuracy, lack of order, contradictions, and absences constituted a good part of the vocabulary describing the testimonies of the Palestinian survivors as documented by Katz in his thesis. Ardinest pointed out that Abu Fahmy, "one of your central witnesses," was eighty-eight years old at the time of the interview (court protocols December 13: 9). Sabha, another witness, told an illusionary story about the occupation of the village that indicated confusion and lack of clarity. Ardinest questioned Katz's reliance on the information provided by these witnesses about the occupation of the village, when these were clearly people incapable of accurate memory.

Contradictions in the accounts of the Tantura survivors were also emphasized in Katz's cross-examination. Whereas Abu Fahmy said that he "collected" the bodies of the dead and wrote the names of ninety-five men and two women, Abu Fahmy had made other statements that did not find their way into Katz's thesis, in which Abu Fahmy denied that he witnessed the killing in Tantura. In his answer to Ardinest's questions, Katz did not attempt to extract some evidence from what seems to be a contradictory story. Instead, he emphasized the contradictions and explained their inevitability:

> I presented, as I could, descriptive quotations from the witnesses; I did not draw conclusions. I presented testimonies as they were said, after forty-nine years. Even if one disregards what [the witnesses] had gone through in that day, during the forty-nine years, they have hung around together, listened and talked to each other. I bring the outcome of what had remained with them, in their thoughts, after forty-nine years. It is impossible for me to take responsibility for the fact that at one moment he [Abu Fahmy] said that they killed, and at the other he said that they did not kill. Therefore, I present what they said, and I do not seek any conclusions.
>
> (COURT PROTOCOLS, December 13: 12)

Memory, in order to pass the requirements of law, should resemble photography. When witnesses are invited to remember, they are expected to describe accurately what happened, after which an attempt is made to counter their version of the facts. The passing of time might not affect the admissibility of memory-based evidence. But it opens up the possibility of questioning the reliability of this evidence. When the main test of the law is one of directness and disinterest, contemporary state documents are destined to be the most reliable. All other evidence is immediately faced with the charge of not being recorded, of not being distant, and of possibly being fabricated. Furthermore, contradictions, lack of order, and multiplicities become invisible when reduced to writing. Oral histories and memories, yet to be reduced to writing, are always guilty of these charges. Hence the insistence that the latter form of evidence reveal the facts, and not an interpretation or construction of them. Judge Pilpel wrote in one of the decisions delivered during the hearings:

> The thesis is supposed to establish, from a factual point of view, the historical truth as to what happened during the occupation of the village of Tantura; was there a massacre of unprotected civilians, or was there not? Facts that constitute historical truth are not interpretations. . . . At the outset, they should be posited as a factual foundation, and after the establishment of a factual foundation—one which is not controversial but a matter of writing down true events that happened in the past—is it possible to write any interpretation.
>
> The establishment of historical events, i.e. reality in our case, should be pure, true and accurate from a factual perspective—as far as one can verify these facts.
>
> (COURT DECISION, June 29, 2000: 5)

Faced with the lack of "convincing" evidence—state documents—and with law's search for factuality, Katz stated that he believed everybody whom he interviewed: the Palestinian survivors, the Alexandaroni veterans, and the documents he consulted. All he had done was gather the information, even if contradictory, and present it in his thesis. He insisted that he did not look for one single truth:

> We live in a period in which historians, in part at least, do not think that in a specific location there was one single truth, that someone can reveal it and establish its singularity. . . . This is a central constituent upon which the historiography of this thesis is based. It is called a history from a constructed story, among other things, from an oral story. As the person who gathered the different testimonies, and who, of course, was not in Tantura in 1948, it did not occur to me to write about what truly happened in Tantura. . . . Therefore, I emphasize both in the introduction and the conclusion that I have no conclusion as to this very specific question [that of the massacre].
>
> (COURT PROTOCOLS, December 13, 2000: 25, 26)

A case that for many Palestinians, and some Israelis, was meant to challenge the denial of the Nakba ended up reasserting its denial, although in a vaguer way.

Bringing Memories to a Historical Closure

In positivist historiography, as in law, memory-based testimonies are meant to establish a factual rendition of the past. This affinity between positivist law and historiography, which excludes a methodology based on understanding, emerged in the sixteenth century. Before that, history was a narrative art. The non-narrative historical work developed in the faculty of law of sixteenth-century France. The humanists set out to establish the exact meaning of the Roman text, which they argued was overlaid with an unmanageable wealth of glosses and commentaries, and this involved a detailed exegesis of the exact meaning of all technical or doubtful words contained in the texts. It was this detailed and conscious historical criticism that made its appearance in the schools of jurisprudence under the name of "grammar"—the science of the meaning and use of words (Pocock 1987).

Julian Franklin explores similar genealogical connections between law and history (Franklin 1963). He traces the sixteenth-century origins of what he calls the "methodological revolution" in the study of law and history in Europe by focusing on the works of French scholars of the later Renaissance. The break with Roman tradition, Franklin argues, came with the work of Jean Bodin, who attempted to reconstruct juristic science on the basis of "universal history" and developed a synthetic comparative method in jurisprudence. He also attempted to establish a "system of internal criticism" within the theory of history that would permit the establishment of a basis of authority for historians and historical sources that would be "independent" of value judgments. Bodin's emphasis on the "actual method of studying the past" brought with it a concern for the "theory of evidence" and accomplished a shift from the "art of writing history" to the "art of reading history."

Patrick Hutton argues that historiography in its ancient beginnings was literally immersed in collective memory, which continuously invoked the presence of the past (Hutton 1993). The trend of modern, and more emphatically postmodern, historiography has been away from reliance on the authority of received tradition. "In our time, we have come to speak of the uses rather than the influences of the past, and its moments are often little more than signatures employed to underscore our present concerns" (Hutton 1993: xxi).

The different degrees of relevance of the past in modern historiography, on the one hand, and collective memory, on the other, signify different temporalities. The temporality of modern historiography faces the future and generates a moment of rupture with the past. It is directed at new possibilities conceived out of present concerns. The second, that of memory, is grounded in the past, which is its founding moment. The past is relived in the present and does not come to an end in the present.

The interviews Katz conducted with the survivors reveal the story of history and the story of memory simultaneously. Some of Katz's questions reveal the positivist historian's conception of a linear progressive history, which separates past from present, focuses on isolated events, locates individual actors, and attempts to discover direct causal relations. The answers of the survivors point to a different conception of time, in which past and present are not separate, and in which the emphasis is not on isolatable and describable events or massacres but on the terror that governed Palestinians' lives during the war. To be sure, Katz's reliance on oral sources distinguishes him from other positivist historians in general and from the dominant historical methodology in Israeli academia. As such, his research constitutes a critical contribution to the literature on the 1948 war. But my concern here is with the ways in which Katz treated these oral testimonies. And this treatment, in order for it to be properly evaluated, needs to be divorced from Katz's political stance and ideology.

I argue that some trends in positivist historical methodology, those dealing with archival records, continued to dominate his treatment of the oral testimonies. For his chapter on Tantura, Katz conducted interviews with some forty men and women: twenty Tantura refugees and twenty Alexandaroni veterans. The research for the thesis started in 1997 and lasted for about a year. The task of collecting the testimonies from the Palestinian survivors was not easy, Katz stated. It was difficult to locate the people still alive who had been in Tantura on the night of its occupation, who remained in what would become Israel or became refugees in the occupied territories, and who were willing to speak about the war.

Some interviews with the Palestinian survivors include Katz's own statements in which he explains that he is interested in learning about the past, about something that happened some fifty years ago, and that the purpose of this learning is to generate knowledge about the past. We are not condemning anybody here, Katz assured an old Palestinian man, we are not looking to show "who was bad and who was good for this is not interesting." What is interesting, Katz elaborated, is to know what had happened so that "my child [can] know in the future about the origins of his state" (Katz's interview with Abu Nayif, February 16, 1997, transcription: 2). The emphasis in these statements was on a future made possible by the generation of historical knowledge that will allow Palestinians and Israelis to live in peace. Understanding past events will enable a process of recovery from the past and make possible a moment of rupture between past and future.

While Katz would reject claims to objectivity and the single-truth theory, he found himself in the same position of positivist historians by reiterating the distinction between past and present. The problem of objectivity in the historical sciences is more than a mere technical perplexity. For Ranke, objectivity, the "extinction of the self" as the condition of "pure vision," means historians must abstain from bestowing either praise or blame, and coupled with an attitude of perfect distance should follow the course of events as they were revealed in their documentary sources. Thus, objectivity, as noninterference and nondiscrimination, necessitates the remoteness of the past (Arendt 1968: 49). Katz sought to break with the past of the Nakba through the historicization of the violence of the 1948 war. His interviews with the survivors are patently skewed toward the identification of individual authors of violence, which entails, as Allen Feldman puts it, "a prosecutional focus on an 'event history'—linear chronologies of acts and actors—who did what to who, when and why" (Feldman 1999).

Events stood at the center of Katz's investigation. The survivors were not usually invited to talk about the structure of emergency and of terror during the 1948 war. This is not to say that the interviewed did not seize the opportunity to talk about larger processes, about life before the war and in its aftermath. The most common question asked by Katz was: "Now, if you can please tell me what you remember from the night during which Tantura was occupied?" His subsequent questions would focus on the exact hour when the village was attacked by the Zionist forces, when the forces entered the village, and the different locations to which they took the women and the children, on the one hand, and the men, on the other. Katz would also ask about whether they knew of an organized killing. What did you see? How many men stood in line? Who shot at them? Where were they standing? Where were the women and the children? When did the killing take place? How did they decide on the men to be killed? Many questions were directed at remembering who the executors were. How many were there? And where did the rest of the Zionist forces stand? Katz, in short, attempted to retrieve all possible details that could enable him to present a picture of the past that was as accurate as possible, for otherwise, he could not refute the official Zionist narrative that denies the bloody ethnic cleansing of Palestinians.

The event-centered historiography also led Katz to articulate a difference between legitimate and illegitimate violence. Faced with some of the survivors' "failure" to remember the exact details of the exceptional acts of killing, in which dozens of men were ordered to stand in line and were systematically shot down, and their continual reference to other forms of killing that accompanied the occupation of their village, Katz pleaded with a number of survivors to remember the specific incident of the organized killing following the surrender of the village. In every war, he said, there are killings and people die. But what is inconceivable is that after people have surrendered, the killing continues. Hence, the unique importance of the exceptional organized killing as opposed to other forms of killing.

But Katz's thesis is not about the organized massacre in Tantura. The killing in Tantura constitutes one part of a whole chapter devoted more generally to the occupation of the village and its depopulation (Pappé 2002: 191).[4] Additionally, the other chapters of his thesis discuss the depopulation of other Palestinian villages during the 1948 war. Katz, thus, situated the exceptional activity in Tantura in the general context of the depopulation and uprooting of these Palestinian villages. However, recognizing the connection between the state of exception and the general structure of war should have consequences for the ways in which we treat the testimonies about the exception. The latter stops being a pure exceptionality standing apart from the general rule. Rather, its existence as an exception is made possible by the general rule (Fitzpatrick 2001; Agamben 1998).[5] Because the exception is rooted in the general rule, the testimonies about it, especially the testimonies of those who experienced it, will also address it as part of the general rule and as indistinguishable from it.

Open-Ended Memories

In the courtroom, Katz was asked why, to his mind, the Tantura refugees were silent for so long. Katz enumerated several reasons. The military rule under which the Palestinian population lived in Israel prevented people not only from moving from one place to another but also from knowing whether they were allowed to speak. This fear continues to dominate the refugees up until today, added Katz. Additionally, people chose to be silent in order to survive in Israel, and they conceived of their silence as a condition for achieving equality in Israel. Silence also functioned to preserve their dignity after their defeat and the sudden transition from being a majority to becoming a minority. Finally, the traumatic events led people to suppress their memories. The massacres in Deir Yassin, another well-known case from 1948, and Kafr Qasim were remembered only because there were immediate reports about the killings that made covering up the events impossible (court protocols: 47, 48).

These motivations, according to Katz, explain the silence of the survivors until the moment when he "revealed" what happened in Tantura. The reasons, however, were not understood by him to structure the memories of the survivors—they remained external to their memories, resulting in either the absence of a narrative or in a contradictory narrative. Katz did not attempt to understand what this silence and these contradictions stood for; he simply pointed to them and based on them his inability to reach final conclusions. The possibility of understanding these contradictions and silences and revealing the evidence already embedded in them was not entertained.

The original "defect" was therefore in the tellers, not the tale, according to Katz. He did not question the tale as such, as other deniers have done; he questioned the ability of the tellers to fully remember. But what if the identity of the teller is given in the articulation of the tale? What if the witness cannot stand outside the tale and assume the role of a teller? What if the tale about the year of conquest has to be told by those who were conquered—the characters of the year of conquest?

Everything was conquered during the year of conquest: land, nature, political projects, social bonds, communities, subjectivities. Together with these, thought was conquered as well, as everything that gave rise to it was occupied. No one could, during the year of conquest, escape the spell of imposed destruction and change. Yes there were villages that were not depopulated; there were Palestinians who did not become refugees. But the majority did. And because individuals and communities did not exist in separation, their destinies overshadowed one another.

What was more radical about that year was that the conqueror assumed an integral role in Palestinians' lives. Soon after the war, the external conquering forces would settle inside Palestinians permanently; they would cease to be external. The war was put to an end, but the conqueror stayed, preventing any attempt at returning some of what had been taken away.

Two constitutive moments, therefore, require some attention when probing an understanding of the conditions under which the memories about Tantura were produced. One is the moment of experiencing/witnessing an atrocity during the year of conquest; another is becoming a witness of that moment and recalling it in its aftermath. These two moments, I suggest, are central for understanding the truth-value of these memories. In the two sections that follow I describe these two moments of witnessing in an attempt to shed light on the memories produced out of them.

Witnessing the Conquest of Tantura

Throughout the interviews, the witnesses had concrete stories to tell about the war, the village, the entry of the Zionist soldiers, the attempts to defend the village, the losses, the killing, the displacement, and the humiliation. One spoke about his uncle who witnessed the killing of his son while attempting to bring him from one of the positions occupied by men from Tantura in order to protect the village against the Zionist invasion.

Riziq, born in 1935, spoke about the many men who lay dead on the streets of Tantura. He described how the bodies were collected: "They took thirty to forty men from the village. They started collecting all the people who died in the village. Where to put them? Can you imagine? They took a cart, they took a cart. Three or four people were pushing the cart and bringing it full, the cart. A cart with horses and four wheels. Where did they throw them? In the cemetery . . . where all the people were sitting, in front of their eyes" (Katz's interview with Riziq, March 9, 1997, transcription: 4).

Riziq explained that one soldier took him to collect bread for the children who gathered on the shore (ibid: 10). On his way, he saw the killing of a woman who was trying to protect her son. "Returning to the shore, I saw those who were killed . . . we passed them . . . a bit farther we saw another group, killed. The same thing . . . maybe fifty, maybe fifty, forty something like this . . . the same thing. Not far from them, maybe fifty meters. Then they took us to a place next to the cemetery. They searched us. You cannot have a watch, you cannot have money, you cannot have clothes. Then they started to clean [us out] . . . and this is how we left, empty. . . . they put us in the cemetery and told us that trucks would come to pick us up. Where would they take us? We did not know where they would take us. . . . They took us, the children and the elderly, to Furaydis" (ibid: 11–12).

Abu Fahmy said that he was asked by the soldiers to collect the bodies from the streets. They gave him two carts and ten men to assist him. They asked him to write the names of those who were killed. Abu Fahmy wrote the names of ninety-five men and two women. The soldiers also asked Abu Fahmy to dig a grave for the dead. Abu Fahmy added that later on they joined the people of the village, who were taken to Zikhron-Ya'kov and from there to the prison.

Rashida told another story of an old man killed by a Zionist soldier. She saw the killing of her uncle when she and the other women and children who remained in the village after its capture were forced to gather on the shore. We could do nothing to help him, she recalled. As for her husband, Rashida insisted that he did not flee to Syria. He stayed because "we are the children of this country, the owners of the land" (Katz's interview with Rashida, March 11, 1997, transcription: 5). Rashida explained that she knows her husband was killed, although she did not see the killing. He was taken with the rest of the men, and the women were taken in another direction. On their way, she saw that they started killing the men.

Sabha, whose nine-month-old child died during the war, talked about her heroic efforts to bring food and water to the children gathered together with the women on the shore and how she stood up to the soldiers who acted against others. There was a guard, she recalled, who stood next to the women and the children. He had a weapon and he fired it. "All the women started to scream. I went to him. I said to him, 'Why are you doing this?' I grabbed him and slapped him. . . . I told him:' Your role is to be a guard,' and said in Hebrew 'Why are you terrifying the children like this?'" (Katz's interview with Sabha, May 10, 1997, transcription: 15).

Anis and Nimr, who were not from Tantura, tried to explain the occupation and the killing of Palestinians. Nimr blamed the inhabitants for refusing to surrender (Katz's interview with Nimr, March 13, 1997, transcription: 4). Anis explained how he delivered a message to the head of the local council asking that Tantura inhabitants relinquish their weapons (Katz's Interview with Anis, March 13, 1997, transcription: 6). Zuhdi also explained that it was the Arabs' fault for under-estimating the power of the Jews in Palestine (Katz's interview with Zuhdi, April 5, 1997, transcription: 2).

Some survivors had stories to tell about good Zionist soldiers who helped them to bring water and food to the children on the shore. Riziq mentioned a soldier who saved the life of his mother. His mother could not walk and when they asked for help from the soldiers, one soldier wanted to kill her. Another soldier came to their aid and prevented the killing (Katz's interview with Riziq, March 9, 1997, transcription: 18).

Most of the survivors insisted on explaining the role that the Jewish settlers from Zikhron-Ya'kov played in stopping the killing in Tantura. The integrity of the Zikhronites was repeatedly affirmed, contrasted with the conduct of the soldiers. They were the ones who saved the survivors. Without them, Muhammad Zaydan insisted, men, women, and children would have been killed (Katz's interview with Muhammad Zaydan, January 8, 1998, transcription: 7).

Not all witnesses could talk definitely about the organized massacre in which men were ordered to stand in line and were then systematically shot. Some could, some could not. Ahmad talked about the massacring of twenty to thirty men who were made to line up and were then shot. He also spoke about the killing of a woman who tried to save her son. Sabha talked about the women and children gathered on the shore. From their location, they could see the killing of the men, who were ordered to stand in line and were shot systematically. Others presented similar accounts about the systematic killing. Zuhdi explained that a Jewish man named Shimshon read out the names of the armed men of Tantura, and these men were taken to their homes by soldiers. The men found to have weapons in their houses either never returned or were gathered and shot dead. Muhammad said that all the men who were armed, and who were taken by the soldiers, never returned. Only his father returned because he could prove to the soldier that his weapon was useless. Muhammad Zaydan spoke of the gathering of groups of twenty, forty, or fifty men at a time next to the wall and their killing. He said that only ten people were killed during the occupation of the village, the rest were systematically shot. Anis recollected that there was a man who covered his face and pointed to some people who were in turn later shot. Twenty-seven men, according to Zaydan, were killed. They had a list of the armed Tantura men, according to which they chose the men to be killed. Among those who could remember, there was no agreement as to the number of the massacred. Numbers, like the accounts, varied.

Various accounts and different concrete stories are the outcome of the impossibility of assuming one subject-position during the occupation of Tantura. The survivors of the conquest of Tantura did not stand outside the event and could not have described it from one vantage point. They were active participants in these events. The disaster that visited the village on the night of occupation in May 1948 touched all the village's inhabitants. The concrete different stories stand for the various ways in which Tantura's inhabitants experienced the conquest of the village. While some of the survivors were spared physical death, either during the invasion stage or during the deadly events that followed, all of them experienced the reality of conquest, all of them experienced the death of others. For this death of others was more than the physical death of a friend or a family member. It brought with it an end to singular relationships that once existed between survivors and deceased. The concrete and various accounts constitute a map with the help of which one is able to read the overreaching effects of the occupation of Tantura, of the Nakba.

The Lasting Conquest of Witnesses

As mentioned above, Katz numerated a few reasons for the "failure" of memories, and for their inadequacy to constitute a narrative fit for positivist historiography. I would like to suggest a different reason why these memories are unwelcome in positivist historical and legal regimes of truth. Death and absence are what render the memories of survivors' narratives unable to fit the linear model of historical time. Death is not simply something that occurs in the past and can be forgotten, or remembered, in the present. Death generates present absence and non-existence. It is something that lives on with its survivors. By death, I do not simply mean physical death, but the death of human relationships, the death of societal bonds, the death of meaning, the death of commonalities—in short, the death of humanity conceived of in concrete terms.

Some of Tantura's inhabitants were massacred, but many of them were also killed during the war, and the majority of them did not stay in what would become Israel and were not allowed to return. Friends were separated and families were torn apart. The village was destroyed and the site of memories disappeared. To understand survivors' memories of the massacre, of this very specific incident of death, one has to understand the partial death of human relationships that Palestinian society was subjected to following the 1948 war and the establishment of the State of Israel.

It is this death, this absence that does not dissipate, that structures the survivors' ability to remember the tragedy of 1948. The word survivor also becomes problematic because it implies a linear temporality in which the moment of surviving is to follow the moment of death. Instead, I suggest using the word survival to mean a continuous process. The remaining inhabitants of Tantura are still surviving every day, so they endure the impossibility of a moment of therapeutic recovery.

The Nakba, resulting in the death of human relationships, structured its lived aftermath, and its effects can never be overcome in the therapeutic sense. David Lloyd makes a similar point about the postcolonial condition and argues that a nontherapeutic relation to the past, structured around the notion of survival or living-on rather than recovery, is what should guide our critique of modernity and ground a different mode of historicization (Lloyd 2000).

Maurice Halbwachs argues that it is the individual as a member of the group who remembers (Halbwachs 1980). Dreams, thus, are different from all other memories, for they lack organization; in them all other human actors who characterize other aspects of waking life are absent. The life of reason, of consciousness and self-consciousness, can be rooted only in waking existence, which is in all cases firmly anchored in the collaboration of other human beings in the group life. Human dignity, human stature, and human distinctiveness can emerge only in the presence of other human beings.

Survivors of the death of human relations are thus capable of a very specific form of memory. They might not be able to tell a unified story with regard to what happened. To be able to tell these stories, one needs others with whom one will be able to piece together a story, to recollect, to be reminded, to think collectively and socially. When society disappears, when family members are absent, memories fall short of the requirements of law and history. If Palestinians had been allowed to preserve their society and their villages, the stories they would be able to tell today would have different dimensions. A woman could talk to her neighbor (who is now a refugee in Syria) while walking in Tantura, facilitating recollection. One part of the story would explain the other, and Sabha could remind Amina of what she had suppressed and forgotten. The absence of a community, but also of institutions to support this endeavor, is an obstacle in the face of memory itself.

But if history and law were concerned with understanding as opposed to establishing facts, these memories would become "admissible." Memories of death would be understood on their terms—not as fragments of a story, but as narratives that were structured under the conditions they are expected to describe. Incoherence, contradictions, and absences should then be understood as signifiers of something that is still present—the death of human relationships, the ethnic cleansing of Palestinians, and the destruction of an entire society. This entails a different reading of the testimonies—a reading that would try to understand the tragedy of a society in the absences and gaps.

The catastrophe, the Nakba, the year of conquest, was a year of death. But it did not destroy the possibility of Tantura's inhabitants remembering it. It rather generated memories that should be understood under the conditions they were produced—between past and present, between death and life. The year of conquest was overreaching, but its survivors lived on out of death. Their memories, as articulated by the silences, the multiple experiences, the various perspectives, are all indicators of the historical, of that which took place. And if the disaster is the erasure of frame and meaning (Blanchot

1995), if the Nakba brought about the death of commonalities and human relationships, then the memories of the Tantura survivors stand in a striking resistance to this disaster. They manifest a will not to be consumed by it. It is, therefore, in the strength of the Tantura inhabitants to recall a disaster, and not to collapse into it, that living on can be located.

Author's Note:

An earlier version of this chapter was published as "1948: Law, History, Memory" *Social Text* 75, vol. 21, no. 2 (Summer 2003): 25–48.

NOTES

1. For historical scholarship on the 1948 war, see Flapan (1987), Khalidi (1992); Masalha (1992); Rogan and Shlaim, (2001), Morris (1988); Morris (2004a [1987]); Sanbar (1984), Tamari (1999). Note that the Hebrew edition of Morris' 1987 book includes sharper conclusions as to the ethnic cleansing of Palestine.

2. I learned about the expected strategies of the Katz team from conversations with some of the lawyers.

3. An example of such a case is one Katz mentions on page 151 of his thesis—there was one Yemenite, Rahamim Levi from Zikhron Ya'kov, who was especially cruel to the Tanturites. Katz relied on one Tanturite for this information. Katz searched for Rahamim Levi, who denied that he was ever in Tantura, though Katz writes that the Zikhronites told him "not to take what he [Rahamim Levi] has to say at face value" (Katz 1998: 151).

4. Writing about the Katz and Tantura affairs, Ilan Pappé (2002) releases himself from the burden of the archives as a point of reference and argues that the testimonies of the survivors should be read in conjunction with the state archives. Both, according to Pappé, are misinterpretations of a given reality, and they offer the historian a considerable space to extract meanings from them. On the basis of this methodology, Pappé is able to establish that there was a massacre in Tantura. The massacre was conducted in two stages: the first, in the streets and the houses of the village; the second, in the systematic killing of men and youths on the shore. This massacre, according to Pappé, was not an exceptional activity but a component in the larger Zionist project of ethnic cleansing.

5. See Fitzpatrick's (2001) discussion of Agamben's work attending, among other things, to the state of exception.

Figure 14 Boys Playing, Shatila Camp, Lebanon, 2005.

10 The Politics of Witness

REMEMBERING AND FORGETTING 1948
IN SHATILA CAMP

Diana K. Allan

Since their displacement from Palestine during the events of the
Nakba in 1948, Palestinian refugees in Lebanon have hovered in an ill-defined
space—out-of-place and between states—as Lebanon denies their natural-
ization and Israel resists their return. In this uncertain context, the political
and institutional value placed on 1948 generation testimonies and practices
commemorating Palestine and the history of the expulsion continues to rise.
While 1948 has remained an important part of Palestinian collective memory
and identity, as the event which marks the loss of Palestine as a physical entity and its birth as a national signifier, its significance as a point of historical
and political orientation toward the future—as founding myth—is relatively
recent. During the early years in exile, the term "the Nakba" had not co-
hered as a national symbol and 1948 was more often viewed as a moment
of weakness and humiliation that needed to be exorcized than as an event
to be actively commemorated. Refugees—or "returnees" as they insisted on
being called—expected that their exile would be temporary, and often actively resisted using the term Nakba because they feared that it lent perma-
nency to their situation. In the 1950s and early 1960s other more euphemistic
terms were employed to describe the events of 1948, among them, *al-ightisab*
(the rape), *al-ahdath* (the events), *al-hijra* (the exodus), *lamma sharna wa tla'na*
(when we blackened our faces and left).[1] While Palestinian nationalism thrived
in Lebanon in the 1970s under the leadership of the Palestine Liberation

Organization (PLO), the focus was on revolution and renewal, making the invocation of 1948 memory neither desirable nor appropriate. It was not, therefore, until the 1990s, largely in response to the perception that Yasir Arafat was on the point of signing away the right of 1948 refugees to return in exchange for Palestinian statehood, that a renewed interest in the Nakba developed among institutions representing Palestinian refugees in Lebanon. This interest was directly linked to the need to publicize to the international community that this right was not negotiable (Sayigh 2001).

The 1998 commemorations to mark the fiftieth anniversary of the Nakba were a politicized reminder of what celebrations of Israeli Independence were denying; the flurry of oral histories, plays, films, art exhibits, and village history books that followed have similarly sought to symbolically reclaim and reify 1948 as a constituting factor of refugee identity.[2] Documenting and performing a history of relation to Palestine is thus intended to counter the dehistoricizing effects of recent "peace" initiatives and the "internationally circulated image of [refugees] as uprooted, temporary sojourners" (Peteet 1995: 170), keeping alive the question of responsibility for the "refugee problem."

Seen in this light, the interest of scholars, nongovernmental organizations (NGOS), and activist networks in the experiences of a passing generation of witnesses appears pragmatic, with the avenues of possible inquiry tied at least implicitly to the escalating urgencies of the present and the desire for retributive justice. What is potentially problematic about this political appropriation of 1948 is that the search for recognition of refugee rights under international law can become confused with the imperative of not forgetting. The question that this essay will seek to address is whether the quest for political agency among refugees might be better served by arguments rooted in the present-day realities of life in the camps rather than those conceived in terms that imply a phantasmic undoing of history.

Even while I pose questions about the ways in which this discourse of witness may be distorting, I believe that documenting refugee memories of 1948—at this point of transition from history as lived to history as text—is critically important. Since 2002 I have been working on an archival project to record testimonies on film with first-generation refugees in camps around Lebanon about their villages prior to 1948, and their experiences during the expulsion.[3] The ethical obligation we have to document the events of the Nakba, however, does not give us the right to speak politically for those whose lives have been determined by 1948. My understanding of the selective ways in which 1948 is being remembered and forgotten, publicly and privately, has been informed not only by my involvement with the archive, but also by the experience of living and working in Shatila camp, where I have been conducting anthropological fieldwork. This brought into focus the residual experiences and suffering of several generations of refugees silenced or left unassimilated by this nationalist history. The ethnographic work I have done in Shatila camp has revealed with great clarity the contradictory ways that 1948 is remembered and the dialectical relations being generated between past and present, memory and motive.

Collectivizing Memory

Within the matrix of Palestinian memory, narratives about the Nakba have emerged as a symbolic lynchpin of collective identity and the bedrock of nationalism. As Rashid Khalidi notes, these parochial loyalties, "an attachment to place, a love of country and a local patriotism . . . were the crucial elements in the construction of nation-state nationalism" (Khalidi 1997: 21). The creation of a Palestinian diaspora and the mass displacement of people has itself been a critical component of nation formation that draws on idioms of home and homelessness. Alienation and exile enhance the need to reconstruct homeland; they generate acts of imagination believed to be essential for the forging of national identity. Writing about the Palestinian diaspora, Edward Said described the impulse to cultural creativity as deriving from this "perilous territory of not-belonging" (Said 1984: 50). In the absence of national institutions, the role of Palestinian intellectuals, activists, and scholars working in the field of Palestine studies has taken on added importance—working to consolidate this nationalist discourse and helping to fashion a vocabulary of authenticity.[4]

Following this logic, nowhere is memory claimed to be—or rhetorically constructed to be—more authentic or vital than among refugees living in the camps. It is the camps, in spite of the poverty and powerlessness of refugees—or perhaps because of it—that emerge as the places in which "the Palestinian national spirit was, and still is, burning. *They are the real Palestinians*" (Klaus 2003: 129, emphasis added). The memorializing consciousness believed to structure refugee experience in exile is often characterized as a compulsive desire to map, through narrative, "every tree, every stone fence, every grave, house, mosque, every street and village square [the refugees] had left behind" (Litvak 1994: 45).[5] Palestinian historian Elias Sanbar takes this one step further, describing this experience in terms that seem almost elegiac: "to rescue their land . . . the refugees would gamble everything on taking it with them, gradually becoming the temporary replacement of their homeland . . . they would live as if they were everything—Palestine and Palestinians, a people and its land" (Sanbar 2001: 90).

Here, Sanbar seems to collapse the distinctions between memory as recollection and memory as cultural reproduction, making it almost indistinguishable from culture or identity. The potency of remembrance that preserves this "internal map" (Khalidi 1997: 205) of Palestine, assumed to lie at the core of refugee identity,[6] is presumably rooted in a model of traumatic memory in which authority and authenticity are grounded in stories of extreme suffering, and where the voicing of pain has itself come to be seen as an empowering act. The rhetorical power of memory is further undergirded by the belief that disempowered communities are somehow preternaturally oriented toward remembering and have a rich, spontaneous, oral tradition—the "social glue" of identity politics—through which to record the injustices and suffering of the past.[7] This assumption that refugees from different generations, with vastly different experiences, continue to cling tenaciously to collective memories of Palestine may, however, speak more to our own anxieties of loss and of letting go of the past—as scholars and activists in sympathy with Palestinian nationalist aims and the rights of refugees—for fear of political defeat and justice not being done.

This heightened sense of a need to bear witness to the events of the Nakba within factions, N G O s, and institutions representing refugee interests within the camps,[8] as well as in academia and international activist networks—at the very moment when "Palestine" as a historical signifier is in danger of losing its signified—must be understood as centrally connected to politics and timing. During the last decade, the battle over the interpretation of 1948 has intensified between scholars and activists calling for further investigation into the human tragedy of 1948 and the war from an ethical perspective[9] and traditional Zionist scholars who continue to view the events of 1948 in terms of *realpolitik*.[10] The collapse of the Oslo peace process and the outbreak of the Al-Aqsa *intifada* have put these "new historians" in Israel under renewed attack. Recent peace initiatives that do not recognize any comprehensive right of return have also raised the historical stakes, and the perceived importance of associating the Palestinian narrative with the question of responsibility for the expulsion in 1948.

Witnessing in this context thus appears to be both retroactive and prospective—in that it looks back to the catastrophe of 1948 and forward to the

possibility of further erasure. In thinking about witness as a way of acknowl-
edging a violent past, calling for redress, or preventing suffering in the future,
however, how might critical thinking be compromised? Based on my work
with refugees in Shatila, I worry that the expedient re-framing of the past in
political terms that seeks to retrieve and consolidate the 1948 narrative—por-
traying refugees as the human remnants of this historic tragedy that strive in
their being for return—may be putting the burden of remembrance on those
with the least resources to realize it.[11] Not only does this collectivized narrative of suffering threaten to elide less legible and localized legacies of 1948
that structure the memory, experience, and hopes of refugees in the diaspora,
but it may also conceal the fact that the intensity of this longing for nation
may now be coming more from the elite echelons of the Palestinian diaspora
than from its base.[12]

The authenticity and legitimacy enacted—and often controlled—by this
increasingly institutionalized understanding of 1948 history and its place
within nationalist discourse clearly comes at a cost. This monument to an idealized past which those of us working in the field may be unintentionally co-
constructing through our research—and which subsequent generations are
expected to bear witness to, and even claim as their own—can be both alien-
ating and oppressive. It is also replacing a sense of history as lived experience
and practice that might evolve, organically, into future possibility. Does this
kind of quasi-institutionalized coercion of memory, in searching for certain
kinds of truths, effect a structural forgetting of others? In approaching eyewit-
nesses as living links with Palestine and their narratives as tools for regenerating collective meanings within a political field, are we in a sense preventing
them from mourning their losses in more personal or permanent terms? Do
institutionalized commemorative practices, or academic studies that compul-
sively look back to this event as the core of national identity, make it harder
for subsequent generations of refugees to articulate a sense of identity and
belonging in terms of present realities and their own hopes for the future?
Merely to pose such questions places one in an acute ethical quandary. Israeli
policy vis-à-vis the Palestinians has often been described in terms of establishing "facts on the ground"; such "facts" can be military and strategic as well
as cultural and historical. The depth of attachment of the Palestinian refugee
diaspora to the land of Palestine is obviously an iconic centerpiece of this
struggle, so the risk exists that bringing it into the light of scrutiny may be
miscast as a concession. Yet this is necessary since what is under scrutiny is as
much the politics of solidarity as the politics of remembrance.

Shatila: Remembering Against the Grain of Archive

The ways that many interviewees responded to our questions about what took place in their villages in 1948 suggested that the past is, in crucial ways, being remembered through the lens of present suffering. In the process of recording several hundred hours of filmed testimony and through my ethnographic research, the gravitational pull that the meta-narrative of the Nakba exerts on personal memory became clearer, as stories fell into and out of discursive alignment with a nationalist master narrative. Particularly illuminating were the different modes of remembrance that I witnessed in Shatila and discrepancies in the way in which the same individual might remember in the course of a formal interview for the archive, and in the more idiomatic contexts of everyday life.

When I first arrived in the camp I was taken to speak with elders, widely recognized to have good or "important" memories. Among the first of these local sages that I met, and subsequently came to know well, was Abu Nayif from Majd al-Krum.[13] After brief introductions, we were seated, and without prompting he launched into a long narrative about his village. Questions or interruptions were not permitted, so we sat and listened to his stylized memoir, which had the air of a well-paced and practiced performance. The narrative showed signs of prescriptive plotting, astutely touching on key political tropes: close relations with local Jewish communities, perfidious Albion, escalating acts of violence, a perilous journey into exile, the hardship of early years in Lebanon, and the establishment of the camp, in which his father had been a major figure.[14] This is not to belittle these experiences or cast doubt over their veracity, more to note the ways in which this narrative—by foregrounding a rhetoric of authenticity and moral edification—seemed marked by an internalization of the protocols of testimony. It was as if Abu Nayif, anticipating the expectations and sympathies of his audience, emphasized those elements of his own history that might generate identification and empathy, and that could be understood in terms of the political interests of the collective. This was also suggested by the fact that his story was structured around episodes marked for some kind of future redemption. As he brought his narrative to a close, he turned and gave us a penetrating look: "If I could go to my village tomorrow I would leave everything I have and walk," he said. Raising his voice a notch, "I would be happy to live under a tree with the sky as my roof and the earth my bed. It would be enough just to die in Palestine.

And then as if on cue, "The right of return is our most important right—we will not give it up for anything." [15]

Over coffee, once the "interview" had formally finished, Abu Nayif showed me a photograph album of images of himself with various delegations, with foreign officials and volunteers from a host of different countries—joking that his house was "like the United Nations." He is clearly proud that representatives from local N G O S regularly take their visitors to see him as part of their tour of Shatila. A local celebrity, he has fashioned his identity as a narrator of the Nakba—and does not disappoint. Through these acts of witness he is both a representative of the community, and an *agent* of collective identity and experience. This might be understood in terms of a poetics of maneuver that allows the "I" to speak for the "we." Through narrative, Abu Nayif tries to evoke solidarity from his audience, interpellating the viewer as secondary witness in this "rhetorical space of intersubjectivity" (Hesford 2004: 105). On the various occasions that I saw him talking with visitors to the camp, the form his narrative took was almost identical; his guests were normally invited to ask questions at the end, sometimes prompted by the "guide"—what, for instance does Abu Nayif think about the right of return? To which his resounding answer would be, "If I could go to my village tomorrow, I would leave everything I have and walk." These strategies of performance and persuasion point to an economy of memory, in which particular versions of the past become standardized and circulate almost as commodities; but they also illustrate the ways in which a transnational discourse of testimony may be shaping local practice, informing the processes by which individual experience becomes social text, and public past (Feldman 2004).

The dissonance between what is being said and what is being felt in the course of these acts of bearing witness must in some sense be a response on the part of the speaker to what they imagine is being—or can be—heard. As I came to know Abu Nayif better in the course of living in the camp, I began to notice how the same events could be discussed in radically different terms in other contexts. His niece became a close friend, and I would often find Abu Nayif talking with her husband when I called to visit. In these informal family settings, his memories (built almost entirely around his experiences in Shatila, and rarely straying as far afield as Majd al-Krum) took on a fluidity and depth—at times a sharp humor—largely absent in the somewhat somber narrations given to visitors. After the Geneva Accords were made public he refused to come with us to a demonstration outside the UN building, telling me—with a certain impatience—that it was a waste of time, and that everyone "knows" that the right of return is impossible. Through these interactions with Abu Nayif and other elders in Shatila, I became more aware of the ways in which this rhetorical language of collective dispossession, struggle, and return that has come to index "Palestinianness"—which finds voice in these more "official" contexts—has lost its resonance, not only in the minds of elders like Abu Nayif, but also, as I came to discover, and which I will discuss below, among younger generations of refugees in the camps.

In the course of everyday conversations with elders and their families, pre-1948 Palestine or the events of the expulsion—when discussed at all—emerged as anecdotal reminiscence that was supple, associative, and more deeply concerned with commenting on the present than memorializing the past. On one occasion it was the aroma of za'tar (wild thyme) that sparked a series of interconnected memories, taking Umm Salih first to Jish and the memory of picking wild za'tar in the mountains with her grandmother—describing how it was used in cooking and the memory of a particular incident when she had seen a snake in their courtyard as a child—before turning to a recent visit with her sister in 'Ayn Hilwa camp where she had seen, and smelt, families pounding their own za'tar. That this unsystematic weaving of events and places at first appeared to me as passing anecdote rather than a narrative about the Nakba, points to my own biases and limits of imagination as to what constituted a historical narrative worth recording. It illustrated for me the way in which prescribed conventions of bearing witness were also shaping what I was listening for—for instance, emotionally charged moments in which national narrative and self-narrative intertwine. Umm Salih's stories, like many others that I have heard since, suggest a refusal to force partial memories into an interpretational schemata—these moments that cannot be sutured into a continuous narrative of moral or cognitive coherence. The value of this fractured reminiscence, however, may lie in its ability to enact a doubling of witness, transmitting not only historical details but also the shattering effects that this history has had on the lives of those who have lived it (see Esmeir, this volume).

However lyrically suggestive these Proustian moments may be in the stories that elders tell, they are essentially deracinated and do not necessarily form good conduits of national memory. While they may form points of reference for elders, are these modes of remembrance crossing generational barriers? Although elders regularly claim—when asked by researchers like myself—to be narrating stories about life in Palestine and the events of 1948, few children know more than the name of, and the most generic facts about, their ancestral village.[16] Muhammad, a thirteen-year-old from Shatila whose grandfather had witnessed the massacre in Safsaf in October 1948, knew only that his relatives in Palestine had not needed money: "People didn't even know what money looked like in those days—they were farmers and grew everything they needed—not like now." When I later asked his grandfather, Abu Waseem, if he had ever described his experiences in detail, he admitted that his grandchildren were more interested in watching television or chatting on the Internet. "Every day my friend Abu Hamadi comes to visit me at 5—we sit and have coffee and sometimes we talk about Palestine, but my grandchildren don't like to sit with us—they'd rather be playing pinball with their friends." Many times when I stopped by Abu Waseem's house in the afternoon I would find him sitting with Abu Hamadi, often in total silence. This at first struck me as odd. Over time, however, it became clear that this ritual meeting that structured their days was a form of exchange and solidarity. These silences— that at times seemed to me agonizingly long, but which they clearly both felt comfortable with—express something deliberate and shared.

Umm Muhammad, who had been sitting with us and had overheard my discussion with her father, later privately acknowledged that she had not encouraged her son to talk with her parents about the past:

> Although my parents used to speak a lot about Palestine when we were young, I don't like to hear these stories now. . . . Sometimes my mother sings to my children about Bint Jbayl, and how families were separated when they first came to Lebanon and it makes us cry. . . . These memories are too painful for her, and for us. . . . I realize it is important for the children to know about Palestine, but I feel that it's good for us to think about how to make their future better rather than to live in the past.
>
> (INTERVIEW, December 16, 2003)

The experience of this family gestures to a shift away from historical transmission through the public performance of personal narrative, to less articulate and ever more private forms of cultural retrieval. Stories do not seem to be a retentive *milieu* for memory or communal solidarity, which instead appear to settle into silent practice, gestures, and repetitive rituals—meeting for coffee, a lullaby. It suggests that remembering Palestine and the events surrounding the expulsion have come to be unconsciously performed where they may have once been actively relayed. It seems also as if speaking directly about these events and experiences has come to represent a form of excess.

In the same way that I had expected to find an active narrative tradition of the Nakba, in which the intensity of verbal recollection, *pace* Sanbar, in some way compensates for the suffering experienced, I was also surprised to discover that many life stories began in the present and worked their way back to the past; genealogies seemed often to be constructed backward, rather than the other way around.[17] Learning to inhabit the world again appears to involve a constant shifting between historical registers. At times this takes the form of simple comparison—like Umm Salih's version of what Shatila is like now with what it used to be. However, this temporal shuttling also gestured to a more sustained interweaving of past and present. For instance, when I'd sit with Umm Jamal in her son's cake shop on the edge of the camp she would begin most recollections about her childhood in Jaffa with a pointed qualification: "But as you know, my dear, I am one of those who say enough! Let's put our hand in the hand of Israel—we've suffered too much and we're tired. Let's be realistic. If I'm not going to go back to Jaffa, then at least I want the right to live well here or somewhere else." In our discussions she rarely spoke to me about the specific events that had led to her family's expulsion from Jaffa—or the death of relatives, which I learned about from her niece. Instead, she took great pleasure in furnishing me with detailed descriptions of her family's wealth and status in Jaffa. For Umm Jamal, constructing a normative picture of her past, as if to somehow draw it back into her present, trumped any narrative of accusation: [18]

I remember how in our house we had two different kinds of bathrooms—we had a foreign one and an Arab one—we had lots of rooms. My grandfather was the president of the port and my father worked with him and they had three ships and did trade with many countries from Addis Ababa to Britain—one time when my father was in England he had a pain in his head, and he went to the doctor—he couldn't speak much English so he said "my head hurt" or something like that, and they said he should remove all his teeth and put in false ones, so he did—it cost a lot of money! If only Jamal could fix his teeth, but we don't have the money—look at them, it's awful! [Jamal, her son has had ongoing problems with his teeth, most of which were broken when the butt of a rifle was smashed into his mouth at an Amal manned checkpoint during the War of the Camps.] But my uncle, now he was *very* educated—he went to the American University in Beirut and studied in schools in Jaffa—he was one of the first people to work at UNRWA. We came here on one of my father's boats—we brought everything with us in boxes the size of this room—the only thing we left behind was the *jarushi* [stone

for grinding wheat] because it was so heavy. We had all our chairs, the old lights—
chandeliers—and we had all the pots—from this big to this small [gesturing with
her hands]. One *tunjara* [cooking pot] from my grandfather's wedding was so big
you could put two whole sheep in it—his wedding lasted for forty days and my
grandmother wore a gown—she had five different ones and I would iron them
and wear them on feast days and dance like Cinderella! [Pause] There were many
people on the boat with us—one woman gave birth on board, so they called the
boy Bahar [sea]. They were shooting at us from the port—I still remember how
the bullets fell on our heads like stars and the sound they made as they hit the
water, like this [she gently taps the table].

(INTERVIEW, June 17, 2004)

In the context of Umm Jamal's stories, references to life in Palestine surface as disconnected fragments, and her account of the events of the expulsion hovered awkwardly at the edge of our conversations. What is striking
about the way this narrative unfolds is the absence of blame: the perpetrators—the Jewish forces—that attacked Jaffa are not named, and the shooting
is mentioned almost as an afterthought. The experience of expulsion seems
contingent, even inexplicable, accentuating a sense of suffering as deriving
from chaotic forces and without meaning. In Veena Das's study (1994) of the
ways suffering is explained and given meaning, she makes the distinction between interpretations predicated on theodicy (justifying suffering as part of
a divine plan) and those that foreground contingency. The latter structures
Umm Jamal's narrative and involves both releasing the perpetrators from
blame and freeing herself from responsibility.[19] Her relation to the past is
toward normalcy; she laments rather than blames.[20] Indeed, Umm Jamal's
emphasis on transformation and continuity outweighs memories of death
and violence. It not only falls short of the juridical requirements of testimony that focuses on particular events, but also seems to go against the genre of
testimony in which, like Abu Nayif's, the rhetorical appeal of the particular,
of the "self," is given meaning through its relation to the collective.[21]

This ambivalent relation of the "I" to the "we" was a feature of a number of the interviews I conducted—both for the archive and in the course of
my own fieldwork. Unwillingness to forfeit communal bonds for any other
kind of identification, epitomized by the well-known saying "my story is the
story of my people," is brought into question by this refocusing on the *individual*. While these two strands of remembrance are clearly not irreconcilable,
there is a sense that what is being foregrounded is not collective harmony or

identification with an increasingly metaphoric Palestinian nation, but rather a longed-for sense of dignity, self-respect, and individual possibility. As a site of collective memory and commemoration, 1948 necessarily also becomes a site "in which individuals must come to terms not only with a *prêt-à-porter* past, but also with their relationship to the collectivity in which they find themselves" (Crapanzano 2004: 172). Umm Jamal's desire not to be submerged in the collective but to retain some sense of distinction and difference, points to the ways in which elders may be regenerating their worlds on their own terms.

The perceived usefulness of practices that salvage authentic culture and align political subjectivities with nationalist goals is at some level being undermined by the community's growing ambivalence toward these acts of national remembrance. When I later spoke of the striking absence of detail about the events of the Nakba in Umm Jamal's stories with Umm Hasan—a friend in her late thirties with whom I lodged in the camp—she laughed and said that it was because Umm Jamal was from *"ahl Yafa"* (the families of Jaffa). She continued:

> These people are good at forgetting the past—throwing it away and starting a new life. They live only for the present without thinking about the future. . . . We have a proverb about Jaffa people, "If you have money in your pocket spend it and God will provide later." . . . Farmers worry about the future, and plan for it. City dwellers have different habits from us—I know a woman from Manshiyya who married someone from Jaffa, and she told me that when they had meat—this was during the invasion, so it was hard to get—her husband would say "Let's eat it all now, don't ration it." But she would always hide some away. One day her husband died while he was working at the port and she was beside herself because she hadn't made him a big meal the day before. She'd hidden some of the meat away. She always tells me this, saying "He was right—better to enjoy what you have when you have it." [Pause] There are differences between us [farmers and city dwellers]—in 1982 it was the families from Jaffa that were the first to leave the camp. Everyone tried to persuade them to stay—"who will liberate Palestine if you leave the resistance?" we'd say. The people who stayed to fight were farmers.
>
> (INTERVIEW, February 16, 2004)

It has been noted how relations between farmers and urbanites, defined by mutual distrust and prejudice, shaped the way in which the physical space of the camps was arranged (Peteet 1995). In Umm Hasan's comments we see how the perceived dissimilarity between rural and urban mentalities has taken on an added twist, here framed in terms of temporal perception.

While Jaffans are seen to live in the moment—recklessly forgetting past and future—farmers (presented here, as the true nationalists) conserve the heritage of the past and struggle for future liberation.

The referential dissonance emerging from the gap between this untimely nationalist discourse and the vicissitudes of everyday life in the camp also registered in the contradictory ways that people responded to the archival project, and the invitation to be interviewed.[22] While some elders were delighted, many were unwilling to talk. This was sometimes out of fear (and I realize that my own position as a British woman, studying at an American university, is probably a significant factor here), and occasionally indifference, or a sense of weariness with the duty to recall. "What's the point?" said one old woman we spoke with in Badawi Camp—"I've done so many interviews now. I've even been on television, and what good has it done?" More often however, this reluctance was a reflection of the fact that for many, these are experiences that have been cordoned off. In Shatila, one friend's mother who had fled her prosperous home outside of Haifa at the age of eleven, could not be persuaded to be interviewed. She listened patiently as we tried to justify the importance of the archive—for future generations, for justice, for historical truth—before politely, but firmly, refusing. Her son, Abu Farah, who was visiting from abroad, was not surprised:

> Whenever I ask her about what happened, she always says, "One day, when I am more comfortable." She doesn't want to remember or talk about what happened [he pauses, visibly upset]. Eventually I had to ask my wife's family who are from the same village—they live near Saida, but outside the camp. It's more relaxed there so they can talk about things; here every single part of this house or alley reminds my parents of what's gone—a reminder that they try to bury. . . . My mother focuses on us, she worries about us—that is her escape from thinking about the past and maybe the future too. . . . My grandfather had a huge amount of land, near Haifa, on the side of a mountain, very fertile land—and they built huge houses—even my mother got an equal share of it along with her brothers because there was such plenty. And then suddenly in one hit they left, leaving everything. And since then my mother has stayed an 11-year-old girl, in a frame, and whatever happens to her now is outside that frame. She brings us inside the frame, but that past is something . . . how to put it—it is the biggest trauma for her. It's like she is looking at the world through a screen, which filters out color and reality—sometimes when I look at her, I feel she is in constant pain.

> (INTERVIEW, July 28, 2004)

This comment illustrates the paradox that lies at the heart of traumatic experience, in which forgetfulness and a breakdown of witnessing are inextricably linked to the act of remembrance, as the event is neither fully recalled nor erased.[23] Abu Farah describes how the condition of inhabiting a world made strange by past violence—in which one can never again feel "comfortable"—stifles memory, creating what Das vividly describes as a "kind of atmosphere that cannot be expelled to an 'outside'"(2000: 69). According to the logic of witness that creates and classifies events as discrete objects to be examined, the necessary distance for bearing witness and the language in which to ground it are lacking. For Abu Farah's mother, it is as if the work of mourning cannot be realized, her experiences frozen somewhere between memory and forgetting. This inability to inscribe memory through substitution in speech may not only derive from a lack of shared language through which to express, or inhabit, trauma but should perhaps also be read as a form of conserving memory, since that which has not been turned into a symbol for recall, cannot be deleted or forgotten.[24]

What is also striking about Abu Farah's analysis of his mother's silence about the past are the synchronic terms he uses to describe historical consciousness; it appears to be associative, embedded in a scarred physical landscape that blends past into present.[25] These comments allude to the ways in which the camp's fraught history, and the structures of social and political exclusion that refugees continue to experience, have come to be seen as part of the same process of erasure that began in 1948, preventing any clear distinction between former and present suffering: *Every single part of this house or alley reminds my parents of what's gone.* The context of narration inescapably inflects memories of 1948, which in turn are filtered through complex local histories that continue to shape the community. As Umm Hasan succinctly expressed it, "For us the Nakba is not a single event, but an ongoing suffering that we experience every day"—suggesting that what it means to be Palestinian may be now understood more in terms of existential bonds of suffering than through a connection to the place itself. Memories of the Nakba seem closer to a lived condition, experienced as a process of survival, rather than as historical possession. As Das suggests, the past can continue to exist as "poisonous knowledge," a knowing by suffering in the world rather than through acts of conscious transmission (Das 2000: 69). Reflecting upon comments like these, we can begin to see how Sanbar's formulation about the refugees having "gambled everything on taking [Palestine] with them, gradually becoming the temporary replacement of their homeland," is both true and untrue.

The loss of public spaces and the increasingly cramped living conditions in the camp have effected other shifts in memory practices in Shatila, as elders find themselves ever more isolated from their friends and the rest of the community. The experience of Abu Aziz, the eighty-three-year-old uncle of a friend, offers a poignant example. Following the War of the Camps in the mid-1980s, the family moved to a building outside the camp in which other former residents were also living. Abu Aziz soon became bored and depressed living in his small apartment. After a while he began to meet with other elders living in the building and they would sit on the wall facing the street and talk. In the last year three members of this impromptu, sidewalk-*diwan* have died, and throughout the summer my friend recounted how his uncle had begun to sit on the opposite side of the street from the remaining two, outside a barber's shop on a borrowed chair. Every day Abu Aziz would hang his *kuffiya* over a nearby bush and sit in silence. When his nephew one day asked why he no longer sat with the others, he said that he was tired of listening to them reminiscing about Palestine: "No amount of talking will ever bring it back." It is as if the collapse of the social context of memory has precipitated the realization that return to his village is extremely unlikely: his response has been to enact remembrance through an intensely private ritual, defiantly unattached to any political agenda.[26] This attempt to reclaim strains of life from memories of overwhelming loss implies some form of redemption. While Abu Aziz may not frame his memories within a familiar language of political activism, he is not "forgiving"—he believes that justice will be done. "There will come a day when all this has to stop," he once told me, " for it can't go on as it is now. God will see to this." Tellingly, he is placing his hopes not in what he regards to be the ineffectual and corrupt domain of international politics, but in the divine.

I was struck by a similar sense of acceptance when I joined a group from Shatila—all originally from Khalisa—when they went to the border to celebrate the liberation of the south in 2004. Khalisa, now called Kiriyat Shmona, is clearly visible from various vantage points near Fatima's Gate, and at one point we were able to make out what we thought may have been the home of one elderly woman in our group. It was the first time, in fact, that she had been to the border, having been too ill to travel in 2000. I was therefore surprised to note how the experience did not seem to stir sad memories, as one might expect, but instead evoked a sense of real joy. She was delighted to see her house and her village, and in the car on the way home she kept smiling and saying how Palestine was even more beautiful than she had remembered. Later, when she was describing the outing to her granddaughter, she said she felt that now she could die in peace since she had seen her home again. It was as if in saying this she was commenting on her relation to the past, to her village, to Palestine as something very important but also as somehow quietly over. What might be viewed here as resigned acceptance, or forgetting, is perhaps better understood as a kind of serenity that completes the process of mourning. Experiences like this trip to the border, or Abu Aziz's enacted ritual—rather than reliving loss—may actually free energies previously invested in marking absence and prolonging "poisonous knowledge" within the community.

The different ways in which these elders in Shatila relate to their memories of Palestine invite us to question the notion that this is a community actively transmitting and preserving local histories that restore Palestine palimpsestically in social memory, or represent a collective call for retributive justice. These various forms of witness that I have described appear to be "antiphonal" (Feldman 2004: 176), expressed in terms that not only alternate between individual and collective, but also between the duty to recall and the desire to forget, between speech and silence, sorrow and joy. These ambivalent discourses of memory and collective meaning-making do not fit extant paradigms for public witness, which presume that a narrative of "what happened" can be communicated and documented.[27] My initial concern that the suffering and loss of 1948 needed to be measured and documented—as materials for political advocacy—presupposed a consensus about a shared understanding of the past and the need to bear witness to it. I was surprised—initially even disappointed—when I discovered that this need to bear witness to 1948 was not foregrounded in people's narratives, but I came to realize how this pointed to the alternative ways that violent history and adversity in this community are being dealt with. This complicates the binary of victimization and agency and should encourage us to recognize more complex and ambiguous processes of semiosis and social action. Clearly these alternate registers of bearing witness suggest other means of coming to terms with the past, and other ways of imagining the future, than those that our own desires for justice might envisage.

Transmission and Transformation:
Commemorating 1948 Among Shatila's Youth

What of the younger generations of refugees in Shatila? What role does the Nakba play in their lives? The dialectical tensions that lie at the heart of this renascent nationalist interest in the history of 1948 that I outlined above were perhaps most vividly revealed to me during an event that I helped organize in Shatila to mark Nakba Day in May 2004. With the help of a local NGO, we mounted a screen against one of the buildings near the main entrance to the camp, squeezed between large posters of two Hamas leaders, Shaykh Ahmad Yassin and Abdel Aziz Rantisi, put up after their assassinations by the Israeli Defense Forces in March and April of that year. The proximity of the screen to these images proved confusing, and initially passersby thought that the event was being organized by the Islamist party, Hamas. The films we had selected—a collection of documentaries, interviews, and features about Palestine and the history of 1948—were to be shown over two evenings. For the opening night, we had chosen a series of six fifteen-minute excerpts from interviews that we had filmed with elders in the camp about their memories of Palestine. The elders had enthusiastically encouraged us, and we thought the interviews would be of interest to their families and the community more generally. A small group of about twenty people gathered—mainly the stars of the show and their friends—perched on plastic chairs, or watching from the balconies that overlooked the street. Kids sat on the hoods of parked cars, enjoying the novelty of street cinema, if not altogether gripped by the subject matter.

About ten minutes into the first interview with Umm Waseem, Muhammad Hasanayn—the brother of Hasan Hasanayn, who, with Shadi Anas of Burj al-Barajna camp, was killed in a demonstration at the border in October 2000—came up to me and asked when we were planning to show "the film about Hasan." I explained that the idea of the event was to commemorate the events of 1948 and that we did not intend to show any films about Hasan. At this point I had to leave to get an extension cable for the projector. When I returned five minutes later, I found that a large crowd had gathered. As I got closer, I realized that the tape had been changed, and instead of Umm Waseem talking about the air attack on her village of Safsaf, we were now watching news footage from Al-Manar (Hizbollah's TV station) of the demonstration in which Hasan was killed. Among the chanting protestors projected above our heads were recognizable faces from the camp—lobbing stones and scurrying away from the clouds of tear gas; some of the more fearless could be seen trying to climb the wire fence. Bullets were fired by panicking Israeli soldiers on the other side, and then ensued a confusion of running bodies and blood: about seventeen people were wounded, two fatally. This footage then cut to images from the camp: Hasan's distraught mother and grieving family, lines of people coming to pay their respects, before culminating in a funeral procession in which several thousand mourners marched, carrying Hasan's coffin through the streets on a wave of anger.

Among those who had gathered to watch and remember, some were animatedly pointing out friends and relatives, while others cursed as the Israeli jeeps darted across the screen; many were crying and visibly upset. The mood was somber—in stark contrast to the distracted manner of the crowd when we projected the first interview. The tension and grief were palpable – it was clear that the Nakba had been upstaged by the representation of these recent events in the camp's history. When Muhammad saw that I had returned, he came over: "Look how many more people there are now" he said, grinning. "People are not interested in watching old people talk about the past— besides we've seen all these stories before." Then, turning to Mahmud—a friend who had helped organize the event—he added, "I'd rather be watching Umm Kulthum [the great Egyptian singer] than these old guys! I also have a video that was made by a doctor who was at the demonstration which shows Hasan going to the hospital—even more people will come tomorrow if you show this one." After we'd packed up, I hung around talking with friends, who, as they put it, had "come to support" me. They were not surprised that the event had not drawn a crowd, noting how few people had even remarked on the significance of the day.

Not only did this experience suggest to me that the significance of rituals that collectively remember 1948 is increasingly in doubt, but that these official forms of remembrance, rather than narrowing the gap between nationalist history and subjective memory in the community, may in fact be pushing these two modes of remembering farther apart. This event—as with others that I attended—clearly seemed to elicit boredom, with factional allegiances further complicating the ability of the community to engage collectively in memorial ceremonies. The manner in which the screening was hijacked by the interests of the audience, however, suggests that such acts of public remembering bring the lived experience of personal memory and collective history into dialogue in ways that may be reconfiguring understandings of self and community. The sense of solidarity generated by the scenes of riot and demonstration presumably derived in part from the emotional reminders of moments where they had been actively involved in events rather than simply being distant observers. As one friend put it to me after the screening, "People like to remember how they felt at this time—there was a lot of hope in the camp then."

The poor attendance at the film screening and the conflict that ensued as to what history should be remembered at this event is indicative of the way in which younger generations born and raised in the diaspora are finding it difficult to absorb these originary narratives as part of their own identity or as a frame for national belonging. This was something that I came to better appreciate through my friendships with second and third-generation refugees. Yusif, a twenty-seven-year-old from Badawi Camp now working as a teacher in an UNRWA school in Shatila, expressed the feeling of historical claustrophobia that the focus on a Palestine of the past engenders:

> Although we are still living the results of the Nakba, my generation didn't experience it, and I refuse to inherit it. . . .When I think of the Nakba and how Palestine used to be, I don't think of it as just some beautiful place where people sat under the trees eating fruit—I think of it as a normal life that I was not part of, but now it has become almost obligatory to turn memories of Palestine into a myth. When I hear elders who lived the Nakba talk about it, and the bad things they experienced, I sympathize with them—but sympathy changes. My memories are different from my father's—and my problems are different from his also. But it's as if all we need to know is the slogan "Palestine is ours"—but to really feel that you are from a place you need to know it. I've learnt about Palestine, but I know and love Lebanon—there's a difference of experience. There is much about our history here that remains hidden and ignored—for instance, why did it take us so long to start a resistance here? We have to ask ourselves this. Why, even after the revolution came here did we fail to liberate Palestine?

(INTERVIEW, November 20, 2003)

This interview is powerfully suggestive of the way in which younger generations are expected to miss keenly something that they themselves have not experienced losing. It questions the efficacy of reviving nationalist discourse through a staging of what historian and critic Mohammed Bamyeh calls a mythological "deep time" (2003: 836). Yusif reveals how this highlighting of 1948 as a productive historical moment is provoking a sense of frustration among second and third-generation refugees who have developed their own forms of rootedness and belonging in Lebanon. His comments suggest that the freighted heritage of the Nakba appears, ironically, to be erasing—rather than bringing into focus—the concrete historical details of 1948. It is as if this fetishization of the national entity, as a "beautiful place in which people sat under trees eating fruit," in which Palestine is signified synecdochically through bucolic imagery, is producing a derivative, and self-conscious sense of solidarity.[28] Here again we sense the referential dissonance of a nationalist discourse out of joint with local and national realities, in which ruptures and inconsistencies are smoothed over. Interestingly, Yusif's reference to the PLO's failed revolution in Lebanon also points to the possibility that an intellectual shift may be taking place—in which a conscious confrontation with the past supersedes an engagement based largely on emotion. As Yusif observes, this has entailed a troubling leveling and streamlining of Palestinian history in which other chapters of violence and loss in Lebanon are obscured or willfully "forgotten" because of their political sensitivity, or because they foreground the divisive ineptitude of the PLO.[29]

In our discussion, Yusif went on to note how the parents of some of the children he taught at UNRWA had expressed similar concerns that the emphasis on what Palestine *was* and what Shatila *is not* in many of the organized activities at school, and through local NGOs, is making it harder for children to acknowledge or appreciate the undeniable strengths of their community:

> In the NGO where my wife was working in Shatila, the children were being told to draw pictures of Palestine rather than things from their own experiences, because these are the kind of activities that get money. . . . But this is wrong—it is as if all Palestinians here have to have the same memory, and the same perspective on who we are or how to resist. Now when I talk about Palestine it makes me sad—because I start to feel as if I am lying too.
>
> (INTERVIEW, November 20, 2003)

What is particularly unsettling is that the factions and NGOs actively inculcating this feeling of loss appear to be bypassing the only members of the community with a legitimate claim to have experienced it. All the organized commemorative activities that I have attended in the camp—with the exception of the organized group visits to the homes of Abu Nayif and others mentioned earlier—are directed at youth, and rarely if ever involve the participation of camp elders. Instead of being the catalyst for discussion about the past in which elders can share their experiences, these institutions appear to be teaching Palestinian youth that by adopting the faculty of nostalgia in relation to the *idea* of Palestine and the events of 1948 they will have memories of a loss that they have not suffered directly. On several occasions I attended lectures organized by a local NGO. I was invited principally because I owned a video camera, since the organizer was eager to put images on the center's website and promotion brochures, "to show the people we are making sure the children know their history." In the talks that I attended, rows of ten-year-olds looked on, bewildered, fidgeting in their seats as the enthusiastic founder lectured on Palestine and the expulsion. It was as if this form of "imagined nostalgia" had become a more efficient means of indexing national authenticity within the community than the messiness of direct experience (Appadurai 1996: 77).

In the context of Shatila this cottage industry of commemoration includes not only the Nakba and Palestinian culture, but the Sabra and Shatila massacre as well. The phenomenon of internationally subsidized activities in the camps reveals the workings of a pragmatic agency on the part of refugees. The simplified narrative of 1948 trumps the ethical quagmire of the present reality in attracting foreign investment in the very institutions (schools, cultural centers, etc.) that, ironically, have come to form the locus of social agency for refugees. The commemorative practices foregrounded by such public institutions should therefore also be understood as part of the economic pragmatics of everyday life, and not merely as abstract models of cultural transmission. We need to consider, however, the extent to which these kinds of activities and our support of them—moral and material—are contributing to a trivialization of memory and cultural practice or, in Yusif's case, even generating a sense of self-deception.

Solidarity, Complicity, and the Symbolic Violence of Testimony

Let us return briefly to the house of Umm Jamal. During one of my last visits before I returned to the United States, I met her youngest son, Mahmud, who was sitting drinking coffee with his friend Farukh. Mahmud is twenty-two years old and works in a factory about an hour outside Beirut that makes bread ovens. He had just returned from work and invited me to join him for a coffee while I waited for his mother to return. Having heard a little about the archival project from his mother, he asked about my research and then turned to me with an air of barely concealed frustration to ask: "What's the point of your research?" As I tried to stumble into an answer, he cut me off:

> What is going to come of this for us? Many foreigners like you come to the camp, and they do research—they ask us questions about the past, about the Nakba, who died, what we felt, about the massacre, about our sadness—and it's like it's a thrill for them. We cry and they profit from our tears, but things stay the same for us. The electricity is still shit, we have no rights and this kind of thing just makes us suffer more. For this reason I don't think any research people like you do will make a difference. Okay, so it's true that many people here don't know the history of Palestine—I think that we should try to solve this through better education. But the problem is people don't really care anymore—and they don't have the time to care. All we do now is think about survival—this kills our desire to be a better people. We don't have time to think about our culture or our history—we are dying in this struggle simply to exist. . . . I believe that after two years there will be no more Palestinians here. I am taking an Australian passport [through a recent marriage to a Lebanese woman living there whom he met online], and my friend Farukh is getting a German passport through his marriage to his cousin there—so you see, soon it will all be gone.
>
> (INTERVIEW, August 10, 2004)

Like Yusif, Mahmud expresses a concern about the opportunistic ways in which the past is being used, and how suffering is the only thing that counts as history. The expectation that increased interest on the part of the international community will lead to intervention or beneficent action on their behalf is being replaced by a perception that these encounters amount to little more than empty talk. There is a sense—as Stevan Weine observes in his analysis of media coverage in Bosnia—that victims are being exposed to "an unwanted parody of genuine witnessing" (Weine 1999: 183). We see how the "victim" status that much of the research in the camps has helped to create is having the troubling effect of making legal tender of the suffering associated with 1948, as well as the massacre in 1982, while devaluing more mundane and everyday experiences of suffering linked to poverty and social and political exclusion.

In the context of my own work, these angry interventions by Yusif, Mahmud, and others forced me to reconsider the implications for younger generations of refugees of producing an archive in which witnessing is framed in such highly exclusive terms. Not only does it necessarily create a hierarchy of admissible and inadmissible memory; it also assumes a set of criteria for what kinds of experiences of suffering have the power to interpellate witnesses. Through these comments we are made aware of the speaker's anxiety at seeing himself outside the frame of witness, reduced to human remnant. As Mahmud explains, *"We are dying in this struggle to exist."*[30] And yet, from these new parameters of life, humans still attempt to create imaginaries, continuities, and futures. This for me suggests an important point of "resistance" to our own theoretical categorization, perhaps even de-humanization, of the informants and friends who shape our work.

What struck me most forcibly about Yusif and Mahmud's sentiments were the uncomfortable questions they provoked about what we—as privileged Westerners—are actually doing when we record narratives of violence or try to bring these subaltern histories into view. There is a sense also in both these comments that people here do not have the luxury to judge or blame—it is a simple matter of survival. If we probe the origins of the "thrill" that Mahmud speaks of, what do we find? It seems to suggest that the very people who purport to be trying to alleviate the suffering of the community—activists, scholars, researchers, etc.—may also be the ones who are minting and circulating this currency of symbolic violence. By documenting histories of violence and suffering in marginalized communities are we facilitating real change in people's lives? Or are we just easing our own consciences—indulging in what Luc Boltanksi calls a "politics of pity" (Boltanski 1999: 3)? The use of testimony as a means of mobilizing solidarity has created the troubling situation in which these intimate and painful memories are authenticated by "making their interiority ever more present, as if experiences were commodities that were being advertised" (Kleinman 2000: 4). Feldman, in his analysis of the role violence plays in "theaters" of witnessing, argues that the validity of these acts depends as much on the violence of the signifier as the signified; it depends, in other words, in part upon the processes by which we, as activists, scholars, and researchers authenticate certain moments of historical memory, or rank some kinds of violence and suffering over others (i.e., through expert knowledge, truth-claiming procedures, and mass media) (Feldman 2004). Farukh, who had been sitting silently on the other side of the room playing with Mahmud's niece, decided at this point to join in:

> Let me tell you a story. When I was a child—after my father was killed during the war—I was able to go to a center in the camp that was created to provide for orphans. Every month we were given money, and once a year some representatives

from the foreign organizations would come to visit the center. When this happened, there were people on the committee that would intentionally ask us not to put on our best clothes—because they thought that it would be better for them if we appeared poor. You could say they were begging off us. . . . You know, ever since I was young, I wanted to be a poet—and I can realize this dream, not like Mahmud who wanted to be a doctor but is not permitted to practice here. I keep my power by going on. I have tried to focus on my education because I feel that I will get another nationality—I don't want to ignore my nationality as a Palestinian but I know that it is impossible for me to return to Jaffa and I don't want to go to the West Bank or Gaza, so why keep talking about this? I am sure that I can do many things if I get German citizenship.

(INTERVIEW, August 10, 2004)

Like Mahmud, Farukh's comments allude to the potential for change being generated by an increasingly heterogeneous community that is being left untapped by a communal solidarity that draws on invocations of shared culture and past. Both Mahmud and Farukh are clearly invested in the lives that they hope are about to begin for them elsewhere. It is as if the idea of emigration serves as an alternative myth of wholeness to the one they have been brought up with. Yusif's identity and aspirations are shaped as much— if not more—by daily communications on email with a brother in Canada, than with his family in Badawi.[31] Simplified representations of refugee identity and aspiration, epitomized in slogans like "return" (al-'awda), are reductive, erasing agency and diversity of opinion. While for first-generation refugees "return" means to a physical place that has been experienced and lost, Farukh's generation appears to understand it in more abstract terms—as a restoration of dignity and justice, the right to respect oneself and be respected (Bamyeh 2003: 841).[32] The role of witness, oriented as it is toward "truth-telling," must accommodate these new political identities and conflicting viewpoints.

Conclusion

In considering the collective memories of catastrophe and injustice, we are reminded that while the political objectives of legal accountability, justice, and restitution may lie at the heart of much of the work being done on memories of the Nakba, social memory in the Palestinian context cannot be reduced to a formula. Collective memory is necessarily made up of a constellation of personal experiences: as such it is dynamic and consists of conflicting temporalities and impulses that find different ways of interacting with their contexts. In the case of Shatila, memory is being configured both within and between generations, creating spaces of remembrance marked by renewal and adaptation. The comments by Umm Hasan, Yusif, Mahmud, Farukh, Abu Farah, and the many others that I have either cited or held in mind while writing, call on us to reflect on the meaning of witness and the politics that inform it. Empathy may draw us to history and a desire that 1948 be neither denied nor forgotten. Empathy, however, may also cause us to lose sight of distinctions—the ways in which the past does, and does not, continue to shape the present. There is clearly a need to move beyond the coercive harmony of a national identity rooted in past history to include emergent forms of subjectivity that increasingly privilege individual aspiration over collective, nationalist imperatives. This suggests a need to rethink the politics of what we witness, and what we regard as constituting testimony.

While much writing on the Palestinian experience—particularly in Shatila—has examined how this community relates to its past, few have explored how refugees imagine the future and what their hopes and aspirations might be. By foregrounding, for political reasons, the need to bear witness to the violent history of 1948, not only are such studies obscuring from view seemingly more mundane—though no less devastating—everyday forms of suffering in the present; they may be eliding the creative ways in which refugees deal with their traumatic past, their sense of hopefulness for the future, and the new subject positions being created in relation to it. This was memorably expressed by Yusif when, during the twentieth anniversary commemorations for the Sabra and Shatila massacre, he led a group of his students in the march to the burial grounds, proudly wearing T-shirts that read, "We are still alive."

Author's Note

I would like to thank Curtis Brown, Sylvain Perdigon, Steven Caton, Michael Fischer and Joyce Dalsheim for their comments on an earlier version of this paper. Some of the ethnographic material for this essay has appeared in a different form in "Mythologizing al-Nakba: Narratives, Collective Identity and Cultural Practice among Palestinian Refugees in Lebanon." *Oral History* 33, no. 1 (Spring 2005): 47–56.

NOTES

1. The repressive measures of the Lebanese Sûreté Générale, and later the Deux-
   ième Bureau, also muted nationalist expression and politically motivated remembrance of the Nakba at this time.
2. See Khalili (2004a and b); Sayigh (1998a); Roberts (1999).
3. The Nakba archive, co-directed by myself and Mahmoud Zeidan, funded by the
   Ford Foundation, the Welfare Foundation, and through private donations, has
   been conducted in all twelve refugee camps in Lebanon, as well as with unreg-
   istered refugees in "gatherings." The project has been undertaken by refugees
   from the camps and is a collaborative endeavor. For more information, visit our
   website: www. Nakba-archive.org.
4. Edward Said along with other intellectuals, artists, and poets—among them
   Mahmoud Darwish, Ghassan Kanafani, Raja Shehadeh, Fadwa Tuqan, Salim
   Jubran, Naji Ali, Ismail Shammout—has played a crucial role in reinforcing collective identity and the creation of national mythologies. Mahmoud Darwish's
   poems are perhaps the best example of this phenomenon, where Palestine and
   the collective suffering of its people are lyrically transformed into indomitable
   archetypes.
5. See also Slyomovics 1998; Swedenburg 1991; Sa'di 2002.
6. Sayigh (1979: 107) also refers to this phenomenon: "The village—with its special
   arrangements of house and orchards, its open meeting places, its burial ground,
   its collective identity—was built into the personality of each individual villager
   to a degree that made separation like an obliteration of self."
7. For a discussion of this phenomenon in oral history see Dakhlia (2001).
8. See the work of 'A'idun ("We will return") founded in 1998; the Al-Jana oral history publications and the work of the Arab Resource Center for Popular Arts
   (ARCPA); Hoqooq, a magazine, produced by the Palestinian Human Rights Organization; the research conducted by CERMOC.
9. Pappé (2003); see also Shlaim (2001), R. Khalidi (1997), and Said (1979).
10. The intensification of debate over 1948 and the explicit linking of history to current political events was well illustrated in the conflicts sparked by Teddy Katz's
   thesis on the massacre at Tantura, and the disciplinary action taken against his
   adviser, Ilan Pappé, at the University of Haifa between December 2000–November 2001 (see Esmeir this volume); and also by Benny Morris' (2002) recantation
   of his former position regarding the war of 1948 published in *The Guardian* and
   Shlaim's (2002) response published in the same paper the following day. See Sa'di
   and Slyomovics (this volume) for more detail on Morris' new position.

11. Klaus makes the important observation in her study of middle-class Palestinians in Lebanon that they "are comfortable enough to consider the possibility for a return ... privately financed sometime in the future. For them ... individual memories of lost villas, conserved in black and white photographs, upheld individualistic thoughts about strategies for a homecoming on civilian grounds, perhaps through business relations. Ironically, then, the relations between intensity of national identity and the notion of return has taken on an inverted logic" (2003: 148).

12. The sense of strain and confusion that people feel toward irredentist, nationalist discourse was vividly revealed to me at a rally outside the UN building in Beirut to protest the Geneva Accord in the spring of 2004. After various elders and camp representatives had spoken about the sacredness of return and their love for their homeland, a woman in the group from Shatila that I had come with was reprimanded by a representative of a Palestinian faction because she had been overhead saying "*khara 'al-'awda– bidna n'ish!*" ("shit to the right of return—we want to live!"). Such vehemence—verging on a kind of political blasphemy—may seem paradoxical; she was there, after all, as a willing participant in a rally the very purpose of which was to protest the abrogation of return. Her outburst is less puzzling, however, when we consider the way in which the symbolism of 1948—and the rhetoric of return, as the only right of Palestinians in Lebanon to have featured on the stage of international consciousness and to have been campaigned for by activists—has come to signify all and nothing: not only the affirmation of refugee rights under international law but also the negation of their civil rights within their host country. Demonstrations for return, in other words, have come to represent the only "legitimate" public arena in which refugees can make visible to a larger audience other less legible—though no less devastating—forms of suffering.

13. Not his real name. Where requested, or where I have felt that the interests of friends and informants might be adversely affected, I have used pseudonyms.

14. This narrative of harmonious relations between Jews and Palestinians prior to the events of 1948 is a phenomenon noted by several scholars who have worked on this period (Sayigh 1979; Swedenburg 1995). Clearly there were close economic and social ties between Palestinian and Jewish communities, particularly those of Arab descent. I would suggest, however, that the theme of coexistence is often foregrounded to accentuate the sense of surprise and betrayal, and to emphasize that this was an event that people were completely unprepared for psychologically, as well as materially. It is also presumably intended to challenge the common stereotype that Palestinians were, and still are, anti-Semitic.

15. Both Sayigh (1998b: 50; this volume) and Slyomovics (1998) note how performance of stories is made more arresting and memorable through the appropriation of mnemonic techniques and the embellishing language of Palestinian folklore. Far from being delegitimating traces of the fantastic, the speaker's ability to build on the expectations of the audience conferred authority by showing them to be adept storytellers.

16. This stands in contrast to the claims often made by scholars and sympathetic commentators that the identity of refugees—even those born in the diaspora, with no direct knowledge of Palestine—remains inseparable from their places of origin. Proof of this affective attachment is frequently adduced by the fact that when asked where they are from, children will invariably respond by naming the communities from which their parents or their grandparents originated, rather than the camp in which they now live. Much of my research suggests that while children may know the name of their ancestral village, the strength of this attachment to place of origin is perhaps more tenuous than is often assumed.

17. These findings contrast to those of Rosemary Sayigh, who in her study of life histories of Palestinian women in Shatila camp found that the starting point of narratives was invariably 1948, not only among those who had actually experienced the events of the expulsion, but also among the younger generation who would have been too young to have personal recollections. If, as I suggest, the political context of remembering is central to what is foregrounded, the political context for Sayigh's piece published in 1998—when the commemoration of the Nakba was at its height—might in part explain the discrepancies in our results (Sayigh 1998: 45).

18. Daniel (1996: 174) and Malkki (1995) both argue that this is an essential component of political agency for refugees—who by foregrounding who they were prior to displacement challenge official representations of what they have become.

19. Das suggests that this emphasis on contingency, in which existence itself is seen as "blameworthy," often "masks the real sources of . . . oppression" (Das 1994: 140).

20. See Paul Ricoeur's distinction between lament and blame, where the former derives from external causes, and the latter is a response to suffering that has an identifiable human source (Ricoeur 1995: 250).

21. In the search for causal relations, an event-based, linear view of history is normally called for—one that differentiates between the past and present. According to this linear model of history the authority and legal value of testimony depend on this distancing as a precondition for objectivity (Feldman 1999; Esmeir, this volume).

22. Clara Han's work on the "untimely" language of socialism in La Pincoya, a poor working-class community in Chile, has been very helpful to my thinking here (Han 2004).

23. Among the key theorists of trauma, Dori Laub and Shoshana Felman argue that the Shoah is an event without witnesses—beyond representability—a quagmire of aporias. In this rather circular argument, in which these lacunae appear almost fetishized, all that can be witnessed is the fact of the breakdown of witnessing (Felman and Laub 1992). Cathy Caruth describes this latency of traumatic memory more helpfully, as positioned "between the elision of memory and the precision of recall" (Caruth 1995: 153). See Bresheeth, this volume, for more on trauma and memory.

24. As Das reminds us, in translating suffering into words, we may deny its reality as effectively as censorship and repression, since discourse all too readily dissolves "the concrete and existential reality of the suffering victim" (Das 1995: 143).

25. It is important to bear in mind that the estrangement of the physical and social spaces of memory is particularly advanced in Shatila because of the violent disruptions that followed the Israeli invasion of Beirut in 1982, the "War of the Camps" between 1985–87, and internal intra-factional disputes during the late 1980s and early 1990s.

26. Debbora Battaglia has argued persuasively that theories of memory need to accommodate the idea of "forgetting as willed transformation of memory"—not in terms of loss, but as carrying its own constructive force (Battaglia 1992: 14).

27. As Leslie Dwyer notes in her study of memories of violence in Bali (1965–66), "The social effects of violence and the realist discourses deployed to address them are often discontinuous, with programs of reconciliation or recovery or social repair faced with more complex cultural forms that may be recognized" (Dwyer 2004: 1–2).

28. This is similar to comments made by Raja Shehadeh about how a standardized vocabulary of national belonging engenders an altered perception of homeland: "Sometimes when I am walking in the hills, say Batn el-Hawa, unselfconsciously enjoying the touch of the hard land under my feet, the smell of thyme and the hills and trees around me, I find myself looking at it, it transforms itself before my eyes into a symbol of samidin, of our struggle, of our loss. And at that very moment, I am robbed of that tree; instead, there is a hollow space into which anger and pain flow" (cited in Parmenter 1994: 86–87).

29. Among them, the Israeli air raid that destroyed Nabatiyya (1973), the attack on Tel al-Za'tar—carried out by Lebanese Christians, with Syrian backing (1976); the "War of the Camps" (1983–1987) when Amal militias besieged Beirut camps—also

with Syrian support; and the "Internal Wars" (1989) when Arafat loyalists were pitted against Syrian-backed Palestinian factions.

30. Giorgio Agamben identifies this mode of subjection as central to the logic of twentieth-century bio-power: "no longer to make die or to make live, but to make survive. The decisive activity of bio-power in our time consists in the production not of life or death, but of a mutable and virtually infinite survival" (Agamben 1999: 155).

31. Efrat Ben Ze'ev makes the point, elegantly, when she says that "Palestinians are a 'classic' diaspora, and yet they also embody post-modern features" (Ben Ze'ev 2005: 127).

32. The shifting attitude of Farukh's generations toward "return" resonates with the controversial claims made by Sari Hanafi about its diminishing significance in refugee communities (Hanafi, 2002; 2005).

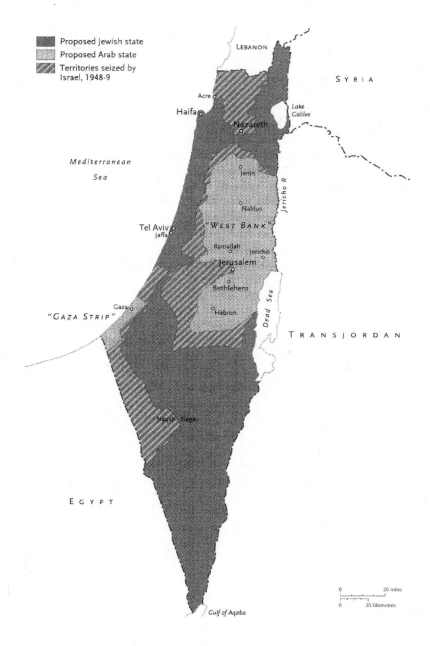

Proposed Jewish state
Proposed Arab state
Territories seized by
Israel, 1948-9

LEBANON

SYRIA

Acre

Haifa

Lake
Galilee

Nazareth

Mediterranean

Sea

Jenin

Nablus

Jericho R

Tel Aviv
Jaffa

"WEST BANK"

Ramallah

Jericho

Jerusalem

Bethlehem

"GAZA STRIP"

Gaza

Dead Sea

Hebron

TRANSJORDAN

EGYPT

Nadab Negev

0   20 miles

0   20 kilometres

Gulf of Aqaba

Figure 15 Additional Palestinian land seized by Zionists in 1948, beyond the 1947 proposed Partition Plan.

Afterword

REFLECTIONS ON REPRESENTATION, HISTORY, AND MORAL ACCOUNTABILITY

Ahmad H. Sa'di

Memory is the diary that we all carry about with us
OSCAR WILDE, The Importance of Being Earnest

The 1948 War over Palestine has had an enduring impact on world affairs. Its ramifications and repercussions have continued to occupy center stage in world politics and news reports since the events unfolded in 1947–48. The issue, controversial and contested, has polarized governments and individuals and made impossible the presentation of a dispassionate history of the events. This essay is not intended to provide a comprehensive history of the struggle over Palestine or the complex unfolding of the Nakba, a truly impossible task. Rather my aim is to explore the relationships among representation, history, and morality. How can one condone the expulsion of one people from its homeland in order to make room for another? This question is usually silenced because it casts doubt on the narratives and claims to morality of the victors of 1948, the Zionists and the State of Israel.

We are now approaching the sixtieth anniversary of both the Nakba and Israel's creation. Will it be marked in the same way the fiftieth anniversary was in 1998? At that time, it was Israel's fiftieth Independence Day that attracted most of the attention in the West. Besides state-sponsored celebrations in Israel and other forms of celebration in Europe, Hollywood put on a show that was transmitted live from coast to coast with the participation of celebrities including U.S. President Bill Clinton. Mainstream Western media coverage replayed the mythical account of the creation of Israel less than a decade after the Holocaust. The story presented was the standard narrative of glorious rebirth, a story of exile and return after millennia, with a people of memory and suffering redeemed by belonging to their own modern nation-state with all its accoutrements: sovereignty, dignity, a flag, an anthem, a mythical past, and future projects. A noble but embattled state. This narrative removed the native Palestinians from the unfolding of history, as their presence would cause embarrassment to a celebration of an otherwise successful colonial mission. This kind of narrative—where the victims disappear from the scene—has comprised one important strategy of un-narration—a strategy that the essays in the book seek to intercept through their analysis of Palestinian memory.[1]

Yet, even in 1998, the seamlessness of this narrative could not be maintained. Nagging questions raised by faint though persistent voices of Palestinians, the victims of the Zionist project, were unsettling. The marches of symbolic return that Palestinians organized in various parts of the world as well as the minute of silence they observed to commemorate the destruction of their society (an act that accompanied the creation of Israel) were sidelined but could not be totally ignored. The refusal of the victims to disappear and to leave the past buried raised anew their moral and political claims. Solidarity groups all over the world, including in Israel, also raised their voices in support of Palestinian rights.[2]

These anniversary events tell us two things about the relationship between morality and narration. First, the question of morality can be explored by highlighting the dialectical relationship between perpetrator and victim. Research on the memories of people who have endured human-inflicted catastrophes tends to draw a sharp polarity between victim and perpetrator and to analyze only the victim's memories. Most of the essays in this book follow this form, looking at Palestinian memories of their uprooting and displacement in 1948, exploring their subjectivity and the ways they counter Israeli time, historiography, and commemoration with a resistant Palestinian time marked by their own reckoning of generations and their own landmark events.[3] However, without the frame of mind, the attitude, the consciousness, and the actions of the perpetrator, the suffering of the victim would not have occurred; it might be said that the will of the former governs the whole interaction. This essay, therefore, will try to sketch, for those unfamiliar with them, the contours of the Zionist project that led to the Palestinians' catastrophe (Nakba), attuned to the way both victims and perpetrators carry with them traces of their antagonist's presence.

Second, we need to examine the moral justifications of perpetrators and to understand how they are related to maintaining the perpetrators' gains. Socrates has most famously referred to this problem in his dialogue with Euthyphro: "I don't think they have the nerve to say or argue that if they are doing wrong they should not pay penalty. What they say, I think, is that they're not doing wrong" (Plato, 1997: 70). In the case of Jewish supporters of the Zionist project today, there appear to be three modes of denial of moral responsibility for the Nakba: denying or hiding the historically documented violence; neutralizing the moral entailments of the Nakba by shifting the focus to less than relevant issues; and hard-heartedly affirming the facts of the Nakba but denying them any moral import. These three modes will be examined in the final section of the essay.

The Palestinian Nakba was an event, a rupture in history, and a tragedy. It was the culmination of a historical development. So the debate about its morality depends on examining both the period that preceded it and the one that followed it. The second section of this essay therefore focuses on the violent path that led to the Nakba, providing a brief counter-history based on now well-established scholarly research. This can be counterposed to the resilient myths about the moral status of the Zionist project, laying the groundwork for a reflection on how Israelis and their supporters now deal—morally, politically, and intellectually—with the cracks historical scholarship and Palestinian memory-work have created in their myths.

Landmarks on the Road to the Nakba

The catastrophe that the Palestinian people experienced as a result of the 1948 War and the creation of the state of Israel began with a vision. In 1895, two years before the convening of the first Zionist Congress, Theodor Herzl, the founder of the Zionist movement, described in his diaries a two-part plan to expel the Palestinians. "We shall try to spirit the penniless population across the border by procuring employment for it in the transit countries, while denying it any employment in our country. . . . Both the process of expropriation and removal of the poor must be carried out discreetly and circumspectly." As for the rich, he added, they would be bought out. "Let the owners of immovable property believe that they are cheating us, selling things for more than they are worth. But we are not going to sell them anything back" (Herzl 1960: 88).

The second part of the plan failed, for Palestinian property owners largely refused to sell land to the Zionists once it was realized that they planned to take over the entire country. So the Zionist project came to depend on the first part of the plan—the involuntary removal of the population, whether penniless or propertied. Thus, a process of colonization and expulsion was put into operation. When Herzl documented these thoughts, Jews constituted less than 5 percent of the population in Palestine. Still further, they were mostly Jews of Arab culture—an identity that has been recently called Arab Jews (Shenhav 2003; Shohat 1999 and 2006)—who opposed Zionism.

Herzl's documented private thoughts were isolated moments of honesty. They would be published only in 1960. His public views carried another message. The indigenous population was promised that Zionist colonization would bring with it prosperity and civilization. This message was most famously expressed in his response to a letter sent to him in 1899 by Yusuf al-Khalidi, then the mayor of Jerusalem, who urged him to look for another country where the Zionist project could be fulfilled. It was articulated more thoroughly in his work of fiction *Altneuland* first published in 1902 (see Sa'di, 1997).

Herzl thought of Zionism as part of Europe's overseas colonial project. In *The Jewish State*, he suggested that "we should there form a part of a wall of defense for Europe in Asia, an outpost of civilization against barbarism" (quoted in Hertzberg 1973: 222). Indeed, since its establishment Zionism has been connected by an umbilical cord to Western imperialist powers despite differences of various sorts.

The main landmarks on the road between the emergence of Zionism as an organized political force on the international stage and the destruction of Palestinian society in 1948, when Israel was established, are the first Zionist Congress and the establishment of the World Zionist Organization in 1897; the Balfour Declaration of 1917, in which Britain announced its decision to support the Zionist colonization of Palestine; Britain's occupation of Palestine in World War I; the defeat by the British of the 1936–39 Palestinian Rebellion; World War II and the Holocaust; and finally the 1947 United Nations Resolution on the Partition of Palestine and the 1948 War that came fast on its heels. These historical events appear to give Zionism a clear trajectory: from the idea of a Jewish Commonwealth in Palestine, to committing the British Empire, the main power, to the Zionist cause, to the destruction of Palestinians' organized resistance by the British Mandatory power, to the changing of patronage from the declining power, Britain, to the United States, the rising superpower in 1942, through to the achievement of international legitimacy and finally the establishment of the Jewish State on 77.8 percent of Palestine's territory (e.g. Hadawi 1967; Kayyali 1978; Said 1979; Pappé 2004).

The establishment of the Jewish state on so much of Palestine was accomplished through the expulsion of the vast majority of the Palestinians who lived there. Despite the vague language of his 1917 declaration—which spoke about a national home for the Jewish people—Balfour envisaged that in the end, British support would lead to the establishment of a Jewish State. He viewed this as "a matter for gradual development in accordance with the ordinary laws of political evolution" (quoted in Nutting n.d.: 4). Moreover, he insightfully anticipated the reaction of Western (at least official) public opinion to the demands, rights, and plight of the Palestinians:

> In Palestine we do not propose even to go through the form of consulting the wishes of the present inhabitants of the country. . . . Zionism, be it right or wrong, good or bad, is rooted in age-old traditions, in present needs, in future hopes, of far profounder import than the desires and prejudices of the 700,000 Arabs who now inhabit that ancient land
>
> (QUOTED IN IBID: 5)

In Palestine, human relations between native Palestinians and Jewish settlers in this early period had been conflictual, even if occasional cooperation and signs of friendship on the individual level also developed. Although the conflicts began with the inception of Zionist settlement in Palestine—as Mandel (1976) meticulously shows—they intensified with the increase in Jewish immigration and the upsurge in the violation of individual Palestinians' rights and their growing national aspirations.

Indeed the conflict between the assertion of rights by the Palestinians, rooted in their long presence on the land, and the Zionist aspirations that, however messianic and restorative for Jews, negated these rights, increasingly occupied center stage in Jewish–Arab relations (Said 1979). The cruelty of this dialectic was described by the Jewish educator Yitzhak Epstein (1907),[4] who witnessed the eviction of the villagers (*fellahin*) of Ja'una and Mutilla following the purchase of their land by the colonizing agency of the Baron Edmond de Rothschild from an absentee landlord:

> And thus, when we come to occupy the land, the question at once arises: what will the *fellahin* do after we buy their fields? . . . From the viewpoint of customary justice and official honesty we are completely righteous, even beyond the strict

letter of the law. But, if we do not want to deceive ourselves with a conventional lie, we must admit that we have driven impoverished people from their humble abode and taken bread out of their mouths. Where will the dispossessed, with only a little money, turn? . . .

The lament of Arab women on the day that their families left Ja'uni—Rosh Pina—to go and settle on the Horan east of the Jordan still rings in my ears today. The men rode on donkeys and the women followed them weeping bitterly, and the valley was filled with their lamentation. As they went they stopped to kiss the stones and the earth.

(DOWTY 2001: 39–41)

The abrogation of justice, the failure of morality, and the consequent need for self-deception to which Epstein refers would only increase along with the development of the Zionist project, for he also described in detail the devious means by which land was acquired at the turn of the century.[5]

These attempts to acquire land could not continue without resistance. They were opposed by the Palestinians and officially contested by the British Mandatory authorities. Moreover, they achieved only limited results. In 1948, when the Mandate was terminated, the lands owned by the Jewish community in Palestine (and by Zionist institutions) purchased or received through state concessions are estimated to have been between 5.6 percent and 7 percent of Mandatory Palestine (Hadawi 1988; Ruedy 1971; Khalidi 1991).

As with cases of European colonization of other world regions during the nineteenth and the early twentieth centuries—Algeria, South Africa, and Rhodesia being notable examples—land was most often acquired by force. The UN resolution of 1947 for the partition of Palestine led to fighting that the Zionist leadership conceived as a golden opportunity to achieve its long-awaited goals. Although the hard facts regarding the developments during 1947–48 that led to the Nakba are well known and documented, the obfuscation by the dominant Israeli story has made recovering the facts, presenting a sensible narrative, and putting them across to the world a formidable task.

To recount these developments briefly, the UN resolution of November 29, 1947, which was only a recommendation, proposed the partition of Palestine into two states: a Jewish state and an Arab one.[6] Although Jews by then constituted only about one-third of the population, the proposed Jewish State was to be established on 56 percent of Palestine's territory and was to have included only a slight Jewish majority of 499,000 Jews versus 438,000 Palestinians. The Arab state was to have been composed of 43 percent of the country and would include 818,000 Palestinians and fewer than 10,000 Jews (Khalidi 1997: 11). Furthermore, in terms of land ownership, the Jewish holdings in the proposed Jewish State were about 11 percent as compared to the 80 percent of land then owned by Palestinians. In the proposed Arab Palestinian state, Jews owned a mere 1 percent of the land (ibid: 13).

Having voted for partition, the UN took no steps to implement it. This enabled the Zionists to implement their own even more one-sided partition plan, with an appearance of UN legitimacy. It also enabled them to incorporate into its implementation the transfer (a euphemism for what we now call ethnic cleansing) of the Palestinians residing within the boundaries of the Jewish state. The imposition of this extreme Zionist plan annuls any legitimacy Israel might claim on the basis of the UN decision.

Not content with the 56 percent of the country offered to them by the UN plan, the Zionists colluded with 'Abdallah, the Emir of Trans-Jordan, to partition the remaining 43 percent proposed for a Palestinian Arab State (Shlaim 1988; 2001; Rogan 2001) and ended up with more than three quarters of the country. Even this was not enough. Zionist leaders have always refused to accept a final demarcation of the Jewish State's borders. This refusal came to light in the debates among the Zionist leadership over an earlier partition plan in 1937.[7] According to the Israeli historian Benny Morris (2001: 138) the two leaders of the Zionist movement, Chaim Weizmann and David Ben-Gurion, "saw partition as a stepping stone to further expansion and eventual takeover of the whole of Palestine." Morris cites a letter that Ben-Gurion sent to his son Amos in which he declared:

> [A] Jewish state in part [of Palestine] is not an end, but a beginning. . . . Our possession is important not only for itself . . . through this we increase our power, and every increase in power facilitates getting hold of the country in its entirety. Establishing a [small] state . . . will serve as a very potent lever in our historical efforts to redeem the whole country.
>
> (IBID)

Ben-Gurion (and mainstream Zionism) remained faithful to this theory of stages, even when he seemed to have accepted a different course. Thus on May 14, 1948, he wrote in his diary: "Take the American Declaration of Independence, for instance. . . . It contains no mention of the territorial limits. We are not obliged to state the limits of our state" (quoted in Khalidi 1997: 17). And, after the end of the 1948 War, reflecting on his decision to stop short of occupying the whole country, he stated: "There was a danger of getting saddled with a hostile Arab majority . . . of entanglement with the United Nations and the powers, and of the State Treasury collapsing. . . . even so, we liberated a very large area, much more than we thought. . . . now we have to work for two or three generations. . . . as for the rest, we'll see later" (Flapan 1987: 52).

The Palestinians' position remained unchanged from the beginning of the British Mandate to its end: they opposed partition and supported the establishment of a political system that would reflect the wishes of the majority. Although they were ready to discuss the modalities of independence, they never doubted their natural right to be the masters in their homeland. Palestinians' sentiments regarding the UN resolution for the partition of Palestine were summarized by the historian Walid Khalidi (1991: 305–6):

> The Palestinians failed to see why they should be made to pay for the Holocaust . . ., and recalled that Zionism was born in the 1880s, long before the advent of the Third Reich. They failed to see why it was not fair for the Jews to be a minority in a unitary Palestinian State, while it was fair for almost half of the Palestinian population—the indigenous majority on its own ancestral soil—to be converted overnight into a minority under alien rule in the envisaged Jewish State.

The conflict of 1948 unfolded in several stages. Soon after the announcement of the UN partition resolution in November 1947, local skirmishes erupted between the two communities. Attacks and retributions escalated into civil strife. With the Cold War developing between the United States and the Soviet Union, the British did not wish to come into conflict with the United States over Palestine. They began preparations to evacuate Palestine on August 1, 1948 (later they declared an earlier date, May 15). However the conflict was abruptly changed at the beginning of April 1948. The Zionist leadership feared an alteration in the U.S. position, abandoning its support for partition in favor of a plan to place Palestine under international trusteeship (Pappé 2004: 130; Morris, 2001b: 204–5). In response, the Hagana, the main Jewish military force, opened a large-scale offensive.

The aim of Plan D, as the offensive was known, was to capture the territories allocated to the Jewish state, as well as areas in Galilee and on the highway between Tel-Aviv and Jerusalem that were part of the proposed Palestinian state (Flapan 1987: 42). The plan, as quoted in Morris (2004a: 164) called for "operations against enemy settlements which are in the rear of, within or near our defense lines, with the aim of preventing their use as bases for an active armed force." However, as Morris points out, given the size of the country, most Palestinians towns and villages within and beyond the proposed Jewish state fell within this category. According to Plan D, the brigade commanders were given "discretion" in what to do with the villages they occupied—that is, to destroy them or leave them standing (Morris 2004a.: 165). On numerous occasions in the execution of Plan D, the Zionist forces expelled people from their towns and villages, committed rape and other acts of violence, massacred civilians, and executed prisoners of war. As we will see, these acts have been widely documented, most forcefully by Israeli historians using military and state archives.

The memories recorded in this book had as their background the kinds of massacres, expulsion, and rape recorded even by some troubled perpetrators. The following testimonies come from soldiers who participated in the occupation of the village of Dawayima in October of 1948. The village was classified before the war as "very friendly" and the occupying force faced only "light resistance." According to a report on the testimony of one Israeli soldier to a MAPAM (United Workers Party) member, "The first [wave] of conquerors killed about 80 to 100 [male] Arabs, women and children. The children they killed by breaking their heads with sticks. There was not a house without dead." He added that a soldier had bragged of raping and shooting a woman, two old women had been blown up in a house, and another woman with her baby were shot (Morris 2004a: 470). Another soldier reported:

> As we got up on the roofs, we saw Arabs running about in the alleyways [below]. We opened fire on them. . . . From our high position we saw a vast plain stretching eastward. . . and the plain was covered by thousands of fleeing Arabs. . . . The machineguns began to chatter and the flight turned into a rout.
>
> (QUOTED IN MORRIS 2004a: 469)

Reflecting on this massacre, the first soldier quoted above remarked that "cultured officers . . . had turned into base murderers and this is not in the heat of battle . . . but out of a system of expulsion and destruction. The less Arabs remained—the better. This principle is the political motor for the expulsion and the atrocities" (quoted in ibid.: 470).

It was not until May 15, a month and a half after the implementation of Plan D, that neighboring Arab states sent in armed forces in an attempt to halt the Zionist seizure of territory and the ethnic cleansing of the population. By then, many acts of expulsion and massacre had occurred, including the widely publicized massacre of Deir Yassin (April 9, 1948); the occupation of cities and the expulsion of their inhabitants in Tiberias (April 18), Haifa

(April 22), Safad (May 11) and Jaffa (May 13). This campaign led to the expulsion of some 380,000 Palestinians, about one-half of the total Palestinian
refugees who would soon be created. In the coastal area between Haifa and
Tel-Aviv, for example, fifty-eight out of the sixty-four villages that had existed
were wiped out (Pappé 2004: 137). By the end of the war only two remained.
In the course of this campaign even villages that maintained good relations
with nearby Jewish settlements and refrained from resorting to violence, such
as Deir Yassin, were not spared. The physical and psychological condition of
the refugees as well as the horror stories they carried intensified the pressures
on Arab leaders to commit their regular armies to the battle.[8]

Although Arab military commanders and some politicians were well
aware of the weakness of their armies, they bent to public pressure and tried
to salvage what they could. The newly independent Arab states, most of
which were still to some degree under the military control of Western powers, were unable to conduct a military campaign. Their national armies were
unprepared for war. They were small, poorly equipped and inexperienced.
Moreover, because of political rivalries between Arab leaders, there was a
failure to coordinate operations (Flapan 1987; Gerges 2001: 151–158; Shlaim
2001). Their intervention came too late, when their ability to tip the balance
of power had already been lost. The Zionist forces were able to repel the
attacks of the Arab armies, to pursue the campaign of conquest, and to continue expelling Palestinians and destroying their villages.

The result was the demographic transformation of Palestine (J. Abu-
Lughod 1971). The proposed partition lines were breached so that the State of
Israel within its first year covered not half of Mandatory Palestine but more
than three-quarters of it. The Arab Palestinian population within its borders
was a fraction of what the Partition Plan had proposed even for the smaller
unit that had not had such an Arab majority. According to J. Abu-Lughod
(1971: 160–61), the Israeli census of November 1948 must have counted only
60,000–64,000 Arabs.[9]

Today, there is little or no academic controversy about the basic course
of events that led to the Zionist victory and the almost complete destruction of Palestinian society. But the popular perception of these events is still
clouded by the myths the Zionist leadership created to hide what it had done.
Simha Flapan, an Israeli revisionist historian and left-wing Zionist activist,
forcefully argues in his book *The Birth of Israel: Myths and Realities* (1990) that
Zionism fostered seven myths around Israel's creation in 1948. According to
these myths, the Zionist movement accepted the UN partition resolution

and planned for peace; the Arabs rejected this resolution and launched a war; the Palestinians fled following orders by their leaders; the Arab states were united in their aim to destroy the Jewish state and annihilate the Yishuv; the Arab armies' invasion of Israel made war unavoidable; Israelis stood with their back to the wall, the few against the many in a heroic war of survival; and finally the Arab states turned down Israeli peace proposals.

These myths survived for a long time and proved instrumental for promoting the internal cohesion of Israeli society and enlisting international sympathy and support (Shlaim 2001: 79). Before reflecting on why Zionist and Western audiences needed this sort of mystification, we might perhaps ask how the Yishuv's success and the disintegration of Palestinian society have been explained. Scholarship shows first that "the transformation of Palestine" (I. Abu-Lughod 1971) would not have occurred had the colonial regime showed less commitment to the Zionist cause. The British nurtured a settler movement that aimed to take over the country and transfer (i.e., expel) the natives. The British supported Zionism until at least 1940, blocking Palestinian efforts to halt Zionist immigration and settlement. Under British rule, the size of the Jewish population grew more than tenfold—from 56,000 in 1914 to about 650,000 in 1948. Their share in the population soared from a mere 9 percent to about 34 percent. Under the British, the Yishuv had established an underground military force that was larger and stronger than anything the Arab states and Palestinian community were able to put up.[10]

Second, plans for a total war with the Palestinians had been conceived as early as 1937. In the summer of that year, in anticipation of a British withdrawal, Ben-Gurion ordered Elimelech Slikowitz (Avnir), the Hagana's commander in Tel-Aviv, to prepare a plan for the occupation of the whole of Palestine. A series of refinements and alterations were then introduced to the plan (A, B, C), which culminated in Plan D, the one employed in 1948 (Khalidi 1997: 6–8). These military preparations were part of a thorough process of institution-building; a process that Zionist historiography refers to as *medina she-ba-derekh* (a state in the making). The institutions included the Jewish Agency; the labor union, Histadrut; the underground armed force, the Hagana; the striking units, Palmach; the Jewish National Fund; the Jewish National Council, Va'ad Leumi; a separate educational system; intelligence services, Shai, etc. This institutional infrastructure established under the Mandate would later constitute the foundations of the Jewish state.

Furthermore, Zionism enjoyed great sympathy among Western policymakers and public opinion. This includes the two major British parties

(Labour and Conservatives) and many leading politicians such as Balfour, Churchill, and Lloyd George. Not only did such politicians support Zionism, but some, like Churchill, held strong anti-Arab views, perhaps a legacy of Orientalism and anti-Islamic sentiment. In the United States, Zionism enjoyed the support of American presidents from the late nineteenth century onward, in part because of anti-Muslim sentiment. President Theodore Roosevelt privately expressed his belief in 1907 that "it is impossible to expect moral, intellectual and material well-being where Mohammedanism is supreme" (quoted in Little 2003: 15). And in July 1918, Roosevelt observed that the allies should "pledge themselves never to make peace until the Turk is driven from Europe, and . . . the Jews [are] given control of Palestine" (ibid).[11] President Wilson was even ready to forgo his principle of self-determination in the case of Palestine. Regarding the contradiction between his principles and his support for the Zionist cause, he assured the Zionist leader Rabbi Stephen Wise, "Don't worry Dr. Wise, Palestine is yours" (Quoted in Davidson 2002: 24). The strongest support in the United States for Zionism—outside some sections of the Jewish community—came from the large evangelical constituency.[12] In the West, support for the Zionist cause also prevailed among liberal public opinion, left-wing parties, and in the social democratic movement. As Kelemen (1996a, 1996b) has shown, Zionism was viewed through the prism of enlightened colonialism. The kibbutz was conceived as the fulfillment of socialist ideals on a virgin soil. In the U.S. the Zionist settlers' experience was sometimes compared with that of the first American settlers.

Finally, the Palestinians reached the final showdown of 1948 after being defeated a decade earlier by the British. Their great rebellion (1936–39), the strongest and the most sustained revolt prior to World War II against British domination in the Middle East and one of the great anticolonial rebellions was, in retrospect, untimely. It occurred during the Spanish civil war (1936–1939) where a mighty struggle took place in Europe and on the eve of World War II. The British put down the rebellion through the use of excessive force (which included the use of air power and heavy artillery) and barbaric methods.[13] When the 1948 war broke out, the Palestinians thus lacked trained cadres and arms.[14]

There were many other contingent factors that affected the unfolding of the last stage before the Nakba—from the continuing crisis over Jewish refugees in Europe to the fact that it was an election year in the United States, where President Harry Truman was fighting a battle for survival and was in desperate need of the Jewish community's support.

Scholars have been increasingly unafraid to recognize that Palestinians bore some responsibility for their debacle as well. Under the British Mandate, they were not encouraged to build national institutions, and no elite was trained to take over after independence, as in other British colonies. Nor were political parties encouraged—parties that could have contributed to political mobilization. Political leadership was also problematic; according to Khalidi (2001), Palestinian society suffered from factionalism and rivalries that divided the elite. The British tradition of divide and rule (Robinson 1972), whereby the colonial administration created beside the local elite a rival one to secure the collaboration of the indigenous powerful groups, did great damage in Palestine. The power struggle between the Husaynis and their arch rivals the Nashashibis was debilitating. And Palestinian notables indeed suffered from a failure of vision, unconnected to emerging social groups. Yet, these failures hardly justify the uprooting of this people from their patrimony or the destruction of their society.

Moral Responsibility

The 1948 War resulted in the destruction of some 420 Palestinian towns and villages, and the expulsion of at least 780,000 Palestinians who were condemned to life in exile. These refugees composed more than 80 percent of the Palestinians who lived in the territories upon which the Jewish State was established; they constituted more than half of the Palestinian population. Yet, the story of their Nakba has hardly been told, and certainly not been well heard. Why has it not found the space where it could take form as a story of (in)justice and (disregard for) human dignity? By that I do not mean an officially sanctioned story of the Nakba that would be encompassed within the cover of a book or a series of books, the walls of a museum, or the boundaries of a park of soulless monuments. Rather, I mean the establishment of a space of legitimacy and understanding within which a pluralistic discourse that would include the multiple voices and experiences of Palestinians could find a hearing, and perhaps contribute to a solution in the future. This failure stems not only from the victims' silences, as discussed in the introduction to the book in terms of an elderly woman's despair about how to "whistle without lips," but also from a general lack of desire by those responsible to deal with the moral weight of the Palestinian catastrophe.

Two audiences are crucial here: the Western world (particularly the United States) and Israeli Jews. It is remarkable how large Western audiences have accepted uncritically the Zionist version of 1948 and the creation of the Palestinian "refugee problem." Besides the legacy of Orientalism that has colored the way in which large segments of Westerners view the Arabs (Said 1978, Little 2003), the question of Palestine touches some powerful elements of Western moral and intellectual culture. Firstly, the Nakba took place in the shadow of the Holocaust, the most disturbing act of inhumanity perpetrated in the heart of modern Europe, an act that brought into question the enlightenment of Western civilization. The Palestinians seem to have been considered insignificant residual victims of this grand history. Their suffering seems to count little compared to the calming of Western conscience. Ben-Gurion understood this very well. He referred to Western support for the partition of Palestine as "Western civilization's gesture of repentance for the Holocaust"(Morris 2001b: 186).

Second, the Zionist narrative is of magisterial dimensions, including many elements that resonate with the Western imagination: the return of the "people of memory" (this label was used, among others, by Nora, 1996: 18) to their ancient land after two millennia of exile, embodying the dialectic of demise-(re)birth, a theme that finds expression in most meaningful stories and theories of the West, from the story of Christ's resurrection to the theories of Marx and Freud. The creation of Israel has been framed as both an outcome of urgent necessity and as an act of heroism. Images of young, healthy, and brave soldiers, of young farmers, craftsmen, and scientists, substituted for those of helpless Jewish men, women, and children herded to their death in the Nazi concentration camps. Beyond that, the 1948 War has been presented as a war of survival of the few against the many; a modern version of the story of David versus Goliath.

As to the ethnic cleansing of Palestinians during the Nakba and its aftermath, it was represented by Israeli and Zionist scholars as a deceitful act of the natives themselves. According to this story, the Palestinians were called upon by their leaders to leave their homes, against the appeals of the Jewish leadership for them to stay and co-exist in peace. Two interrelated logics for this conspiracy were given: to smear the Jews and to prevent a situation in which Palestinian civilians would hinder the advancement of the invading Arab armies. Already during the war of 1947–48 this misinformation campaign had begun to operate in full swing (see Khalidi, 2005; Esber 2003: 129–32).[15]

This version of the 1948 War and the creation of the Palestinian refugee problem has had wide credibility among Western audiences, despite the emergence of more and more well-documented accounts that attested to its speciousness. The works of W. Khalidi (1959a; 1959b), Childers (1961, 1971); Nazzal (1978) were among the earlier ones. Ironically, however, the most comprehensive evidence against the Zionist version of the War of 1948 has come from the Israeli archives, particularly from the Israeli Army archive. From these sources, the victims' narratives have begun to gain some credibility because they have been corroborated by reports by the perpetrators of the expulsions: army commanders, officers, and soldiers who took active part in causing the Nakba. Morris has made the most thorough use of these sources in his study of what he calls, euphemistically, "the birth of the Palestinian refugee problem" (Morris 1987; 2004a). This evidence has not diminished the chorus of the minstrels for the Zionist cause, but it does open up a space for the victims of this particular set of events to tell their own story, and perhaps for it to begin to be heard.

The most resistant audience for this emerging story is composed of Israeli Jews, who seem—officially, collectively, and in the vast majority of cases, individually—unwilling to deal with their moral responsibility for the Nakba. Charles Peguy has written, "It is not given for a man to make for himself another cradle" (quoted in Booth, 1999: 255). His point is that the past is both nonelective and unalterable. However, when the cradle has involved the destruction, death, and uprooting of others, how should a group that considers itself a "community of fate" and a "community of suffering" relate to the genesis of this situation and to its victims? How should Israeli Jews, and those outside of Israel who support them, cope with their messy past?

A small story of an event that took place in the Negev desert just after the end of the 1948 War sheds light on one method for dealing with the past— keeping it hidden. The story, as reported in the British newspaper, the *Guardian* a few years ago, is as follows:

> In August 1949, an army unit stationed at Nirim in the Negev shot an Arab man and captured a Bedouin girl with him. Her name and age remain unknown, but she was probably in her mid-teens. In the following hours she was taken from the hut and forced to shower naked in full view of the soldiers. Three of the men then raped her.
>
> After the Sabbath meal the platoon commander, identified . . . as a man called Moshe. . . . proposed a vote on what should be done with her. Most of the 20 or so soldiers present voted for the alternative by chanting: "We want to . . . "

The commander organised a rota for groups of his men to gang rape the girl over the next three days. Moshe and one of his sergeants went first, leaving the girl unconscious. Next morning, she complicated matters by protesting about her treatment. Moshe told one of his sergeants to kill her. She was forced into a patrol vehicle with several soldiers, two carrying shovels, and they drove off into the dunes. When the girl realised what was about to happen she tried to run, but only made it a few paces before she was shot by a Sergeant Michael. Her body was buried in a grave less than a foot deep.

(MCGREAL 2003)

What is interesting about this story, which appeared as a single entry in the diary of Ben-Gurion—the first prime minister of Israel and one of its founding fathers—is that it was classified until recently as a secret document in the army archive (McGreal 2003). As Slyomovics and Khalili and Humphries discuss in this volume, Morris (2004a) reports that there were "about a dozen" cases of documented rape, often followed by murder. As he notes, "We have to assume that the dozen cases of rape that were reported . . . are not the whole story. They are just the tip of the iceberg" (Morris, 2004b: 39). Morris (2004a) also mentions twenty-four cases of massacre, while Palestinian scholars using oral historical methods have documented more than sixty (Abdel Jawad, n.d.). Yet, as with the case of the Bedouin girl, these were silenced, shelved, hidden, removed from the public eye, or denied.

The same strategy was employed with regard to the expulsion of Palestinians during the 1948 War and its aftermath. Yitzhak Rabin, who epitomized the 1948 generation (Dor Tashah) described the expulsion of the inhabitants of the towns of Lydda and Ramlah as follows:

While the fighting was still in progress (in the front), we have to grapple with a troublesome problem: the fate of the populations of Lod [Lydda] and Ramleh, numbering some fifty thousand civilians. Not even Ben-Gurion could offer any solution, and during the discussions at the operational headquarters, he remained silent, as was his habit in such situation. . . . We walked outside, Ben-Gurion accompanied us. Alon repeated his question: "What is to be done with the population?" Ben-Gurion waved his hand in a gesture that said: Drive them out! . . . There was no way of avoiding the use of force and warning shots in order to make the inhabitants march the 10–15 miles.

(QUOTED IN KIDRON 1988: 91–92)

Rabin omitted from his account the fact that the journey took place in late July in the summer heat, during which at least 335 civilians died (Palumbo 1987: 137; for a personal account of this journey, see Busailah 1981).

As with Rabin's description of Ben-Gurion's attitude, Morris (2004a) describes orders by Moshe Carmel, the Northern front commander, to expel the Palestinians from the villages in the Galilee captured in "Operation Hiram." The order "was apparently issued while Carmel and Ben-Gurion—who came to visit—were meeting in Nazareth, or minutes after their meeting; one may assume that it was authorized, if not actually authored, by the prime minister" (Morris 2004a: 464). This, however, did not prevent the prime minister from asserting that "Israel has never expelled a single Arab" (quoted in Finkelstein 1995: 53).

While the truth about the inhabitants and their tragedy has been denied or obfuscated, deliberate efforts were made to conceal the former localities of the expelled Palestinians from the public eye. Moshe Dayan—one of Israel's most influential military and political figures between 1948 and the late 1970s—wanted to believe that the obliteration of the Palestinian landscape had reached a level of perfection. In a lecture given before the Israel Technological Institute in 1969 and reported in Ha'aretz on April 4, 1969, he declared:

> Jewish villages were built in the place of Arab villages. You do not even know the names of these villages, and I don't blame you, since these geography books no longer exist. Not only the books do not exist—the Arab villages are not there either.
>
> (DAYAN 1969)

However, this strategy could not be employed across the board, since in many cases Israeli Jews lived in Palestinian houses, used their furniture, ate the fruit of their groves and gardens, plowed their fields, drank from their wells, and walked in the alleyways and the streets they paved.

The novelist Yizhar Smilansky, known by his penname S. Yizhar, was among the very few to question the morality of the expulsion of Palestinians. His novel *Hirbet Hiz'ah*, (a fictionalized name of a Palestinian village) based on his wartime experience, grapples with this reasoning and the morality of the expropriations and expulsions. The defining moment for Yizhar and the climax of the novel is when the protagonist is asked to take part in the expulsion. He writes:

If we have to do this, let others do it. And if we have to defile ourselves let others defile their hands—I can't. Plainly no. However, immediately another voice from inside me sang [cynically]: high-souled, high-souled. . . . I hesitated and debated with myself, encouraged, and told Moshe [the field commander] "Does this mean we must expel them? What can these people do: who can they harm?"

Ha! Moshe answered me with affection. "This is what is written in the orders concerning this operation." "But this is not right," I said without knowing which of the arguments or the lectures I had in mind to bring as overwhelming proof. Thus I repeated "This really is not right."

(YIZHAR 1989: 65–66, all translations from the Hebrew by AHS)

But why should morality interfere with the realist logic embedded in Moshe Dayan's above-mentioned lecture? Indeed the other Moshe (the field commander in the novel) gave a similar answer to Yizhar in 1948:

"Listen to what I am going to tell you," Moshe said while trying to look straight into my eyes. "To this Hirba, whatever its name, immigrants will come, will take this land and work it and everything will be fine!"

(YIZHAR: 76)

S. Yizhar mocks this reasoning:

Of course how did I not think about this in the first place? Our Hirbet Hiz'ah. . . . We shall open a grocery shop, establish a learning institute, and maybe a synagogue too. . . . Long live Hebrew Hirbet Hiz'ah! Who will think that once there was a [Palestinian] Hirbet Hiz'ah from which we expelled [the residents] and also inherited [them]? We came, shot, burned, blew up, drove out, exiled.

(YIZHAR: 76–77)

Yizhar Smilansky proclaims that despite the difficulty in stepping out of line, he couldn't join

"the community of liars—who pretended ignorance, utilitarian apathy and self-ishness, without feeling shameful—and turned a great justice up-side-down by a clever shake of the shoulder by a longstanding criminal."

(YIZHAR: 33)

However, Yizhar is almost unique in his generation. Self-reflection and self-criticism rarely found expression in the discussions around the founding premises of Israeli society, despite the opposition to Zionism among some European intellectuals.[16]

Resilient Mythologies and Forms of Denial

Gabriel Garcia Marquez reminds us that human beings are not helpless in the face of their pasts: "Human beings are not born once and for all on the day their mothers give birth to them, but that life obliges them to give birth to themselves" (Quoted in Said 2004: 86). This highlights the challenge of responsibility. People must face responsibility in order to constitute themselves as moral subjects, and to construct their collective identity as a moral community. If the past cannot be changed, the question is what to do with its legacy. The "cradle makers" of Israeli Jewish society, along with their sons and daughters, have had to begin to face the founding moment of their nation following the appearance of a considerable literature since the 1980s demystifying this past. Works such as Tom Segev's (1984/1986) *1949—the First Israelis*; Simha Flapan's (1987/1990) *The Birth of Israel: Myths and Realities*; Benny Morris's (1988; 2004a) *The Birth of the Palestinian Refugee Problem*; Benjamin Beit-Hallahmi's (1992) *Original Sins: Reflections on the History of Zionism and Israel*; and Ilan Pappé's long list of books and articles (e.g. Pappé 1988; 1994; 1999; 2004), among many others, have been unsettling the picture the founding fathers worked so energetically to paint and to institutionalize as the hegemonic account of 1948. How are they responding?

Discussing techniques used in constructing myths, Barthes analyzes a photograph of a black soldier giving the French salute. The photograph is meant to convey the myth "that France is a great Empire, that all her sons, without any colour discrimination, faithfully serve under her flag, and that there is no better answer to the detractors of an alleged colonialism than the zeal shown by this Negro in serving his so-called oppressors" (Barthes 2000: 116). The mythological qualities of this photograph, according to Barthes, lie in its depoliticized posture. It creates false causes and effects that are removed from the thrust of history. Instead it presents a façade of naïveté. He goes on to argue that "myth does not deny things . . . simply it purifies them, it makes them innocent, it gives them a natural and eternal justification . . . it abolishes the complexity of human acts, it gives them the simplicity of essence, it does away with all dialectics" (ibid.: 143).

Just as this photograph conveys the image of French domination in Africa as a multiracial egalitarian empire, the story of the creation of Israel has been presented as the heroic act of a persecuted minority returning to its homeland who had to repel villainous Arabs in an act of self-defense. Facts such as the takeover of the homeland of another people, the destruction of their society, the expulsion of civilians, rapes, and massacres could not be tolerated. Whenever they come to light, attempts are made to nullify them. In this saga the binaries are sharp: Zionist leaders are heroes while Palestinians who oppose Zionism are depraved creatures (terrorists, Nazis, primitives, gangsters etc.).

However, we have already encountered in this essay the mythic heroes like Ben-Gurion and Rabin. We have seen their close involvement in the transfer of civilians that led to so many deaths, such dispossession, loss of property, and large-scale Palestinian exile. We have glimpsed their knowledge of what was happening and their attempts to cover up. The same can be said about Menachem Begin, who was rehabilitated in Israeli historiography in the late 1960s and raised to the status of national hero after his election as a prime minister in 1977, and even later was awarded the Nobel Peace Prize. Begin was the leader of the armed underground group of IZL (the Irgun), who fought for the expulsion of the British. Groups under his command contributed to the deterioration of the security situation in Palestine during 1947–48 by their murderous tactics, which reached their apex in the infamous massacre of innocent civilians in Deir Yassin.[17] This massacre is often highlighted because the village had nonaggression agreements with adjacent Jewish settlements and the *mukhtar* (village leader) not only rejected proposals by Arab militias to station themselves in the village but also passed on information to the Hagana regarding the movement of Arab forces in the area. Following the massacre, Begin sent a letter to his commanders saying: "Accept congratulations on this splendid act of conquest. . . . Tell the soldiers you have made history in Israel" (quoted in Palumbo 1987: 55).

Yet, as noted above, the myth of Israel's creation is now harder to sustain, both because of the work of a generation of historians and the internal questioning by peace activists and some intellectuals. What new arguments have been advanced to deal with Israel's role in the Nakba and the problem of morality? Ideological modes of thought, it would seem, can survive refutations as long as the sociopolitical order to which they give expression continues to prevail. I now reflect on three current modes of dealing with the morality of the past, comparing them to the responses of several other nations' to their own troubled pasts.

The first strategy for Zionists has been to revert to the old myth of "a land without people for a people without land." The best example is Alan Dershowitz's *The Case for Israel* (2003). Dershowitz's book draws upon an earlier version of the myth advanced by Joan Peters (1984) in her pseudo-historical book, *From Time Immemorial: The Origin of the Jewish-Arab Conflict Over Palestine*. Peters' thesis is simple: the majority of refugees were not natives of Palestine. Rather, they were immigrant Arab workers from the adjacent countries who came during the Mandate period to work in the prosperous Jewish enterprises. When the 1948 War broke out, they simply returned to their countries. Through denial of the other's existence, this formulation did away with the colonization-uprooting dialectic and was therefore widely appreciated by Zionists and many Israeli intellectuals, politicians, and organizations. However, Peters' statistical manipulations, misquotations, and twisting of facts could not pass as sound scholarship (for the Peters affair see e.g. Said 1988: 23–31; Finkelstein 1995: 21–50).[18] Nonetheless the recent surge of anti-Arab and anti-Muslim racism in the West following the events of 9/11 and the United States' pursuant wars in Afghanistan and Iraq enabled Dershowitz to resurrect these myths, requiring Finkelstein (2005) to painstakingly debunk them yet again.[19]

The problem for Israelis is that manifestations of the Nakba surround them, in the history, the geography, the archaeology, the architecture, the language, and the Palestinians who remained.[20] How can they be removed from consciousness? Mostly, responsibility is evaded by attempting to remove the Palestinians from the history of the country before and during 1948. Dalsheim found that this was what the history lessons in a kibbutz high school where she conducted three years of field research were designed to achieve. This is the same framework organizing the exhibit at the Disney-style Palmach Museum, dedicated to the pre-state elite unit of the Hagana. Dalsheim concludes:

> Contrary to what we might expect, for members of this group [secular, liberal Israelis], Palestinians are not their significant other. . . . they are instead an uncanny other, not fully recognised, not fully known, somehow magically imagined away, and for all these reasons that much more frightening. This is perhaps the current version of "a land without people for a people without land," a way in which the logic of separation/elimination central to the settler-colonial project can be expressed while maintaining a morally accepted self-portrait among descendants.
>
> (DALSHEIM 2004: 166–67)

The second emerging trend for dealing with the morality of the Nakba is to recognize that it took place but to deny that it carries any moral or practical implications. Writing on the need to go "beyond the destruction of the other's collective memory" as an overture for Israeli-Palestinian coexistence and reconciliation, Gur-Ze'ev, for example, argues that the moral ground of Palestinians and Israelis is equal. In arguing against Palestinians who assert the universal pedagogical lessons of the Holocaust, he writes: "Central to this trend is the avoidance of treating the Muslim and Arab involvement in the Nazi army (and the special role of the Mufti)" (Gur-Ze'ev and Pappé 2003: 103). He argues that Palestinians do not recognize "the injustice inflicted on the Jews throughout their history in the Diaspora and the Palestinian part in their present tragedy" (ibid). There is no victim–perpetrator dialectic at play here; consequently, there is no Palestinian moral claim. Despite his "critical" rhetoric, Gur-Ze'ev creates a misleading picture both of Arab–Nazi relations and the violence in Palestine.

Some of these claims have deeper roots in Zionist and Israeli propaganda and modes of representation than Gur-Ze'ev might wish to reveal. He alludes to a major trend in Zionism that has presented Palestinian/Arab/ Zionist relations as a continuation of Nazi-Jewish relations. Thus the historical relations between Arabs and Nazi Germany are exaggerated. One example relates to Hajj Amin al-Husayni's asylum in Berlin during World War II. Does his asylum make the Palestinian leader responsible for or even a sharer in the Nazis' crimes? Does it matter that Nazi racist ideology saw Arabs as subhuman? Hajj al-Husayni was, after the eruption of the 1936–39 Palestinian rebellion, a fugitive. He escaped a British order of arrest, fearing imprisonment, exile, or even execution—the fate of other rebel leaders. Like many in British colonies (see, e.g., Appadurai, 1996: 158–77) he hoped that a British defeat would lead to independence. Yet even if, like many anticolonials, the Hajj al-Husayni made an opportunistic alliance in order to pursue resistance to the British, the moral question that still imposes itself is: Does the relationship of the Mufti (who was originally appointed by the British) with Nazi Germany vindicate the destruction of Palestinian society? Mainstream Zionism says it does. In the Holocaust museum in Jerusalem (Yad Vashem) the Palestinian leader "is shown being greeted by Heinrich Himmler and inspecting Muslim volunteers in the Wehrmacht" (Swedenburg, 1995: 45). Indeed as Swedenburg argues "Yad Vashem recalls the Palestinian leader simply as a collaborator with Hitler; through his image the entire Palestinian people is metonymically implicated in the crimes of Nazism. The effect of such propagandistic association according to Israeli commentator Boaz Evron, has been to make most Israelis feel that 'there is no difference between an illiterate Palestinian refugee and an SS trooper'" (ibid.).

But what if the same propaganda line were to be taken one step further? Do the agreements that the leading Zionist organizations—the World Zionist Organization and the Jewish Agency—signed with Nazi Germany—known as the transfer (Ha'vara) agreements—make these groups responsible in any way for Nazi Germany's crimes?

Beside the relations with Germany, Gur-Ze'ev raises the issue of violence in Palestine, arguing that it has been one-sided. Yet historical research has shown that Palestinian violence grew out of the experience of colonization and expulsion (Mandel 1976). The following testimony given by the head of the (Jewish) Farmer's Union, Mr. Smilansky, in a closed session of a committee appointed by the Jewish Agency Executive in 1940 to study Jewish–Palestinian relations gives a good example of this process. His testimony refers to the fate of evicted Palestinian peasants from the Hula area, following the takeover of their land by Jewish settlers:

> How is it possible to believe in establishing brotherly relations (with an Arab) when the Jewish farmer takes his land, which he has worked for years and gives him instead a few pennies. And when I go to the grove, I see the armed Jewish young man beats him badly. How is it possible to bring together the two parties and how is it possible to find a solution?
>
> (QUOTED IN GOZANSKY 1987: 165–66, translated from Arabic by AHS)

Pappé, who co-authored the article with Gur-Ze'ev, understands the relationship between violence and justice in the colonial context differently. He writes that "although there was violence, no injustice was inflicted by the Palestinians on the Israelis, just as no injustice was inflicted by the Algerians on the French colonialists although there certainly was violence" (Gur-Ze'ev and Pappé 2003: 104).

The third Zionist strategy for dealing with 1948 addresses the moral weight of the Palestinian Nakba unapologetically. Benny Morris has articulated this position most clearly. No Israeli researcher has studied the critical period in which the colonization-expulsion took place as thoroughly as he has. In the first edition of his book *The Birth of the Palestinian Refugee Problem* (1987), he presents in a detached style enormous detail about the acts of transfer and the massacres that took place in 1948. Morris drew his data from Israeli archives, mainly of the army. The source of his material, the comprehensiveness of his research, and the descriptive style gave his book credibility among scholars and the general public. He tried to substitute a new myth regarding the causes of the Palestinian refugee problem for the old Zionist one—namely, that the Palestinian refugee problem was born out of war rather than long-term design. Nevertheless, Morris made a significant contribution by resolving one acrimonious debate regarding 1948—whether the Palestinians left as a result of calls by Arab leaders for them to do so, as part of a military plan, or as a result of expulsion. Morris's (2004a) research confirms what Palestinians have argued all along; he shows definitively that active expulsion by the Jewish forces, the flight of civilians from the battle zones following the attacks of Jewish forces, psychological warfare, and fear of atrocities and random killing by the advancing Jewish forces were the main causes for the Palestinian refugee problem.

But there are two problems with his work and position. As Slyomovics shows in her essay in this volume, Morris validates written documents as the definitive source for the historian and devalues personal testimony. Remarking on his own method Morris writes: "While contemporary documents may misinform, distort, omit or lie, they do so in my experience, far less than interviewees recalling highly controversial events some 40–50 years ago" (Morris 2004a: 4). Since Palestinian society disintegrated as a political entity during the war, and thus has not established national archives, it is unable, according to Morris, to put together a credible narrative regarding its own Nakba.[21]

Yet researchers who have based their understandings of the past on memories of Palestinians who survived the war and on archival materials—the same archival material Morris used—have reported that the two sources complement rather than contradict each other. For example Ben-Ze'ev, who studied the village of Ijzim during the war argues, "What is common to the two sources—the villagers' accounts and the army documents—is that they derive from people who witnessed the war events. They are predominantly first-hand accounts. . . . The fact that oral accounts are a reflection does not necessarily suggest that they are unreliable or distorted accounts" (Ben-Ze'ev 2002: 13–14)

What is the real reason for Morris's refusal to accept Palestinian testimony and memory? That it might be part of something unrelated to the historian's craft is given some credence by his later statement on the ethnic cleansing he documented in his book. In an interview in *Ha'aretz*[22] (also discussed by Slyomovics), he expresses the ultimate form of denial of moral responsibility for the Nakba: he deplores the fact that the job was not completed. "Ben-Gurion was right," he said. "If he had not done what he did, a state would not have come into being. That has to be clear. It is impossible to evade it. Without

the uprooting of the Palestinians, a Jewish State would not have arisen here"
(Morris 2004b: 41).

The requirements of creating the state trump morality, for Morris. As he
says,

> The need to establish this state [Israel] in this place overcomes the injustice that
> was done to the Palestinians by uprooting them. . . . Even the great American
> democracy could not have been created without the annihilation of the Indians.
> There are cases in which the overall, final good justifies harsh and cruel acts that
> are committed in the course of history.
>
> (MORRIS 2004b: 43)

He goes on to suggest that it might have been better

> if Ben-Gurion had carried out a large expulsion and cleansed the whole coun-
> try—the whole land of Israel, as far as the Jordan River. It may yet turn out that
> this was his fatal mistake.
>
> (MORRIS 2004b: 44)[23]

These are three methods by which Zionists even today try to rationalize
the Nakba. These methods do not acknowledge the morally tainted genesis
of the Jewish State or question its founding fathers. Yet this is not the only
way nations can deal with their pasts. Other nations have related to events
in their past in a variety of ways. The French official position was to bracket
the Vichy regime and its legacy of collaboration with the Nazis. It has considered French history, morals, and responsibility as identical with what, after
the war, De Gaulle called "une certaine idée de la France" (Booth 1999: 250);
thus, French governments have refused to take upon themselves the moral
responsibility of the collaborationist regime. The Israelis cannot follow this
strategy, since it would demand the denunciation of the founding fathers of
the state as well as Israeli history since 1948. In the case of Israel there has
been no rupture nor a radical shift of political or moral regime that would
render this easy position possible. The Germans, on the other hand, have
taken upon themselves the moral responsibilities of the World War II generation, drawing the lesson of "Never again!" (Booth 1999: 256). They have taken
significant compensatory measures: restitution of property, compensation,
or rehabilitation of victims and/or their families. Given the mythical quality
of the Israeli official narrative described so far, this strategy is unthinkable by
either the Israeli government or the wider public. Nor have Israelis accepted
any political solution that could then lead to a process of clearing up the past

through a body such as South Africa's Truth and Reconciliation Commission, formed to investigate the past and acknowledge injury.

Rather, the three trends described above suggest that most Israelis continue to bury, suppress, or ignore the past, translating existing power relations and continuing practices of governance and control into fixed sociopolitical realities and consciousness.[24] As Orwell said, "Whoever controls the present controls the past." Yet the moral tragedy in this case lies in the relationship between the colonizer and the expelled. A historical photograph that is reprinted in Segev's book from an article published in the Israeli weekly *Haolam Hazeh* on June 22, 1950, amidst the continuing campaign of expulsion and fruitless attempts by refugees to sneak back across the borders reveals the terrible form this dialectic has taken in Palestine/Israel.

The photograph shows Palestinians standing single file, most wearing traditional peasant clothes but with one in a European suit. Two armed soldiers supervise them. One of the photographs in the article is captioned, according to Segev: "Note the number tattooed on the guarding soldier's arm" (Segev 1986: 63). The photograph conveys the message that the soldier who survived the European concentration camps came to build a new life on the property of the Palestinians, who had to be kept out if this was to happen. The article reports, "Many of the immigrants who have been through the hell of the European concentration camps lack the proper attitudes toward the Arab captives of the State" (ibid.). Responding to a question by one reader about whether everything known to the editor about this situation was published, the latter answers ominously: "There are some things which are better left unpublished" (ibid).

How long will it take for the memories of those standing in single file under the watch of the brutalized and now brutal soldier to be heard? Or to be allowed to have moral weight?

NOTES

1. Many of the public memories the authors analyze were produced around the commemoration of the fiftieth anniversary of the Nakba.
2. For example, contrary to the official celebrations in Israel, a left-wing group of Israeli academics centered around the journal *Teoria Ve-bikoret* (Theory and Critique) published a special issue on the occasion entitled "50 to 48."
3. The stark differences in times and realities are captured sadly in Ghassan Kanafani's novel *'A'id ila Hayfa* (A Returnee to Haifa).

4. In analyzing the text I used the Hebrew version of the article, yet I quote from the English translation by Alan Dowty.

5. His descriptions of the devious method used in such deals speak for themselves: "And in the village of Metullah were more than a hundred Druze families on leased land that had changed ownership several times. The last owner was a certain pasha who loathed his tenants. . . . The pasha tried to sell the estate, but found no buyer, because no one wanted to take on or to expel by force such tenants who had grown old on the land (they dwelled there some ninety years). And behold the purchase was proposed to the pekidut [the officials who worked for the colonising agency of the Baron Edmond de Rothschild]. . . . The negotiations continued for four years, and perhaps even then would not have concluded except for an extraordinary event. In the year 1895–1896 the last Druze rebellion broke out; it lasted for a year, the tribal chiefs were exiled to Constantinople—and the pekidut made use of the emergency to complete the purchase. The village elders received substantial rewards, and in the circumstances violent resistance was not possible. Nevertheless many of the villagers refused to leave their homes and rejected even the most generous offers for their houses and gardens. And the day came to pass when the settlement official came to Metullah with a bag of gold coins in his carriage, and as though by chance there also appeared an army officer with troops, who came to arrest those evading military service—there are many of these among the Druze and the government does not pursue them diligently—and they were ready to command the hold-outs to sign the bills of sale. All of them of course signed, and within a few days more than six hundred souls left the village of their birth. . . . and within a week some sixty Jewish farmers, the pick of settlement workers, gathered there and occupied the Druze houses" (Dowty 2001: 44–45).

6. This decision would not have passed had the United States not used its full pressure, including threats of boycott against many states (Morris 2001: 184–85).

7. Following the eruption of the Palestinian rebellion in 1936, the British government sent a fact-finding committee to investigate the revolt and to submit political recommendations. The committee, chaired by Lord William Peel, a former secretary of state for India, recommended the establishment of a Jewish State on the fertile 33 percent of the country. The rest of the country should be annexed to Jordan but small enclaves, mainly mixed, and holy cities should remain in the hands of the British. Moreover it recommended (as a result of Zionist influence) the transfer of some quarter million Palestinians from the Jewish State, and some 1,250 Jews from the Arab part.

8. Hasso (2000) sums up the crucial importance of honor in nationalism and fear of the violation of women in Palestinian flight.

9. For newer and more complex documentation, see Abu-Sitta (2004).

10. In 1946, the Hagana Commander told the Anglo-American Committee of Inquiry, "There is no doubt that the Jewish force is superior in organisation, training, planning and equipment and that we ourselves will be able to handle any attack or rebellion from the Arab side without calling any assistance from the British or the Americans. If you accept the Zionist solution but are unable or unwilling to enforce it, please don't interfere, and we ourselves will secure its implementation" (quoted in Esber 2003: 115).

    This force was not built overnight; the Hagana was established in 1920. On various occasions the British played a vital role in training and arming Jewish forces. During the 1936–39 Palestinian rebellion, a special strike unit was formed under the command of the British Capt. C.O. Wingate and included British soldiers, Jewish policemen, and Hagana members. Its tactics of murderous night raids on Palestinian villages had an important influence in shaping the Hagana's doctrine (Morris, 2001: 148–49). In 1941 the British assisted the Hagana in establishing the Palmach (shock companies), an elite mobile unit of some two thousand men and women (ibid.: 174) that played a decisive role in the 1948 War. Moreover during World War II some 25,000 to 28,000 Jewish men and women enlisted in the British Army and auxiliary police, thus gaining invaluable training and experience (ibid: 166). In comparison, the Arab Legion (the Jordanian Army), the most effective Arab Army, had no more than 8,000 soldiers (ibid.: 222–23).

11. President Roosevelt went as far as to describe himself in the Yalta conference (held in February 1945) as "a Zionist" (Morris, 2001: 171).

12. For example, the evangelist William Blackstone organized a pro-Zionist lobby in 1891 by enlisting the major newspapers from the Atlantic to the Mississippi to publish editorials urging President Benjamin Harrison to support the establishment of a Jewish State in Palestine (Wagner 2002: 53–54).

13. Over 10 percent of the adult Palestinian male population was killed, wounded, imprisoned, or exiled. Moreover, the British confiscated large quantities of arms and ammunition during the revolt and continued to do so until the final stage of the Mandate (Khalidi 2001: 27). The British also destroyed some two thousand houses, in addition to many groves and orchards. As a result of British suppression, the Palestinians were left leaderless and bitterly divided. And in the final stage of the revolt the British established a local militia affiliated with the Palestinian opposition to combat the guerrillas (Morris 2001: 158–59).

14. They had limited quantities of small arms (mainly rifles and revolvers) and in some villages, negligible numbers of sub-machine guns. The following account of weapons in Al-Tira—a large village adjacent to Haifa, where many British army depots existed—exemplifies the dire military condition of the Palestinians. According to a report by HIS [Hagana Intelligence Service], in Al-Tira there were 40 revolvers, 64 rifles (20 of which were old Turkish rifles or hunting ones), 4 light sub-machine guns and a medium-size one; no ammunition was available for the sub-machine guns. The situation in Jaffa, a major Palestinian city of 70,000 inhabitants was not much better. There were 400–500 rifles and 30–40 sub-machine guns, most of which were in bad condition; and no heavy machine guns or artillery were on hand (Gelber 2004: 42–43).

   Following the passing of the Partition Resolution, a British commander in Haifa (the hometown of approximately 80,000 Palestinians) noted that Palestinian inhabitants "were not organized in any military sense" (quoted in Esber 2003: 116). The defenders numbered some 450 men armed mostly with World War I vintage rifles and 15 submachine guns, facing the larger and trained forces of the Carmeli or Second Brigade (ibid.: 121). The only Arab with serious military experience was a Lebanese commander (Amin Bey 'Iz al-Din) who took up his post as the Commander of the Defenders on March 27 but left on April 21—one day before the fall of the city. This left the command in the final showdown to Yunis Nafa'a, a sanitary engineer "with no military experience whatsoever" (Ibid: 121–29).

15. Walid Khalidi (2005: 43–44) argues: "If I were to place my finger on a single person who is responsible for systematizing the story. . .I would probably place it on a certain American Zionist by the name of Dr. Joseph Schechtman, a leading member of the Zionist revisionist wing. He is almost certainly responsible for the drafting of two mimeographed pamphlets that appeared in 1949 under the auspices of the Israel Information Center, New York." Esber (2003: 130) reports, "The Zionist narrative alleging that the Arabs left on Arab orders took roots early. The Jewish Agency was quoted by The Times of London on 23 April as saying that 'this exodus [from Haifa] has been carried out deliberately by the Arabs to besmirch the Jews, to influence the Arab Governments to send more help, and to clear the ground for an attack by regular Arab forces later.'"

16. Those who registered concern were considered threatening dissenters, as Jacqueline Rose (2005: 58–107) eloquently argues was the case for those like Martin Buber, Hannah Arendt, and Hans Kohn, and one could add, George Steiner much later (1985), who questioned political Zionism and saw a grave danger to Jewish values and Jewish life in the exclusive, militarized nation-state where justice

was not the key value. Important echoes of this early questioning of the morality of the nation-state project for Jews can be found in Steven Spielberg's controversial 2005 film, *Munich*.

17. See McGowan and Ellis 1998.

18. See Finkelstein (2005) for a detailed critique of the revival of these arguments in
Dershowitz (2003).

19. For a refutation see also Michael Neumann's (2005) *The Case Against Israel*. See
also Norman Finkelstein's findings on his webpage: *http://www.normanfinkel-
stein.com/article.php?pg = 11&ar = 1*

20. Small efforts are now getting underway to invite Palestinians back to their semi-
destroyed villages, or to former areas now inhabited by others, to give tours to
Israeli Jews to teach them about the Nakba, which Bronstein (2005: 11) calls "a
ghost that continues to walk through our space and time." Bronstein works with
a small organization called *Zochrot* (Remembering).

21. The effects of this inequality of archival resources are apparent in Esmeir's analysis (this volume) of the trial of Teddy Katz.

22. I used the original interview published in *Ha'aretz* in Hebrew as "Waiting for
the Barbarians" for the analysis of Morris's arguments. An electronic version is
available on line at http://www.haaretz.co.il/hasite/objects/pages/PrintArticle.
jhtml?itemNo = 380119. I quote from an English version of the interview that appeared as "On Ethnic Cleansing" in the *New Left Review*.

23. See Massad and Morris (2002) for a discussion of Morris's views.

24. In this, they resemble more closely the Turkish state that has tried to deny the
genocide of the Armenians in 1915. Although there is currently tremendous debate in Turkey on the issue, with intellectuals and journalists trying to explore
the past, it is nevertheless the case that criminal charges were brought against
the internationally known Turkish writer Orhan Pamuk in 2005 for "denigrat-
ing" Turkish identity by talking about the murder of Kurds and Armenians in
1915–1917 (charges dropped in January 2006) and that a conference on the Armenians in Turkey in December 2005 had to be moved from a public university to a
private one. See Shafak (2005).

BIBLIOGRAPHY

Abdel Jawad, Saleh. 1994. "Introduction." In *Qaryat Qaqun*. Birzeit: Markaz Dirasat wa Tawthiq al-Mujtama' al-Filastini.

———. 2003. "Massacres and the Creation of the Palestinian Refugee Problem in the 1948 War." Acts of the international conference: Israel and the Palestinian Refugees, Max Planck Institute for Comparative Public and International law, Heidelberg. 103 ms. pages.

———. 2004. "Le témoignage des victims palestiniennes entre l'historiographie israélienne et l'historiographie arabe: Le cas de 1948." In Catherine Coquio, ed. *L'histoire trouée, négation et témoignage*. Nantes: L'Atalante.

———. Forthcoming. *Why the Palestinians "Left" Their Paradise? Rewriting the Creation of the Palestinian Refugee Tragedy*.

Abdo, Nahla and Ronit Lentin. 2002. *Women and the Politics of Military Confrontation: Palestinian and Israeli Gendered Narratives of Dislocation*. New York: Berghahn Books.

Abu Eishe Anwar, ed. 1982. *Mémoires Palestiniennes: la terre dans la tête*. Paris: Editions Clancier-Guerod.

Abu El-Haj, Nadia. 2001. *Facts on the Ground: Archaeological Practice and Territorial Self-Fashioning in Israeli Society*. Chicago: University of Chicago Press.

———. 2002. "Producing (Arti)Facts: Archaeology and Power During the British Mandate of Palestine." *Israel Studies* 7, no.2, 33–61.

Abu Ghosha, 'Abd al-Majid. 1990. *'Imwas*. Beisan Press: Jerusalem.

Abu Hadba, 'Abd al-'Aziz. 1990. *Qaryat Dayr Aban* [The Village of Dayr Aban]. al-Bira: In'ash al-Usra.

Abu, Iyad and Eric Rouleau. 1981. *My Home, My Land: A Narrative of the Palestinian Struggle*. Translated by Linda Butler Koseoglu. New York: Times Books.

Abu Khiyara, ʿAziz, Salih Fannush, Mahmud Sulayman, and Musa ʿAshur. 1993. *Al-Walaja: Hadara wa Tarikh* [Al-Walaja: Culture and History]. Amman, Jordan: al-Walaja Cooperative Society.

Abu-Lughod, Ibrahim, ed. 1971.*The Transformation of Palestine: Essays on the Origin and Development of the Arab-Israeli Conflict.* Evanston, IL: Northwestern University Press.

Abu-Lughod, Janet L. 1971. "The Demographic Transformation of Palestine." In Ibrahim Abu-Lughod, ed. *The Transformation of Palestine: Essays on the Origin and Development of the Arab-Israeli Conflict.* Evanston, IL: Northwestern University Press, 139–63.

———. 1988. "Palestinians: Exiles at Home and Abroad." *Current Sociology* 36, no.2 (Summer): 61–69.

Abu-Lughod, Lila. 1993. *Writing Women's Worlds: Bedouin Stories.* Berkeley and Los Angeles: University of California Press.

———. 2001. "My Father's Return to Palestine." *Jerusalem Quarterly File*, 11–12. *www.jqf-jerusalem.org/journal/2001/jqf11–12/*

———. 2005. "About Politics, Palestine, and Friendship: A Letter to Edward from Egypt." In *Edward Said: Continuing the Conversation.* Ed. Homi Bhabha and W. J. T. Mitchell. Chicago: University of Chicago Press, 17–25.

Abu-Sitta, Salman. 2000. "The Palestinian Nakba—1948: The Register of Depopulated Localities in Palestine." London: Palestinian Return Center.

———. 2004. *Atlas of Palestine, 1948.* London: Palestine Land Society.

al-Adharba, Ahmad. 1997. *Qaryat al-Dawayima.* Birzeit: Markaz Dirasat wa-Tawthiq al-Mujtamaʿ al-Filastini.

Agamben, Giorgio. 1998. *Homo Sacer: Sovereign Power and Bare Life.* Translated by Daniel Heller-Roazen. Stanford, CA: Stanford University Press.

———. 1999. *Remnants of Auschwitz: The Witness and the Archive.* New York: Zone Books.

Ahmed-Fararjeh, Hisham. 2003. *Ibrahim Abu-Lughod: Resistance, Exile and Return. Conversations with Hisham Ahmed-Farajeh.* Birzeit: Ibrahim Abu-Lughod Institute for International Studies, Birzeit University.

Alexandaroni Society v. Theodore Katz. 2000. C.C.1686/2000. Tel Aviv District Court (court proceedings protocol. December 13, 14, 2000).

Alexandaroni Society v. Theodore Katz. 2000. C.C.1686/2000. Tel Aviv District Court (court decision, June 29, 2000).

Alexander, Livia. 2002. "Let Me In, Let Me Out, Going Places and Going Back." *Framework* 43, no. 2 (Fall): 157–77.

al-ʿAli, ʿAbd al-Majid Fadl. 2002. *Kuwaykat: Ihda Sharayin Filastin* [Kuwaykat: One of the Arteries of Palestine]. Beirut: n.p.

Ali, Tariq. 1994. "An Interview with Edward Said." Channel 4 YV. UK: December 15.

Alonso, Ana María. 1992. "Gender, Power, and Historical Memory: Discourses of *Serrano* Resistance." In Judith Butler and Joan W. Scott, eds., *Feminists Theorize the Political.* New York: Routledge.

Anderson, Benedict. 1983. *Imagined Communities.* London: Verso.

Anderson, Caroline and Thomas Benson. 1991. *Documentary Dilemmas: Frederick Wiseman's "Titicut Follies."* Carbondale and Edwardsville: Southern Illinois University Press.

Anderson, Scott. 2002. "Paving over Peace? Canuck-Built Road Helps Israel Cement Control." *Now* online edition, 21, no. 39. *http://www.nowtoronto.com/issues/2002-05-30/news_story3.php*.

Antonius, Soraya. 1979. "Fighting on Two Fronts: Conversations with Palestinian Women." *Journal of Palestine Studies* 8, no. 3, 26–45.

Appadurai, Arjun. 1996. *Modernity at Large: Cultural Dimensions of Globalization*. Minneapolis: University of Minnesota Press.

Aql, Abd Al-Salam. 1995. "Palestinian Refugees of Lebanon Speak." *Journal of Palestine Studies* 25, no.1, 54–60.

Arendt, Hannah. 1968. *Between Past and Present*. New York: Penguin.

Asad, Talal. 1986. "The Concept of Cultural Translation in British Social Anthropology." In James Clifford and George Marcus, eds., *Writing Culture: The Poetics and Politics of Ethnography*. Berkeley and Los Angeles: University of California Press.

'Atiyya, 'Atiyya 'Abdallah. 1992. *'Ayn Karim: al-Haqiqa wal-Hulm* [Ayn Karim: the Reality and the Dream]. Amman: n.p.

Auerbach, Erich. 1971. *Mimesis: The Representation of Reality in Western Literature*. Princeton: Princeton University Press.

Augé, Marc. 2004. *Oblivion*. Translated by Marjolijn De Jager. Minneapolis: University of Minnesota Press.

Augustin, Ebba, ed. 1993. *Palestinian Women: Identity and Experience*. London: Zed Books.

Avissar, Miriam and Eliyahu Shabo. 2000. "Qula." *Excavations and Surveys in Israel* 20: 51–53, 74–76.

'Awad, Hanan. 2004. *Fi al-Bad' anti Filastin: "Yawmiyyat al-Hisar"* [In the Beginning, You Palestine: "Daily Memoirs of the Siege"]. Ramallah: Dar Al-Shuruq.

Aymard, Maurice. 2004. "History and Memory: Construction, Deconstruction and Reconstruction." *Diogenes* 51, no.1, 7–16.

Azaryahu, Maoz. 1995. *Pulhane medinah: hagigot ha-'atsma'ut he-hantsa'hat ha-noflim, 1948–1956* [State Cults: Celebrating Independence and Commemorating the Fallen, 1948–1956]. Sedeh Boker: Ben Gurion University.

Bal, Mieke L., Jonathan Crewe, and Leo Spitzer, eds. 1999. *Acts of Memory: Cultural Recall in the Present*. Hanover: University Press of New England.

Bamyeh, Mohammed. 2003. "Palestine: Listening to the Inaudible." *The South Atlantic Quarterly* 102, no. 4, 825–49.

Bardenstein, Carol B. 1997. "Raped Brides and Steadfast Mothers." In Alexis Jetter, Annelise Orleck, and Diana Taylor, eds., *The Politics of Motherhood: Activist Voices From Left to Right*. Hanover: University Press of New England, 170–81.

——. 1999. "Trees, Forests, and the Shaping of Palestinian and Israeli Collective Memory." In Mieke L. Bal, Jonathan Crewe and Leo Spitzer, eds., *Acts of Memory: Cultural Recall in the Present*. Hanover: University Press of New England, 148–68.

Baron, Beth. 1997. "Nationalist Iconography: Egypt as a Woman." In James Jankowski and Israel Gershoni, eds., *Rethinking Nationalism in the Arab Middle East*. New York: Columbia University Press.

Baroud, Ramzy, ed. 2003. *Searching Jenin: Eyewitness Accounts of the Israeli Invasion 2002*. Seattle: Cune Press.

Barthes, Roland. 2000. *Mythologies*. London: Vintage.

Bar-Zohar, Michael and Eitan Haber. 1983. *The Quest for the Red Prince*. New York: William Morrow.

Bassiouni, Mohamed Cherif. 1996. *The Law of the International Criminal Tribunal for the Former Yugoslavia*. Irvington-on-Hudson, NY: Transnational.

Battaglia, Debbora. 1992. "The Body and the Gift: Memory and Forgetting in Sabari Mortuary Exchange." *American Ethnologist* 19, no. 1, 3–18.

Beinin, Joel. 2004. "No More Tears: Benny Morris and the Road Back from Liberal Zionism." *MERIP*. http://www.merip.org/mer/mer230/230_beinin.html.

Beit-Hallahmi, Benjamin. 1992. *Original Sins: Reflections on the History of Zionism and Israel*. London: Pluto Press.

Benhabib, Seyla. 1999. "Critical Theory and Postmodernism: On the Interplay of Ethics, Aesthetics, and Utopia in Critical Theory." *Cardozo Law Review* 11: 1435–49.

Benjamin, Walter. 1966. *Angelus novus. Ausgewählte Schriften*. Frankfurt a. M.: Suhrkamp. (English-language edition, 1968.)

———. 1969 [1936]. *Illuminations*. Translated by Harry Zohn. Hannah Arendt, ed. New York: Schocken Books.

Benvenisti, Meron. 1970. *The Crusaders in the Holy Land*. Jerusalem: Israel Universities Press.

———. 2000. *Sacred Landscape: The Buried History of the Holy Land Since 1948*. Berkeley: University of California Press.

Ben Ze'ev, Efrat. 2000. *Narratives of Exile: Palestinian Refugee Reflections on Three Villages: Tirat Haifa, 'Ein Hawd, and Izjim*. D.Phil. Thesis. Oxford University.

———. 2002. "The Palestinian Village of Izjim During the 1948 War: Forming an Anthropological History Through Villagers' Accounts and Army Documents." *History and Anthropology* 13, no. 1, 13–30.

———. 2003. "Al-Nakha wa al-Ra'iha fi Tuqus al-'Awda" [Flavors and Smells in Return Rituals]. *Al-Karmil*, nos. 76–77, 107–22.

———. 2005. "Transmission and Transformation: The Palestinian Second Generation and the Commemoration of the Homeland." In Alex Weingrod and André Levy, eds., *Homelands and Diasporas: Holy Lands and Other Places*. Stanford: Stanford University Press.

Ben Zvi, Tal. 1999. "Aval ani ve-rak ani asaper et ha-sipur sheli" [But I and only I can tell my story]. *Plastika*, no. 3 (Summer): 75–81.

Beverley, John. 1992. "The Margin at the Center: On 'Testimonio'." In Sidoni Smith and Julia Watson, eds. *Decolonizing the Subject: The Politics of Gender in Women's Autobiography*. Minneapolis: University of Minnesota Press.

Bishara, Amahl. 2003. "Examining Sentiments about and Claims to Jerusalem and its Houses." *Social Text* 75, no. 21 (Summer): 141–62.

Bishara, Azmi. 1995. "Ha-aravim ve-ha-shoah: nituah bayatiyuta shel ot hibur" [The Arabs and the Holocaust: An Analysis of the Problematics of Conjunction]. *Zemanim* 53 (Summer): 54–71.

Blanchot, Maurice. 1995. *The Writing of the Disaster*. Translated by Ann Smock. Lincoln, NE: University of Nebraska Press.

Bock, Gisela and Pat Thane. 1994. Maternity and Gender Policies: Women and the Rise of the European Welfare States, 1880s–1950s. New York: Routledge.

Bokae'e, Nihad. 2003. *Palestinian Internally Displaced Persons Inside Israel: Challenging the Solid Structures*. Bethlehem: Badil Resource Center.

Boltanski, Luc. 1999. *Distant Suffering: Morality, Media and Politics*. Translated by Graham Burchell. Cambridge: Cambridge University Press.

Boose, Lynda E. 2002. "Crossing the River Drina: Bosnian Rape Camps, Turkish Impalement, and Serb Cultural Memory." *Signs* 28, no. 1 (Autumn): 71–96.

Booth, James W. 1999. "Communities of Memory: On Identity, Memory, and Debt." *American Political Science Review* 93, no. 2, 249–63.

Bowersock, G. W. 1998. "Palestine: Ancient History and Modern Politics." In Edward Said and Christopher Hitchens, eds., *Blaming the Victims*. London: Verso.

Bowman, Glen. 1994. "A Country of Words: Conceiving the Palestinian Nation from the Position of Exile." In Ernesto Laclau, ed., *The Making of Political Identities*. London: Verso.

Bresheeth, Haim. 1989. "Self and Other in Zionism: Palestine and Israel in Recent Hebrew Literature." In *Palestine: A Profile of an Occupation*. Khamsin Series. London: Zed Books.

———. 1997. "The Great Taboo Broken: Reflections on the Israeli Reception of Schindler's List." In Yosefa Loshitzky, ed., *Spielberg's Holocaust: Critical Reflections on Schindler's List*. Bloomington: Indiana University Press.

———. 2001. "Gvulot ha-zikaron ha-falastini: Bayit ve-galut, zehut ve-he'almut ba-akolnoa ha-falastini he-hadash" [The Boundaries of Palestinian Memory: Home and Exile, Identity and Disappearance in New Palestinian Cinema.] *Teoria Ve-bikoret* [Theory and Critique] 18, 77–102.

———. 2002a. "A Symphony of Absence: Borders and Liminality in Elia Suleiman's Chronicle of a Disappearance." *Framework* 43, no. 2 (Fall): 71–84.

———. 2002b. "Telling the Stories of *Heim* and *Heimat*, Home and Exile: Recent Palestinian Films and the Iconic Parable of Invisible Palestine." *New Cinemas* 1, no.1, 24–39.

———. 2003. "Givaat Aliyah ke-mashal: shlosha hebetim" [Givaat Aliyah as a Parable: Three Aspects]. In Yehuda Shenhav, ed., *Space, Land, Home*. Jerusalem: Van Leer Institute, 251–56.

Bronstein, Eitan. 2005. "Studying the Nakba and Reconstructing Space in the Palestinian Village of Lifta." Working Paper of the European University, The Robert Schuman Centre for Advanced Studies. *http://www.eui.eu/RSCAS/WP-Texts/05_35.pdf*

Brown, Nathan. 2002. "Democracy, History, and the Contest Over the Palestinian Curriculum." http://www.nad-plo.org/textbooks/textbooks.html. First accessed March 27.

Bruce, Charles. 1998. *In Search of Palestine*. London: British Broadcasting Company.

Burch, Noel. 1990. "A Primitive Mode of Representation?" In Thomas Elsasser, ed., *Early Cinema*. London: British Film Institute.

Busailah, Reja-e. 1981. "The Fall of Lydda." *Arab Studies Quarterly* 3, no.2 (Spring): 123–51.

Butalia, Urvashi. 2000. *The Other Side of Silence: Voices from the Partition of India.* Durham, N.C.: Duke University Press.

Caruth, Cathy. 1995. *Trauma: Explorations in Memory.* Baltimore: John Hopkins University Press.

———. 1996. *Unclaimed Experience: Trauma, Narrative and History.* Baltimore: John Hopkins University Press.

———. 2001. "Parting Words: Trauma, Silence and Survival." *Cultural Values* 5, no. 1, 7–19.

Casey, Edward S. 1997. *The Fate of Place: A Philosophical History.* Berkeley and Los Angeles: University of California Press.

———. 2004. "Public Memory in Place and Time." In Kendall R. Phillips, ed., *Framing Public Memory.* Tuscaloosa: The University of Alabama Press.

Censor, Dany. 2000. *http://www.ee.bgu.ac.il/~censor/katz-directory/*

Certeau, Michel de. 1984. *The Practice of Everyday Life.* Trans. Steven Rendall. Berkeley: University of California Press.

Childers, Erskine. 1961. "The Other Exodus." *The Spectator* no. 6933 (May 12): 672–75.

———. 1971. "The Wordless Wish: From Citizens to Refugees." In Ibrahim Abu-Lughod, ed., *The Transformation of Palestine.* Evanston, IL: Northwestern University Press, 165–202.

Cohen, Hillel. 2003. "Land, Memory, and Identity: The Palestinian Internal Refugees in Israel." *Refuge: Canada's Periodical on Refugees* 21, no. 2, 6–13.

Cohen, Saul. 1986. *The Geopolitics of Israel's Border Question.* Boulder, CO: Westview Press.

Cohen, Shaul Ephraim. 1993. *The Politics of Planting.* Chicago: University of Chicago Press.

Collard, Anna. 1989. "Investigating 'Social Memory' in a Greek Context." In Elizabeth Tonkin, Maryon McDonald, and Malcolm Chapman, eds., *History and Ethnicity.* ASA Monographs 7. London: Routledge.

Collins, Larry and Dominique Lapierre. 1972. *O Jerusalem!* New York: Simon and Schuster.

Connerton, Paul. 1989. *How Societies Remember.* Cambridge: Cambridge University Press.

Coony, Mark. 1994. "Evidence as Partisanship." *Law and Society Review* 28, no. 4, 832.

Crane, Susan. 2000. "Introduction: Of Museums and Memory." In Susan Crane, ed., *Museums and Memory.* Stanford: Stanford University Press.

Crapanzano, Vincent. 2004. *Imaginary Horizons: An Essay in Literary-Philosophical Anthropology.* Chicago: University of Chicago Press.

al-Dabbagh, Mustafa. 1972–1986. *Biladuna Filastin* [Our Homeland Palestine]. 11 vols. Hebron: Matbu'at Rabitat al-Jami'iyin bi-Muhafizat al-Khalil.

Dakhlia, Jocelyne. 2001. "New Approaches in the History of Memory?" In Angelika Neuwirth and Andreas Pflitsch, eds., *Crisis and Memory in Islamic Societies.* Orient Institute: Beirut.

Dalsheim, Joyce. 2004. "Settler Nationalism, Collective Memories of Violence and the 'Uncanny Other.'" *Social Identities* 10, no. 2, 151–70.

Daniel, E. Valentine. 1996. *Charred Lullabies.* Princeton: Princeton University Press.

Daniel, E. Valentine and John Knudsen eds. 1996. *Mistrusting Refugees*. Berkeley and Los Angeles: University of California Press.

Darwish, Mahmoud. 2001. "Ibrahim Abu-Lughud: Tariq al-'Awda hiya Tariq al-Ma'rifa" [Ibrahim Abu-Lughod: The Path of Return is the Path of Knowledge]. Eulogy at the commemoration in Ramallah, May 26. 2001. Later published in *Akhbar Yafa* 11, May 31, p. 4.

Das, Veena. 1994. "Moral Orientations to Suffering: Legitimation, Power, and Healing." In Lincoln C. Chen, Arthur Kleinman, and Norma C. Ware eds., *Health and Social Change in International Perspective*. Cambridge: Harvard University Press.

———. 1995. *Critical Events: An Anthropological Perspective on Contemporary India*. Delhi: Oxford University Press.

———. 2000. "The Act of Witnessing: Violence, Poisonous Knowledge, and Subjectivity." In Arthur Kleinman, Veena Das, Mamphela Ramphele, and Pamela Reynolds, eds., *Violence and Subjectivity*. Berkeley: University of California Press.

Davidson, Lawrence. 2002. "The Past as Prelude: Zionism and the Betrayal of American Democratic Principles." *Journal of Palestine Studies* 31, no.3, 21–35.

Davis, Rochelle. 2002. "The Attar of History: Palestinian Narratives of Life Before 1948." Ph.D. diss. University of Michigan.

———. 2004. "Palestinian Memorial Books as Collective Autobiographies." Unpublished paper delivered at a conference on Autobiography and Social History of the Levant. Beirut, December.

Dayan, Moshe. 1969. "Extracts from Dayan's Lecture Given Before the Israel Technological Institute." *Ha'aretz* April 4.

Delbo, Charlotte. 1990. *Days and Memory*. Translated and with a preface by Rosette Lamont. Marlboro, Vt.: Marlboro Press.

Deleuze, Gilles and Elias Sanbar. 2001. "The Indians of Palestine." *The MIT Electronic Journal of Middle East Studies* 1 (Spring): 72–75. http://web.mit.edu/cis/wwv/mitejmes/issues/200105/deleuze-sanbar.htm

Dershowitz, Alan. 2003. *The Case for Israel*. Hoboken, N.J.: John Wiley and Sons.

Dirbas, Sahira. 1993. *Salama*. Ramallah: N.p.

Diyab, Imtiyaz and Hisham Sharabi. 1991. *Yafa: 'Itr Madina* [Jaffa: The Perfume of a City]. Cairo, Egypt: Dar al-Fata al-'Arabi.

Doumani, Beshara. 1992. "Rediscovering Ottoman Palestine: Writing Palestinians into History." *Journal of Palestine Studies* 21, no. 2(Winter): 5–28.

———. 1995. *Rediscovering Palestine: Merchants and Peasants in Jabal Nablus, 1700–1900*. Berkeley: University of California Press.

Dowty, Alan. 2001. "A Question that Outweighs All Others: Yitzhak Epstein and Zionist Recognition of the Arab Issue." *Israel Studies* 6, no. 1, 35–54.

Dwyer, Leslie. 2004. "The Intimacy of Terror: Gender and the Violence of 1965–1966 in Bali." *Intersections: Gender, History and Culture in the Asian Context* 10, 1–18.

Enloe, Cynthia. 2000. *Maneuvers: The International Politics of Militarizing Women's Lives*. Berkeley: University of California Press.

Epstein, Yitzhak. 1907. "Ha-she'ela ha-ne'lamit." [The Hidden Question]. *Ha-shiloah* (July-December): 193–206.

Esber, Rosemarie M. 2003. "The 1948 Palestinian Arab Exodus from Haifa." *The Arab Geographer* 6, no. 2,112–141.

Esmeir, Samera. 2003. "Law, History, Memory." *Social Text* 21, no. 2, 25–48.

Ewick, Patricia and Susan Silbey. 1995. "Hegemonic Narratives, Subversive Tales." *Law and Society Review* 29, no. 2, 197.

Fabian, Johannes. 1983. *Time and the Other: How Anthropology Makes its Object*. New York: Columbia University Press.

Falah, Ghazi. 1996. "The 1948 Israeli-Palestinian War and its Aftermath: The Transformation and De-Signification of Palestine's Cultural Landscape." *Annals of the Association of American Geographers*, 256–85.

Farah, Randa. 1997. "Crossing Boundaries: Reconstructions of Palestinian Identity in Al-Baq'a Refugee Camp, Jordan." In Riccardo Bocco, Blandine Destramau, and Jean Hannoyer, eds.. *Palestine, Palestiniens: Territoire national, espaces communautaires*. Beirut: CERMOC.

Fasl al-Maqal . 2001. (Newspaper, in Arabic) June 1, 7.

Feldman, Allen. 1999. "The Event and Its Shadow: Figure and Ground in Violence." *Transforming Anthropology* 8, no. 1–2, 3–11.

———. 2004. "Memory Theaters, Virtual Witnessing and the Trauma-Aesthetic" *Biography* 27, no. 1, 163—202.

Felman, Shoshana and Dori Laub. 1992. *Testimony: Crises of Witnessing in Literature, Psychoanalysis, and History*. New York: Routledge.

Fentress, James and Chris Wickham. 1992. *Social Memory*. Oxford: Blackwell Publishing.

Finkelstein, Norman. 1995. *Images and Realities of the Israeli-Palestinian Conflict*. London: Verso.

———. 2005. *Beyond Chutzpah: On the Misuse of Anti-Semitism and the Abuse of History*. Berkeley and Los Angeles: University of California Press.

Fitzpatrick, Peter. 2001. "Bare Sovereignty: *Homo Sacer* and the Insistence of Law." *Theory and Event* 5, no.2. http://muse.jhu.edu/journals/theoryandevent/v005/5.2fitzpatrick. html

Flapan, Simha. 1987. *The Birth of Israel: Myths and Realities*. London: Croom Helm.

———. 1990. Lidat Yisrael: Mitos ve-mitsi'ut [The Birth of Israel: Myths and Realities]. Personally published.

Fleischmann, Ellen L. 1996. "The Nation and Its 'New' Women: Feminism, Nationalism, Colonialism, and the Palestinian Women's Movement, 1920–1948." Ph.D. dissertation. Georgetown University.

———. 2003. *The Nation and Its "New" Women: the Palestinian Women's Movement 1920–1948*. Berkeley: University of California Press.

Franklin, Julian. 1963. *Jean Bodin and the Sixteenth-Century Revolution in the Methodology of Law and History*. New York: Columbia University Press.

Friedländer, Saul. 1993. *Memory, History, and the Extermination of the Jews of Europe*. Bloomington: Indiana University Press.

Freud, Sigmund. 1991 [1917]. "Mourning and Melancholia." In *On Metapsychology*. Penguin Freud Library, vol. 11. London: Penguin Books.

——. 1991 [1920]. "Beyond the Pleasure Principle." In *On Metapsychology*. Penguin Freud Library, vol. 11. London: Penguin Books.

——. 1991 [1930]. "Civilization and Discontents." In *Civilization, Society and Religion*, Penguin Freud Library, vol. 12. London: Penguin Books.

Gedi, Noa and Yigal Elam. 1996. "Collective Memory. What is it?" *History and Memory* 8, no. 2, 30–50.

Gelber, Yoav. 2004. *Komemiyut ve-Nakba* [Independence and Nakba]. Or Yehuda: Kinneret, Zmora-Bitan, Dvir Publishing.

Genet, Jean. 1986. *Un Captif Amoureux*. Paris: Éditions Gallimard.

Gerges, Fawaz. 2001. "Egypt and the 1948 War: Internal Conflict and Regional Ambitions." In Eugene L. Rogan and Avi Shlaim, eds. *The War for Palestine: Rewriting the History of 1948*. Cambridge: Cambridge University Press, 151–77.

Gilat, Amir. 2000."Ha-Tevah be-Tantura" [The Massacre in Tantura]. *Ma'ariv*, January 21, p. 9.

Giles, Judy. 2002. "Narratives of Gender, Class, and Modernity in Women's Memories of Mid-Twentieth Century Britain." *Signs* 28, no.1 (Autum): 21–41.

Gilloch, Graeme. 2002. *Walter Benjamin: Critical Constellations*. Cambridge: Polity Press.

Gorkin, Michael. 1991. *Days of Honey, Days of Onion: The Story of a Palestinian Family in Israel*. Berkeley: University of California Press.

Gorkin, Michael and Rafiqa Othman. 1996. *Three Mothers, Three Daughters: Palestinian Women's Stories*. Berkeley: University of California Press.

Gozansky, Tamar. 1987. *Tatawwur al-Ra'as Maliyya fi Filastin* [Formation of Capitalism in Palestine]. Haifa: Al-Ittihad.

Granqvist, Hilma. 1931, 1935. *Marriage Conditions in a Palestinian Village*. Helsinki: Societas Scientiarium Fennica, 2 volumes.

Gregory, Derek. 2004. *The Colonial Present*. Oxford: Blackwell.

Gross, David. 2002."Vanishing Worlds: On Dealing with What is Passing Away." *Telos* 124, 55–70.

Guérin, Victor. 1874. *Description géographique, historique et archéologique de la Palestine*. Paris: Imprimé par autorisation du gouvernement à l' Imprimerie Nationale.

Gur-Ze'ev, Ilan and Ilan Pappé. 2003. "Beyond the Destruction of the Other's Collective Memory: Blueprint for a Palestine/Israel Dialogue." *Theory, Culture & Society* 20, no. 1, 93–108.

Habiby, Emile. 1969. *Sudasiyyat al-ayyam al-sitta* [Sextet on the six days]. N.p.

——. 1992. "The Odds-and-Ends Woman." Translated by Roger Allen and Christopher Tingley. In Salma Khadra Jayyusi, ed., *Anthology of Modern Palestinian Literature*. New York: Columbia University Press, pp.454–59.

——. 2002. *The Secret Life of Saeed: The Pessoptimist*. Translated by Salma Khadra Jayyusi & Trevor LeGassick. New York: Interlink Books.

Hadawi, Sami. 1967. *Bitter Harvest: Palestine between 1914–1967*. New York: New World Press.

——. 1988. *Palestinian Rights and Losses in 1948*. London: Al-Saqi.

Halbwachs, Maurice. 1980. *Collective Memory*. New York: Harper and Row.

———. 1992 [1914]. *On Collective Memory*. Translated and edited by Lewis A. Coser. Chicago: The University of Chicago Press.

Halper, Jeff. 2000. "The 94 Percent Solution: A Matrix of Control." *MERIP Middle East Report* 216. http://www.merip.org/mer/mer216/216_halper.html

———. 2002. "The Message of the Bulldozer." *http://www.icahd.org/eng/articles.asp?menu = 6&submenu = 2&article = 58*. Accessed September 8.

Hammad, Suheir. 1996. *Born Palestinian, Born Black*. New York: Harlem River Press.

Hammami, Rema. 2003. "Gender, *Nakbe* and Nation: Palestinian Women's Presence and Absence in the Narration of 1948 Memories." In Ron Robin and Bo Stråth, eds., *Homelands: Poetic Power and the Politics of Space*. Brussels: P.I.E. Peter Lang.

Hammer, Juliane. 2001. "Homeland Palestine: Lost in the Catastrophe of 1948 and Recreated in Memories and Art." In *Crisis and Memory in Islamic Societies*. Proceedings of the third Summer Academy of the Working Group Modernity and Islam. Beirut: Orient-Institut der Deutschen Morgenlandischen Gesellschaft; Wurzbug: Ergon, pp. 453–81.

Han, Clara. 2004. "The Work of Indebtedness: The Traumatic Present in Late Capitalist Chile." *Culture, Medicine and Psychiatry* 28, no. 2, 169–87.

Hanafi, Sari. 2002. "Opening the Debate on the Right of Return." *Middle East Report* 222 (March).

———. 2005. "Social Capital and Refugee Repatriation: A Study of Economic and Social Transnational Kinship Networks in Palestine/Israel." In Ann M. Lesch and Ian S. Lustick, eds., *Exile and Return: Predicaments of Palestinians and Jews*. Philadelphia: University of Pennsylvania Press, 57–84.

Hasso, Frances S. 2000. "Modernity and Gender in Arab Accounts of the 1948 and 1967 Defeats." *International Journal of Middle East Studies* 32, no.4, 491–510.

Hazin, Salah. 1998. "Al-Balad allati lam Azurha" [The Village that I Have Never Visited]. *Al-Karmil*, 162–74.

Hershatter, Gail. 2002. "The Gender of Memory: Rural Chinese Women and the 1950s." *Signs* 28, no. 1 (Autumn): 43–70.

Herskovits, Melville. 1963. *Cultural Anthropology*. New York: Knopf.

Hertzberg, Arthur. ed. 1973. *The Zionist Idea: A Historical Analysis and Reader*. New York: Temple Books.

Herzl, Theodor. 1960. *The Complete Diaries of Theodor Herzl*. Vol.1 (edited by Raphael Patai). New York: Herzl Press and Thomas Yoseloff.

Hesford, Wendy. 2004. "Documenting Violations: Rhetorical Witnessing and the Spectacle of Distant Suffering." *Biography* 27, no. 1, 104–44.

Hill, Tom. 2005. "Historicity and the Nakba Commemorations of 1998." Working paper of the European University, Robert Schuman Centre for Advanced Studies, http://www.eui.eu/RSCAS/wp__Texts/05_33

Hirsch, Marianne. 1997. *Family Frames: Photography, Narrative, and Postmemory*. Cambridge: Harvard University Press.

————. 1999. "Projected Memory: Holocaust Photographs in Personal and Public Fantasy." In Mieke Bal, Jonathan Crewe, and Leo Spitzer, eds., *Acts of Memory: Cultural Recall in the Present*. Hanover: University Press of New England.

Hirsch, Marianne, and Valerie Smith. "Feminism and Cultural Memory: An Introduction." *Signs* 28, no. 1 (Autumn 2002): 1–19.

Hourani, Faysal. 2004. *Al Hanin: Hikayat 'Awda* [Longing: A Tale of Return]. Ramallah: Shaml-Palestinian Diaspora and Refugee Center and Institute for Jerusalem Studies.

al-Hout, Shafiq. 1998. "Reflections on al-Nakba." *Journal of Palestine Studies* 28, no.1 (Autumn): 23–27.

Hovsepian, Nubar. 2004. "Palestinian State Formation, Political Rent, and Education Policy: Development and the Construction of Identity." Ph.D. dissertation. City University of New York.

Humphries, Isabelle. 2000. "Race, Gender and Oppression: A Case Study of Arab Women in Israel." Master's Thesis. University of Durham.

Husayn, Rashid. 1968. *Yafa* [Jaffa]. In Yusuf al-Khatib, ed., *Diwan al-Watan al-Muhtal* [Anthology from the Occupied Homeland]. Damascus: Dar Filastin.

Hütteroth, Wolf-Dieter and Kamal Abdulfattah. 1977. *Historical Geography of Palestine, Transjordan and Southern Syria in the Late 16th Century*. Erlangen, Germany: Frankische Geographische Gesellschaft, Palm und Enke.

Hutton, Patrick. 1993. *History as an Art of Memory*. Hanover, N.H.: University Press of New England.

Huyssen, Andreas. 1995. *Twilight Memories: Making Time in a Culture of Amnesia*. London: Routledge.

Jammal, Laila. 1985. *Contributions by Palestinian Women to the National Struggle for Liberation*. Washington D.C.: Middle East Public Relations.

Al-Jana. 1998. "Participants' Responses to ARCPA's 1948 Uprooting Oral History Project." *Al-Jana*. May. Beirut: Arab Resource Centre for Popular Arts.

————. 2002. "File on Palestinian Oral History." Beirut: Arab Resource Centre for Popular Arts.

Jarrar, Husni and Khalid Sa'id. 2003. *Al-Mukhayyam wa Jenin: Malhamat al-Sumud wa al-Butula: Al-Ma'arik ma' al-Yahud, 1948–2002* [The Camp and Jenin: Epic of Steadfastness and Heroism: The Battles with the Jews, 1948–2002]. Amman: Al-Sabil Newspaper.

Jayyusi, Lena. 1984. *Categorization and the Moral Order*. London: Routledge.

————. 1988. "Toward a Socio-Logic of the Film Text." *Semiotica* 68, no. 3–4, 217–296.

————. 1995. "The Grammar of Difference: The Palestinian/Israeli Conflict as a Moral Site." In Annelies Moors, Toine van Teeffelen, Sharif Kanaana, and Ilham Abu Ghazaleh, eds., *Discourse and Palestine: Power, Text, and Context*. Amsterdam: Het Spinhuis.

Jayyusi, Salma K. 1987. *Modern Arabic Poetry: An Anthology*. New York: Columbia University Press.

Jedlowski, Paolo. 2001. "Memory and Sociology: Themes and Issues." *Time and Society* 10, no. 1, 29–44.

Kallam, Mahmud 'Abd Allah. 2003. *Sabra wa Shatila: Dhakirat al-Dam* [Sabra and Shatila: Blood's Memory]. Beirut: Beisan Publishing.

Kamen, Charles S. 1988. "After the Catastrophe II: The Arabs in Israel, 1948–51." *Middle Eastern Studies* 24, no. 1 (January): 68–109.

Kammen, Michael. 1995. "Review of *Frames of Remembrance: The Dynamics of Collective Memory.*" *History & Theory* 34, no. 3, 245–61.

Kanaana, Sharif. 1989. "Methodology in 'The Destroyed Palestinian Villages Project.'" Paper delivered at the Carleton-Bir Zeit Workshop. Carleton University. Ottawa, Ontario: March 8–9.

———. 1992. *Still on Vacation! The Eviction of the Palestinians in 1948.* Jerusalem: Jerusalem International Center for Palestinian Studies.

———. 1994. "The De-Arabization of Palestine." In *Folk Heritage of Palestine.* Tayibeh: Research Center for Arab Heritage, pp 47–54.

Kanaana, Sharif and Lubna 'Abd al-Hadi. 1986. *Salama.* Birzeit University Markaz al-Watha'iq wa-al-Abhath.

Kanaana, Sharif and Bassam al-Ka'bi. 1987. *'Ayn Hawd.* Birzeit University: Markaz al-Watha'iq wa-al-Abhath.

Kanaana, Sharif and Rashad al-Madani. 1987. *Majdal 'Asqalan.* Birzeit University Markaz al-Watha'iq wa-al-Abhath.

Kanaaneh, Rhoda Ann. 2002. *Birthing the Nation: Strategies of Palestinian Women in Israel.* Berkeley: University of California Press.

Kanafani, Ghassan 1970. *'A'id ila Hayfa [A Returnee to Haifa].* Beirut: Dar-Al-'Awda.

———. 1976. *Rijal fi al-Shams* [Men in the Sun]. Jerusalem: Salah Al-Din Publications.

———. 1992. *All That's Left to You: A Novella and Other Stories.* Translated by May Jayyusi and Jeremy Reed. Cairo: The American University of Cairo Press.

Karmi, Ghada. 1999. "After the Nakba: An Experience of Exile in England." *Journal of Palestine Studies* 28, no. 3, 52–63.

———. 2002. *In Search of Fatima: A Palestinian Story.* London and New York: Verso Press.

Kassabian, Anahid and David Kazanjian. 1999. "Melancholic Memories and Manic Politics: Feminism, Documentary, and the Armenian Diaspora." In Diane Waldman and Janet Walker, eds., *Feminism and Documentary.* Minneapolis: University of Minnesota Press.

Katz, Kimberly. 1998. "School Books and Tourism Brochures: Constructions of Identity in Jordan." Paper presented at the Research Fellows Lecture Series, Bi-National Fulbright Commission, Amman, Jordan, April 23, 1998.

Katz, Sheila H. 2003. *Women and Gender in Early Jewish and Palestinian Nationalism.* Gainesville: University Press of Florida.

Katz, Theodore. 1998. "The Exodus of Arabs from the Villages at the Foot of Southern Mount Carmel in 1948." Master's thesis. University of Haifa.

Kawar, Amal. 1996. *Daughters of Palestine: Leading Women of the Palestinian National Movement.* Albany: State University of New York Press.

Kayyali, A.W. 1978. *Palestine: A Modern History.* London: Croom Helm.

Kelemen, Paul. 1996a. "Zionism and the British Labour Party 1917–1939." *Social History* 21, no. 1, 71–78.

————. 1996b. "In the Name of Socialism: Zionism and European Social Democracy in the Inter-War Years." *International Review of Social History* 41, no. 3, 331–50.

Khalidi, Rashid. 1997. *Palestinian Identity: The Construction of Modern National Consciousness.* New York: Columbia University Press.

————. 2001. "The Palestinians and 1948; The Underlying Causes of Failure." In Eugene L. Rogan and Avi Shlaim, eds. *The War for Palestine: Rewriting the History of 1948.* Cambridge: Cambridge University Press, 12–36.

Khalidi, Walid. 1959a. "Why Did the Palestinians Leave? An Examination of the Zionist Version of the Exodus of 48." *Middle East Forum* 34 (July): 21–24.

————. 1959b. "The Fall of Haifa." *Middle East Forum* 35 (December): 22–32.

————. 1971. *From Haven to Conquest.* Beirut: Institute for Palestine Studies.

————. 1986. "The Arab Perspective." In William Roger Louis and Robert W. Stookey, eds. *The End of the Palestine Mandate.* London: I. B. Tauris.

————. 1991. *Before Their Diaspora: A Photographic History of the Palestinians 1876–1948.* Washington DC: Institute for Palestine Studies.

————. 1997. "Revisiting The UNGA Partition Resolution." *Journal of Palestine Studies* 27, no. 1, 5–21.

————. 2005. "Why Did the Palestinians Leave, Revisited." *Journal of Palestine Studies* 34, no. 2, 42–54.

Khalidi, Walid, ed. 1992. *All That Remains: The Palestinian Villages Occupied and Depopulated by Israel in 1948.* Washington DC: Institute for Palestine Studies.

Khalidi, Walid and Jill Khadduri, eds. 1974. *Palestine and the Arab-Israeli Conflict.* Beirut: Institute of Palestine Studies.

Khalili, Laleh. 2004a. "Citizens of an Unborn Kingdom: Stateless Palestinian Refugees and Contentious Commemoration." Ph.D. diss. Columbia University.

————. 2004b. "Grassroots Commemorations: Remembering the Land in the Camps of Lebanon." *Journal of Palestine Studies* 34, no. 1 (Fall): 6–22.

Khleifi, Michel. 1980. *Athakira al-Khasba* [Fertile Memory]. Belgium: Marisa Films.

Khoury, Elias. 2006. *The Gate of the Sun.* Translated by Humphrey Davies. Brooklyn, N.Y.: Archipelago Books.

Kidron, Peretz. 1988. "Truth Whereby Nations Live." In Edward Said and Christopher Hitchens, eds. *Blaming the Victims: Spurious Scholarship and the Palestinian Question.* London: Verso, 85–96.

Klaus, Dorothée. 2003. *Palestinian Refugees in Lebanon – Where to Belong?* Berlin: Klaus Schwartz Verlag.

Klein, Kerwin Lee. 2000. "On the Emergence of Memory in Historical Discourse." *Representations* 69 (Winter):127–50.

Kleinman, Arthur. 2000. "Introduction." In Arthur Kleinman, Veena Das, Mamphela Ramphele, and Pamela Reynolds, eds., *Violence and Subjectivity.* Berkeley and Los Angeles: University of California Press.

Kracauer, Siegfried. 1995. *History: The Last Things Before the Last.* Princeton: Markus Wiener Publishing.

Kugelmass, Jack and Jonathan Boyarin. 1998. *From a Ruined Garden.* Bloomington, Ind.: Indiana University Press.

LaCapra, Dominick. 1994. *Representing the Holocaust: History, Theory, Trauma*. Ithaca, NY: Cornell University Press.

———. 1998. *History and Memory after Auschwitz*. Ithaca, NY: Cornell University Press.

Lehn, Walter with Uri Davis. 1988. *The Jewish National Fund*. London: Kegan Paul.

Lessing, Doris. 1981. *African Stories*. New York: Simon and Schuster.

Levine, Mark. 2005. *Overthrowing Geography: Jaffa, Tel Aviv, and the Struggle for Palestine, 1880–1948*. Berkeley and Los Angeles: University of California Press.

Little, Douglas. 2003. *American Orientalism: The United States and the Middle East Since 1945*. London: I.B. Tauris.

Litvak, Meir. 1994. "A Palestinian Past: National Construction and Reconstruction." *History and Memory* 6, 24–56.

Lloyd, David. 2000. "Colonial Trauma/Postcolonial Recovery?" *Interventions* 2, no. 2, 212–28.

Loshitzky, Yosefa. 2001. *Identity Politics on the Israeli Screen*. Austin: University of Texas Press.

Loshitzky, Yosefa, ed. 1997. *Spielberg's Holocaust: Critical Perspectives on Schindler's List*. Bloomington: Indiana University Press.

Malkki, Liisa. 1994. "Citizens of Humanity: Internationalism and the Imagined Community of Nations." *Diaspora* 3, no. 1, 41–68.

———. 1995. *Purity and Exile: Violence, Memory and National Cosmology Among Hutu Refugees in Tanzania*. Chicago: University of Chicago Press.

Mandel, Neville. 1976. *The Arabs and Zionism Before World War I*. Berkeley: University of California Press.

Marx, Karl and Frederick Engels. 1985. *The German Ideology*. Edited by C.J. Arthur. London: Lawrence & Wishart.

Masalha, Nur. 1992. *The Expulsion of Palestinians: The Concept of 'Transfer' in Zionist Political Thought, 1892–1948*. Washington, D.C.: Institute for Palestine Studies.

———. 2003. *The Politics of Denial: Israel and the Palestinian Refugee Problem*. London: Pluto Press.

———. 2005. *Catastrophe Remembered: Palestine, Israel and the Internal Refugees*. London: Zed Books.

Massad, Joseph. 1995. "Conceiving the Masculine: Gender and Palestinian Nationalism." *Middle East Journal* 49, no. 3, 467–83.

Massad, Joseph and Benny Morris. 2002. "History on the Line: 'No Common Ground': Joseph Massad and Benny Morris Discuss the Middle East." *History Workshop Journal* 53: 205–16.

al-Mawsu'a al-Filastiniyya [Palestine Encyclopedia]. 1984. 4 vols. Damascus: Hay'at al-Mawsu'a al-Filastiniyya.

Mazzawi, André. 1997. "Memories and Counter-Memories: Production, Reproduction and Deconstruction of Some Palestinian Memory Accounts about Jaffa." Presented at the annual meetings of the Middle East Studies Association, San Francisco, November.

McClintock, Anne. 1995. *Imperial Leather: Race, Gender, and Sexuality in the Colonial Conquest*. New York: Routledge.

McGowan, Daniel and Marc H. Ellis, eds. 1998. *Remembering Deir Yassin: The Future of Israel and Palestine*. New York: Olive Branch Press.

McGreal, Chris. 2003. "Israel Learns of a Hidden Shame in its Early Years: Soldiers Raped and Killed Bedouin Girl in the Negev." *The Guardian* (November 4). http://www.guardian.co.uk/international/story/0,,1077103,00.html

Melucci, Alberto. 1998. "Inner Time and Social Time in a World of Uncertainty." *Time & Society* 7, no.2, 179–91.

Menon, Ritu and Kamla Bhasin. 1998. *Borders and Boundaries: Women in India's Partition*. New Brunswick: Rutgers University Press.

Merleau-Ponty, Maurice. 1962. *Phenomenology of Perception*. Translated by Colin Smith. New York: Humanities Press.

———. 1968. *The Visible and the Invisible*. Translated by Alphonso Lingis. Evanston, Ill.: Northwestern University Press.

Misztal, Barbara. 2003. *Theories of Social Remembering*. Philadelphia: Open University Press.

Mitchell, Timothy. 1988. *Colonising Egypt*. Cambridge: Cambridge University Press.

Moors, Annelies. 1995. *Women, Property and Islam: Palestinian Experiences, 1920 – 1990*. Cambridge: Cambridge University Press.

———. 2000. "Embodying the Nation: Maha Saca's Post-Intifada Postcards." *Ethnic and Racial Studies* 23, no. 5, 871–87.

Morris, Benny. 1987. *The Birth of the Palestinian Refugee problem, 1947–1949*. Cambridge: Cambridge University Press.

———. 1988. "Israel: The New Historiography." *Tikkun* (November–December): 19–24.

———. 1997. *Israel's Border Wars 1949–1956*. Oxford: Clarendon Press.

———. 2001a. "Revisiting the Palestinian Exodus of 1948." In Eugene Rogan and Avi Shlaim, eds. *The War for Palestine: Rewriting the History of 1948*. Cambridge: Cambridge University Press.

———. 2001b. *Righteous Victim: A History of the Zionist-Arab Conflict, 1881–2001*. New York: Vintage.

———. 2002. "Peace? No Chance." *Guardian*. February 21, G2.

———. 2004a. *The Birth of the Palestinian Refugee Problem Revisited*. Cambridge: Cambridge University Press.

———. 2004b. "Mikhake la-barbarim" [Waiting for the Barbarians]. *Ha'aretz* January 6. *http://haaretz.co.il/hasite/objects/pages/PrintArticle.jhtml?itemNo = 380119*

———. 2004c. "On Ethnic Cleansing: Introduction and Interview by Ari Shavit." *New Left Review*. 26: 37–51.

Moughrabi, Fouad. 2001. "The Politics of Palestinian Textbooks." *Journal of Palestine Studies* 31, no. 1, 5–19.

Mu'assasat al-Ta'awun. 2000. *Mathaf al-Dhakira al-Filastiniyya: Wathiqat al-Mashru'* [Palestinian Memory Museum: Project Document]. Welfare Association, November.

al-Mudawwar, 'Abd al-Rahim Badr. 1994. *Qaryat Qaqun*. Birzeit University: Markaz Dirasat wa-Tawthiq al-Mujtama' al-Filastini.

Muhammad, Zakariya. 1995. "'An Yafa . . . wa al-Mowt . . . wa al-Farah . . . wa al-Hazima . . . wa al-Amal. Abu-Lughud: Khuft an Amut dun an Ara Filastin fa Qarrart al-

'Awda" [On Jaffa. . .and Death . . . and Happiness . . . and Defeat . . . and Hope: Abu-Lughod: I Feared that I Would Die Without Seeing Palestine So I Decided to Return]. *Al-Ayyam,* December 25 and 26, p.14 in each.

Muhawi, Ibrahim and Sharif Kanaana. 1989. *Speak, Bird, Speak Again.* Berkeley: University of California Press.

Naficy, Hamid, ed. 1999. *Home, Exile, Homeland: Film, Media, and the Politics of Place.* London: Routledge.

Najjar, Orayb Aref. 1992. *Portraits of Palestinian Women.* Salt Lake City: University of Utah Press.

Najmabadi, Afsaneh. 2005. *Women with Mustaches and Men without Beards : Gender and Sexual Anxieties of Iranian Modernity.* Berkeley and Los Angeles: University of California Press.

Nassar, Hala. 2002. "The Invocation of Lost Places." *The Open Page: Theatre/Women/Travel* 7 (March): 36–39.

Natour, Salman. *Dhakira* [Memory]. Unpublished manuscript.

Nazzal, Nafez. 1974. "The Zionist Occupation of Western Galilee, 1948." *Journal of Palestine Studies* 3, no. 3: 58–76.

———. 1978. *The Palestinian Exodus from Galilee, 1948.* Beirut: The Institute for Palestine Studies.

Neumann, Michael. 2005. *The Case Against Israel.* Oakland, CA: AK Press.

Nichols, Bill. 1991. *Representing Reality.* Bloomington: Indiana University Press.

Nora, Pierre. 1989. "Between Memory and History: *Les lieux de mémoire.*" Translated by Marc Roudebush. *Representations* 26 (Spring): 7–24.

Nora, Pierre, ed. 1996. *Realms of Memory, Volume I: Conflicts and Divisions.* Translated by Arthur Goldhammer. New York: Columbia University Press.

———. 1997. *Realms of Memory, Volume II: Traditions.* Translated by Arthur Goldhammer. New York: Columbia University Press.

———. 1998. *Realms of Memory, Volume III: Symbols.* Translated by Arthur Goldhammer. New York: Columbia University Press.

———. 2001. *Rethinking France: Les lieux de mémoire. Vol. I: The State.* Translated by Mary Trouille. Chicago: The University of Chicago Press.

Nunn, Kenneth. 1996. "Personal Hopefulness: A Conceptual Review of the Relevance of the Perceived Future to Psychiatry." *British Journal of Medical Psychology* 69: 227–45.

Nutting, Sir Anthony. n.d. *Balfour And Palestine: A Legacy of Deceit.* London: The Council for the Advancement of Arab-British Understanding.

'Odeh, 'Abdallah. 1980. *al-Kababir.* Shafa 'Amr: Dar al-Mashriq.

'Odeh, 'Aysha. 2004. *Ahlam bil-Hurriyya: Al Juz' Al-Awwal min Tajribat I'tiqal Fatah Filastiniyya* [Dreams of Freedom: Part I of the Prison Experience of a Palestinian Girl]. Ramallah: Muwatin.

Olick, Jeffrey K. 1999. "Genre Memories and Memory Genres: A Dialogical Analysis of May 8, 1945 Commemorations in the Federal Republic of Germany." *American Sociological Review* 64, no. 3, 381–403.

Olick Jeffrey and Joyce Robbins. 1998. "Social Memory Studies: From 'Collective Memory' to the Historical Sociology of Mnemonic Practices." *Annual Review of Sociology* 24: 105–40.

Palumbo, Michael. 1987. *The Palestinian Catastrophe: the 1948 Expulsion of a People from Their Homeland*. London, Boston: Faber and Faber.

Pandey, Gyanandren. 2001. *Remembering Partition: Violence, Nationalism, and History in India*. Cambridge, Eng.: Cambridge University Press.

Pappé, Ilan. 1988. *Britain and the Arab-Israeli Conflict, 1948–1951*. London: Macmillan.

———. 1994. *The Making of the Arab-Israeli Conflict, 1948–1951*. London: I. B. Tauris.

———. 1999. *The Israel/Palestine Question*. London: Routledge.

———. 2001. "The Tantura Case in Israel: The Katz Research and Trial." *Journal of Palestine Studies* 30, no. 3, 19–39.

———. 2002. "Parashot Katz ve-Tantura: historia, historiographia, mishpat ve-akademia." (The Katz and the Tantura Affairs: History, Historiography, the Court, and the Israeli Academia.) *Teoria Ve-bikoret* [Theory and Criticism] 20: 191.

———. 2003. "Humanizing the Text: Israeli 'New History' and the Trajectory of the 1948 Historiography." *Radical History Review*, no. 86, 102–22.

———. 2004. *A History of Modern Palestine: One Land, Two Peoples*. Cambridge: Cambridge University Press.

Parmenter, Barbara. 1994. *Giving Voice to Stones: Places and Identity in Palestinian Literature*. Austin: University of Texas Press.

Peteet, Julie. 1991. *Gender in Crisis: Women and the Palestinian Resistance Movement*. New York: Columbia University Press.

———. 1995. "Transforming Trust: Dispossession and Empowerment among Palestinian Refugees." In E. Valentine Daniel and John Knudsen, eds., *Mistrusting Refugees*. Berkeley: University of California Press.

———. 1997. "Icons and Militants: Mothering in the Danger Zone." *Signs* 23, no. 1, 103–29.

———. 2005. *Landscape of Hope and Despair: Palestinian Refugee Camps*. Philadelphia: University of Pennsylvania Press.

Peters, Joan. 1984. *From Time Immemorial: The Origin of the Jewish-Arab Conflict Over Palestine*. New York: Harper and Row.

Phillips. Kendall R, ed. 2004. *Framing Public Memory*. Tuscaloosa: The University of Alabama Press.

Plato. 1997. *Symposium and the Death of Socrates*. Translated by Tom Griffith with an introduction by Jane O'Grady. Ware, Hertfordshire: Wordsworth.

Pocock, J. 1987. *The Ancient Constitution and Feudal Law*. Cambridge: Cambridge University Press.

Popular Memory Group. 1982. "Popular Memory: Theory, Politics, Method." In Richard Johnson, Gregor McLennan, Bill Schwartz, David Sutton eds., *Making Histories: Studies in History-Writing and Politics*. London: Hutchinson.

Portelli, Alessandro. 1997. *The Battle of Valle Giulia: Oral History and the Art of Dialogue*. Madison: The University of Wisconsin Press.

Pringle, Denys. 1997. *Secular Buildings in the Crusader Kingdom of Jerusalem: An Archaeological Gazetteer*. New York: Cambridge University Press.

Prosecutor v. Tadic (Case No. IT-94-1-T), Opinion and Judgment (May 7, 1997), 36 ILM 908, 112 ILR 1, para. 555.

Proust, Marcel. *Swann's Way*. 2002. [1928, 1981 translation] Translated by C.K. Scott Montcrieff. New York: Dover Publications.

Al-Qalqili, 'Abd al-Fattah. 2004. *Al Ard fi Thaakirat al-Filastiniyyin: I'timadan 'ala al-Tarikh al-Shafawi fi Mukhayyam Jenin* [Land in Palestinian Memory: Based on Oral Histories in the Jenin Refugee Camp]. Ramallah: Shaml, Palestinian Diaspora and Refugee Center.

Al-Qattan, Omar. 1991. *Ahlam fi Faragh* [Dreams and Silence]. Belgium: Sourat Films.

———. 1995. *Al-'Awda* [Going Home]. UK: Sindibad Films and Café Productions.

Rabinowitz, Dan and Khawla Abu-Baker. 2005. *Coffins on our Shoulders: The Experience of the Palestinian Citizens of Israel*. Berkeley: University of California Press.

Rabinowitz, Dan and Itay Vardi. Forthcoming. *Kohot meni'im: Kvish hotze Yisra'el, globalizatsya ve-'itsuvam me-hadash shel ha-merhav veha-hevra be-Yisra'el*. (Driving Forces: The Trans-Israel Highway, Globalization and the Reshaping of Space and Society in Israel). Tel-Aviv: Ha-Kibbutz Ha-Me'uhad and Van-Leer Jerusalem Foundation.

Ramadanovic, Petar. 2001. "From Haunting to Trauma: Nietzsche's Active Forgetting and Blanchot's Writing of the Disaster." *Postmodern Culture* 11, no. 2. http://muse.jhu.edu/journals/pmc/v011/11.2ramadanovic.html.

Ricoeur, Paul. 1984. *Time and Narrative*. Chicago: University of Chicago Press.

———. 1995. *Figuring the Sacred: Religion, Narrative and Imagination*. Trans. by David Pellauer. Indianapolis: Fortress Press.

Riley, Denise. 1988. *"Am I That Name?" Feminism and the Category of Women in History*. Minneapolis: University of Minnesota Press.

Roberts, Rebecca. 1999. *Bourj al Barajneh: The Significance of Village Origins in a Palestinian Refugee Camp*. Master's thesis. University of Durham.

Robinson, Ronald. 1972. "Non-European Foundations of European Imperialism: Sketch for a Theory of Collaboration." In Roger Owen & Bob Sutcliffe (eds.) *Studies in the Theory of Imperialism*. Longman, 117–42.

Rogan, Eugene, L. 2001. "Jordan and 1948: the Persistence of an Official History." In Eugene L. Rogan and Avi Shlaim, eds. *The War for Palestine: Rewriting the History of 1948*. Cambridge: Cambridge University Press, 104–24.

Rogan, Eugene and Avi Shlaim, eds. 2001.*The War for Palestine: Rewriting the History of 1948*. Cambridge: Cambridge University Press.

Rogers, Mary Eliza. 1989 [1862]. *Domestic Life in Palestine*. London: Kegan Paul International.

Rose, Jacqueline. 2005. *The Question of Zion*. Princeton: Princeton University Press.

Rotha, Paul. 1952. *Documentary Film*. 2nd ed. London: Faber.

Rouff, Jeffrey Keith. 1998. "A Bastard Union of Several Forms: Style and Narrative in an American Family." In Barry Grant and Jeannette Sloniowsky, eds., *Documenting the Documentary: Close Readings of Documentary Film and Video*. Detroit: Wayne State University Press.

Ruedy, John. 1971. "Dynamics of Land Alienation in Palestine." In Ibrahim Abu-Lughod, ed., *The Transformation of Palestine*. Evanston: Northwestern University Press, 119–38.

Rumman, Muhammad Sa'id Muslih. 2000. *Suba: Qarya Maqdisiyya fil-Dhakira* [Suba: A Jerusalem Village in Memory]. Jerusalem: 'Ayn Rafa Press.

Russell, Catherine. 1999. *Experimental Ethnography: The Work of Film in the Age of Video*. Durham: Duke University Press.

Sabbagh, Suha, ed. 1998. *Palestinian Women of Gaza and the West Bank*. Bloomington: Indiana University Press.

Sacks, Harvey. 1972. "An Initial Investigation of the Usability of Conversational Data for Doing Sociology." In David Sudnow, ed., *Studies in Social Interaction*. New York: The Free Press.

Sa'di, Ahmad H. 1997. "Modernization as an Explanatory Discourse of Zionist Palestinian Relations." *British Journal of Middle Eastern Studies*. 24 (1), 25–48.

——. 2002. "Catastrophe, Memory and Identity: Al-Nakbah as a Component of Palestinian Identity." *Israel Studies* 7, no. 2, 175–98.

Safranski, Rüdiger. 2002. *Nietzsche: A Philosophical Biography*. Translated by Shelley Frisch. New York: W.W. Norton & Company.

Said, Edward. 1978. *Orientalism*. New York: Pantheon.

——. 1979. *The Question of Palestine*. New York: Vintage Books.

——. 1984. "The Mind of Winter: Reflections on Life in Exile." *Harper's Magazine* 269 (September): 49–55.

——. 1985. *After the Last Sky: Palestinian Lives*. Photographs by Jean Mohr. New York: Pantheon.

——. 1988. "Conspiracy of Praise." In Edward Said and Christopher Hitchens, eds., *Blaming the Victims: Spurious Scholarship and the Palestinian Question*. London: Verso, 23-31.

——. 1994a. "Permission to Narrate." In *The Politics of Dispossession*. New York, Pantheon.

——. 1994b. *Culture and Imperialism*. London: Vintage.

——. 1999. *Out of Place: A Memoir*. New York: Knopf.

——. 2000a. "Invention, Memory, and Place." *Critical Inquiry* 26, no. 2 (Winter): 175–192.

——. 2000b. *Reflections on Exile and Other Essays*. Cambridge: Harvard University Press.

——. 2001. "My Guru." *London Review of Books* 23, no. 24 (December): 19–20.

——. 2004. *Humanism and Democratic Criticism*. New York: Columbia University Press.

Said, Edward and Christopher Hitchins, eds. 2001. *Blaming the Victims: Spurious Scholarship and the Palestinian Question*. New York: Verso.

Sanbar, Elias. 1984. *Palestine 1948: L'expulsion*. Paris: Institute for Palestine Studies.

——. 2001. "Out of Place, Out of Time." *Mediterranean Historical Review* 16, no.1, 87–94.

Sawalha, Aseel. 1996. "Identity, the Self, and the Other: In a Poor Neighborhood in East Amman." In Anthony Marcus, ed. *Anthropology for a Small Planet: Culture and Community in a Global Environment*. St. James, NY: Brandywine Press, 19–30.

Sayigh, Rosemary. 1979. *Palestinians: From Peasants to Revolutionaries*. London: Zed Books.

——. 1994. *Too Many Enemies: The Palestinian Experience in Lebanon*. London: Zed Books.

——. 1998a. "Oral History for Palestinians—the Beginning of a Discipline." *Al-Jana*: The Harvest. May.

——. 1998b. "Palestinian Camp Women as Tellers of History." *Journal of Palestine Studies* 27, no. 2, 42–58.

———. 1999. "Gendering the Nationalist Subject: Palestinian Camp Women's Life Stories." *Subaltern Studies X*. New Delhi: Oxford University Press.

———. 2001. "Palestinian Refugees in Lebanon: Implantation, Transfer or Return?" *Middle East Policy* 8, no. 1, 95–105.

———. 2002a. "The History of Palestinian Oral History: Individual Vitality and Institutional Paralysis." *Al-Jana: The Harvest* 2–4, 64–72.

———. 2002b. Interview with Saleh Abdel Jawad. *Al-Jana: The Harvest*, 30–34.

———. 2002c. "Remembering Mothers, Forming Daughters: Palestinian Women's Narratives in Refugee Camps in Lebanon." In Nahla Abdo and Ronit Lentin, eds., *Women and the Politics of Military Confrontation: Palestinian and Israeli Gendered Narratives of Dislocation*. New York and Oxford: Berghahn.

Schabas, William. 2001. *An Introduction to the Study of the International Criminal Court*. Cambridge: Cambridge University Press.

Schutz, Alfred. 1962. *Collected Papers, Vol. I*. The Hague: Martinus Nijhoff.

Schwartz, Barry. 1982. "The Social Context of Commemoration: A Study in Collective Memory." *Social Forces* 61, no. 2, 374–402.

———. 1991. "Social Change and Collective Memory: The Democratization of George Washington." *American Sociological Review* 56, no. 2, 221–36.

Scott, Joan W. 1988. *Gender and the Politics of History*. New York: Columbia University Press.

———. 1992. "'Experience.'" In Judith Butler and Joan W. Scott, eds., *Feminists Theorize the Political*. New York: Routledge.

Seed, Patricia. 1999. "The Key to the House." In Hamid Naficy, ed., *Home, Exile, Homeland: Film, Media, and the Politics of Place*. London: Routledge 87–94.

Segev, Tom. 1984. *1949 – Ha-Yisraelim Ha-Rishunim* [1949—The First Israelis]. Jerusalem: Domino Press.

———. 1986. *1949 – The First Israelis*. New York: The Free Press.

———. 2001. "The Return of Ibrahim Abu-Lughod." *Ha'aretz* June 1.

Shafak, Elif. 2005. "In Istanbul, a Crack In the Wall of Denial: We're Trying to Debate the Armenian Issue." *Washington Post* September 25, B03.

Shamir, Ronen. 1996. "Suspended in Space: Bedouins under the Law of Israel." *Law and Society Review* 30, no. 2, 231–58.

Shammas, Anton. 1988. "The Retreat from Galilee." *Granta* 23 (Spring): 46–68.

Sharoni, Simona. 1995. *Gender and the Politics of Israeli-Palestinian Conflict: The Politics of Women's Resistance*. Syracuse: Syracuse University Press.

———. 1997. "Motherhood and the Politics of Women's Resistance: Israeli Women Organizing for Peace." In Alexis Jetter, Annelise Orleck, and Diana Taylor, eds., *The Politics of Motherhood: Activist Voices From Left to Right*. Hanover, NH: University Press of New England.

Shavit, Ari. 2004. "Survival of the Fittest." *Ha'aretz*. January 9.

Shenhav, Yehuda. 2003. *Ha-yehudim ha-'aravim: leumiyut, dat vi-etniyut* [The Arab-Jews: Nationalism, Religion and Ethnicity]. Tel-Aviv: Am Oved.

Shlaim, Avi. 1988. *Collusion Across the Jordan : King Abdullah, the Zionist Movement, and the Partition of Palestine*. New York: Columbia University Press.

————. 2000. *The Iron Wall: Israel and the Arab World*. New York: Norton.

————. 2001. "Israel and the Arab Coalition in 1948." In Eugene L. Rogan and Avi Shlaim, eds., *The War for Palestine: Rewriting the History of 1948*. Cambridge: Cambridge University Press, 79–103.

————. 2002. A Betrayal of History. *Guardian* February 22.

Shohat, Ella. 1989. *Israeli Cinema: East-West and the Politics of Representation*. Austin: University of Texas Press.

————. 1999. "The Invention of the Mizrahim." *Journal of Palestine Studies* 29, no. 2, 5–20.

————. 2006. *Taboo Memories, Diasporic Voices*. Durham: Duke University Press.

Slyomovics, Susan. 1991. "Review of the *Destroyed Palestinian Village* Series." *Journal of American Folklore* 104, no. 413, 385–87.

————. 1993. "Discourses on the pre-1948 Palestinian Village: The Case of Ein Hod/Ein Houd." *Traditional Dwellings and Settlements Review* 4, no. 2, 27–37.

————. 1994. "The Memory of Place: Rebuilding the Pre-1948 Palestinian Village." *Diaspora: A Journal of Transnational Studies* 3, no. 2, 157–68.

————. 1998. *The Object of Memory: Arab and Jew Narrate the Palestinian Village*. Philadelphia: University of Pennsylvania Press.

Smilansky, Yizhar. 1989. "Hirbet Hiz'ah." In Yizhak Smilansky, *Hirbet Hiz'ah*. Tel-Aviv: Zmora Bitan.

Smith, Charles. 2004. *Palestine and the Arab-Israeli Conflict*. 5th ed. Boston: Bedford/St. Martin's.

Srouji, Elias. 2003 "The Last Days of 'Free Galilee:' Memories of 1948." *Journal of Palestine Studies* 33, no.1 (Fall): 55–67.

————. 2004. "The Fall of a Galilean Village During the 1948 War: An Eyewitness Account." *Journal of Palestine Studies* 33, no. 2, 71–80.

Stanley, Jo. 1996. "Including the Feelings: Personal Political Testimony and Self-Disclosure." *Oral History* 24, no. 1 (Spring): 60–67.

Steiner, George. 1985. "Our Homeland, the Text." *Salmagundi* 66 (Winter–Spring): 4–25.

Stoler, Ann Laura and Karen Strassler. 2000. "Castings for the Colonial: Memory Work in 'New Order' Java." *Comparative Studies in Society and* History 42, no. 1, 4–48.

Sturken, Marita. 1997. *Tangled Memories: The Vietnam War, the AIDS Epidemic, and the Politics of Remembering*. Berkeley: University of California Press.

Suleiman, Jaber. 2001. "The Palestine Liberation Organization: From the Right of Return to Bantustan." In Naseer Aruri, ed. *Palestinian Refugees: The Right of Return*. London: Pluto Press.

Sumrayn, Ghalib Muhammad. 1993. *Qaryati Qalunya: Al-Ard wa-al-Judhur (Filastinuna bi Qissat Qarya)* [My Village Qalunya: Land and Roots (Our Palestine in the Story of a Village)]. Amman: n.p.

The Survey of Western Palestine 1882–1888. 1998. Reprint. Slough, England: Archive Editions in Association with Palestine Exploration Fund.

Swedenburg, Ted. 1990. "The Palestinian Peasant as National Signifier." *Anthropological Quarterly* 63, no.1, 18–30.

———. 1991. "Popular Memory and the Palestinian National Past." In Jay O'Brien and William Roseberry, eds., *Golden Ages, Dark Ages*. Berkeley: University of California Press, 52–79.

———. 1992. "Seeing Double: Palestinian-American Histories of the Kufiya." *Michigan Quarterly Review* 31, no.4, 557–77.

———. 1995. *Memories of Revolt: The 1936–9 Rebellion and the Struggle for a Palestinian National Past*. Minneapolis: University of Minnesota Press.

Tal, Alon. 2002. *Pollution in a Promised Land: An Environmental History of Israel*. Berkeley: University of California Press.

Tamari, Salim. 1999. *Jerusalem 1948: The Arab Neighbourhoods and Their Fate in the War*. Jerusalem and Bethlehem: The Institute for Jerusalem Studies and Badil Resource Center.

———. 2003. "Bourgeois Nostalgia and the Abandoned City." *Comparative Studies of South Asia, Africa and the Middle East* 23, nos. 1–2, 1–11.

Tamari, Salim and Rema Hammami. 1998. "Virtual Return to Jaffa." *Journal of Palestine Studies* 27, no. 4 (Summer): 65–79.

Tansman, Alan. 2004. "Catastrophe, Memory, and Narrative: Teaching Japanese and Jewish Responses to Twentieth Century Atrocity." *Discourse* 25, no. 1, 248–271.

Tarkosky, Andrei and Tonino Guera. 2003. *Tempo di Viaggio (1984)*. Distributed by Artificial Eye Film Company.

Thompson, Thomas L., ed. 2003. *Jerusalem in Ancient History and Tradition*. London: Continuum.

Thorse, Karen. 1990. *The Price of a Ticket*. California Newsreel, American Masters and Yaysles Films.

Tibawi, Abdul Latif. 1956. *Arab Education in Mandatory Palestine: A Study of Three Decades of British Administration*. London: Luzac.

Tonkin, Elizabeth. 1992. *Narrating Our Past: The Social Construction of Oral History*. Cambridge University Press.

Trouillot, Michel-Rolph. 1995. *Silencing the Past: Power and the Production of History*. Boston: Beacon Press.

Turki, Fawaz. 1998. "Reflections on Al-Nakba." *Journal of Palestine Studies* 28, no. 1 (Autumn): 9–14.

Wagner, Don. 2002. "For Zion's Sake." *Middle East Report* 223 (Summer): 52–57.

Walker, David B. 2003. "The Displaced Self: The Experience of Atopia and the Recollection of Place." *Mosaic* 36, no. 1, 21–32.

Warnock, Kitty. 1990. *Land Before Honour: Palestinian Women in the Occupied Territories*. New York: Monthly Review Press.

Weine, Stevan. 1999. *When History is a Nightmare: Lives and Memories of Ethnic Cleansing in Bosnia-Herzegovina*. New Brunswick: Rutgers University Press.

Weir, Shelagh. 1989. *Palestinian Costume*. London: Trustees of the British Museum.

Weizman, Eyal. 2003. "The Politics of Verticality: The West Bank as an Architectural Construction." In *Territories: Islands, Camps and Other States of Utopia*. Berlin: KW, Institute for Contemporary Art.

Whitelam, Keith W. 1996. *The Invention of Ancient Israel: The Silencing of Palestinian History*. London: Routledge.

Winston, Brian. 1995. *Claiming the Real: The Documentary Film Revisited*. London: British Film Institute.

al-Yamani, Ahmad Hussayn, et al. n. d. *Suhmata: Zahra min Riyad al-Jalil al-A'la* [Suhmata: Flower from the Garden of the Upper Galilee]. n.p.

Ya'qub, Nasr and Fahum Shalabi. 1995. *Qaryat Abu Shushah*. Under the editorial supervision of Saleh Abdel Jawad and Walid Mustafa. Birzeit: Markaz Dirasat wa-Tawthiq al-Mujtam' al-Filastini.

Yehezka'el, Ariel. 2001. *Dinei reayot* [Rules of Evidence]. Pardes Chana: A.D. Mishpatim.

Yizhar, S. [Yizhar Smilanski]. 1989. "Hirbet Hiz'ah" In S. Yizhar, *Hirbet Hiz'ah* (A collection of stories). Tel Aviv: Zmora Bitan.

Young, James E. 1993. *The Texture of Memory: Holocaust Memorials and Meaning*. New Haven: Yale University Press.

———. 2001. "Memory and Counter-Memory: The End of the Monument in Germany." *Harvard Design Magazine*. http://www.gsd.harvard.edu/research/publications/hdm/back/9young.pdf

Zertal, Idit. 2002. *Ha-uma ve-ha-mavet: historia, zikaron, politika* [Death and the Nation: History, Memory, Politics]. Or Yehuda: Dvir.

Zerubavel, Yael. 1995. *Recovered Roots: Collective Memory and the Making of Israeli National Tradition*. Chicago: University of Chicago Press.

CONTRIBUTORS

LILA ABU LUGHOD: Professor of Anthropology and Director of the Institute for Research on Women and Gender at Columbia University. She has published widely on women, gender, and cultural politics in the Middle East. Her first books were based on ethnographic work in Egypt. These include *Veiled Sentiments* (1986/2000); *Writing Women's Worlds* (1993); and *Dramas of Nationhood* (2005). She has also edited or co-edited *Remaking Women: Feminism and Modernity in the Middle East* (1998) and *Media Worlds: Anthropology on New Terrain* (2000). Although she has had a lifelong interest in Palestine, she has only recently begun to do scholarly research on the subject.

DIANA K. ALLAN: Co-director of The Nakba Archive and Director of Lens on Lebanon, a grassroots media collective documenting the long-term effects of the 2006 conflict with Israel. She is the producer of the documentaries *Chatila, Beirut* (2002), and *Nakba Archive* (2006), and is currently working on a film installation, *Still Lives*, and a book project, Photo48, while completing a doctorate in anthropology and film at Harvard University. Her publications include "Mythologizing al-Nakba: Narratives, Collective Identity, and Cultural Practice Among Palestinian Refugees in Lebanon," *Oral History* 33, no. 1 (Spring 2005) 47–56 and "Photo48: Looking at Palestine" *Bidoun*, September 2005.

HAIM BRESHEETH: Professor of Media and Cultural Studies at the University of East London. He is the co-editor of *Cinema and Memory: Dangerous Liaisons* (In Hebrew, 2004) and (with Nira Yuval-Davis) of *The Gulf War and the New World Order* (Zed Books, 1991), and co-author (with Stuart Hood) of *Introducing the Holocaust* (Icon Books, 1993, 2001). He has made a number of documentary films, notably "A State of Danger" (BBC2, 1989) on the Palestinian Intifada. Currently he works on the topic of the other and stranger in European cinema, and on history and memory in Palestinian cinema. He is completing a book titled *Art in Exile*, centered on the acquisition of ancient artifacts by Western museums.

ROCHELLE DAVIS: Assistant Professor of Arab Culture and Society in the Center for Contemporary Arab Studies at Georgetown University. She completed a combined Ph.D. in Cultural Anthropology and Near Eastern Studies at the University of Michigan in 2002, and has been a postdoctoral fellow in the Stanford University Introduction to the Humanities Program and at the Center for Middle Eastern Studies at the University of California, Berkeley. Areas of interest are Palestinian history, oral history, transnationalism, urban history, and travel literature. Her publications include: "Language and Loss, Or How to Bark like a Dog and Other Lessons from al-Jahiz," *Critique*, Spring 2004; "Commemorating Education: Recollections of the Arab College in Jerusalem, 1918-1948," *Comparative Studies of South Asia, Africa and the Middle East* 23, nos.1–2 (2003).

SAMERA ESMEIR: Former lawyer who received a Ph.D. from the Law and Society Program, New York University, and is now Assistant Professor of Rhetoric at the University of California at Berkeley. She is the co-founder, and was the co-editor, of *Adalah's Review*, a socio-legal journal published in Arabic, Hebrew, and English that focuses on the Palestinian minority in Israel. She is a regular contributor to the journal and has published in *Social Text*, *PMLA*, and *Journal of Law and Society*. She is currently working on a book manuscript on colonial Egypt with the working title, *Juridical Humanity*.

ISABELLE HUMPHRIES: Doctoral student researching contemporary narratives of displacement among Palestinian refugees in the Galilee with the Holy Land Research Project, St Mary's College, University of Surrey. Since 2000, she has been situated in Jerusalem, Cairo, and Nazareth at various times. She has worked as consultant with both local NGOs and UNDP, and written for a variety of publications such as *Holy Land Studies: A Multidisciplinary Journal*, *Middle East Report Online*, *Haq Al Awda* (Badil Resource Centre, Jerusalem), *Daily Star* (Beirut), *Cairo Times*, *Washington Report for Middle East Affairs*, and *Znet*. Her research in Nazareth features in her chapter of *Catastrophe Remembered: Palestine, Israel, and the Internal Refugees*, edited by Nur Masalha (Zed, 2005).

LENA JAYYUSI: A Palestinian educated in the UK, currently Associate Professor in the College of Communication and Media Sciences at Zayed University and Director of Research for the Zayed University Media Center in the UAE. Chair of the Department of Communication Studies at Cedar Crest College in Pennsylvania 1990-94, she has been an Annenberg Scholar as well as an SSRC Research Fellow and a Ford Foundation grantee. She has been a Senior Research Fellow with Muwatin: The Palestinian Institute for the Study of Democracy in Ramallah, Palestine, since 1995, and has also served as Senior Media Consultant for the UNPD in Jerusalem, and as Director of the Oral History Program at Shaml: The Palestinian Diaspora and Refugee Center. Her research interests are media studies, the microsociology of knowledge, visual studies, cultural studies, and Palestinian national discourse. Author of *Categorization and the Moral Order* (Routledge and Kegan Paul, 1984), and translator/narrator of *The Adventures of Sayf ben Dhi Yazan: An Arab Folk Epic* (Indiana University Press, 1996), she is currently working on a book on the subject of Palestinian media and national discourse during the Oslo years, and preparing an edited collection on the transformation of Arab Jerusalem during the twentieth century, as well as an Arabic-language reader for Muwatin on the subject of Media and Democracy.

LALEH KHALILI: Lecturer in Middle East History at the School of Oriental and African Studies (SOAS), University of London. She is the author of *Heroes and Martyrs of Palestine: The Politics of National Commemoration* (Cambridge University Press, 2007), and several articles published in *Comparative Studies in Society and History, Journal of Palestine Studies, Critical Sociology* and other journals, as well as several book chapters on Palestinian nationalism and commemorative practices. She is currently researching extraterritorial prisons in the Middle East and their colonial/imperial roots.

OMAR AL-QATTAN: British-Palestinian film-maker. His first film, *Dreams and Silence* (1991) won the prestigious Joris Ivens Award and was one of the first documentaries to examine political Islam. In 1995, he made *Going Home*, a portrait of a British officer who served in Palestine during the 1948 War. In 2000–2001, he worked as director on *Muhammad – Legacy of a Prophet*, a two-hour biographical film broadcast on PBS. He has also produced several films by Michel Khleifi and other directors. Since 1999, he has been active in the field of cultural development in Palestine where he directed the Culture and Science Programme (1999-2004) and the Palestinian Audio-visual Project (2004-2006) at the A.M. Qattan Foundation. He has also written in both Arabic and English for the *New Statesman, Al-Hayat*, Opendemocracy.net, the *Jordan Times*, and *Counterpunch* and is a contributor to a book on Palestinian cinema, *Dreams of a Nation*, edited by Hamid Dabashi (Verso 2006).

AHMAD H. SA'DI: Senior lecturer in the department of Politics and Government at Ben-Gurion University. He has published many articles examining myriad aspects of the conflict over Palestine/Israel in referee journals in English, Arabic, Hebrew, and Japanese including: *Sociology; Work, Employment and Society; International Journal of Intercultural Relations; Social Identities; Arab Studies Quarterly; Asian Journal of Social Sciences; Social Text; The Japan Center For Area Studies Review; Annals of Japan Association for Middle East Studies; Israel Studies;* and *British Journal of Middle Eastern Studies*. Moreover, he has contributed ten chapters to collective volumes (in English, Hebrew, and German).

ROSEMARY SAYIGH: Anthropologist and oral historian living in Lebanon, currently engaged in writing an Internet book based on recording displacement narratives of Palestinian women. She is the author of *Palestinians: From Peasants to Revolutionaries* (London: Zed Books, 1979) and *Too Many Enemies: The Palestinian Experience in Lebanon* (London: Zed Books, 1994), as well as many articles in referee journals. She edited a special issue of *Al-Jana* (Beirut) on Palestinian oral history in 2002.

SUSAN SLYOMOVICS: Professor of Anthropology and Near Eastern Languages and Cultures at the University of California, Los Angeles. She is the author of *The Merchant of Art: An Egyptian Hilali Epic Poet in Performance* (1988), *The Object of Memory: Arab and Jew Narrate the Palestinian Village* (1998), winner of the 1999 Albert Hourani Book Award, given by the Middle East Studies Association, and the 1999 Chicago Folklore Prize; and *The Performance of Human Rights in Morocco* (2005). She is also co-editor of *Women and Power in the Middle East* (2001) and editor of *The Walled Arab City in Literature, Architecture and History: The Living Medina in the Maghrib* (2001).

INDEX